He's My Only Vampire 7
Aya Shouoto

Translation: Su Mon Han † Lettering: Alexis Eckerman

This book is a work of fiction. Names, characters, places, and incidents are the product of the author's imagination or are used fictitiously. Any resemblance to actual events, locales, or persons, living or dead, is coincidental.

HE'S MY ONLY VAMPIRE Volume 7 © 2013 Aya Shouoto. All rights reserved. First published in Japan in 2013 by Kodansha Ltd., Tokyo. Publication rights for this English edition arranged through Kodansha Ltd., Tokyo.

Translation © 2016 by Hachette Book Group, Inc.

Yen Press
Hachette Book Group
1290 Avenue of the Americas, New York, NY 10104

www.HachetteBookGroup.com
www.YenPress.com

Yen Press is an imprint of Hachette Book Group, Inc. The Yen Press name and logo are trademarks of Hachette Book Group, Inc.

The publisher is not responsible for websites (or their content) that are not owned by the publisher.

Library of Congress Control Number: 2016932696

First Yen Press Edition: June 2016

ISBN: 978-0-316-34582-8

10 9 8 7 6 5 4 3 2 1

BVG

Printed in the

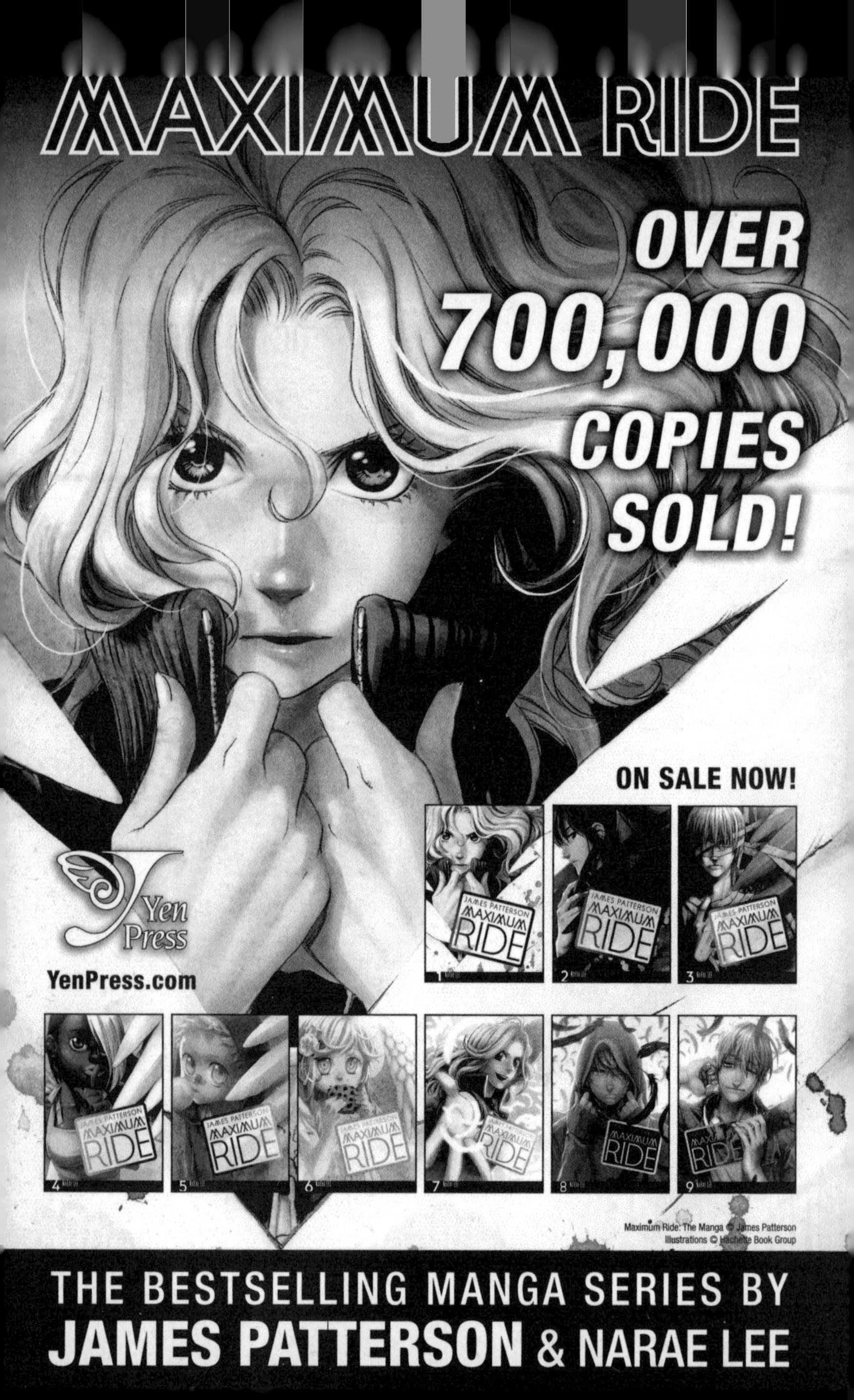
MAXIMUM RIDE
OVER 700,000 COPIES SOLD!
ON SALE NOW!
Yen Press
YenPress.com
Maximum Ride: The Manga © James Patterson
Illustrations © Hachette Book Group
THE BESTSELLING MANGA SERIES BY
JAMES PATTERSON & NARAE LEE

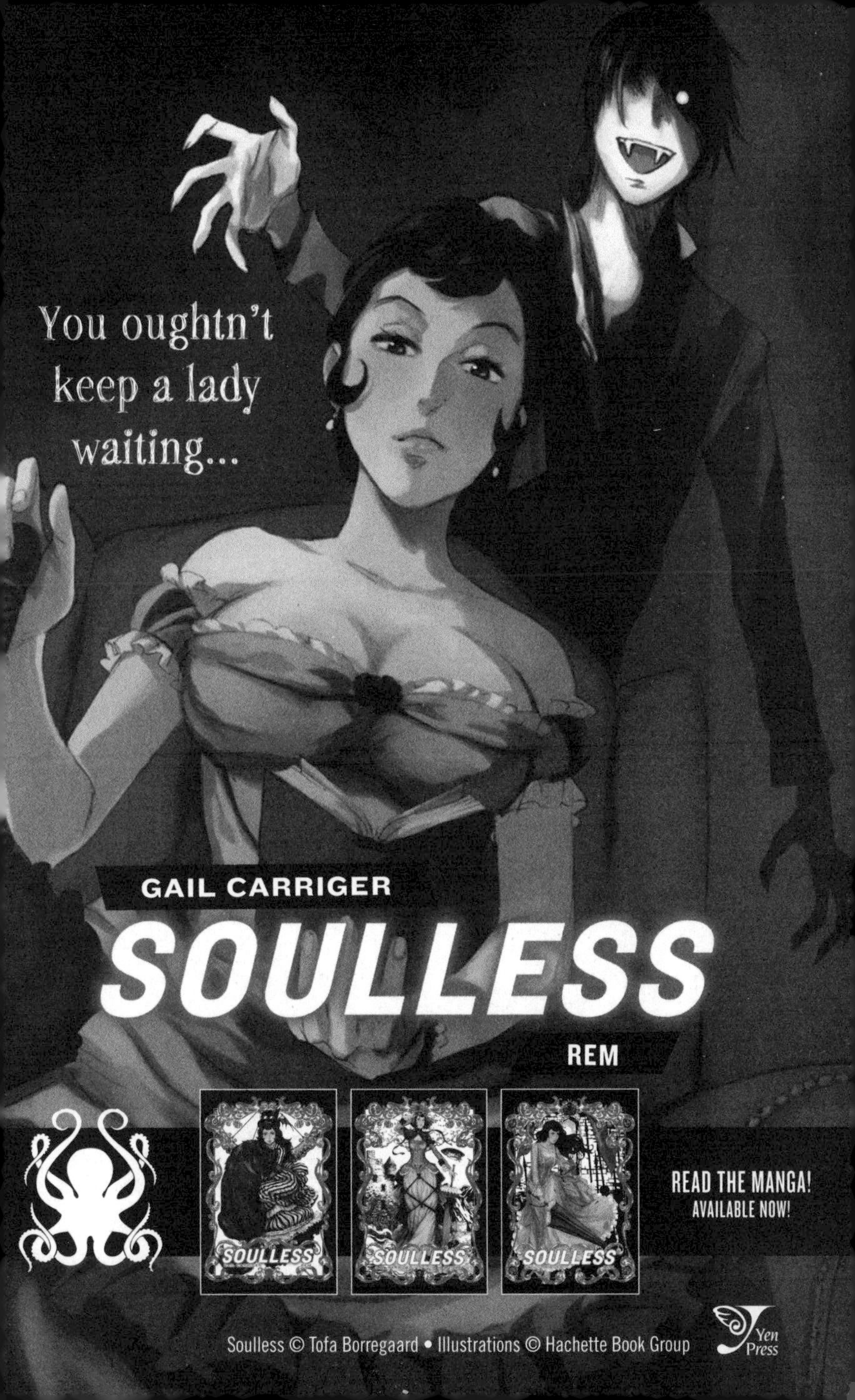
You oughtn't keep a lady waiting...
GAIL CARRIGER
SOULLESS
REM
SOULLESS
SOULLESS
SOULLESS
READ THE MANGA!
AVAILABLE NOW!
Soulless © Tofa Borregaard • Illustrations © Hachette Book Group
Yen Press

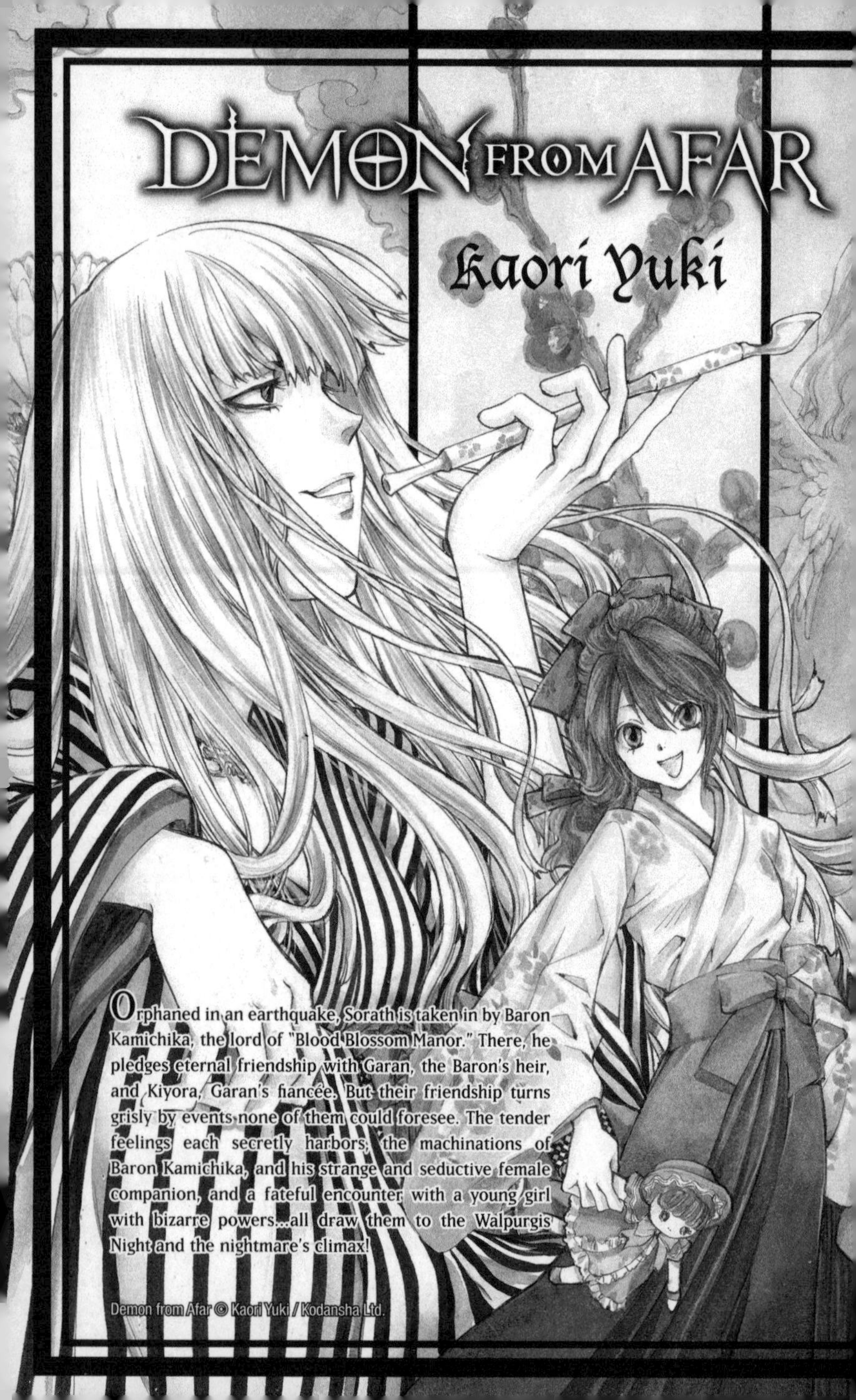
DEMON FROM AFAR
Kaori Yuki
Orphaned in an earthquake, Sorath is taken in by Baron Kamichika, the lord of "Blood Blossom Manor." There, he pledges eternal friendship with Garan, the Baron's heir, and Kiyora, Garan's fiancée. But their friendship turns grisly by events none of them could foresee. The tender feelings each secretly harbors, the machinations of Baron Kamichika, and his strange and seductive female companion, and a fateful encounter with a young girl with bizarre powers...all draw them to the Walpurgis Night and the nightmare's climax!
Demon from Afar © Kaori Yuki / Kodansha Ltd.

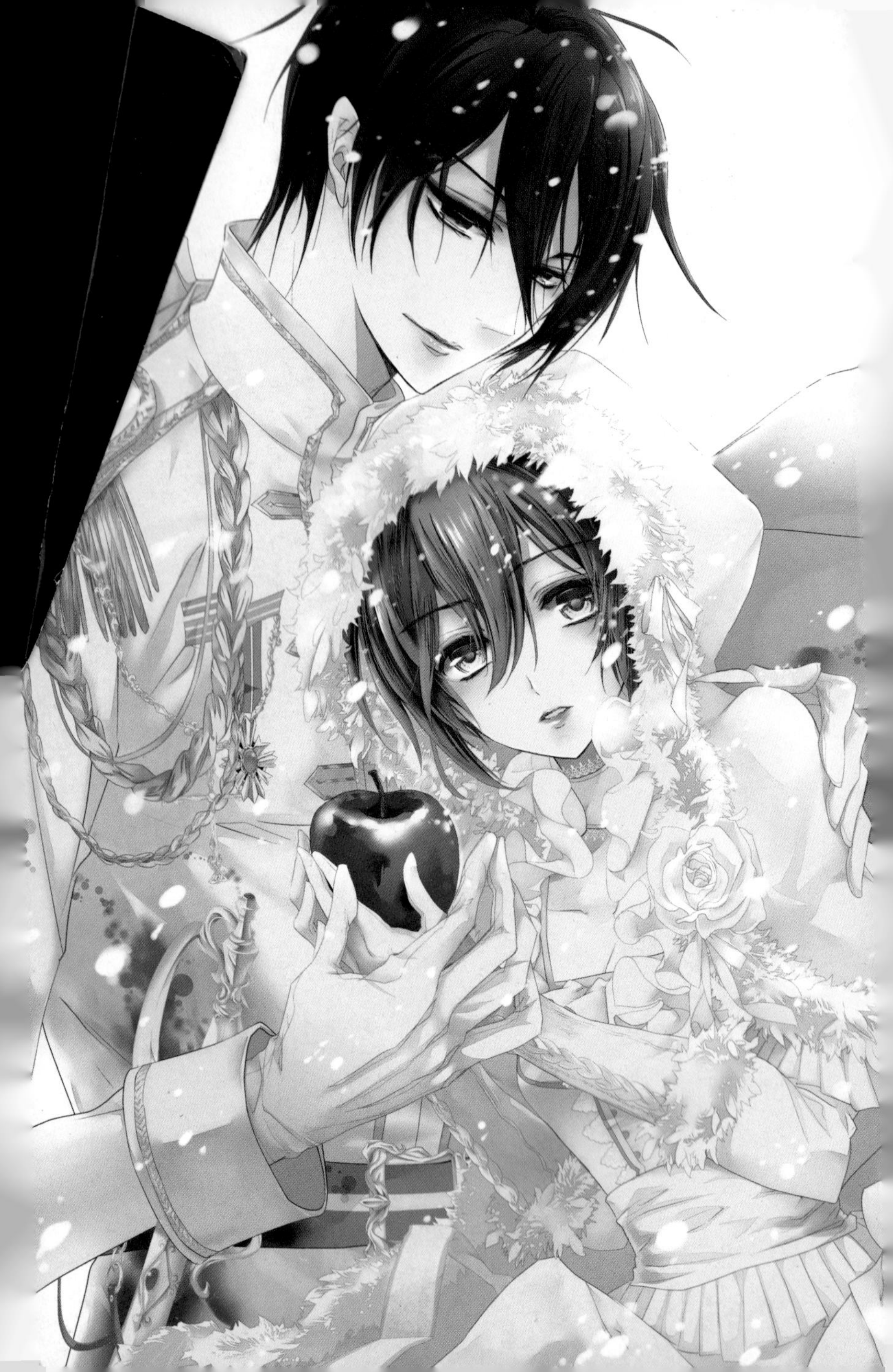

c o n t e n t s

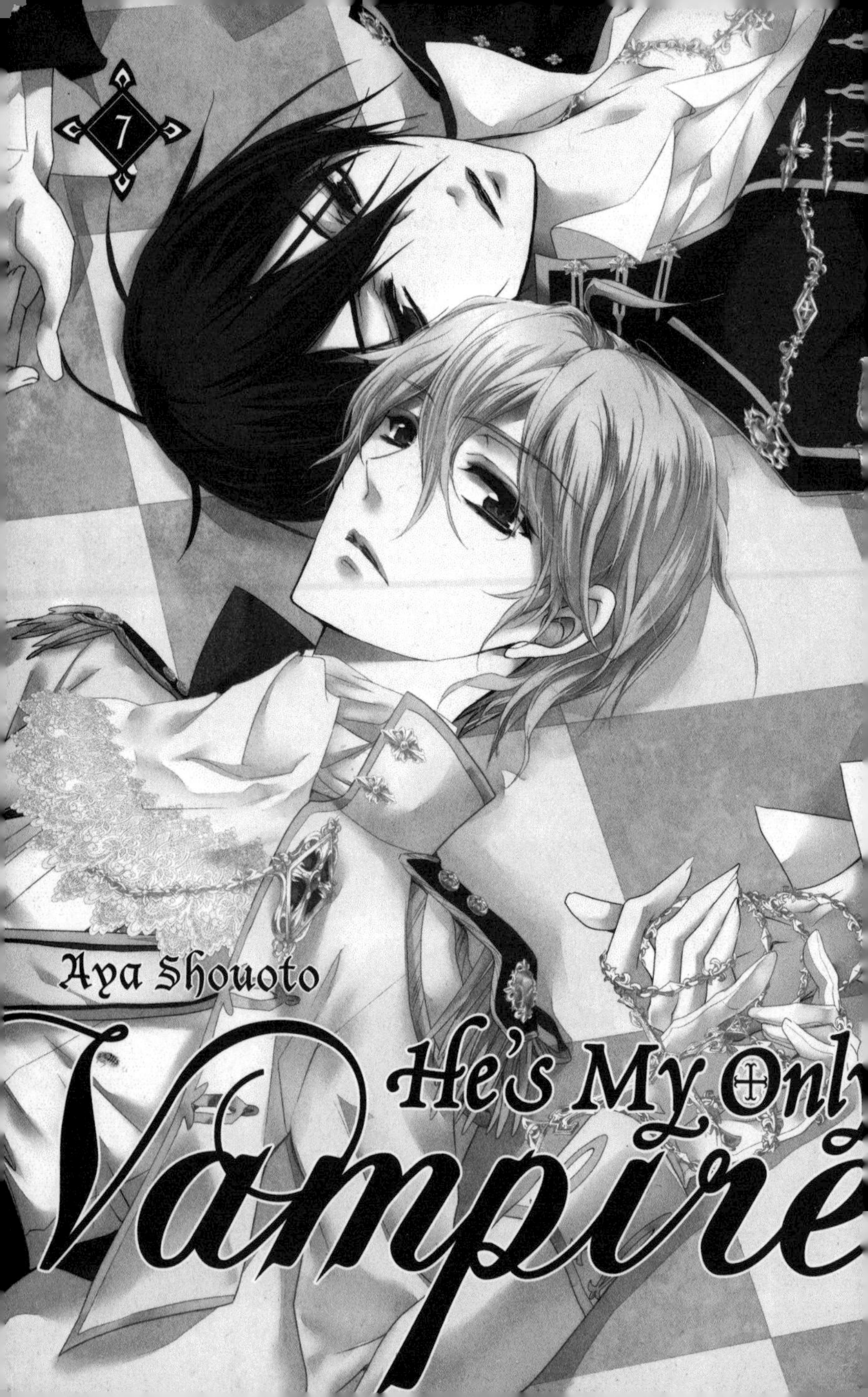
7
Aya Shouoto
He's My Only Vampire

Characters and Story

"Thrall"

One who is ageless and deathless, and shall surrender the entirety of their being to their vampire master for all of eternity...

THIS IS THE STORY OF THE VAMPIRE AKI AND HIS THRALL, KANA. AKI CAME TO KANA'S TOWN IN ORDER TO WIN A GAME TO COLLECT THE SEVEN STIGMAS AND USE THEIR POWER TO WAKE HIS SLUMBERING BROTHER, ERIYA. AKI AND KANA, ALONG WITH THEIR FRIEND JIN, FORMED A SCHOOL CLUB CALLED THE "CURIOUS EVENTS CLUB" TO GATHER INFORMATION ON THE STIGMAS, AND AKI SUCCESSFULLY OBTAINED TWO MORE OF THEM.

IN DUE COURSE, THE GROUP IS SUDDENLY ATTACKED BY THE TSUBAKIIN CLAN, WHICH CARRIES KANA OFF TO THEIR VILLAGE. THERE, THEY INDUCE KANA TO REGAIN HER LOST MEMORIES OF THE EVENTS FROM SEVEN YEARS EARLIER AND TO FULLY REALIZE THAT SHE IS IN LOVE WITH AKI. MEANWHILE, TO RECLAIM KANA, AKI SURRENDERS HIS "LUST" STIGMA TO THE TSUBAKIINS. HOWEVER, THE PRICE THAT "LUST" EXACTS FROM ITS OWNER IS THE LOSS OF ALL THEIR MEMORIES OF THE PERSON WHO IS MOST IMPORTANT TO THEM.

THUS, AKI LOSES ALL MEMORY OF KANA...

JIN SHIRANUI
(SECOND YEAR)

KANA'S CLASSMATE AND A WELL-KNOWN DELINQUENT. HE IS ACTUALLY A LYCAN-THROPE. POSSESSOR OF THE "GREED" STIGMA.

DEALER SWALLOW

AKI'S SENTRY AND A JUDGE IN THE GAME OF THE SEVEN STIGMAS. HIS TRUE FORM IS THAT OF A TENGU DEMON.

ISUKA BERNSTEIN
(THIRD YEAR)
HITAKI MIYAJIMA
(THIRD YEAR)

ST. AGATHA ACADEMY'S STUDENT COUNCIL PRESIDENT AND VICE PRESIDENT. IN TRUTH, THEY ARE ANGELS. HITAKI IS IN POSSESSION OF A STIGMA, WHILE ISUKA IS HIS DEALER.

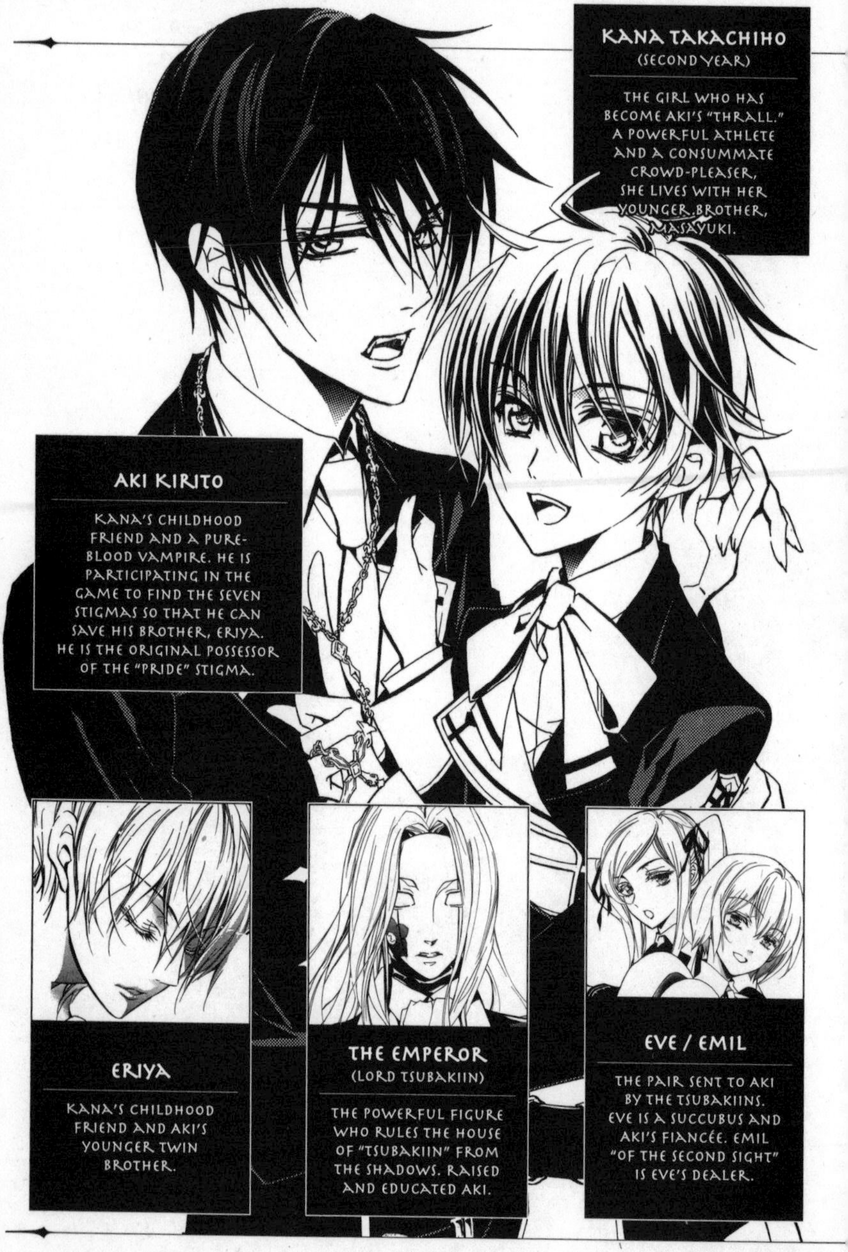
KANA TAKACHIHO
(SECOND YEAR)
THE GIRL WHO HAS BECOME AKI'S "THRALL." A POWERFUL ATHLETE AND A CONSUMMATE CROWD-PLEASER, SHE LIVES WITH HER YOUNGER BROTHER, MASAYUKI.
AKI KIRITO
KANA'S CHILDHOOD FRIEND AND A PURE-BLOOD VAMPIRE. HE IS PARTICIPATING IN THE GAME TO FIND THE SEVEN STIGMAS SO THAT HE CAN SAVE HIS BROTHER, ERIYA. HE IS THE ORIGINAL POSSESSOR OF THE "PRIDE" STIGMA.
EVE / EMIL
THE PAIR SENT TO AKI BY THE TSUBAKIINS. EVE IS A SUCCUBUS AND AKI'S FIANCÉE. EMIL "OF THE SECOND SIGHT" IS EVE'S DEALER.
THE EMPEROR
(LORD TSUBAKIIN)
THE POWERFUL FIGURE WHO RULES THE HOUSE OF "TSUBAKIIN" FROM THE SHADOWS. RAISED AND EDUCATED AKI.
ERIYA
KANA'S CHILDHOOD FRIEND AND AKI'S YOUNGER TWIN BROTHER.

~moon phase~28

First Love Eclipse

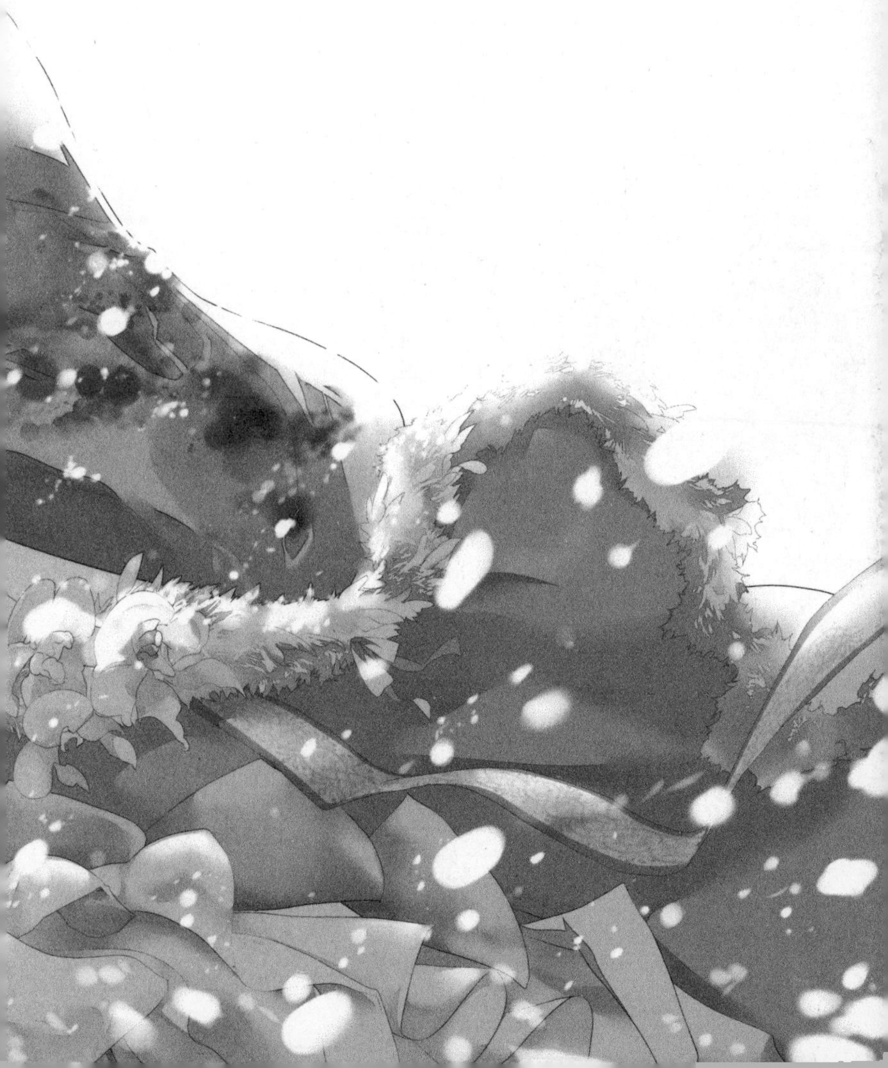

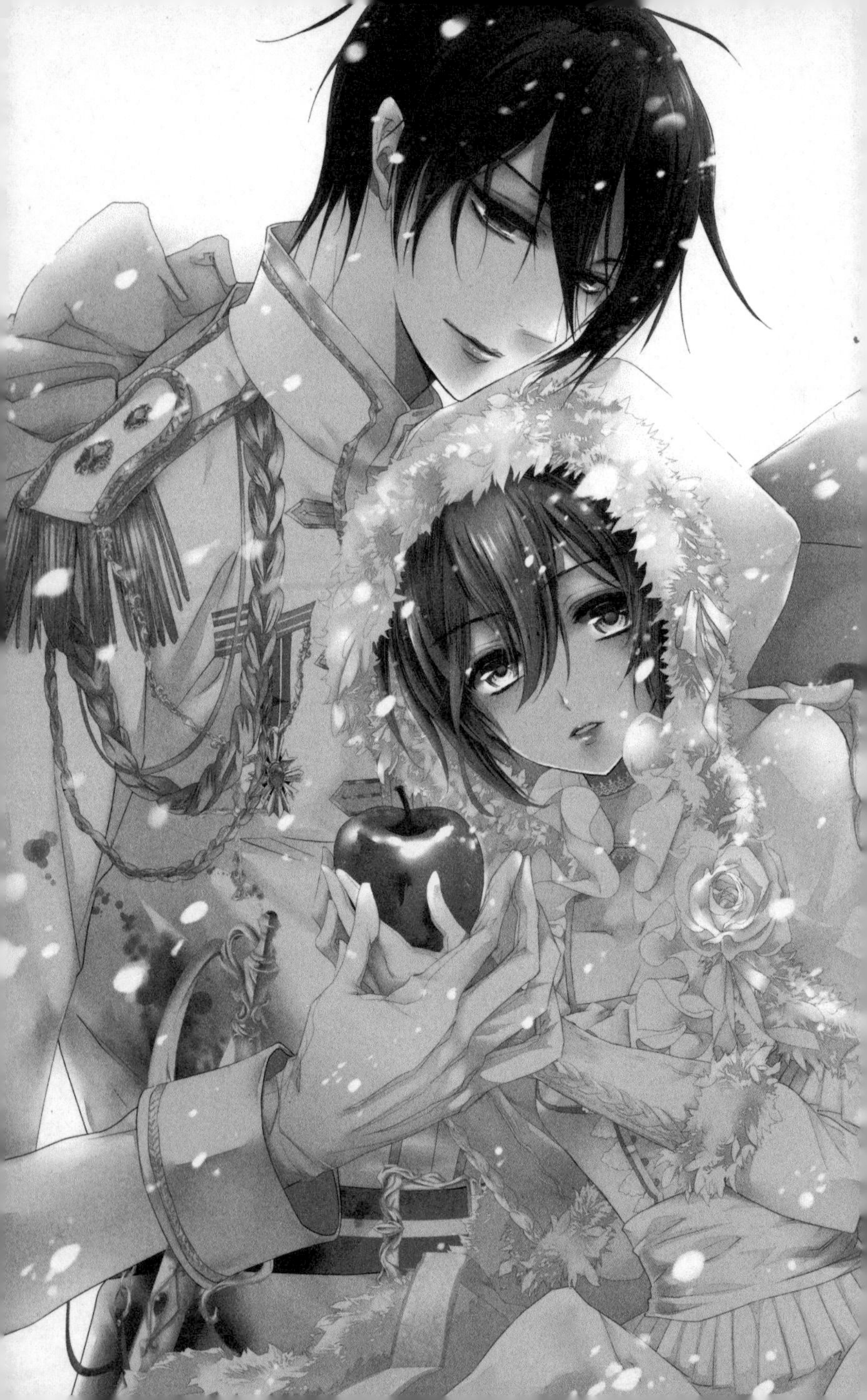

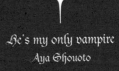

He's my only vampire
Aya Shouoto

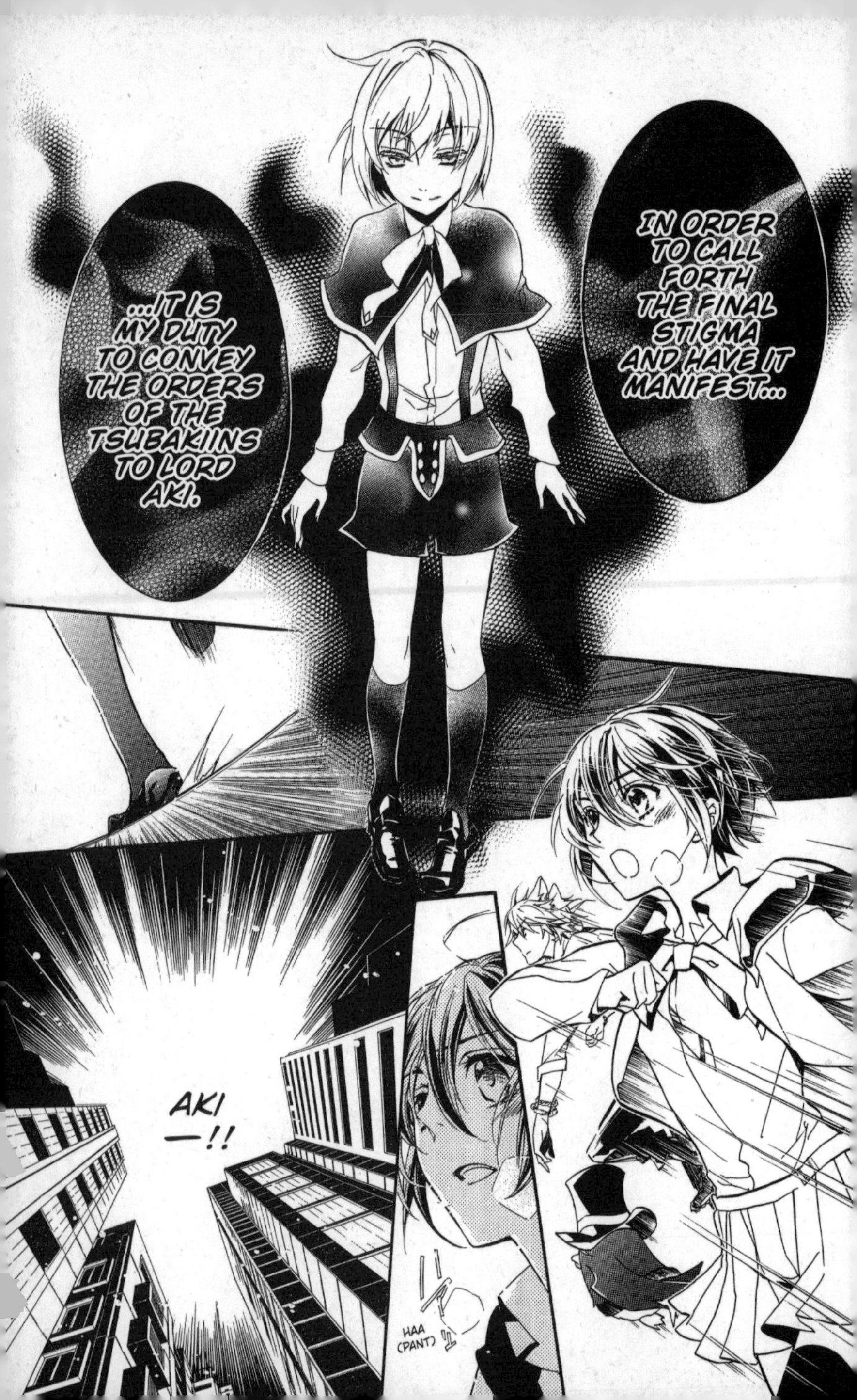
IN ORDER TO CALL FORTH THE FINAL STIGMA AND HAVE IT MANIFEST...
...IT IS MY DUTY TO CONVEY THE ORDERS OF THE TSUBAKIINS TO LORD AKI.
HAA (PANT)
AKI—!!

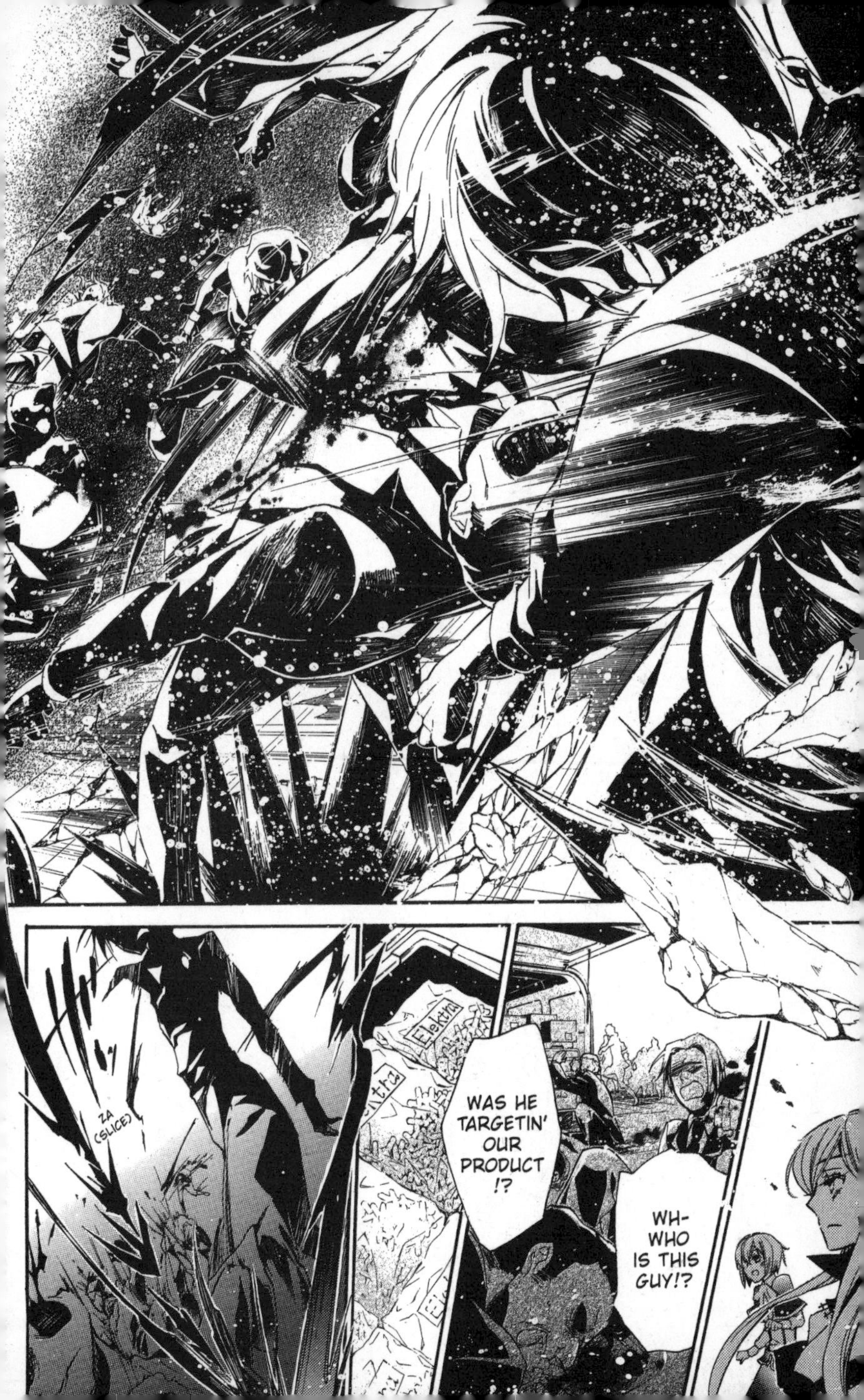
WH- WHO IS THIS GUY!?
WAS HE TARGETIN' OUR PRODUCT !?
Elektra
ZA (SLICE)

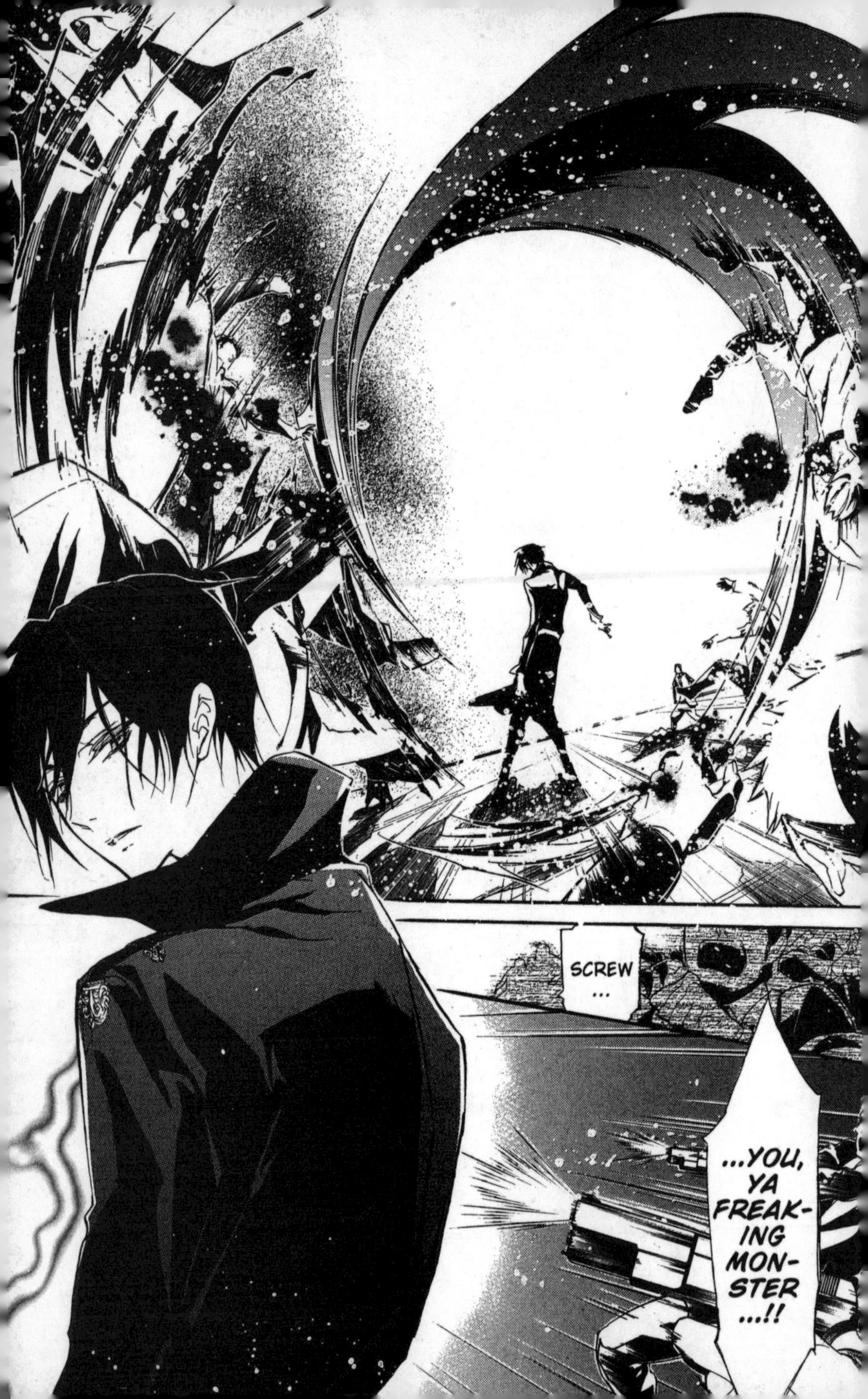
SCREW ...
...YOU, YA FREAK-ING MON-STER ...!!

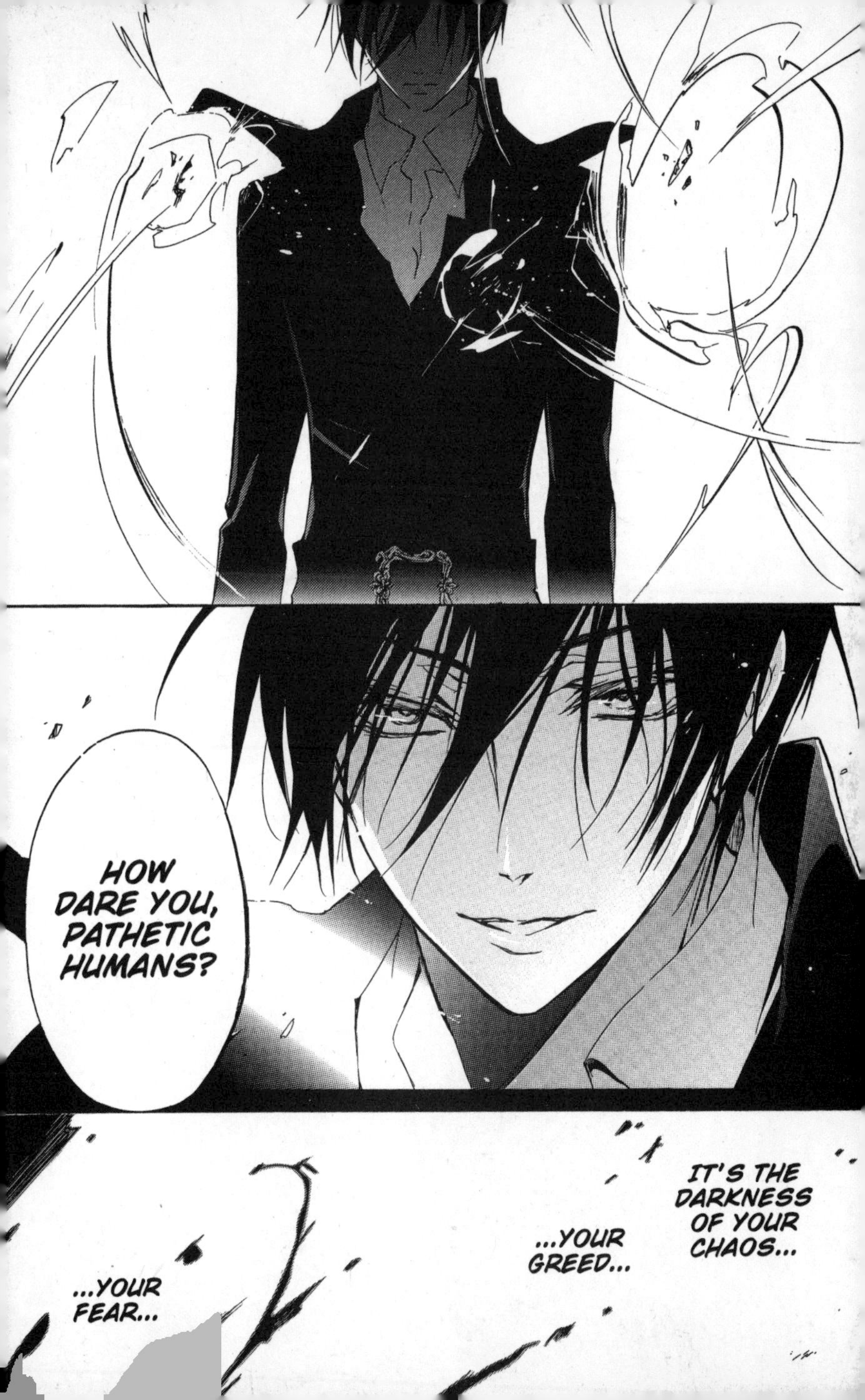
HOW DARE YOU, PATHETIC HUMANS?
IT'S THE DARKNESS OF YOUR CHAOS...
...YOUR GREED...
...YOUR FEAR...

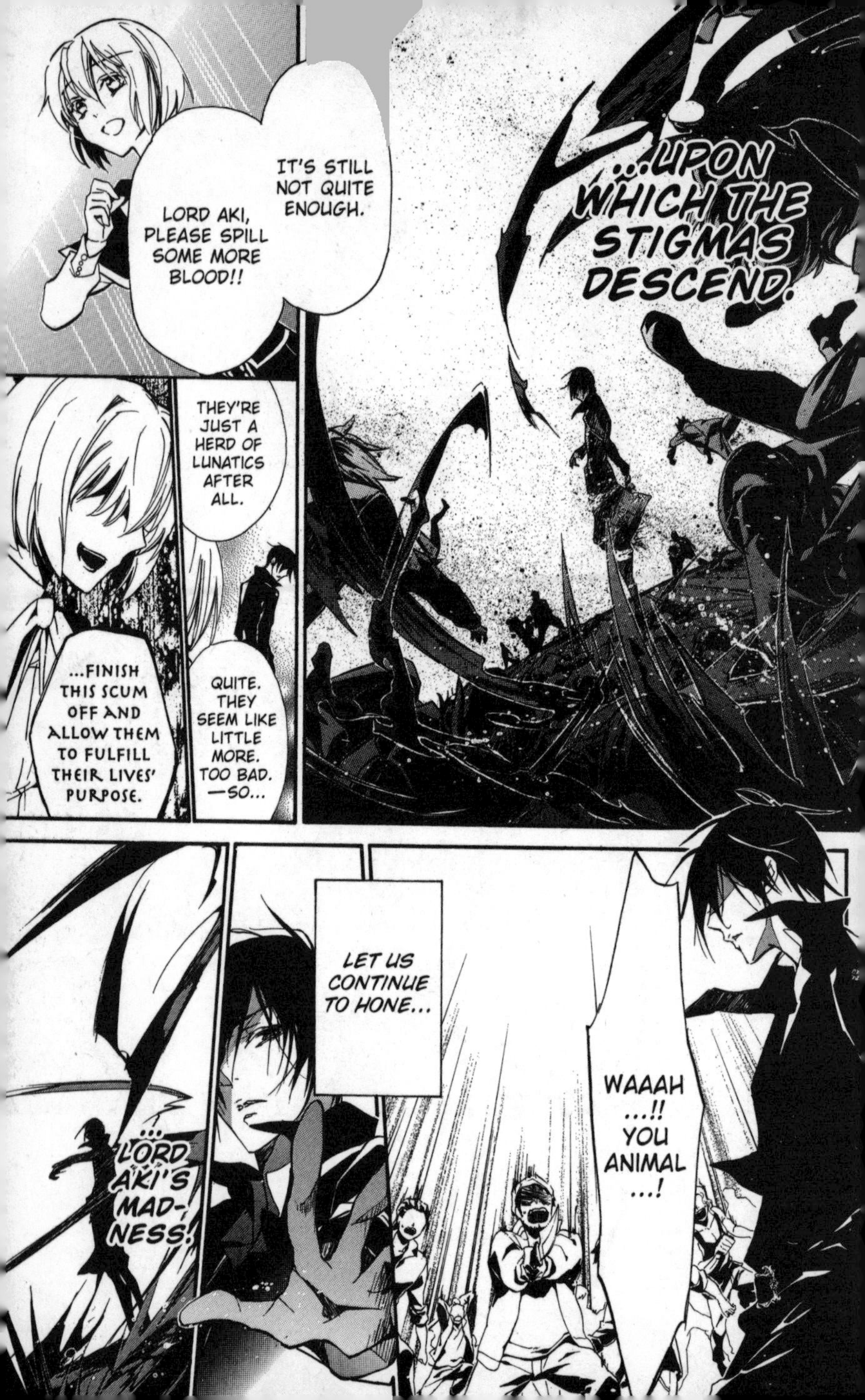
...UPON WHICH THE STIGMAS DESCEND.
IT'S STILL NOT QUITE ENOUGH.
LORD AKI, PLEASE SPILL SOME MORE BLOOD!!
THEY'RE JUST A HERD OF LUNATICS AFTER ALL.
QUITE. THEY SEEM LIKE LITTLE MORE. TOO BAD. —SO...
...FINISH THIS SCUM OFF AND ALLOW THEM TO FULFILL THEIR LIVES' PURPOSE.
WAAAH ...!! YOU ANIMAL ...!
LET US CONTINUE TO HONE...
...LORD AKI'S MAD-NESS!

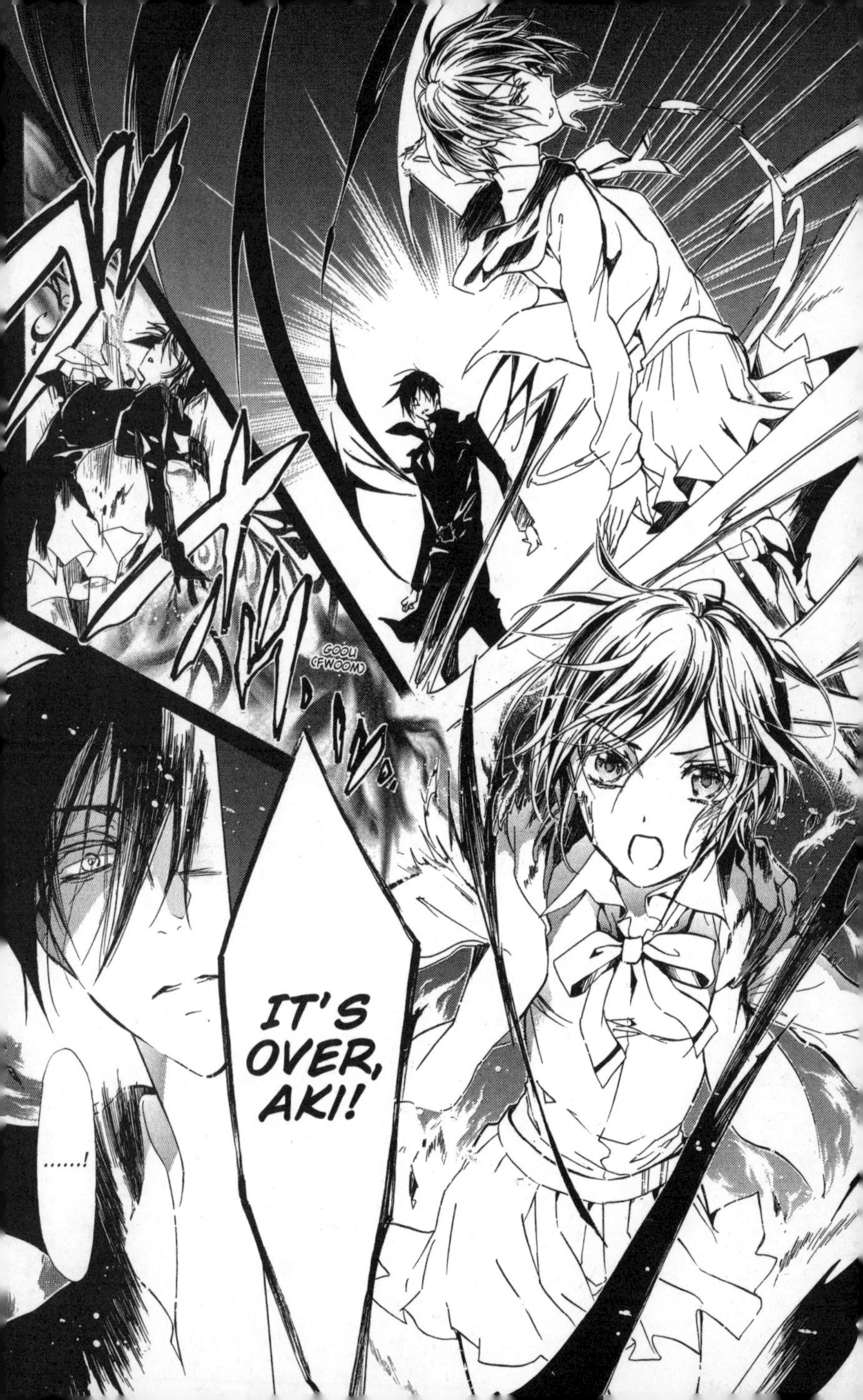
GOOU
(FWOOM)
IT'S OVER, AKI!
......!

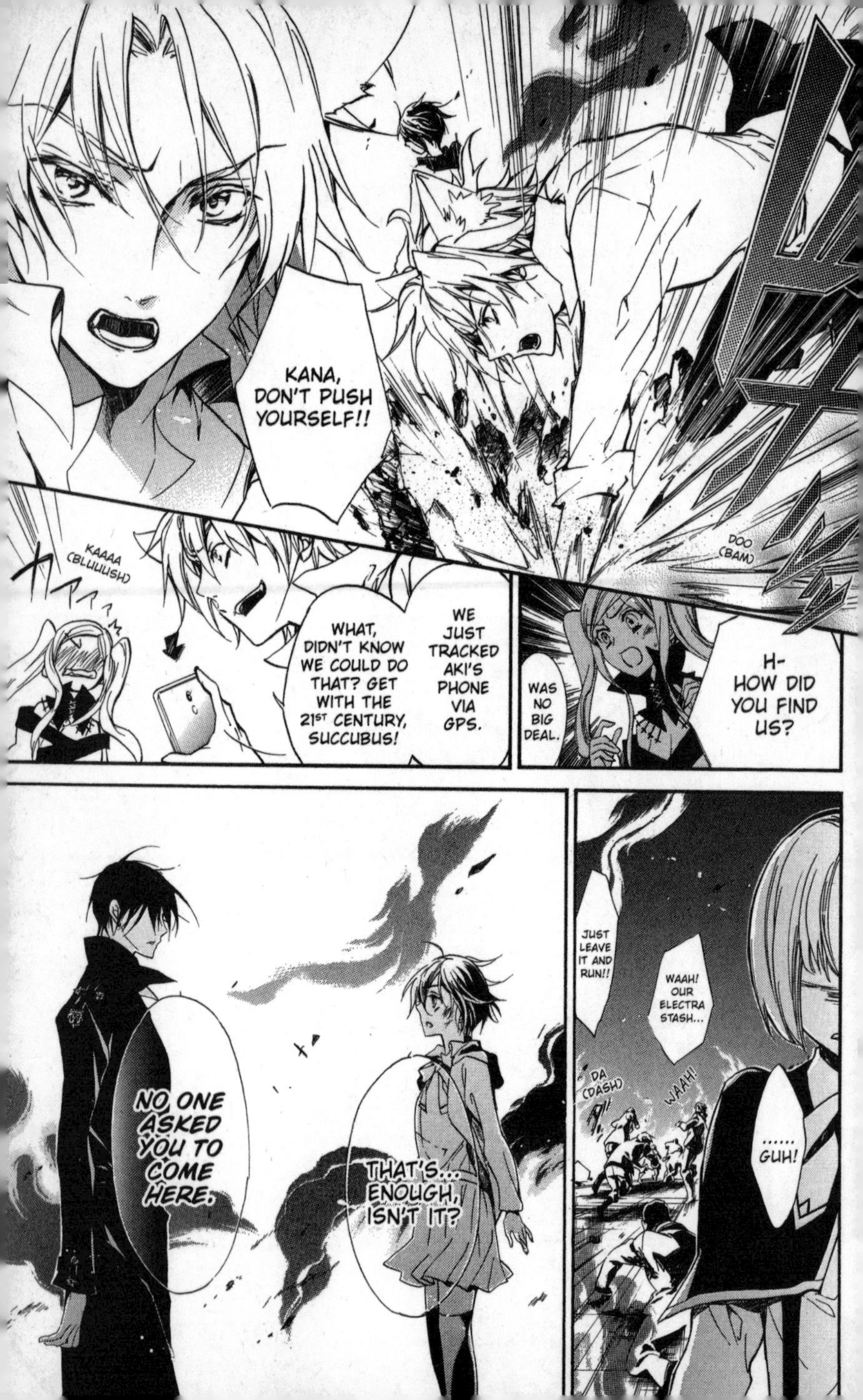
DOO (BAM)
KANA, DON'T PUSH YOURSELF!!
H- HOW DID YOU FIND US?
WAS NO BIG DEAL.
WE JUST TRACKED AKI'S PHONE VIA GPS.
WHAT, DIDN'T KNOW WE COULD DO THAT? GET WITH THE 21ST CENTURY, SUCCUBUS!
KAAAA (BLUUUSH)
......GUH!
WAAH! OUR ELECTRA STASH...
JUST LEAVE IT AND RUN!!
WAAH!
DA (DASH)
THAT'S... ENOUGH, ISN'T IT?
NO ONE ASKED YOU TO COME HERE.

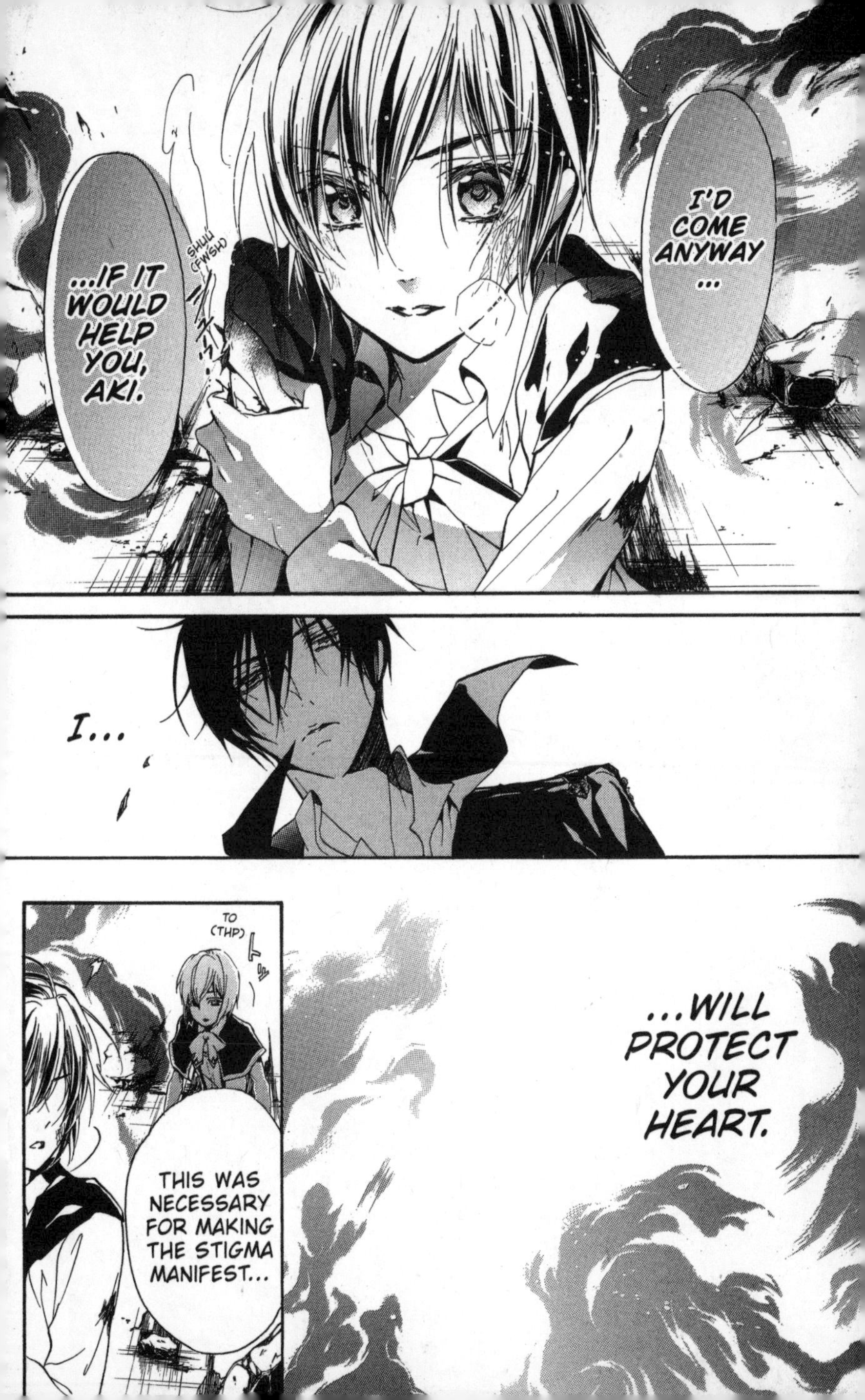
I'D COME ANYWAY...
SHUU (FWSH)
...IF IT WOULD HELP YOU, AKI.
I...
...WILL PROTECT YOUR HEART.
TO (THP)
THIS WAS NECESSARY FOR MAKING THE STIGMA MANIFEST...

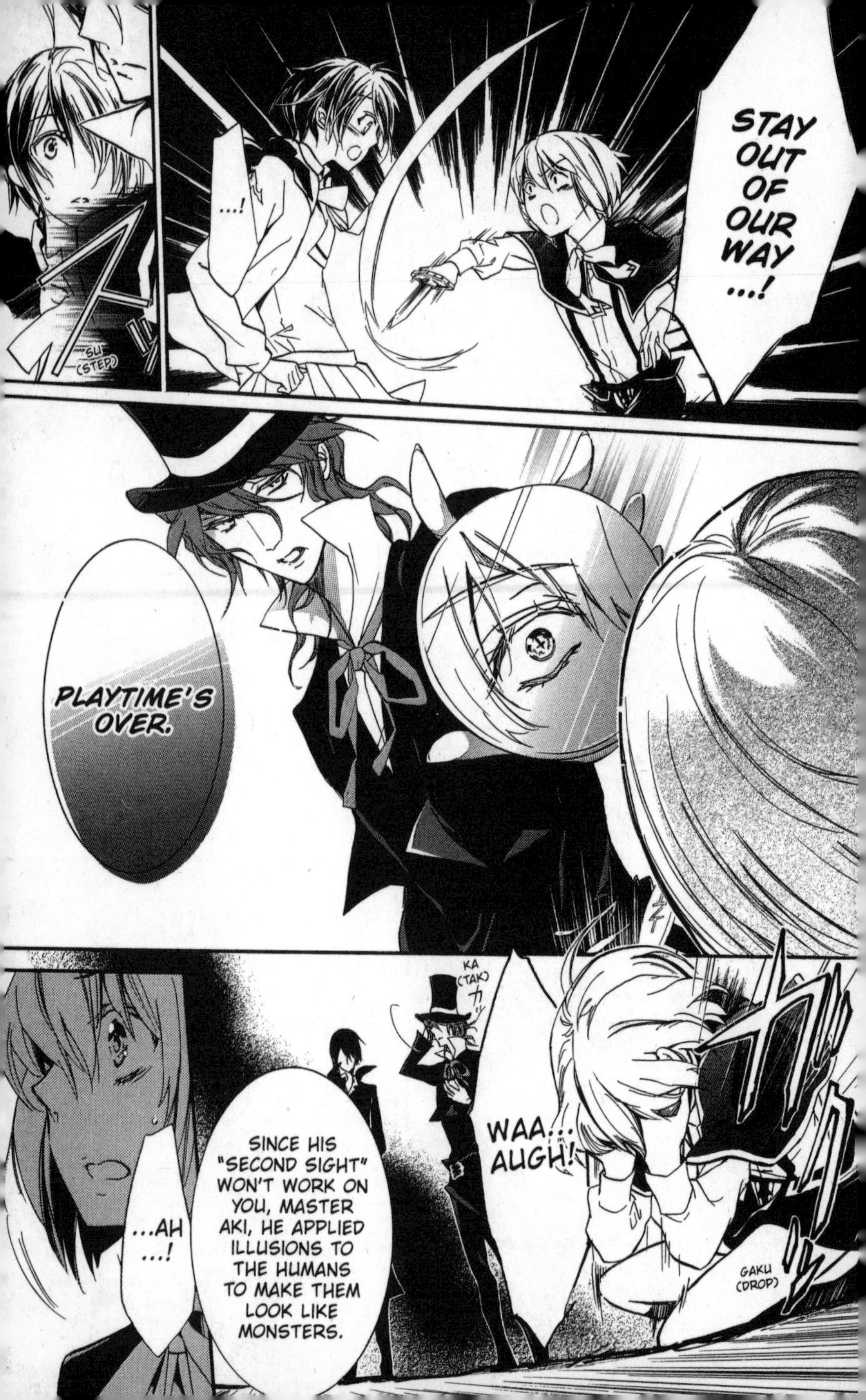
STAY OUT OF OUR WAY ...!
...!
SU (STEP)
PLAYTIME'S OVER.
KA (TAK)
WAA... AUGH!
GAKU (DROP)
SINCE HIS "SECOND SIGHT" WON'T WORK ON YOU, MASTER AKI, HE APPLIED ILLUSIONS TO THE HUMANS TO MAKE THEM LOOK LIKE MONSTERS.
...AH ...!

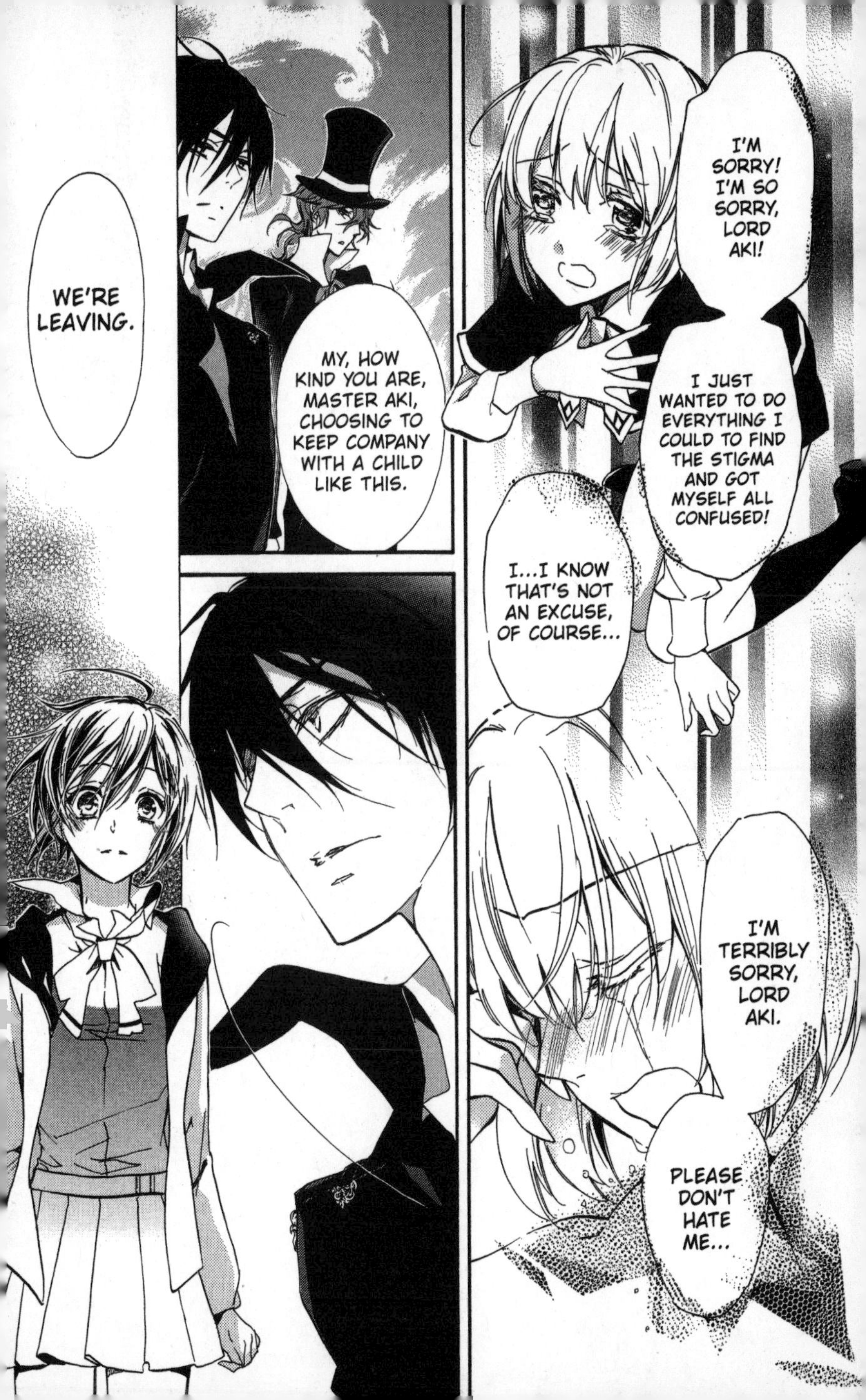
I'M SORRY! I'M SO SORRY, LORD AKI!
I JUST WANTED TO DO EVERYTHING I COULD TO FIND THE STIGMA AND GOT MYSELF ALL CONFUSED!
I...I KNOW THAT'S NOT AN EXCUSE, OF COURSE...
I'M TERRIBLY SORRY, LORD AKI.
PLEASE DON'T HATE ME...
MY, HOW KIND YOU ARE, MASTER AKI, CHOOSING TO KEEP COMPANY WITH A CHILD LIKE THIS.
WE'RE LEAVING.

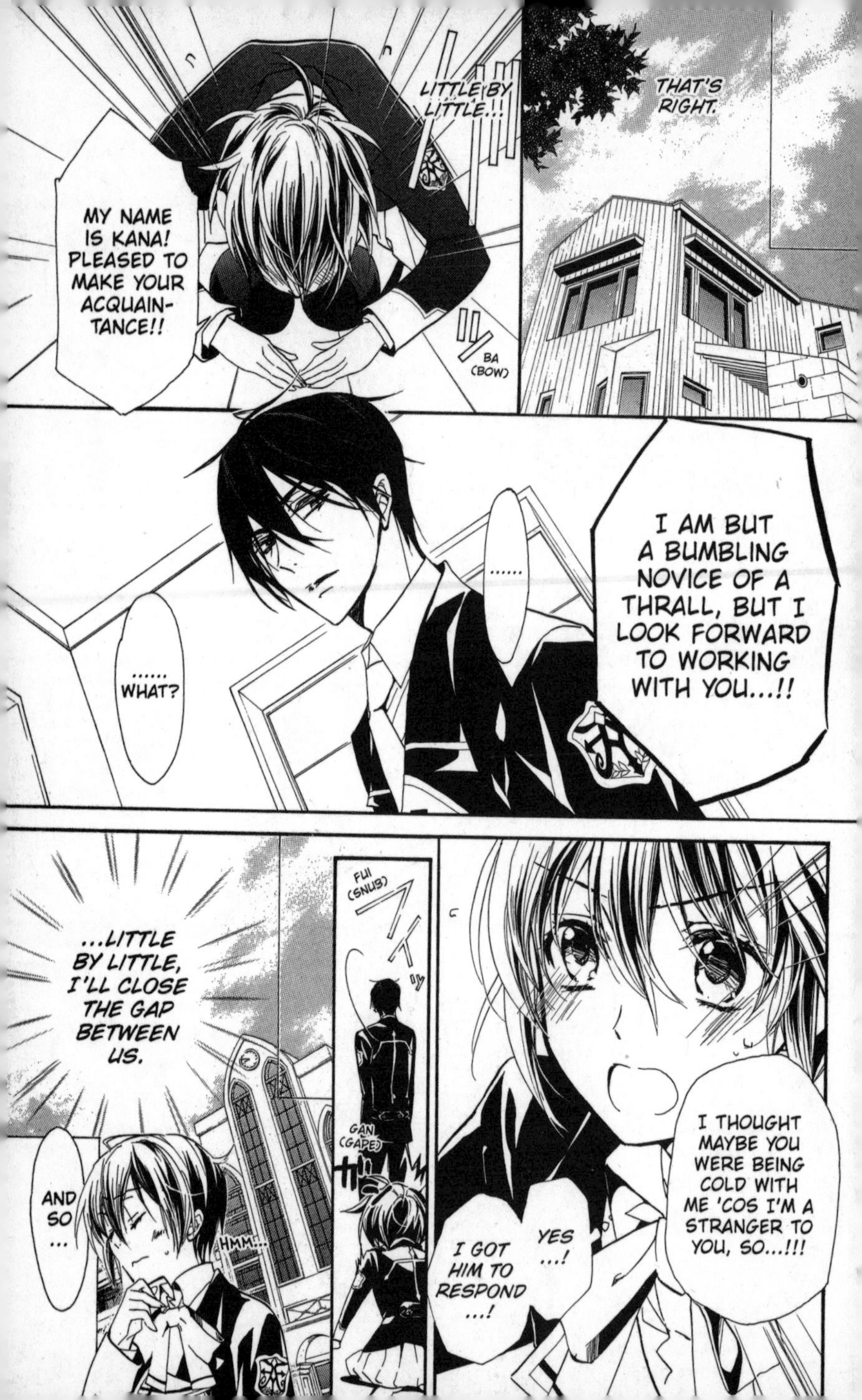
THAT'S RIGHT.
LITTLE BY LITTLE...!!
BA (BOW)
MY NAME IS KANA! PLEASED TO MAKE YOUR ACQUAINTANCE!!
I AM BUT A BUMBLING NOVICE OF A THRALL, BUT I LOOK FORWARD TO WORKING WITH YOU...!!
......
...... WHAT?
I THOUGHT MAYBE YOU WERE BEING COLD WITH ME 'COS I'M A STRANGER TO YOU, SO...!!!
YES ...!
I GOT HIM TO RESPOND ...!
FUI (SNUB)
GAN (GAPE)
...LITTLE BY LITTLE, I'LL CLOSE THE GAP BETWEEN US.
AND SO ...
HMM...

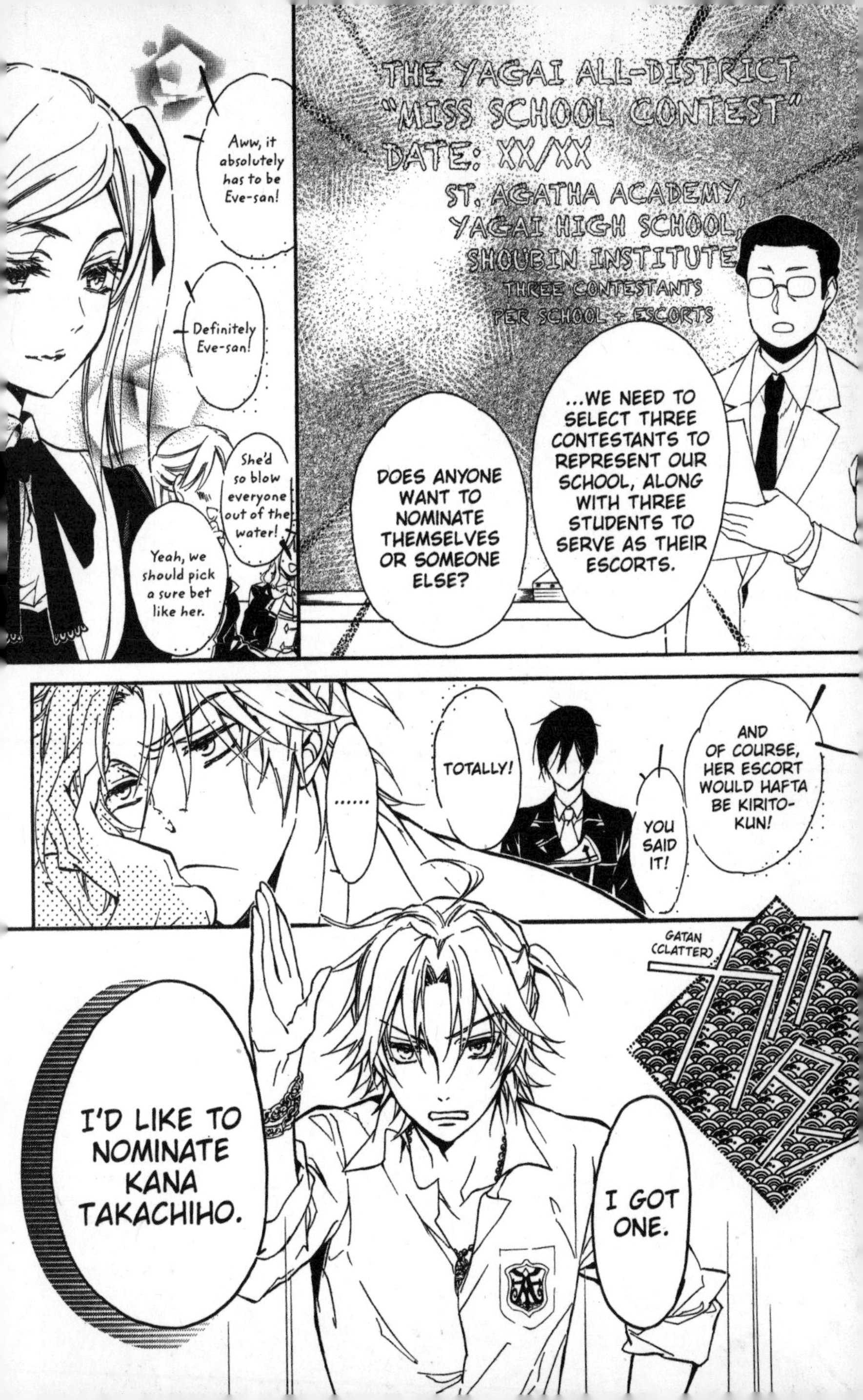
THE YAGAI ALL-DISTRICT "MISS SCHOOL CONTEST"
DATE: XX/XX
ST. AGATHA ACADEMY, YAGAI HIGH SCHOOL, SHOUBIN INSTITUTE
THREE CONTESTANTS PER SCHOOL + ESCORTS
...WE NEED TO SELECT THREE CONTESTANTS TO REPRESENT OUR SCHOOL, ALONG WITH THREE STUDENTS TO SERVE AS THEIR ESCORTS.
DOES ANYONE WANT TO NOMINATE THEMSELVES OR SOMEONE ELSE?
Aww, it absolutely has to be Eve-san!
Definitely Eve-san!
She'd so blow everyone out of the water!
Yeah, we should pick a sure bet like her.
AND OF COURSE, HER ESCORT WOULD HAFTA BE KIRITO-KUN!
YOU SAID IT!
TOTALLY!
......
GATAN (CLATTER)
I GOT ONE.
I'D LIKE TO NOMINATE KANA TAKACHIHO.

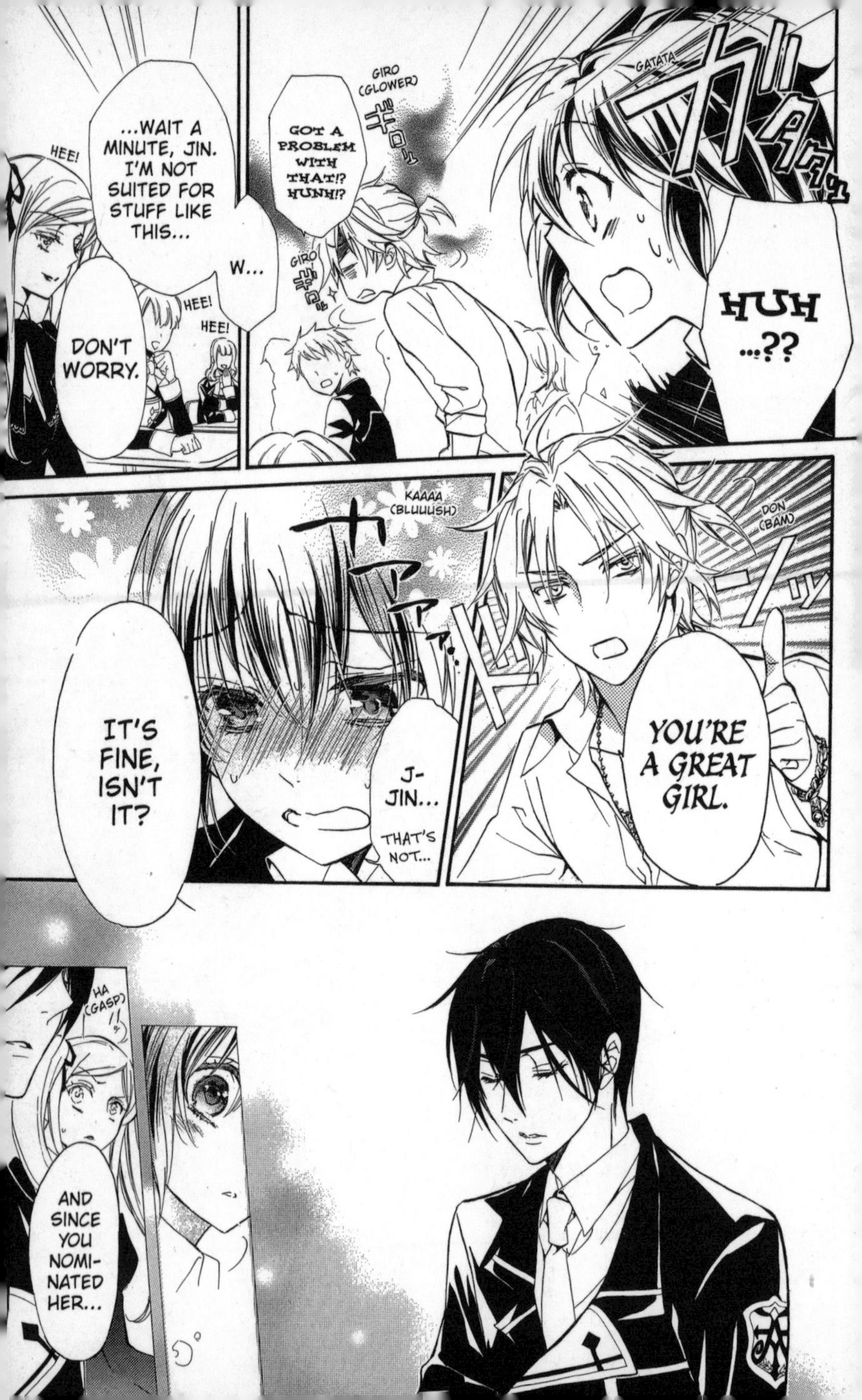
GATATA
HUH ...??
GIRO (GLOWER)
GOT A PROBLEM WITH THAT!? HUNH!?
GIRO
W...
...WAIT A MINUTE, JIN. I'M NOT SUITED FOR STUFF LIKE THIS...
HEE!
HEE!
HEE!
DON'T WORRY.
DON (BAM)
YOU'RE A GREAT GIRL.
KAAAA (BLUUUSH)
J-JIN...
THAT'S NOT...
IT'S FINE, ISN'T IT?
HA (GASP) !!
AND SINCE YOU NOMINATED HER...

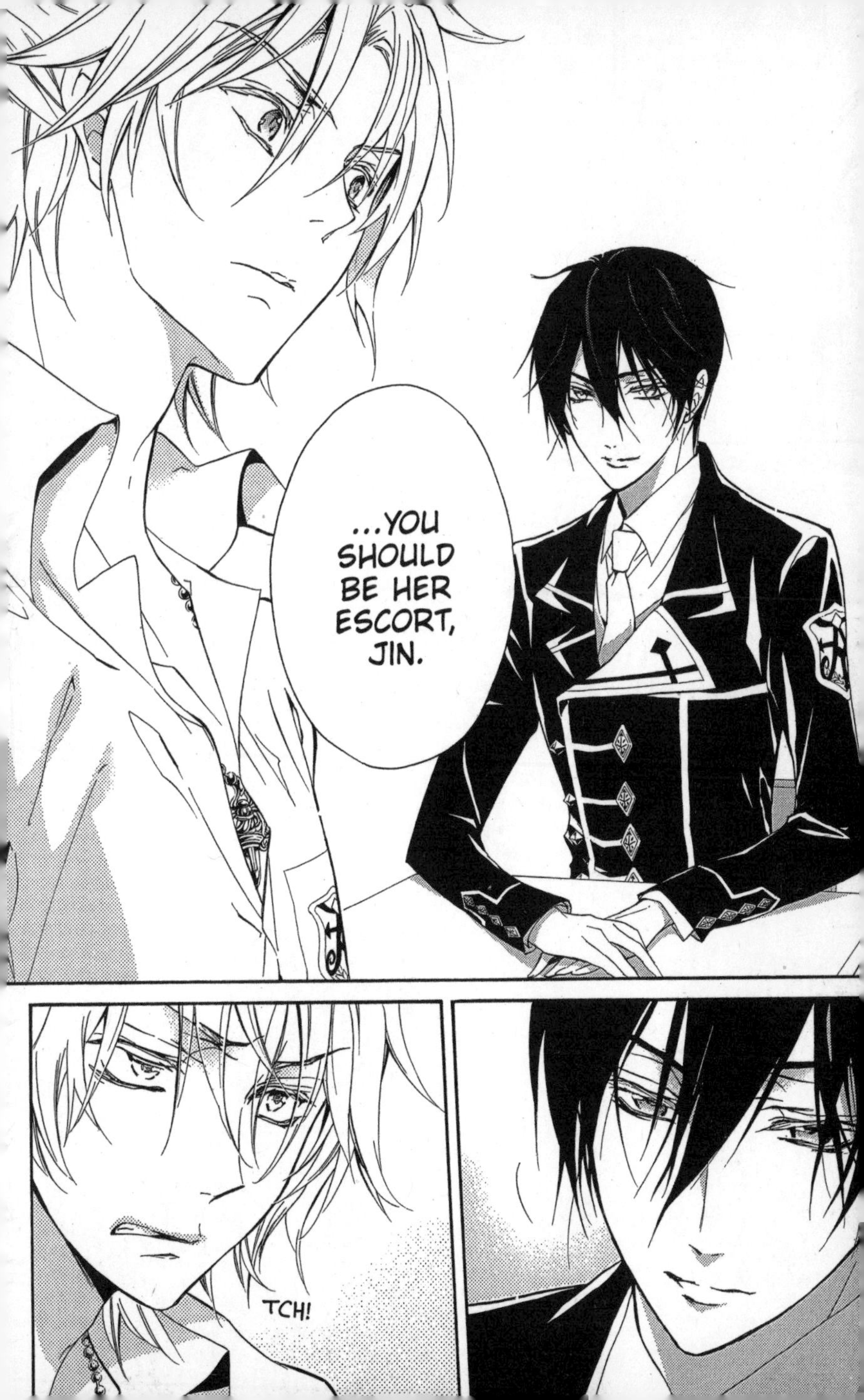
...YOU SHOULD BE HER ESCORT, JIN.
TCH!

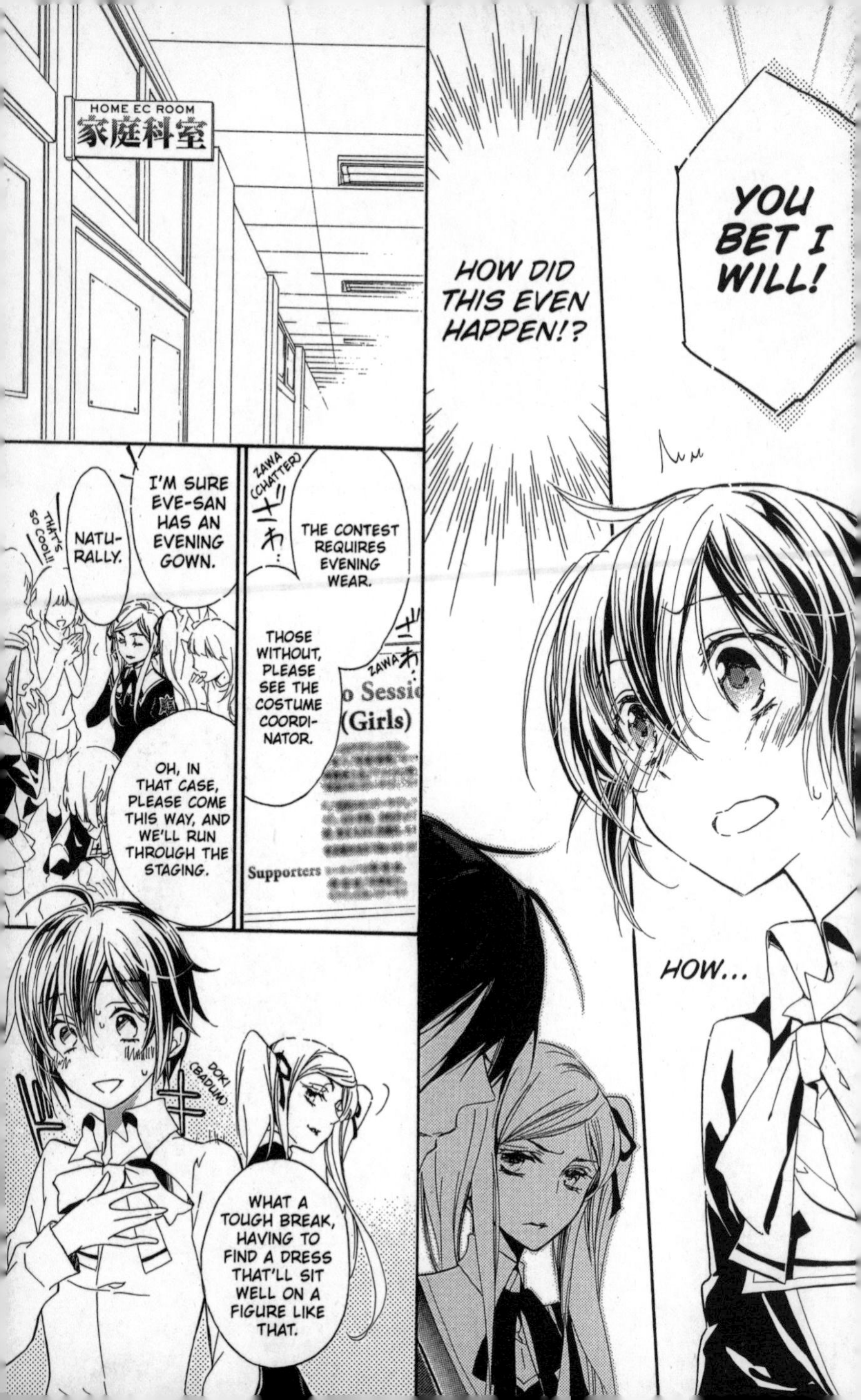
YOU BET I WILL!
HOW...
HOW DID THIS EVEN HAPPEN!?
HOME EC ROOM
家庭科室
ZAWA (CHATTER)
THE CONTEST REQUIRES EVENING WEAR.
THOSE WITHOUT, PLEASE SEE THE COSTUME COORDINATOR.
ZAWA
(Girls)
Supporters
I'M SURE EVE-SAN HAS AN EVENING GOWN.
NATURALLY.
THAT'S SO COOL!!
OH, IN THAT CASE, PLEASE COME THIS WAY, AND WE'LL RUN THROUGH THE STAGING.
DOKI (BADUM)
WHAT A TOUGH BREAK, HAVING TO FIND A DRESS THAT'LL SIT WELL ON A FIGURE LIKE THAT.

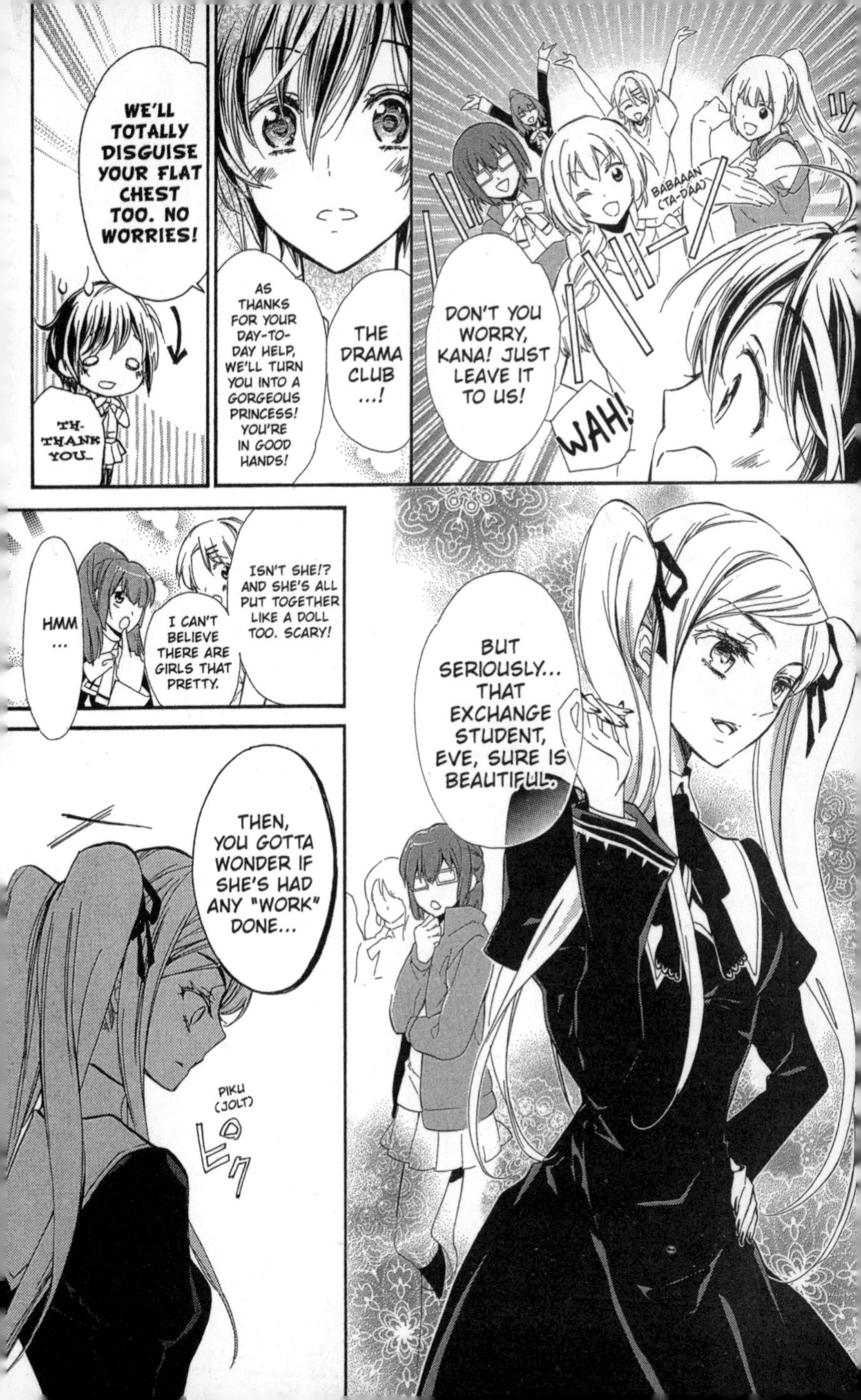
BABAAAN (TA-DAA)
WAH!
DON'T YOU WORRY, KANA! JUST LEAVE IT TO US!
THE DRAMA CLUB ...!
AS THANKS FOR YOUR DAY-TO-DAY HELP, WE'LL TURN YOU INTO A GORGEOUS PRINCESS! YOU'RE IN GOOD HANDS!
WE'LL TOTALLY DISGUISE YOUR FLAT CHEST TOO. NO WORRIES!
TH-THANK YOU...
BUT SERIOUSLY... THAT EXCHANGE STUDENT, EVE, SURE IS BEAUTIFUL.
ISN'T SHE!? AND SHE'S ALL PUT TOGETHER LIKE A DOLL TOO. SCARY!
I CAN'T BELIEVE THERE ARE GIRLS THAT PRETTY.
HMM ...
THEN, YOU GOTTA WONDER IF SHE'S HAD ANY "WORK" DONE...
PIKU (JOLT)

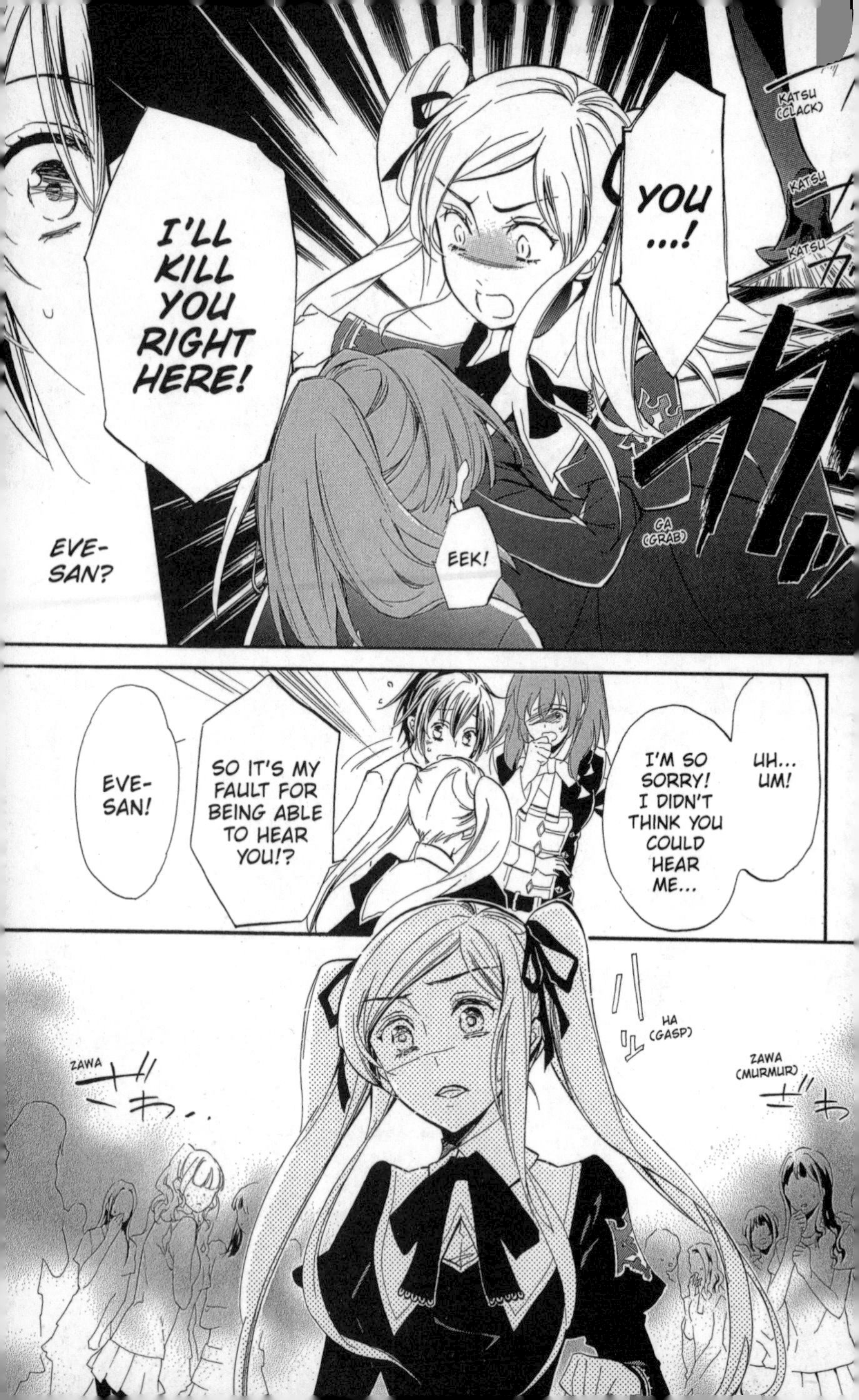
KATSU (CLACK)
KATSU
KATSU
YOU...!
GA (GRAB)
EEK!
I'LL KILL YOU RIGHT HERE!
EVE-SAN?
UH... UM!
I'M SO SORRY! I DIDN'T THINK YOU COULD HEAR ME...
SO IT'S MY FAULT FOR BEING ABLE TO HEAR YOU!?
EVE-SAN!
ZAWA (MURMUR)
HA (GASP)
ZAWA

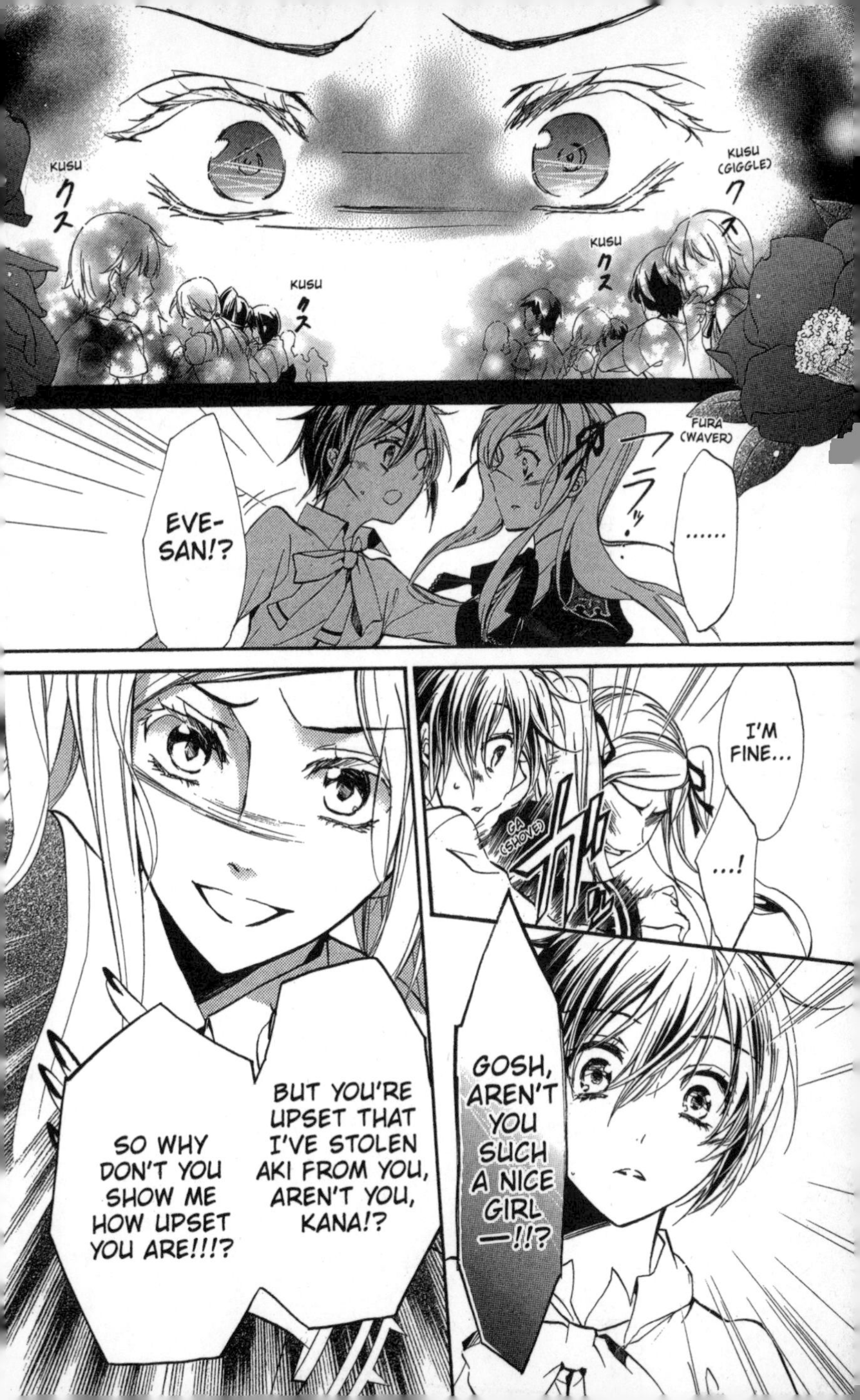
KUSU (GIGGLE)
クス
KUSU
クス
KUSU
クス
KUSU
クス
FURA (WAVER)
フラッ
......
EVE-SAN!?
I'M FINE...
GA (SHOVE)
ガッ
...!
GOSH, AREN'T YOU SUCH A NICE GIRL—!!?
BUT YOU'RE UPSET THAT I'VE STOLEN AKI FROM YOU, AREN'T YOU, KANA!?
SO WHY DON'T YOU SHOW ME HOW UPSET YOU ARE!!!?

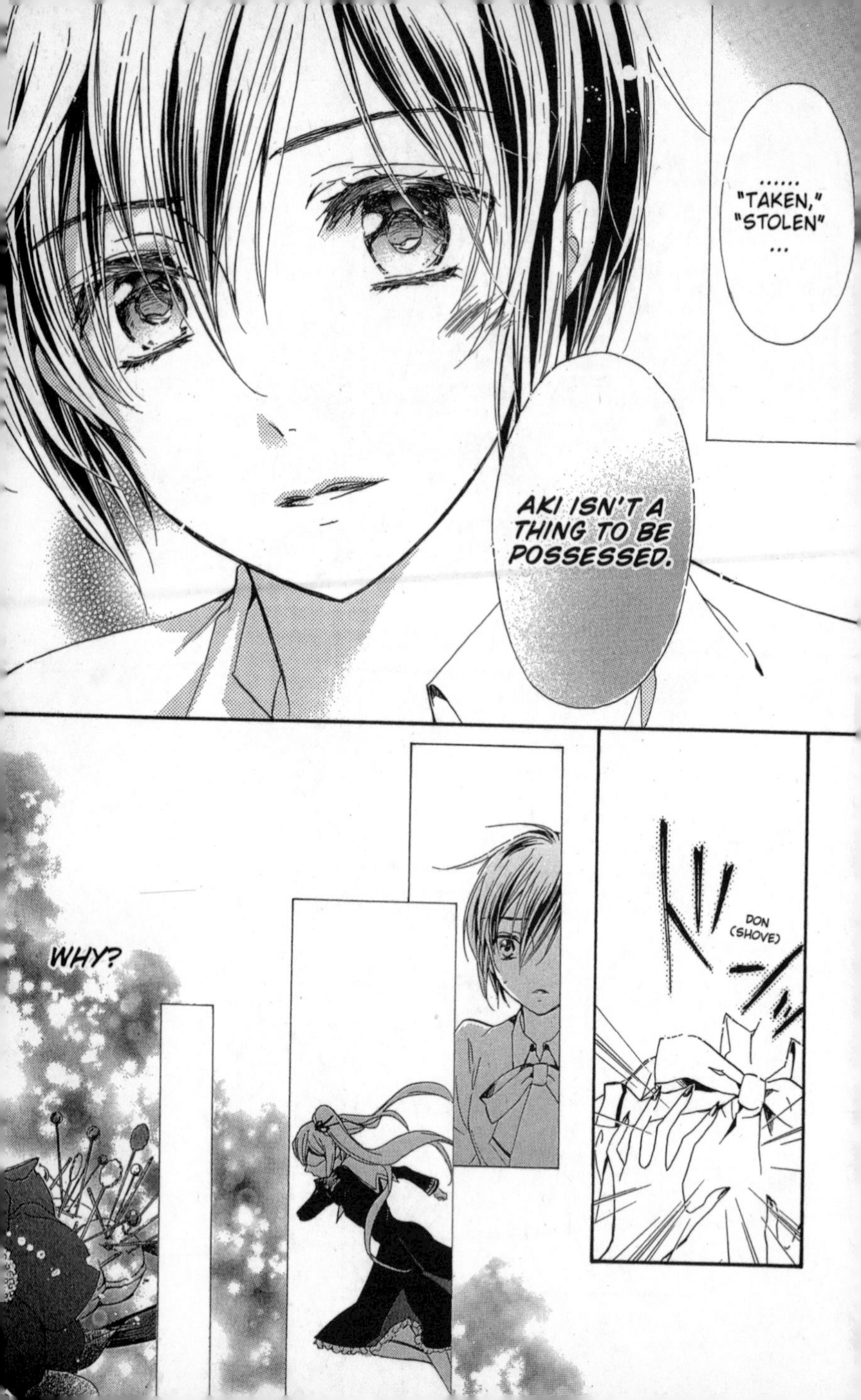
......
"TAKEN,"
"STOLEN"
...
AKI ISN'T A THING TO BE POSSESSED.
DON (SHOVE)
WHY?

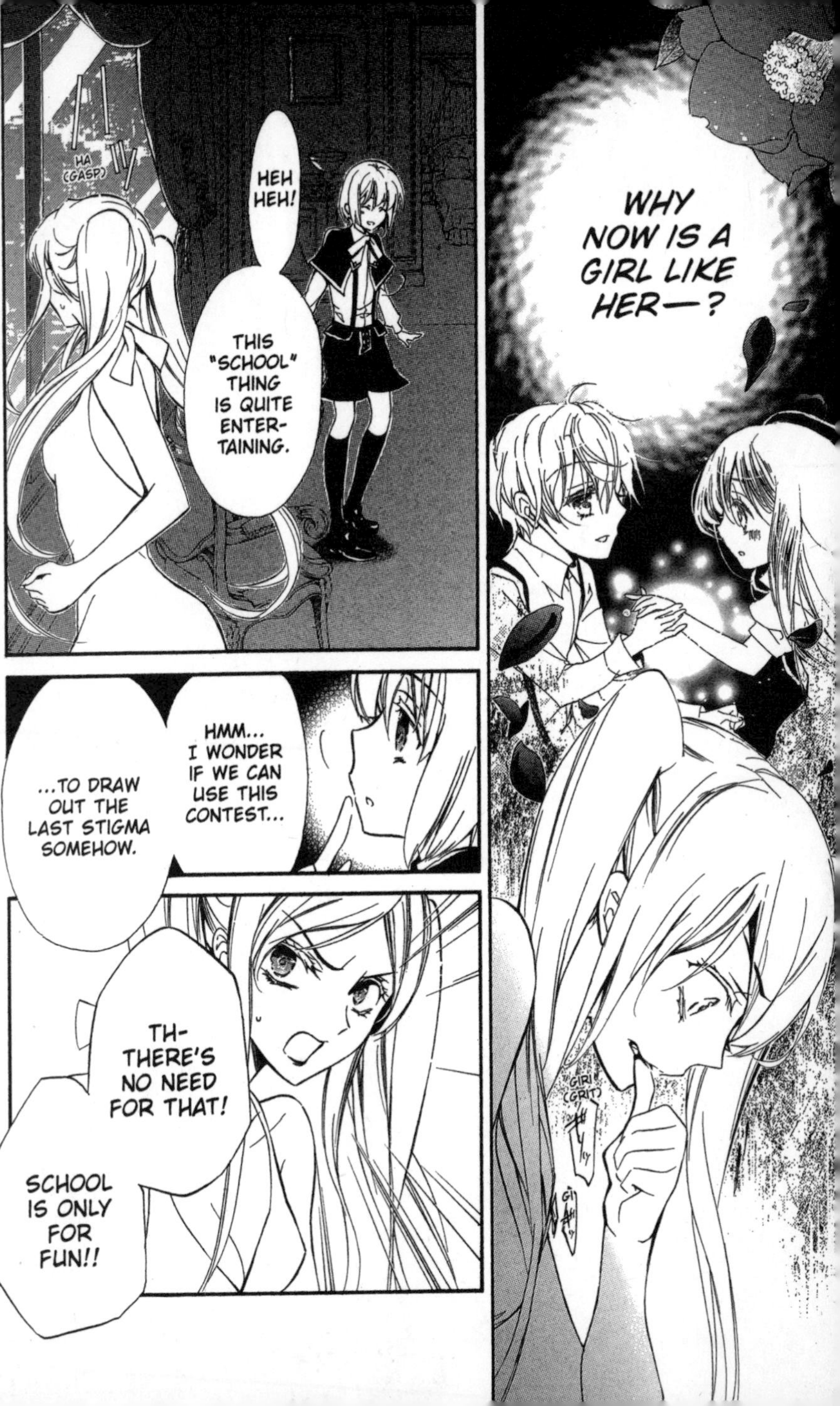
WHY NOW IS A GIRL LIKE HER—?
GIRI (GRIT)
HEH HEH!
THIS "SCHOOL" THING IS QUITE ENTERTAINING.
HA (GASP)
HMM... I WONDER IF WE CAN USE THIS CONTEST...
...TO DRAW OUT THE LAST STIGMA SOMEHOW.
TH-THERE'S NO NEED FOR THAT!
SCHOOL IS ONLY FOR FUN!!

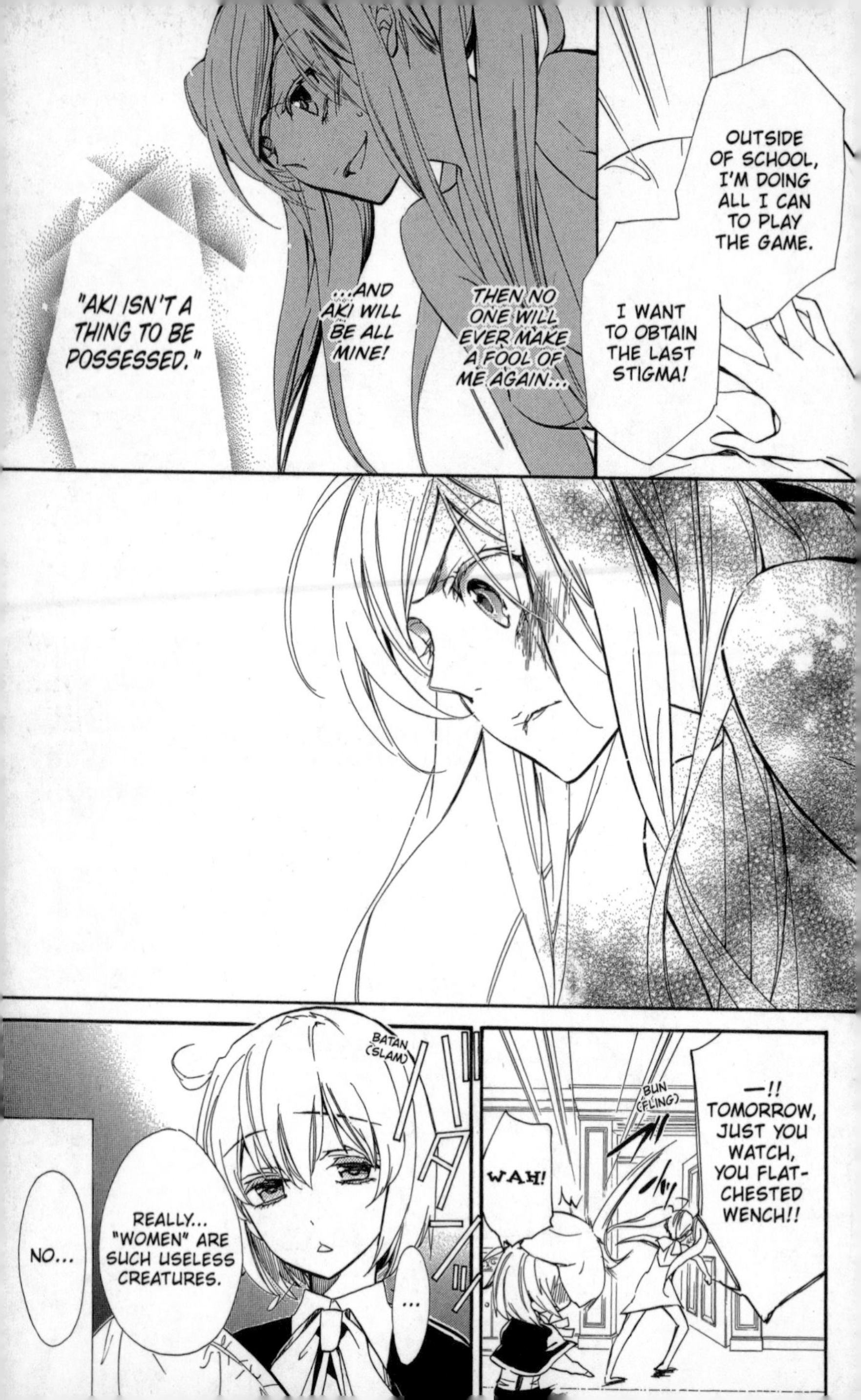
OUTSIDE OF SCHOOL, I'M DOING ALL I CAN TO PLAY THE GAME.
I WANT TO OBTAIN THE LAST STIGMA!
THEN NO ONE WILL EVER MAKE A FOOL OF ME AGAIN...
...AND AKI WILL BE ALL MINE!
"AKI ISN'T A THING TO BE POSSESSED."
—!! TOMORROW, JUST YOU WATCH, YOU FLAT-CHESTED WENCH!!
BUN (FLING)
WAH!
BATAN (SLAM)
...
REALLY... "WOMEN" ARE SUCH USELESS CREATURES.
NO...

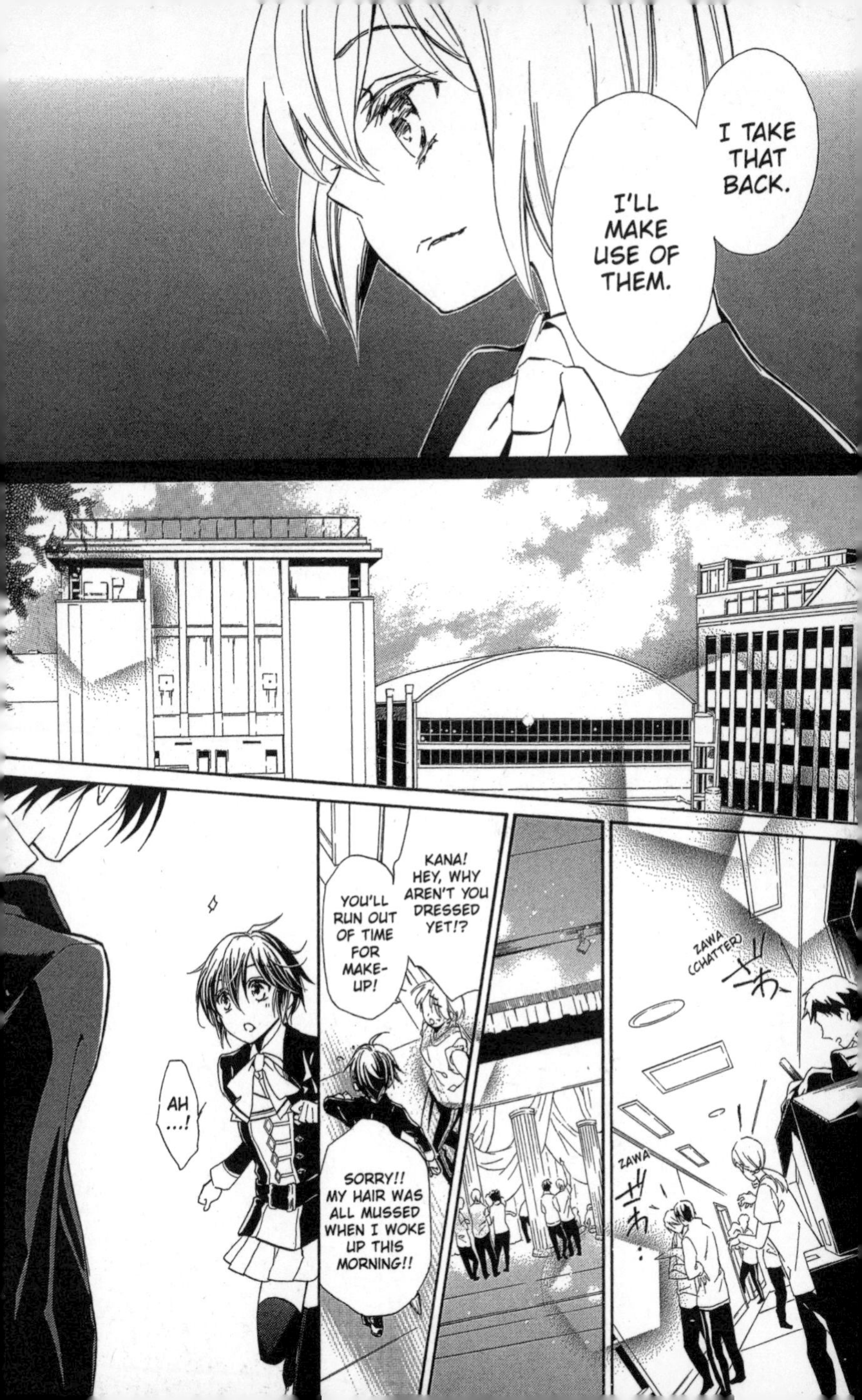
I TAKE THAT BACK.
I'LL MAKE USE OF THEM.
ZAWA (CHATTER)
ZAWA
KANA! HEY, WHY AREN'T YOU DRESSED YET!?
YOU'LL RUN OUT OF TIME FOR MAKE-UP!
SORRY!! MY HAIR WAS ALL MUSSED WHEN I WOKE UP THIS MORNING!!
AH ...!

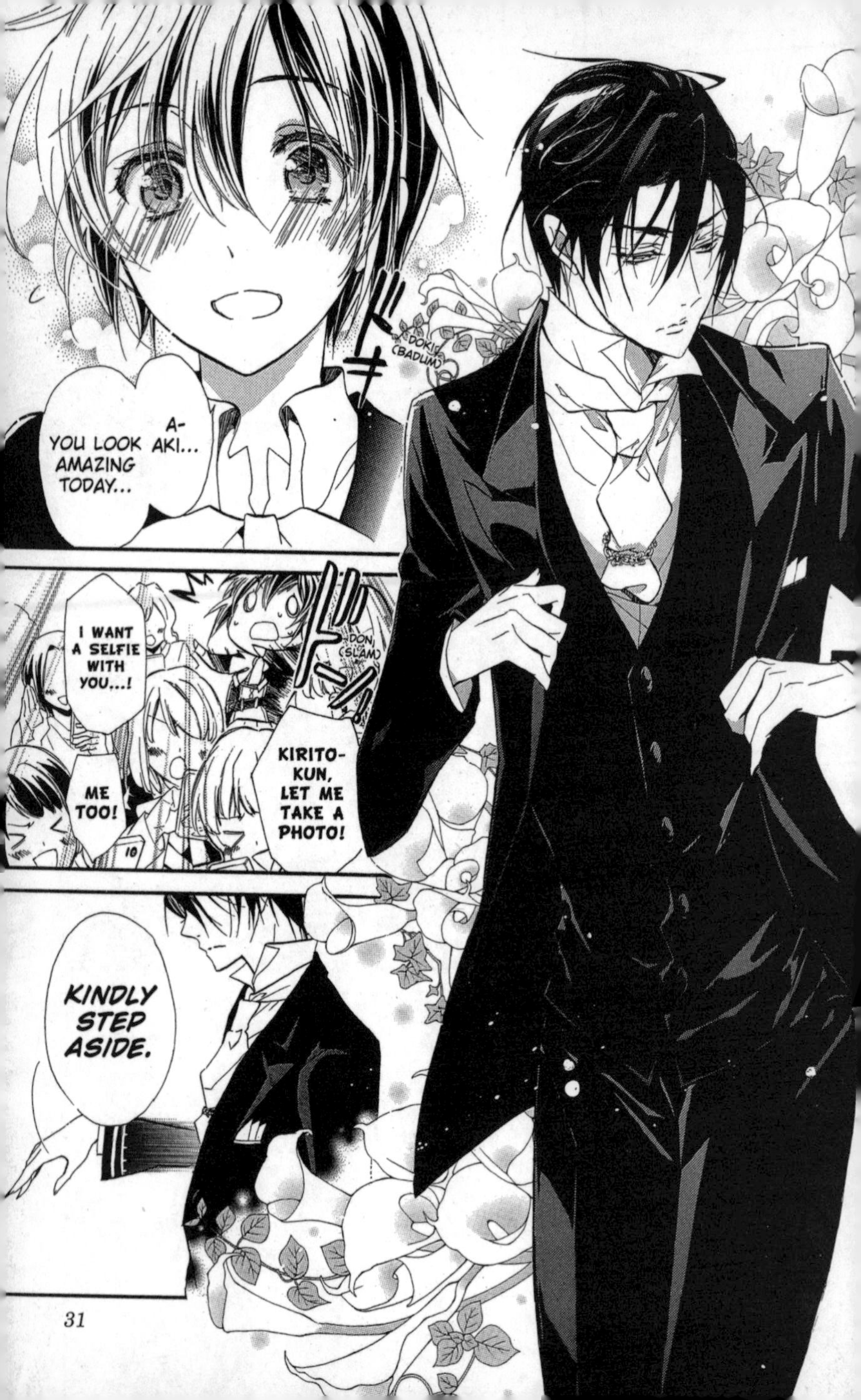
DOKI (BADUM)
A- AKI... YOU LOOK AMAZING TODAY...
DON (SLAM)
KIRITO-KUN, LET ME TAKE A PHOTO!
I WANT A SELFIE WITH YOU...!
ME TOO!
KINDLY STEP ASIDE.

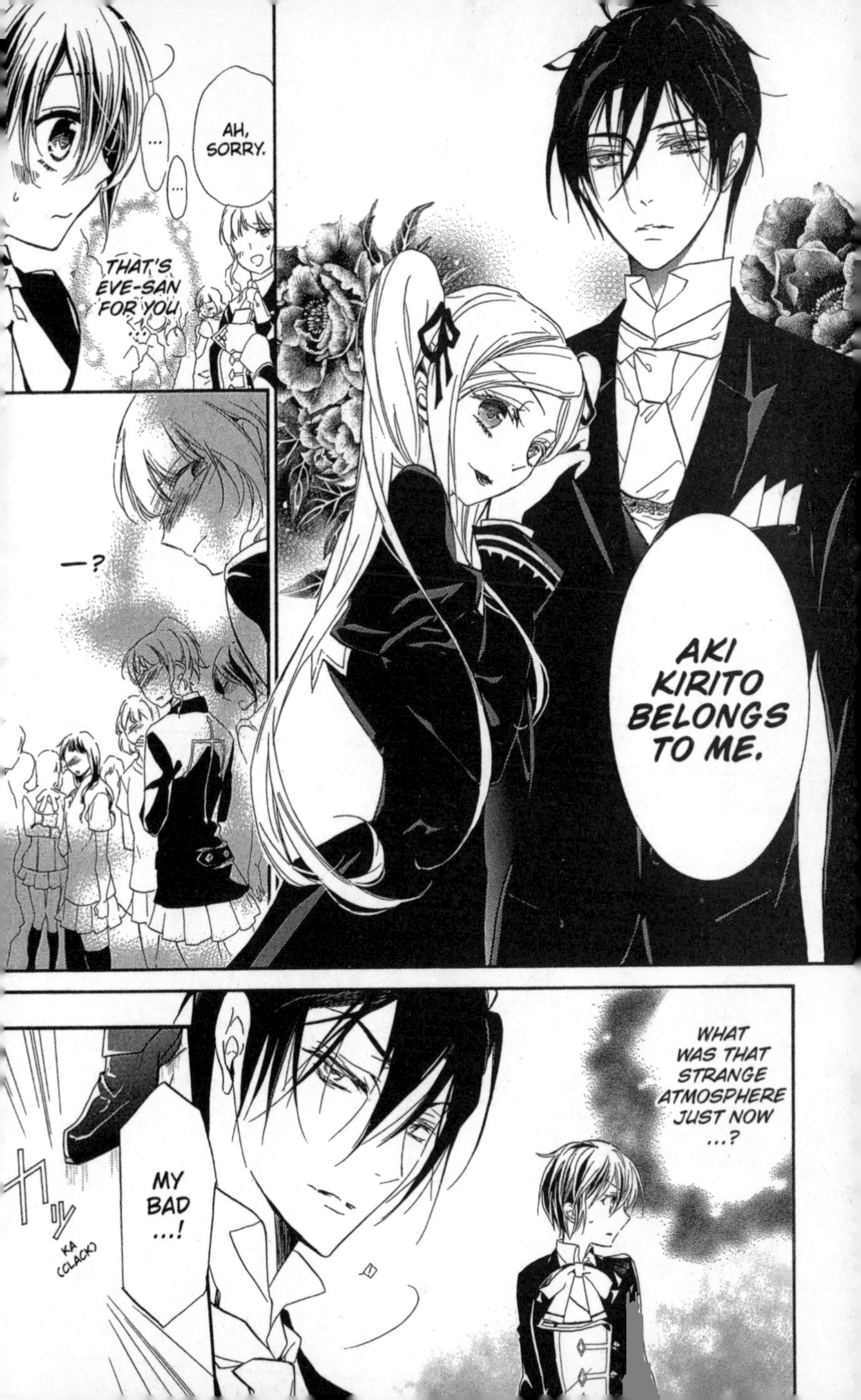
AKI KIRITO BELONGS TO ME.
AH, SORRY.
...
...
THAT'S EVE-SAN FOR YOU
—?
WHAT WAS THAT STRANGE ATMOSPHERE JUST NOW ...?
MY BAD ...!
カッ
KA (CLACK)

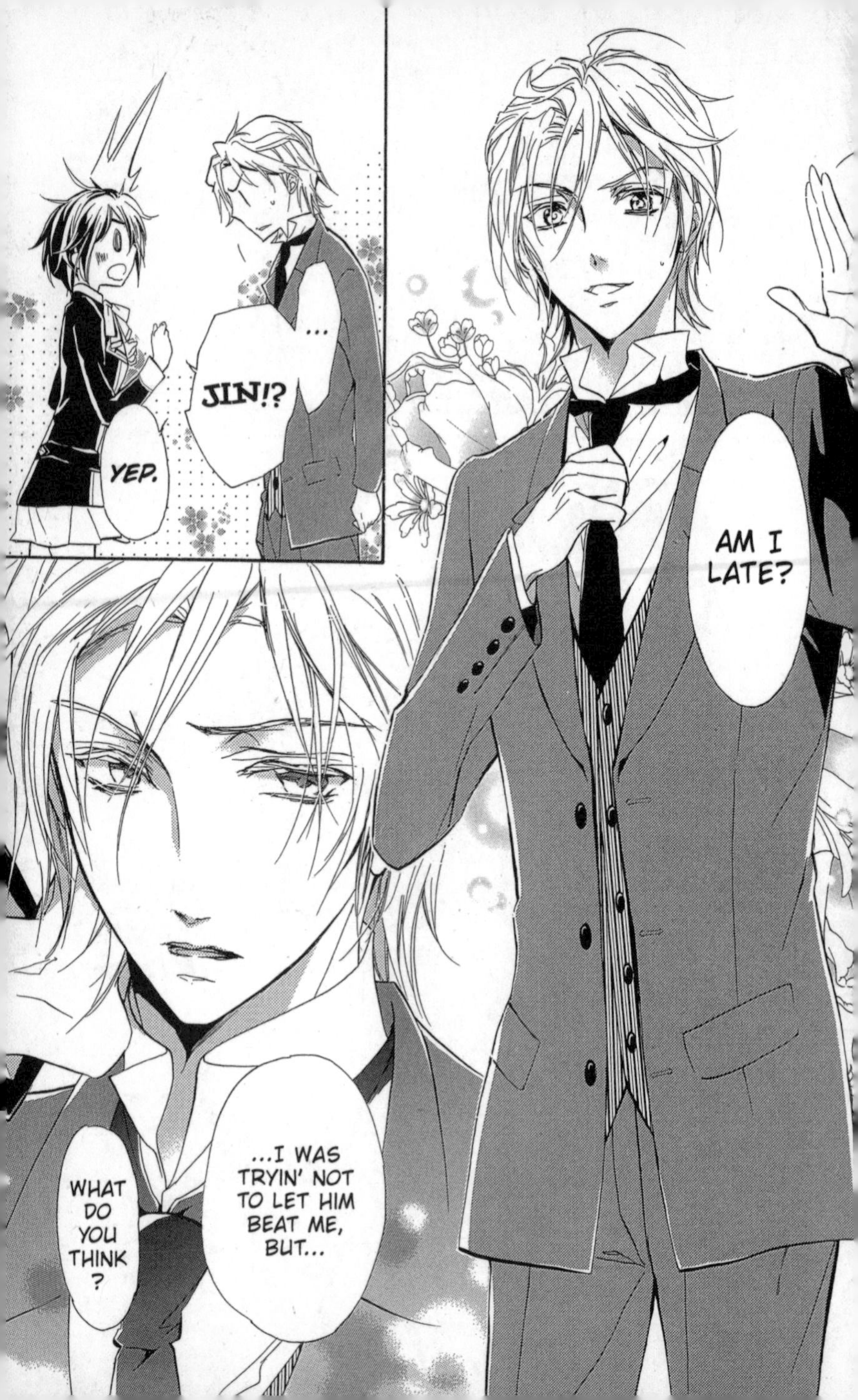
AM I LATE?
...
JIN!?
YEP.
...I WAS TRYIN' NOT TO LET HIM BEAT ME, BUT...
WHAT DO YOU THINK?

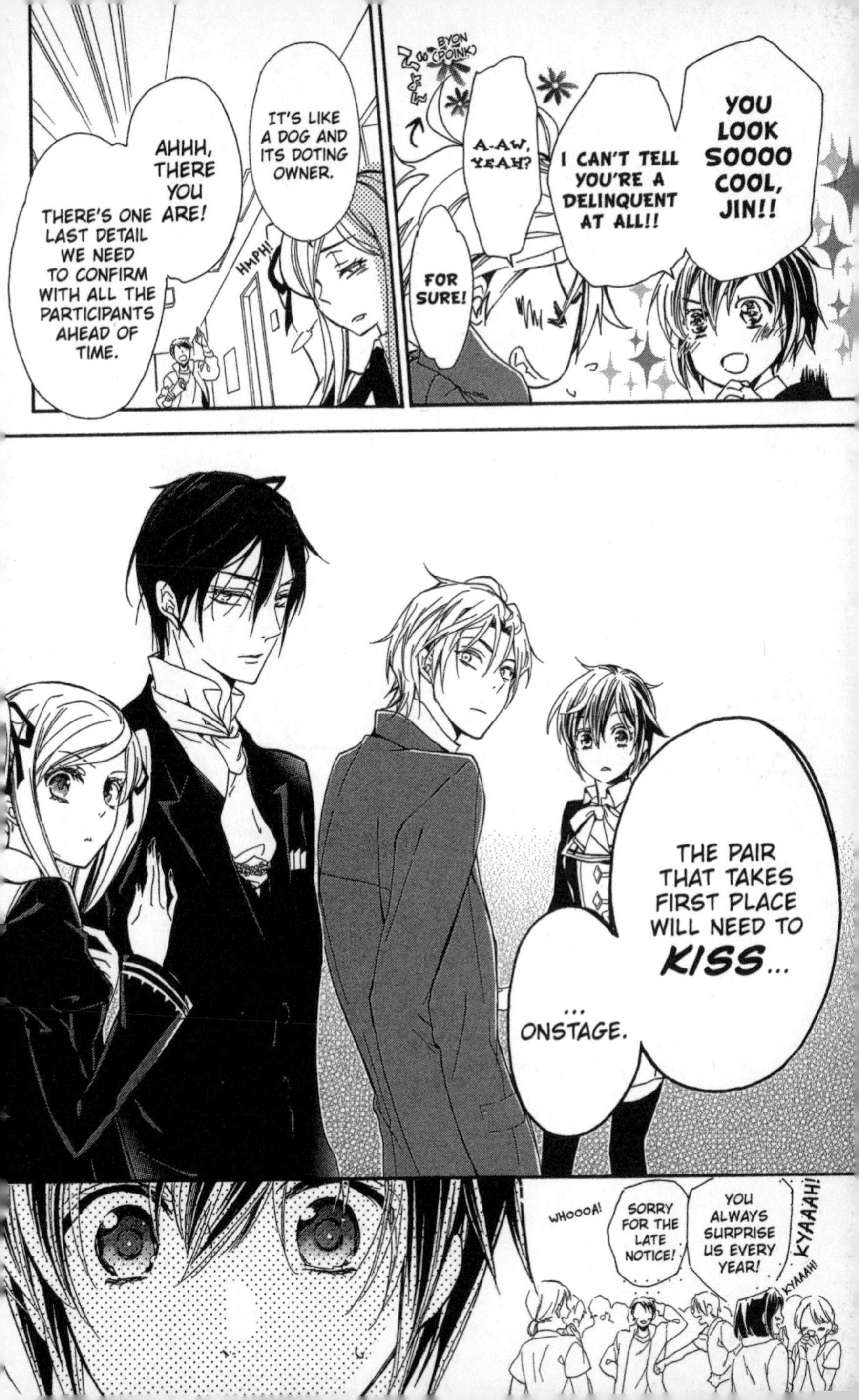
BYON (POINK)
YOU LOOK SOOOO COOL, JIN!!
I CAN'T TELL YOU'RE A DELINQUENT AT ALL!!
A-AW, YEAH?
FOR SURE!
IT'S LIKE A DOG AND ITS DOTING OWNER.
HMPH!
AHHH, THERE YOU ARE!
THERE'S ONE LAST DETAIL WE NEED TO CONFIRM WITH ALL THE PARTICIPANTS AHEAD OF TIME.
THE PAIR THAT TAKES FIRST PLACE WILL NEED TO KISS...
... ONSTAGE.
KYAAAH!
YOU ALWAYS SURPRISE US EVERY YEAR!
SORRY FOR THE LATE NOTICE!
WHOOOA!
KYAAAH!

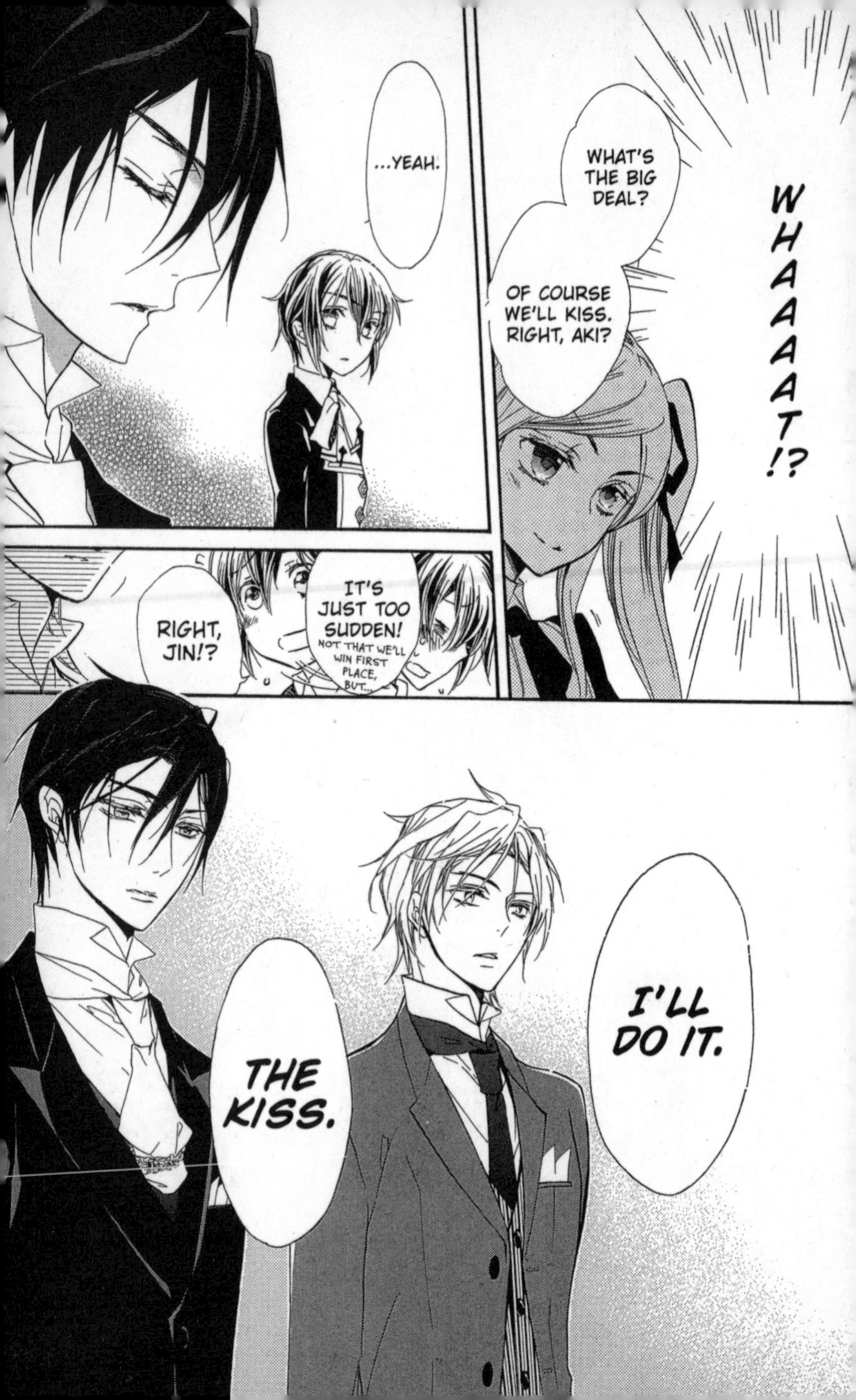
WHAAAAAT!?
WHAT'S THE BIG DEAL?
OF COURSE WE'LL KISS. RIGHT, AKI?
...YEAH.
IT'S JUST TOO SUDDEN! NOT THAT WE'LL WIN FIRST PLACE, BUT...
RIGHT, JIN!?
I'LL DO IT.
THE KISS.

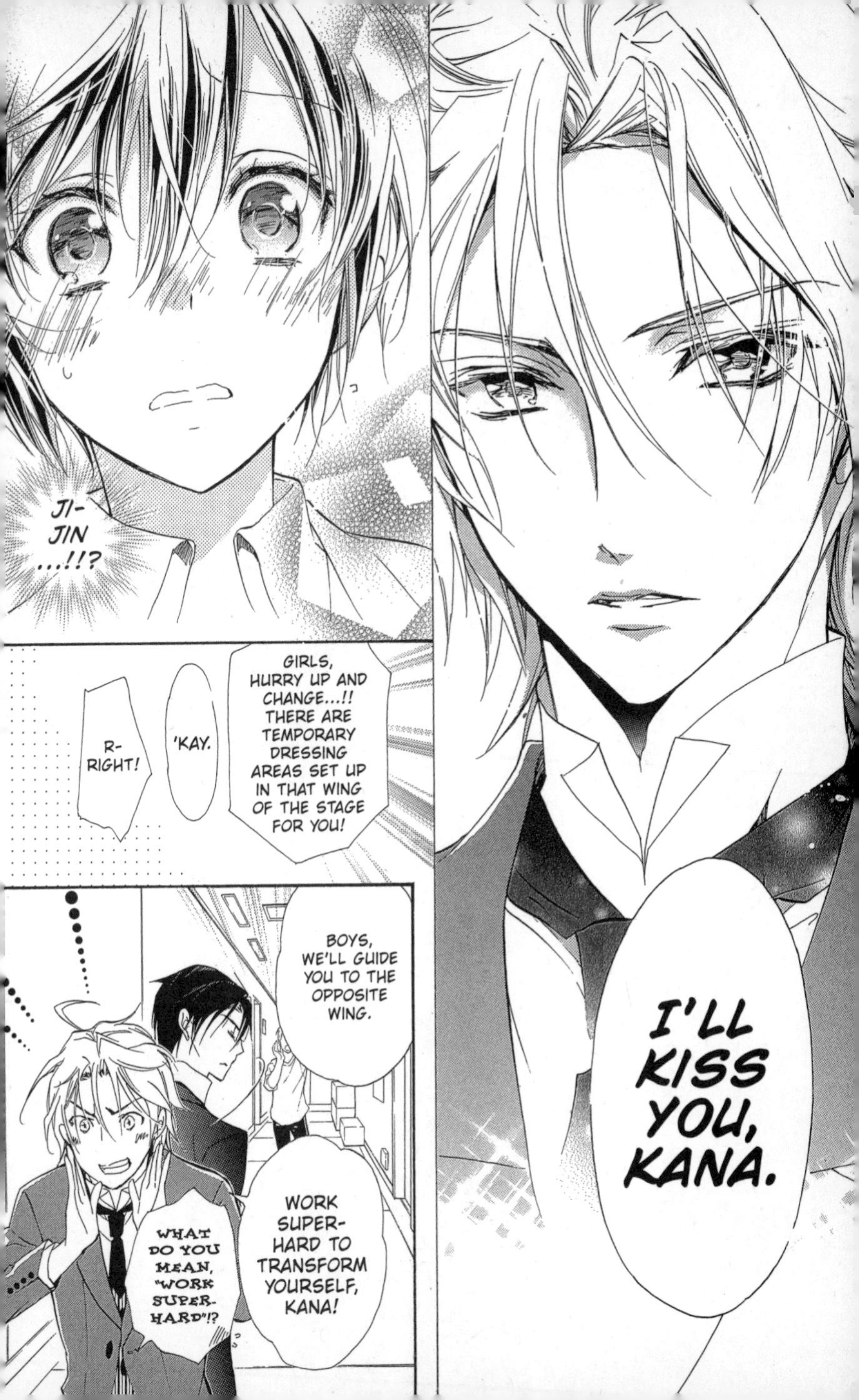
I'LL KISS YOU, KANA.
JI-JIN ...!!?
GIRLS, HURRY UP AND CHANGE...!! THERE ARE TEMPORARY DRESSING AREAS SET UP IN THAT WING OF THE STAGE FOR YOU!
'KAY.
R-RIGHT!
BOYS, WE'LL GUIDE YOU TO THE OPPOSITE WING.
WORK SUPER-HARD TO TRANSFORM YOURSELF, KANA!
WHAT DO YOU MEAN, "WORK SUPER-HARD"!?

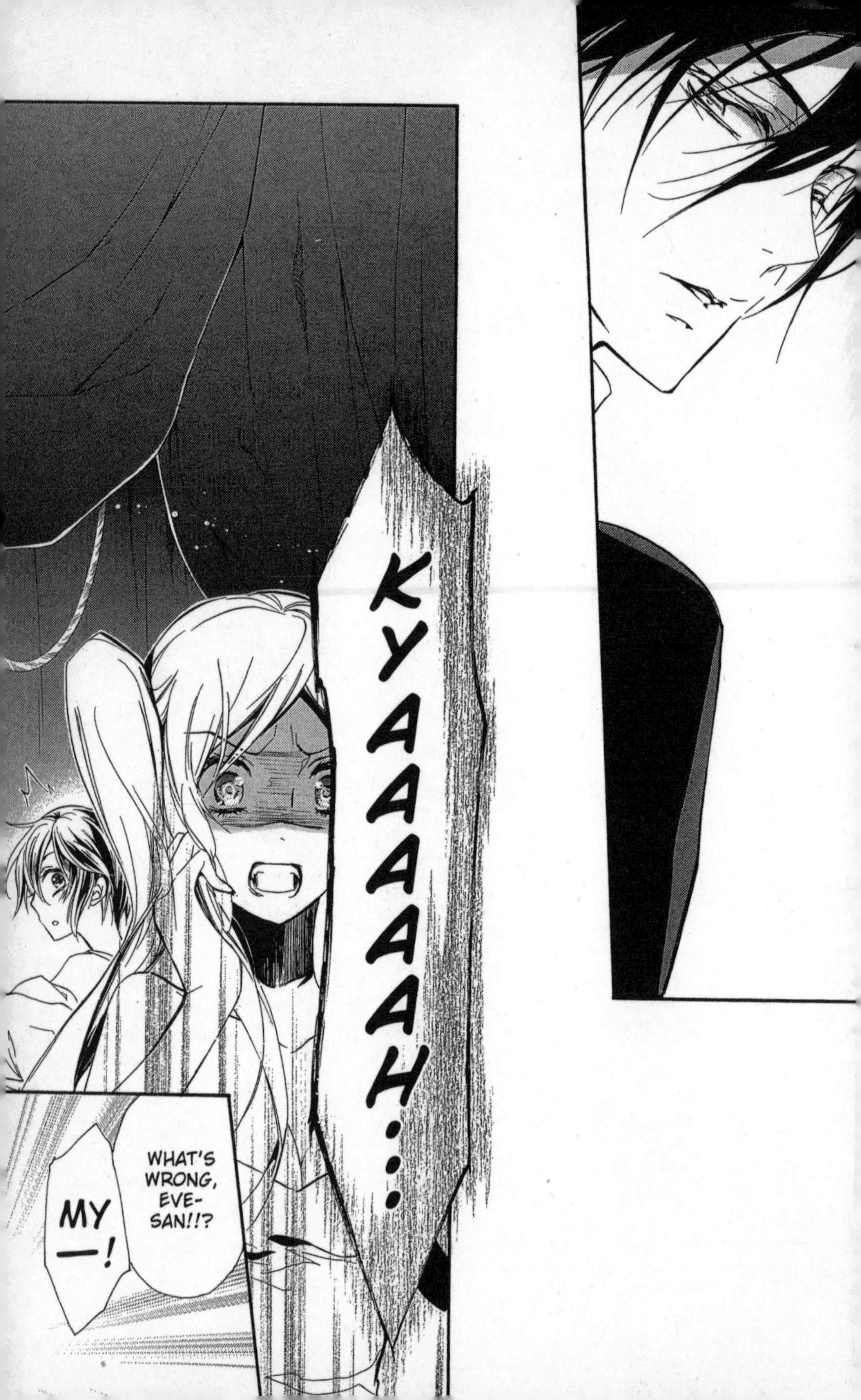
KYAAAAAH...
WHAT'S WRONG, EVE-SAN!!?
MY —!

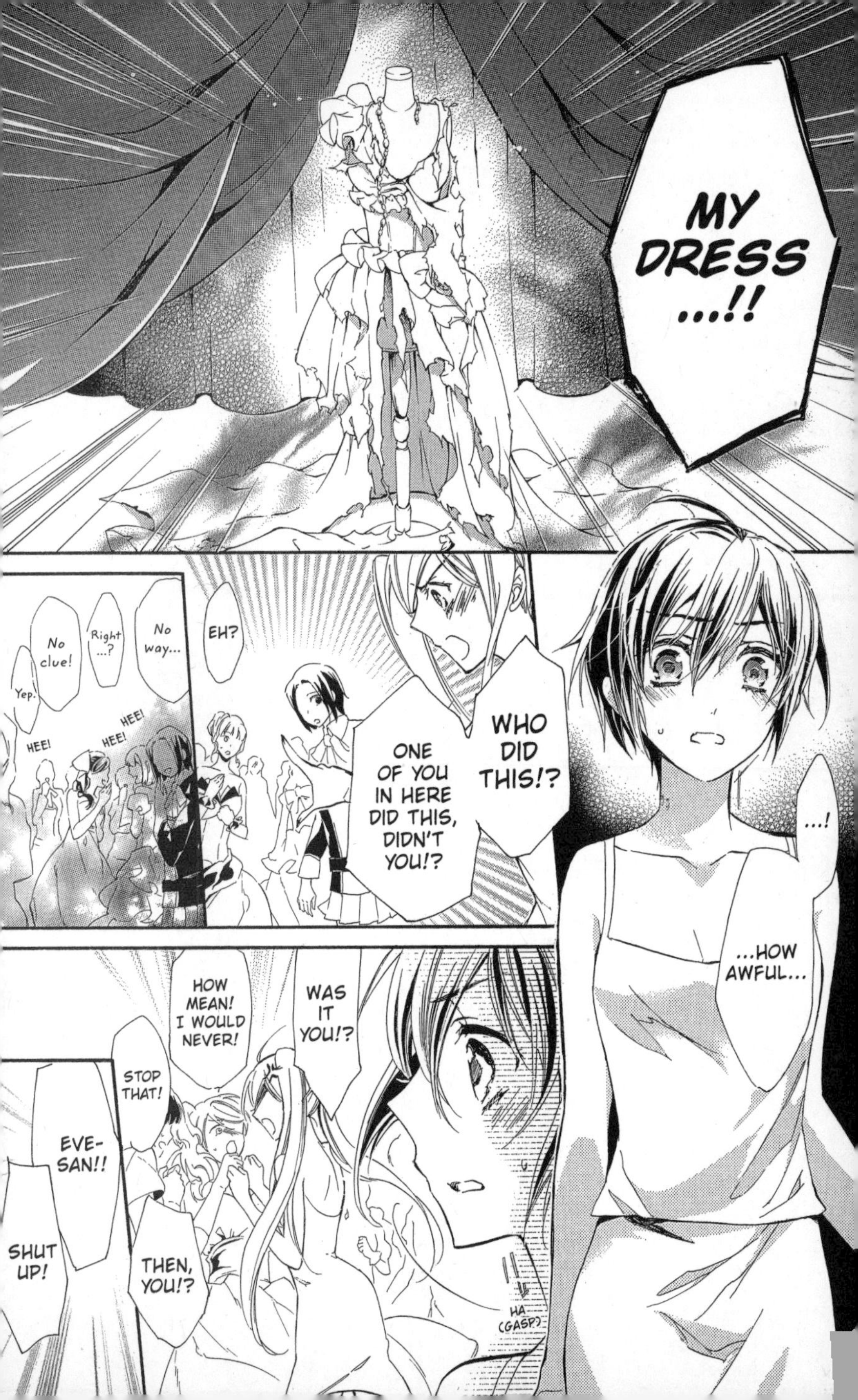
MY DRESS ...!!
...!
...HOW AWFUL...
WHO DID THIS!?
ONE OF YOU IN HERE DID THIS, DIDN'T YOU!?
EH?
No way...
Right ...?
No clue!
Yep.
HEE!
HEE!
HEE!
WAS IT YOU!?
HOW MEAN! I WOULD NEVER!
STOP THAT!
EVE-SAN!!
THEN, YOU!?
SHUT UP!
HA (GASP)

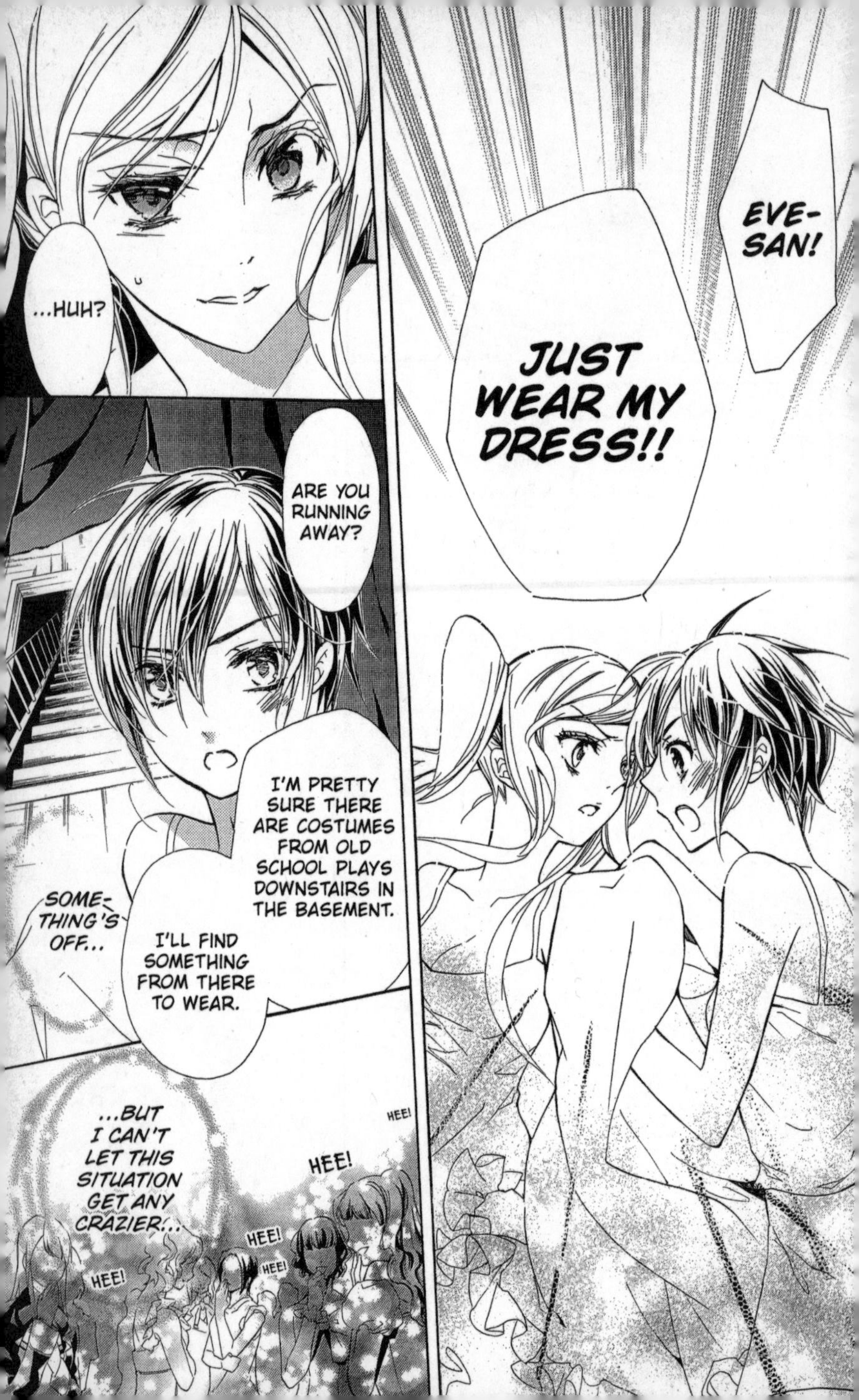
EVE-SAN!
JUST WEAR MY DRESS!!
...HUH?
ARE YOU RUNNING AWAY?
I'M PRETTY SURE THERE ARE COSTUMES FROM OLD SCHOOL PLAYS DOWNSTAIRS IN THE BASEMENT.
I'LL FIND SOMETHING FROM THERE TO WEAR.
SOME-THING'S OFF...
...BUT I CAN'T LET THIS SITUATION GET ANY CRAZIER...
HEE!
HEE!
HEE!
HEE!
HEE!

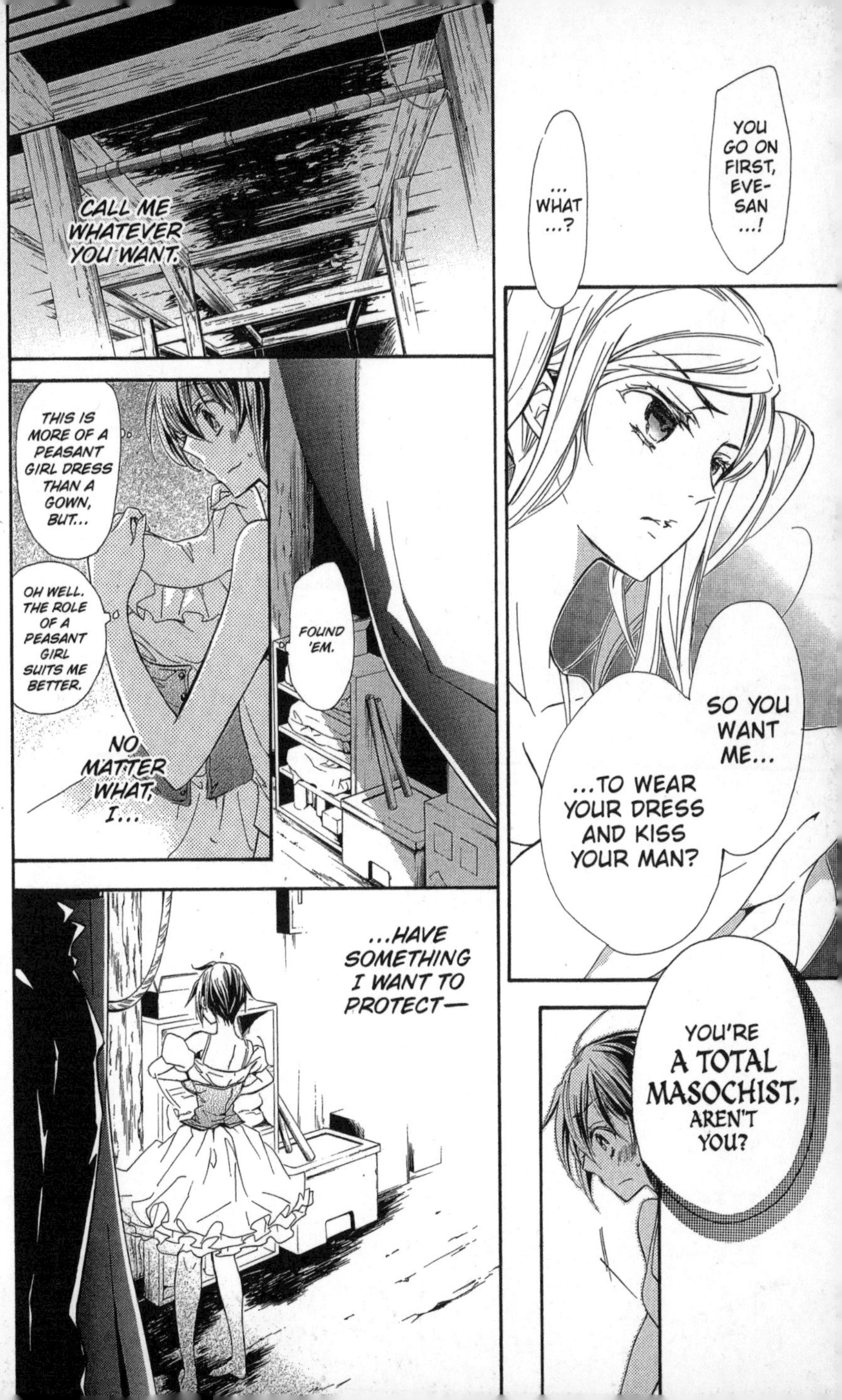
YOU GO ON FIRST, EVE-SAN ...!
... WHAT ...?
SO YOU WANT ME...
...TO WEAR YOUR DRESS AND KISS YOUR MAN?
YOU'RE A TOTAL MASOCHIST, AREN'T YOU?
CALL ME WHATEVER YOU WANT.
FOUND 'EM.
THIS IS MORE OF A PEASANT GIRL DRESS THAN A GOWN, BUT...
OH WELL. THE ROLE OF A PEASANT GIRL SUITS ME BETTER.
NO MATTER WHAT, I...
...HAVE SOMETHING I WANT TO PROTECT—

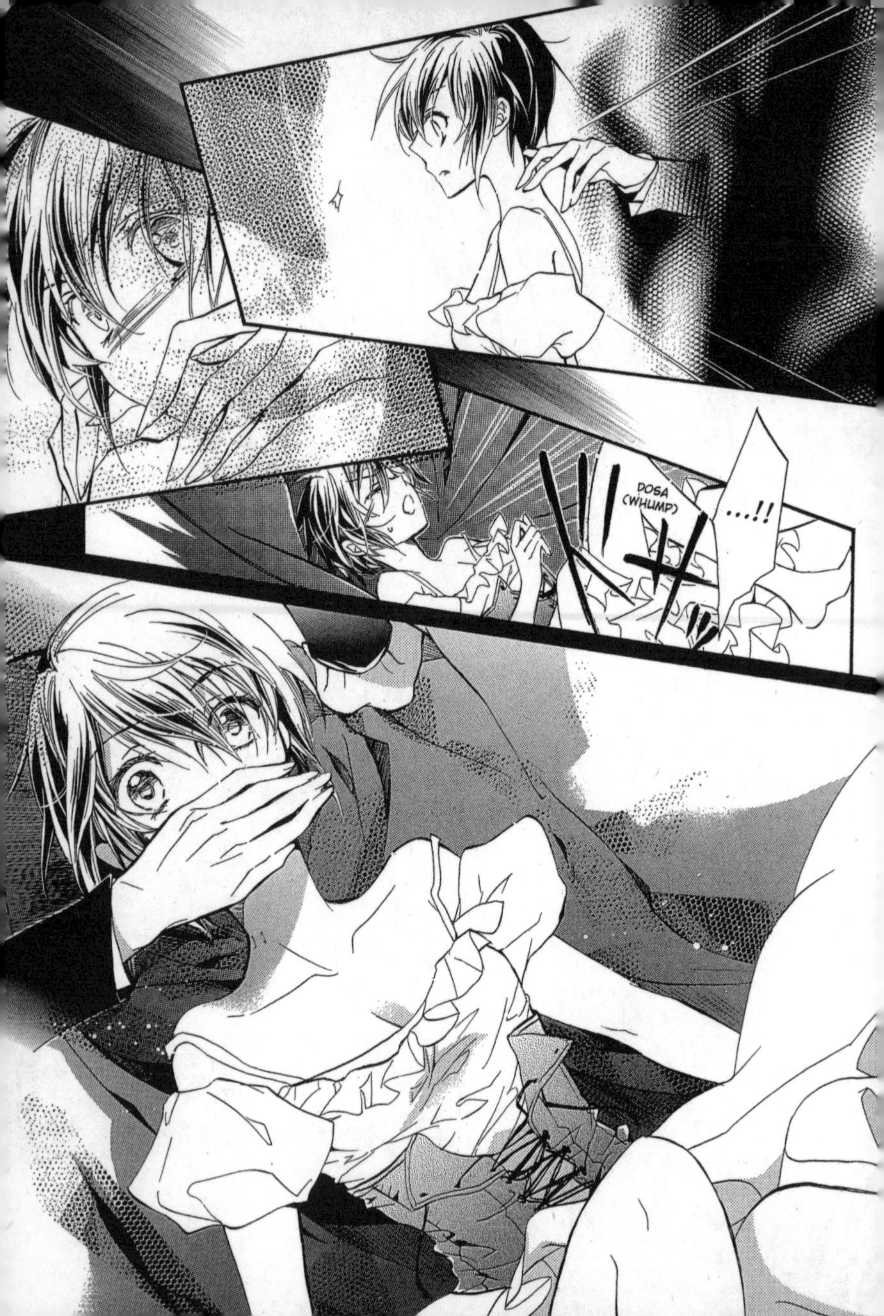
...!!
DOSA (WHUMP)

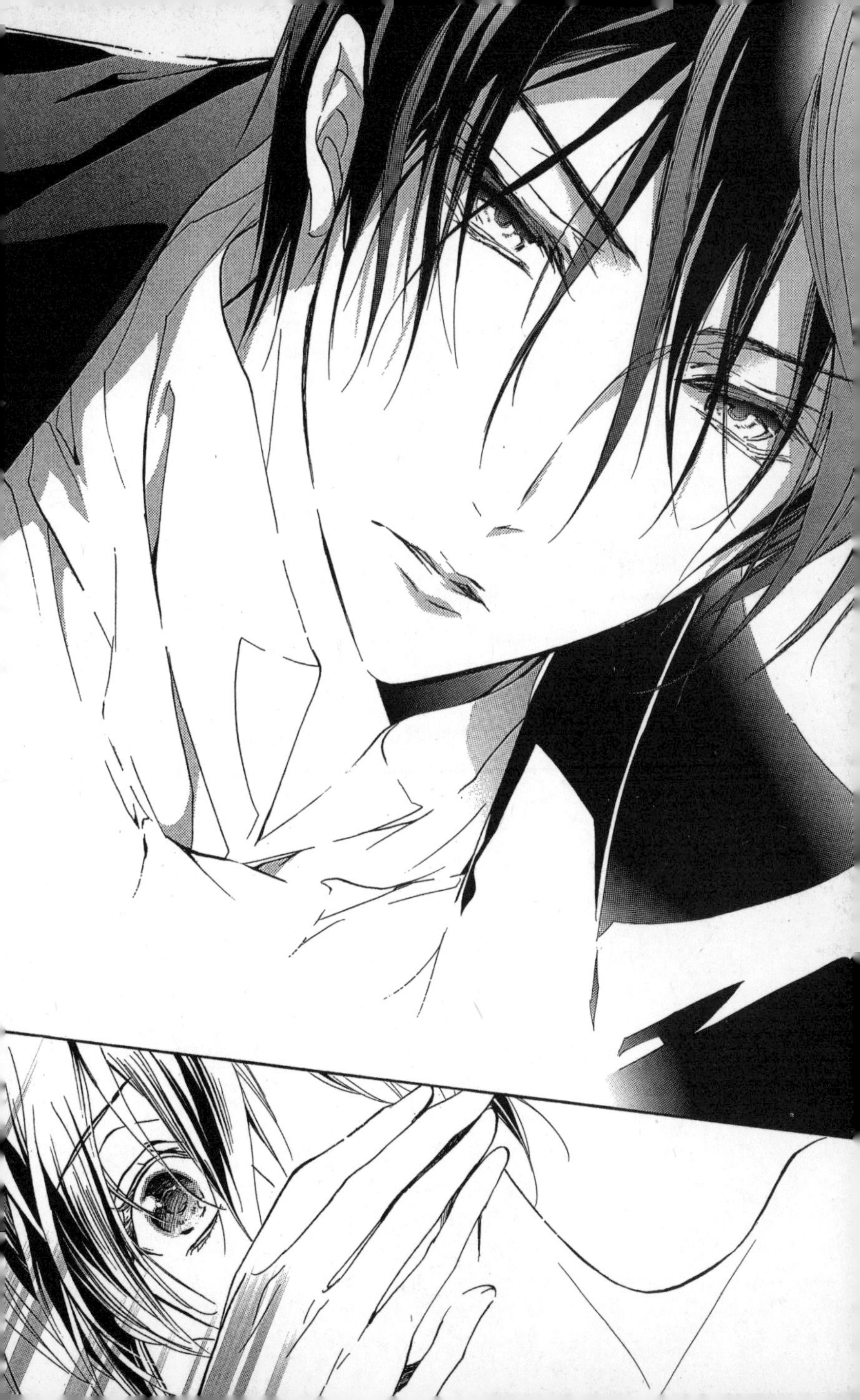

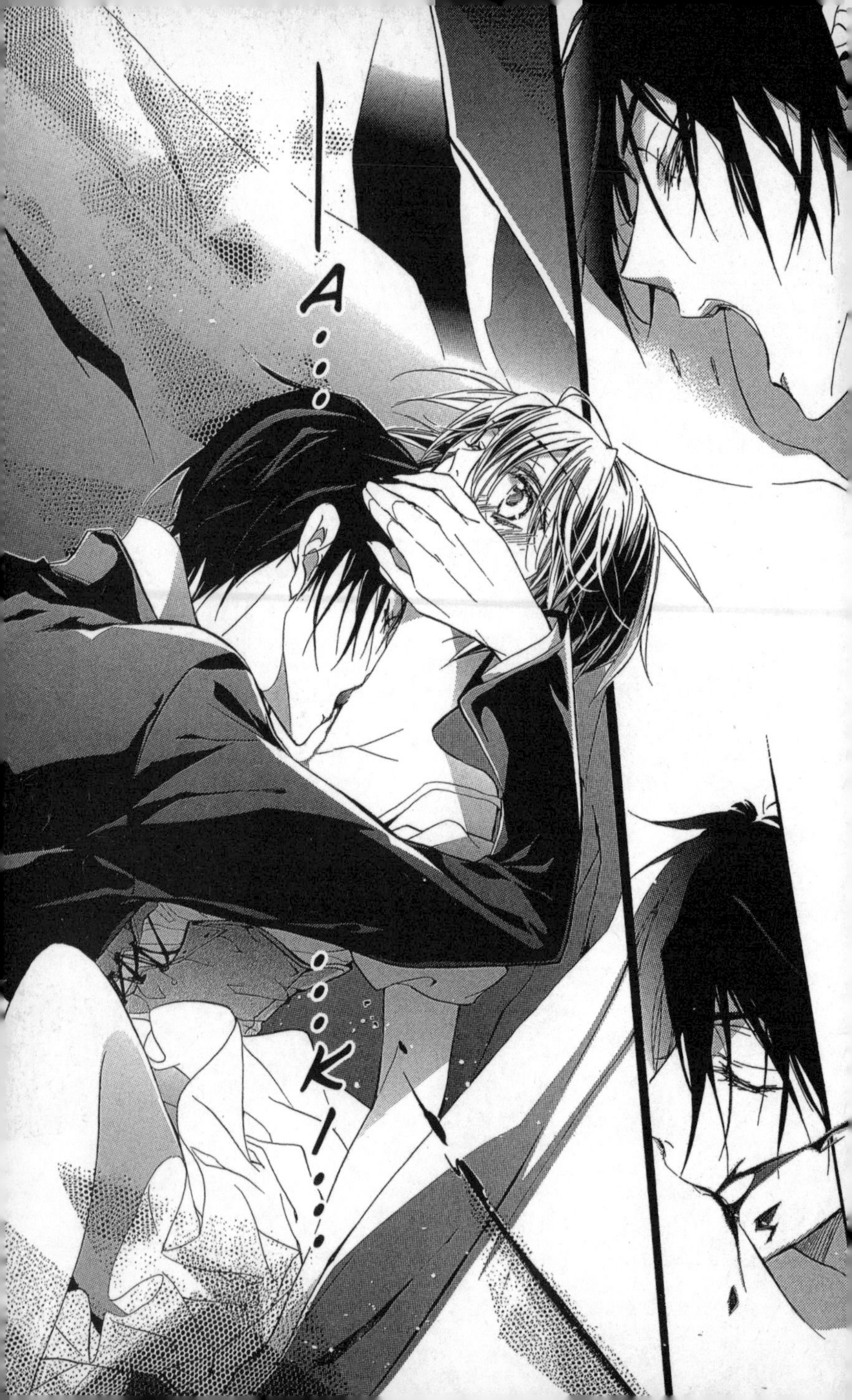
—A...
...ooo...K...I...

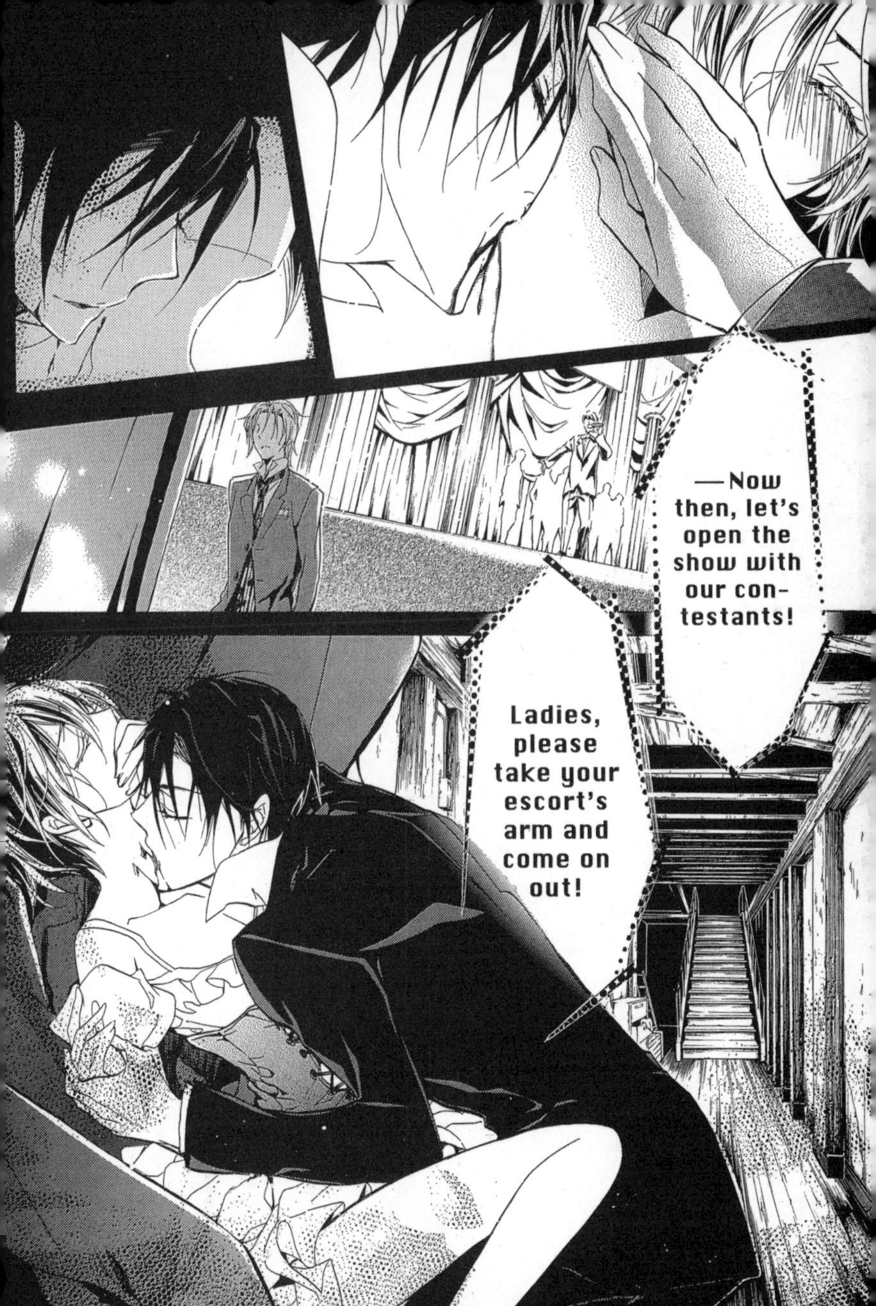
—Now then, let's open the show with our contestants!
Ladies, please take your escort's arm and come on out!

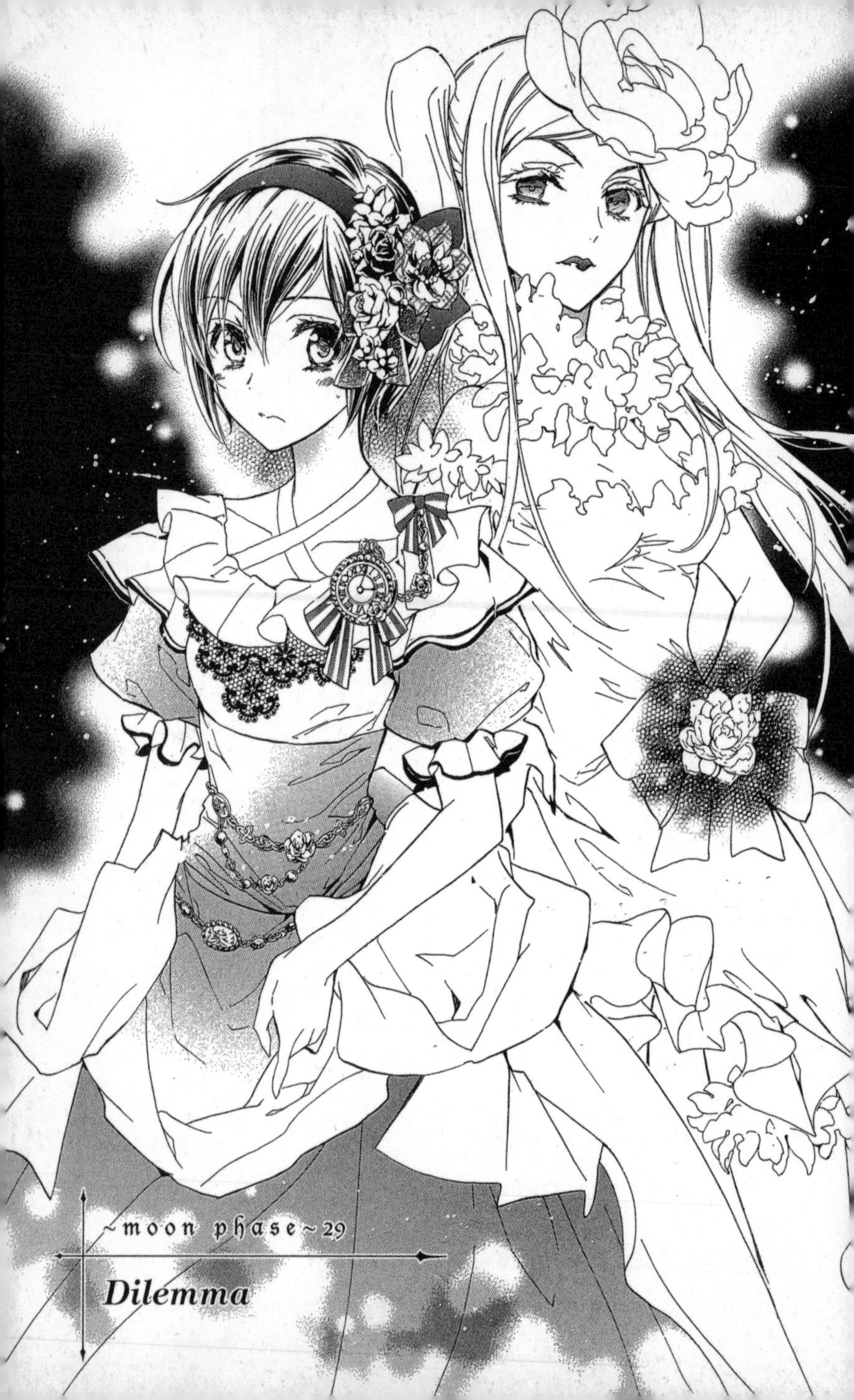

~moon phase~29

Dilemma

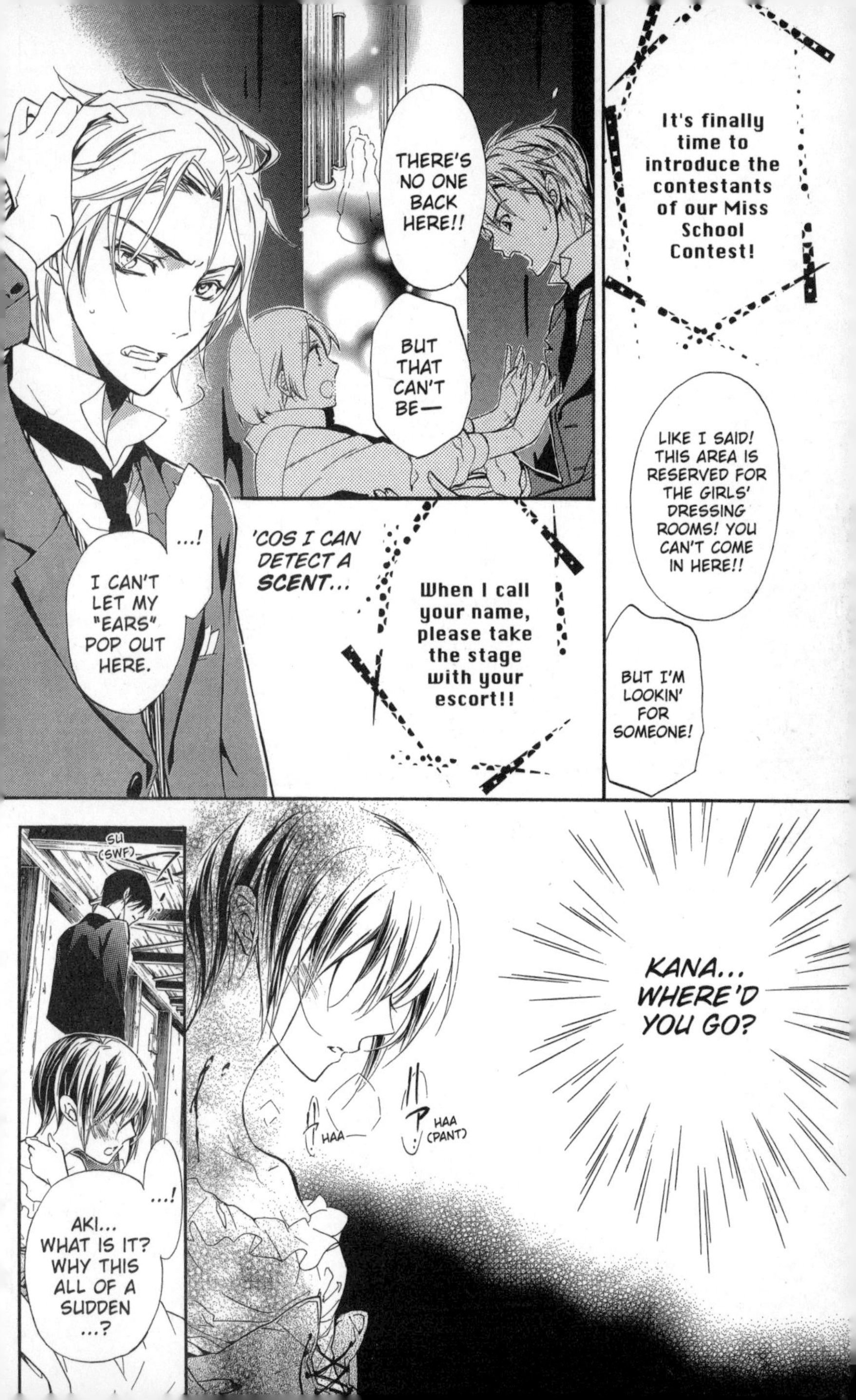
It's finally time to introduce the contestants of our Miss School Contest!
LIKE I SAID! THIS AREA IS RESERVED FOR THE GIRLS' DRESSING ROOMS! YOU CAN'T COME IN HERE!!
BUT I'M LOOKIN' FOR SOMEONE!
THERE'S NO ONE BACK HERE!!
BUT THAT CAN'T BE—
When I call your name, please take the stage with your escort!!
'COS I CAN DETECT A SCENT...
...!
I CAN'T LET MY "EARS" POP OUT HERE.
KANA... WHERE'D YOU GO?
HAA (PANT)
HAA—
SU (SWF)
...!
AKI... WHAT IS IT? WHY THIS ALL OF A SUDDEN ...?

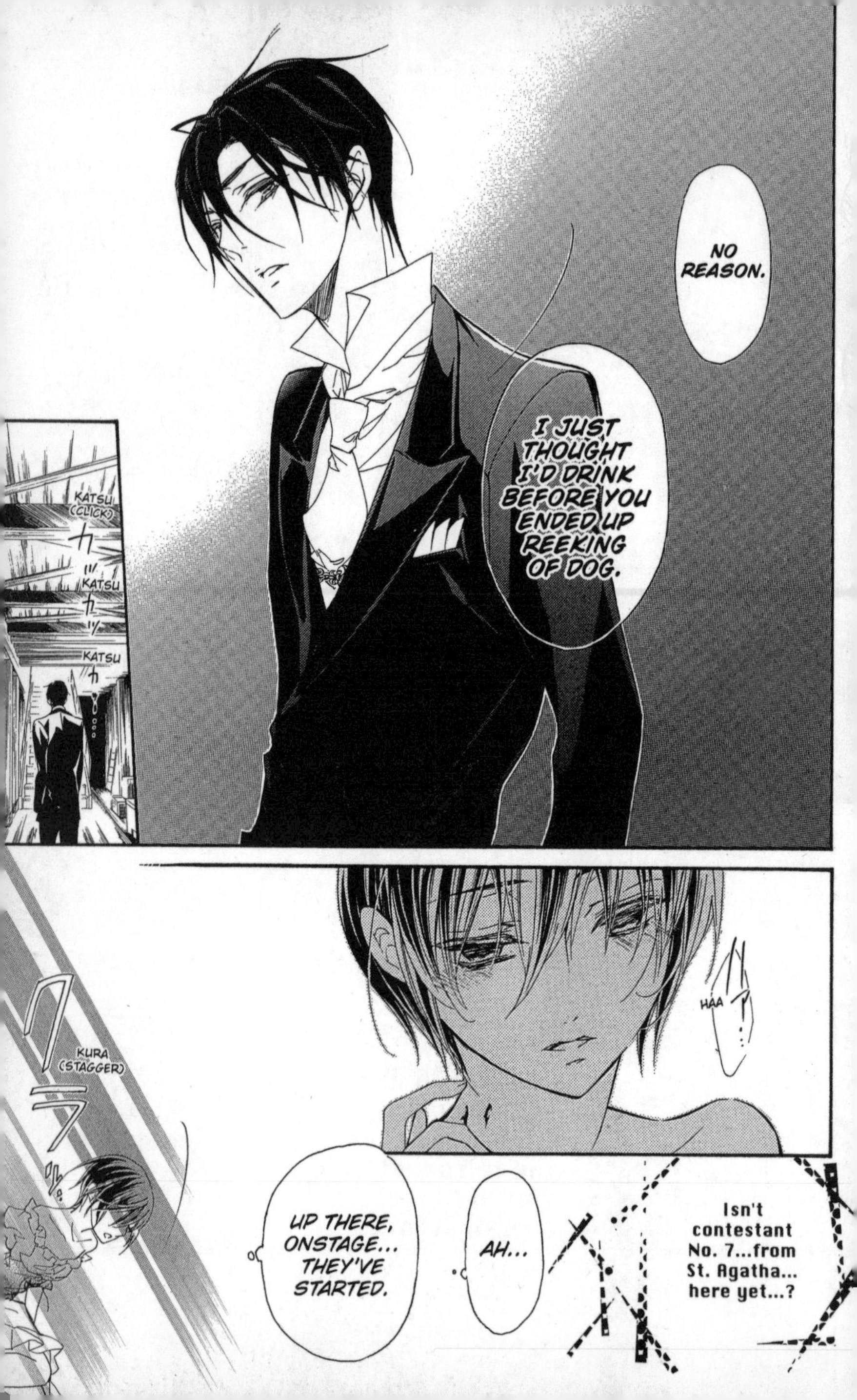
NO REASON.
I JUST THOUGHT I'D DRINK BEFORE YOU ENDED UP REEKING OF DOG.
KATSU (CLICK)
KATSU
KATSU
HAA
KURA (STAGGER)
Isn't contestant No. 7...from St. Agatha... here yet...?
AH...
UP THERE, ONSTAGE... THEY'VE STARTED.

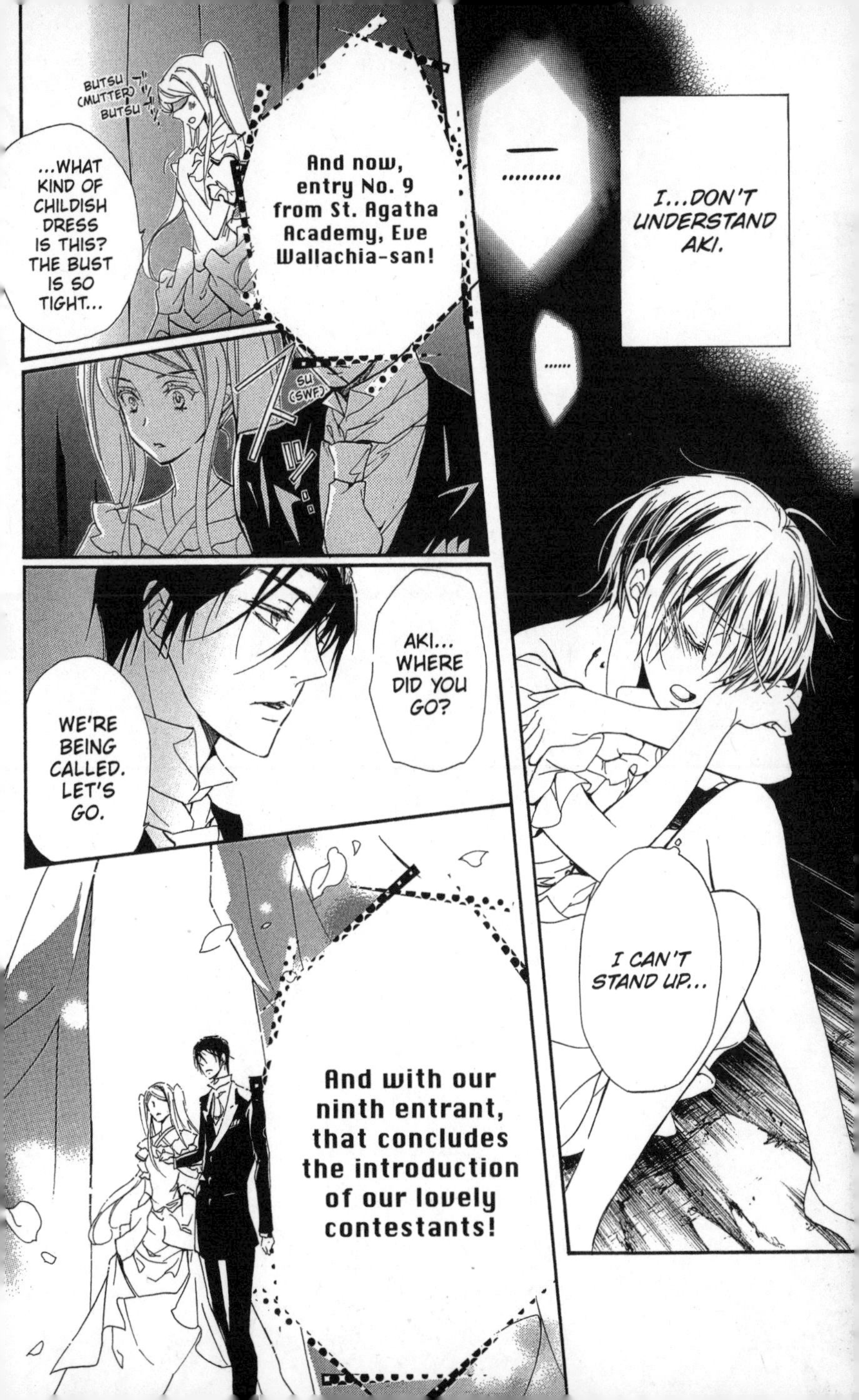
—
....
I...DON'T UNDERSTAND AKI.
......
I CAN'T STAND UP...
And now, entry No. 9 from St. Agatha Academy, Eve Wallachia-san!
BUTSU (MUTTER) BUTSU
...WHAT KIND OF CHILDISH DRESS IS THIS? THE BUST IS SO TIGHT...
SU (SWF)
AKI... WHERE DID YOU GO?
WE'RE BEING CALLED. LET'S GO.
And with our ninth entrant, that concludes the introduction of our lovely contestants!

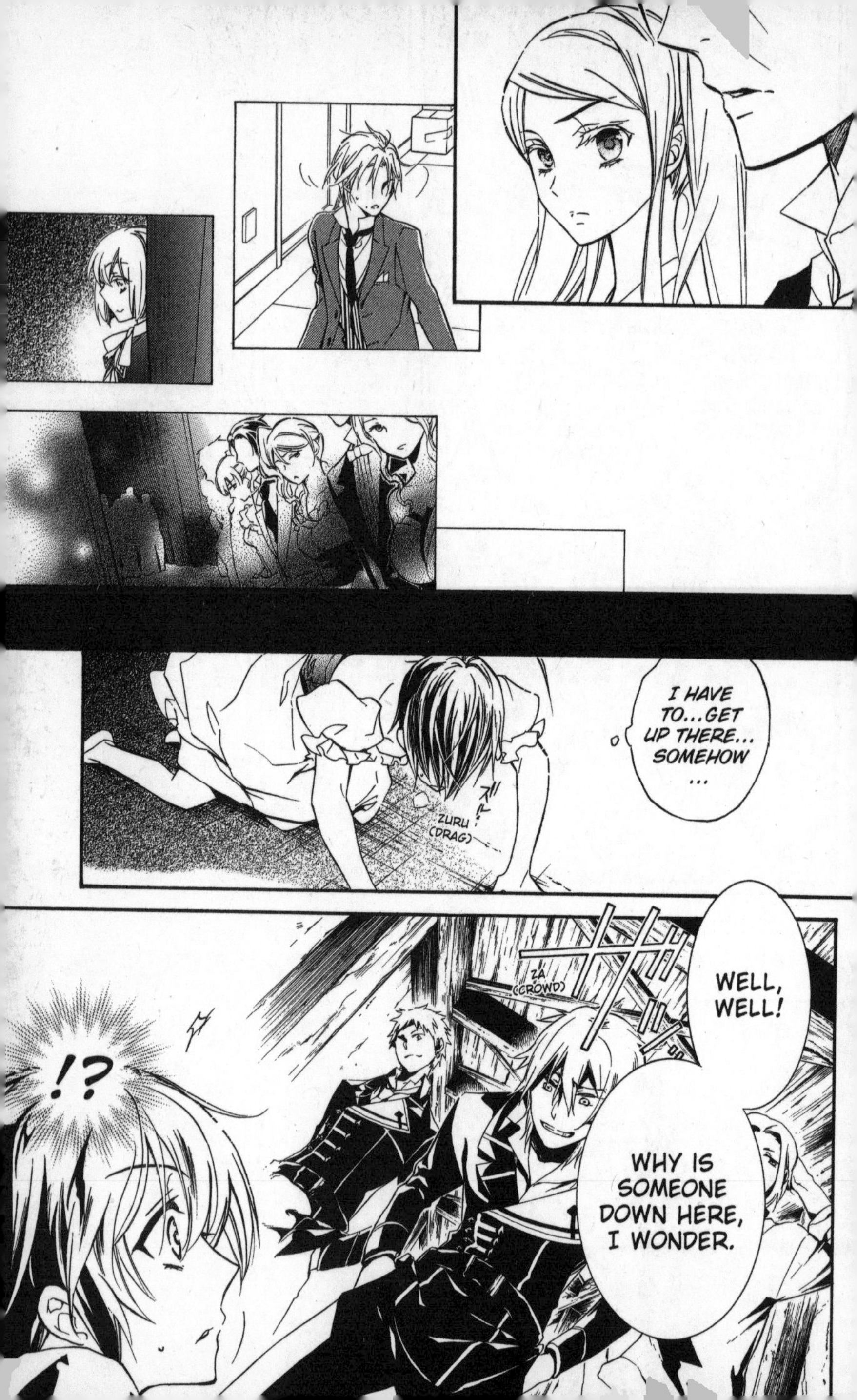

I HAVE TO...GET UP THERE... SOMEHOW ...
ZURU (DRAG)
WELL, WELL!
WHY IS SOMEONE DOWN HERE, I WONDER.
ZA (CROWD)
!?

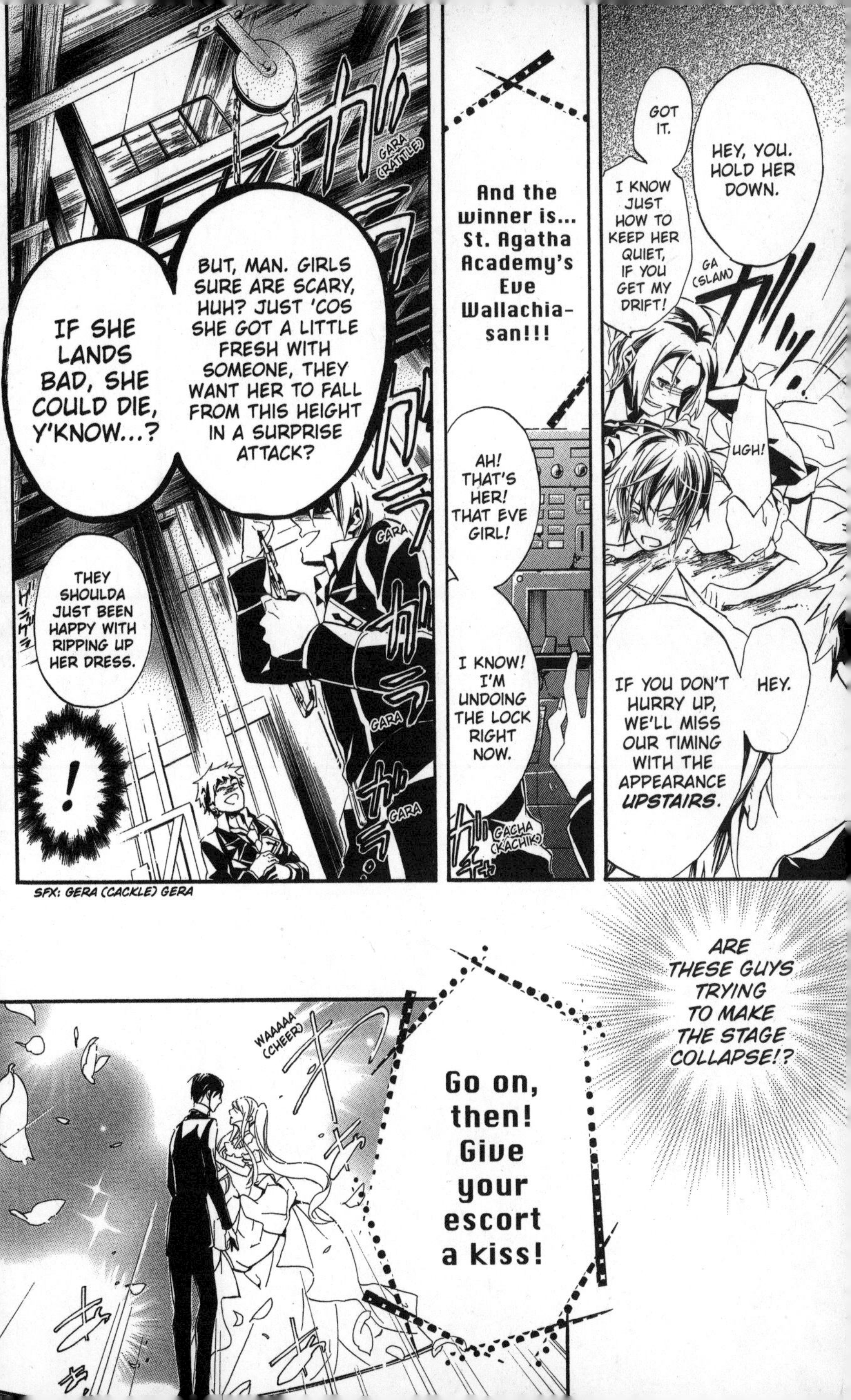
HEY, YOU. HOLD HER DOWN.
GOT IT.
I KNOW JUST HOW TO KEEP HER QUIET, IF YOU GET MY DRIFT!
GA (SLAM)
UGH!
HEY.
IF YOU DON'T HURRY UP, WE'LL MISS OUR TIMING WITH THE APPEARANCE UPSTAIRS.
And the winner is... St. Agatha Academy's Eve Wallachia-san!!!
AH! THAT'S HER! THAT EVE GIRL!
I KNOW! I'M UNDOING THE LOCK RIGHT NOW.
GACHA (KACHIK)
GARA (RATTLE)
BUT, MAN. GIRLS SURE ARE SCARY, HUH? JUST 'COS SHE GOT A LITTLE FRESH WITH SOMEONE, THEY WANT HER TO FALL FROM THIS HEIGHT IN A SURPRISE ATTACK?
IF SHE LANDS BAD, SHE COULD DIE, Y'KNOW...?
GARA
THEY SHOULDA JUST BEEN HAPPY WITH RIPPING UP HER DRESS.
GARA
GARA
!
SFX: GERA (CACKLE) GERA
ARE THESE GUYS TRYING TO MAKE THE STAGE COLLAPSE!?
Go on, then! Give your escort a kiss!
WAAAAA (CHEER)

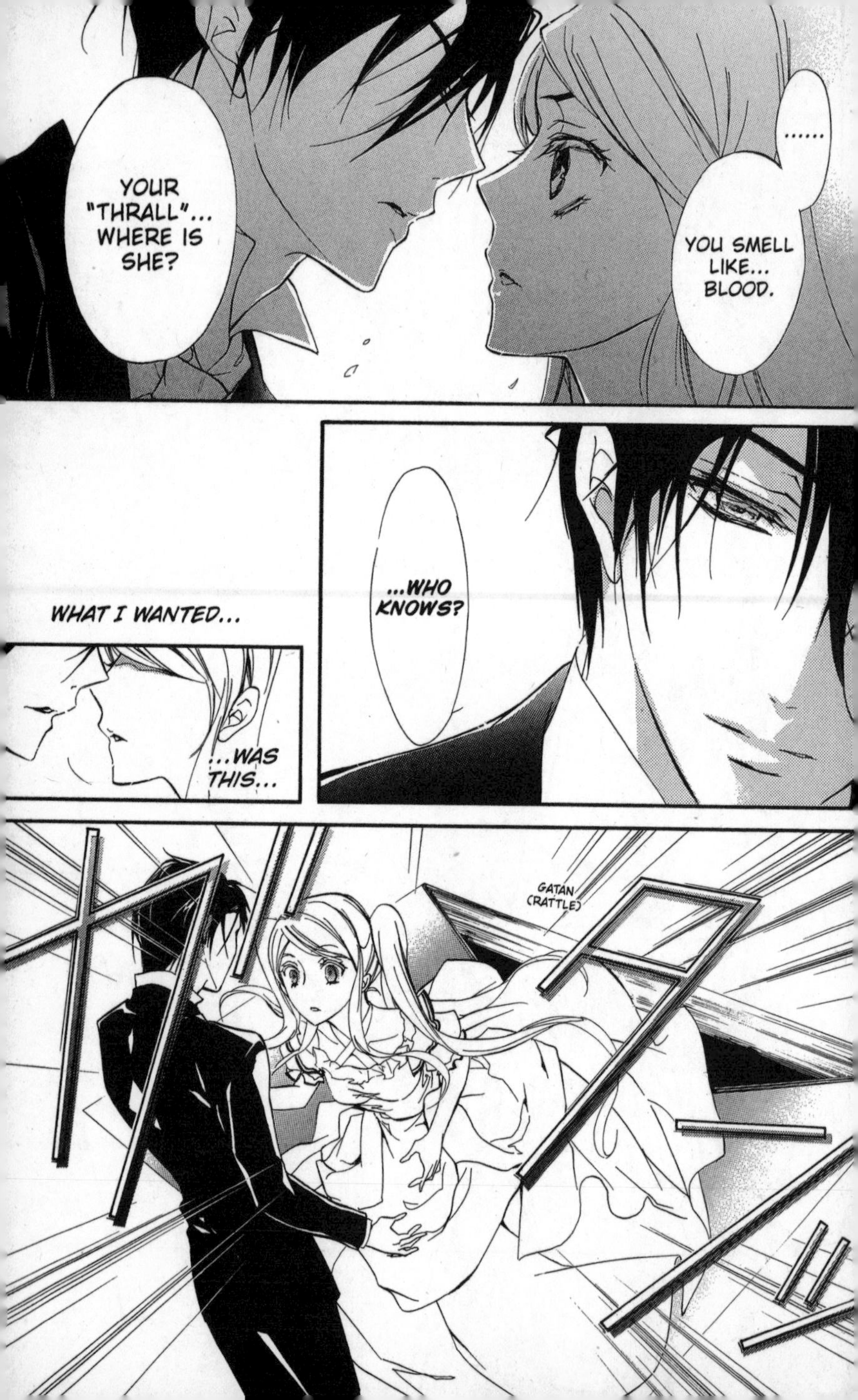
......
YOU SMELL LIKE... BLOOD.
YOUR "THRALL"... WHERE IS SHE?
...WHO KNOWS?
WHAT I WANTED...
...WAS THIS...
GATAN (RATTLE)

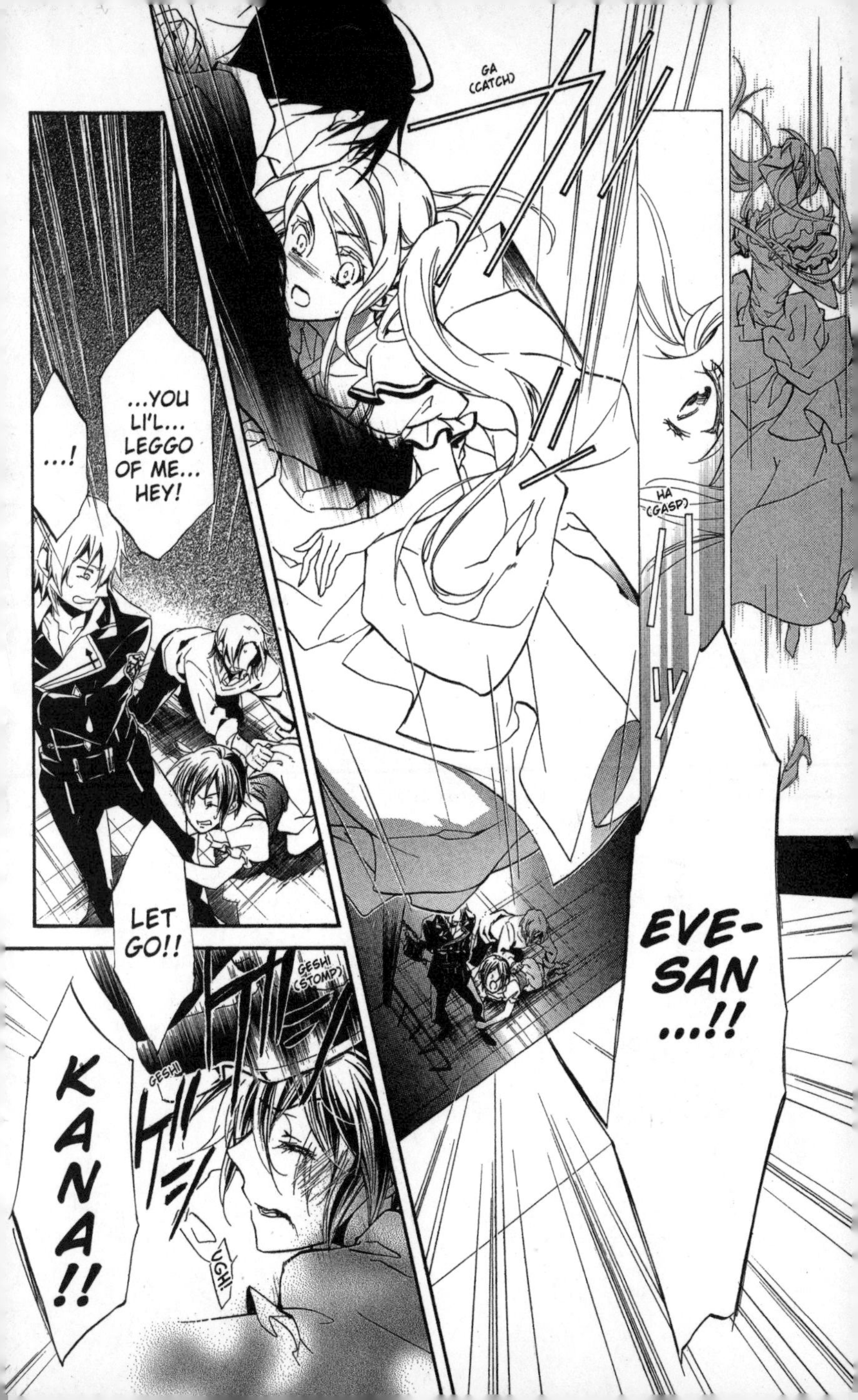
GA (CATCH)
HA (GASP)
EVE-SAN...!!
...YOU LI'L... LEGGO OF ME... HEY!
...!
LET GO!!
GESHI (STOMP)
GESHI
UGH!
KANA!!

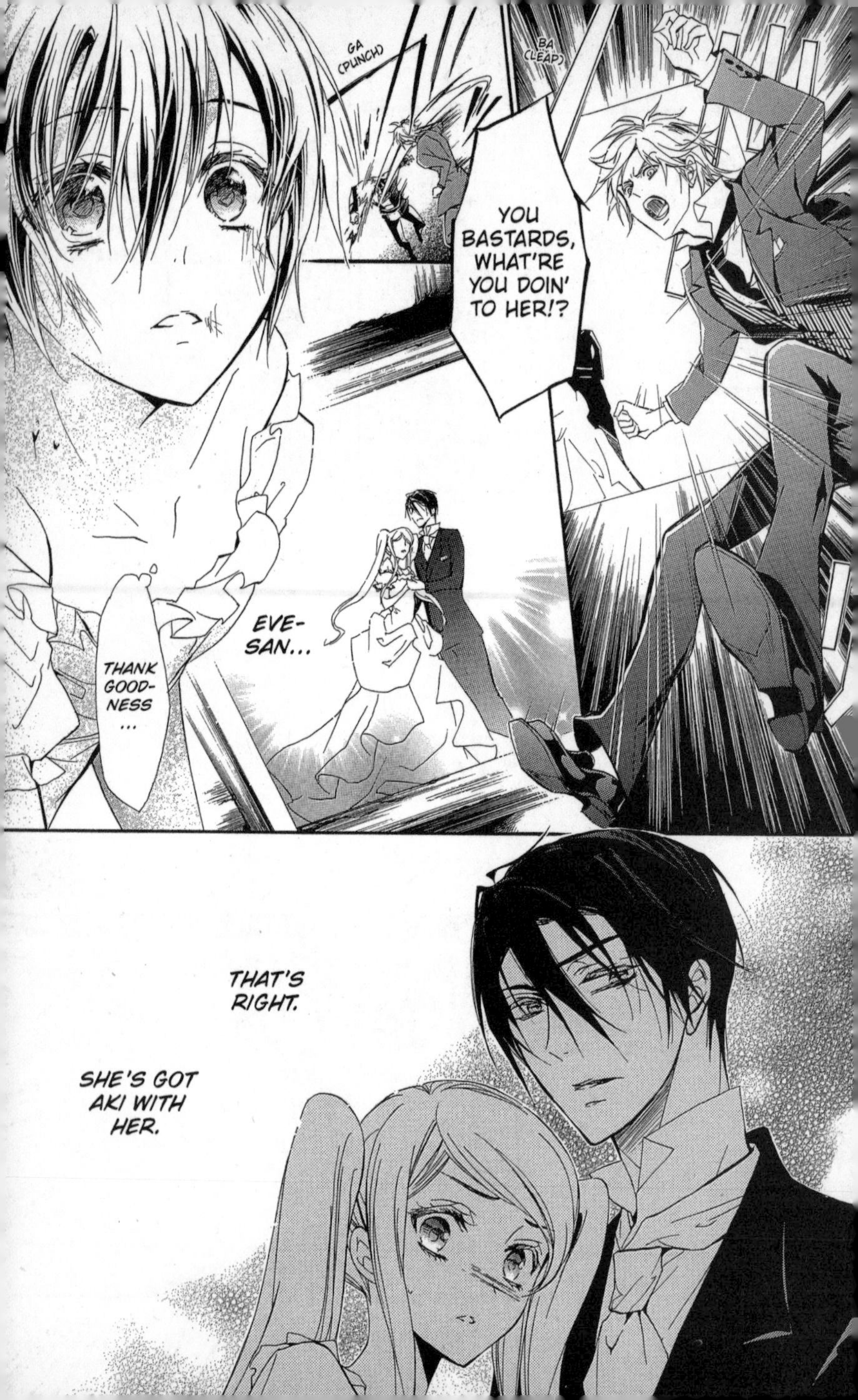
BA (LEAP)
YOU BASTARDS, WHAT'RE YOU DOIN' TO HER!?
GA (PUNCH)
EVE-SAN...
THANK GOODNESS...
THAT'S RIGHT.
SHE'S GOT AKI WITH HER.

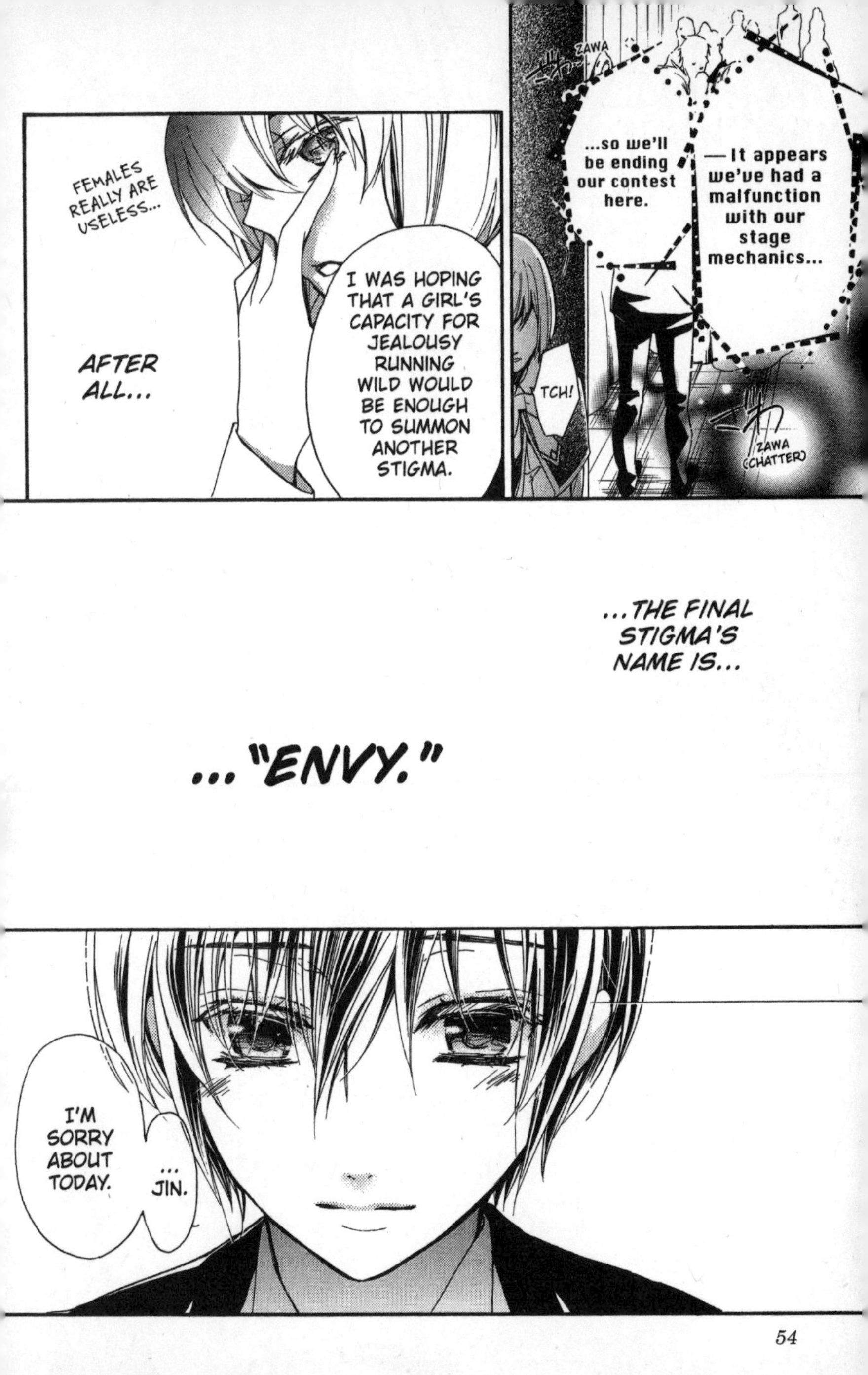
—It appears we've had a malfunction with our stage mechanics...
...so we'll be ending our contest here.
ZAWA
TCH!
ZAWA (CHATTER)
I WAS HOPING THAT A GIRL'S CAPACITY FOR JEALOUSY RUNNING WILD WOULD BE ENOUGH TO SUMMON ANOTHER STIGMA.
FEMALES REALLY ARE USELESS...
AFTER ALL...
...THE FINAL STIGMA'S NAME IS...
..."ENVY."
...JIN.
I'M SORRY ABOUT TODAY.

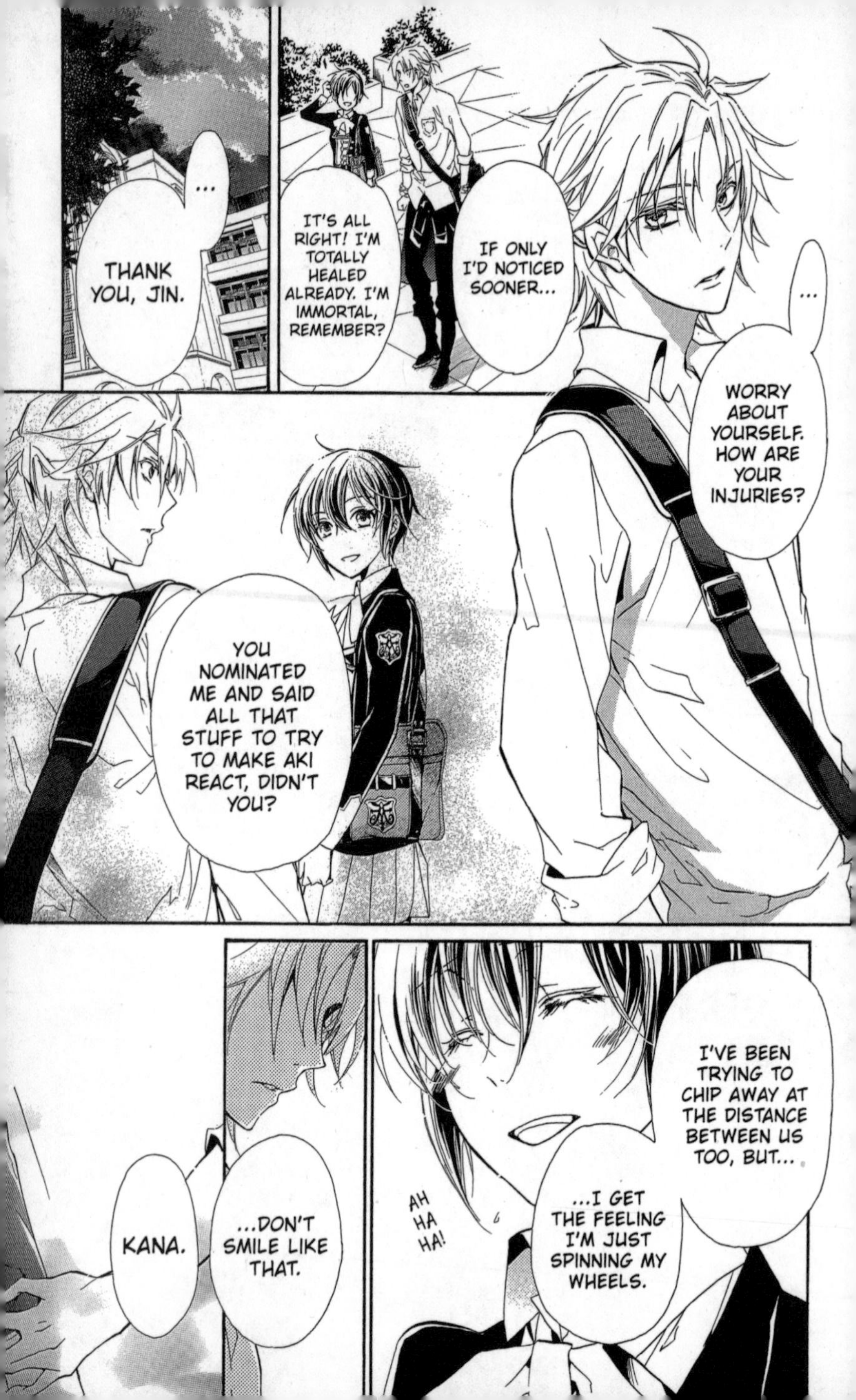
...
WORRY ABOUT YOURSELF. HOW ARE YOUR INJURIES?
IF ONLY I'D NOTICED SOONER...
IT'S ALL RIGHT! I'M TOTALLY HEALED ALREADY. I'M IMMORTAL, REMEMBER?
...
THANK YOU, JIN.
YOU NOMINATED ME AND SAID ALL THAT STUFF TO TRY TO MAKE AKI REACT, DIDN'T YOU?
I'VE BEEN TRYING TO CHIP AWAY AT THE DISTANCE BETWEEN US TOO, BUT...
...I GET THE FEELING I'M JUST SPINNING MY WHEELS.
AH HA HA!
...DON'T SMILE LIKE THAT.
KANA.

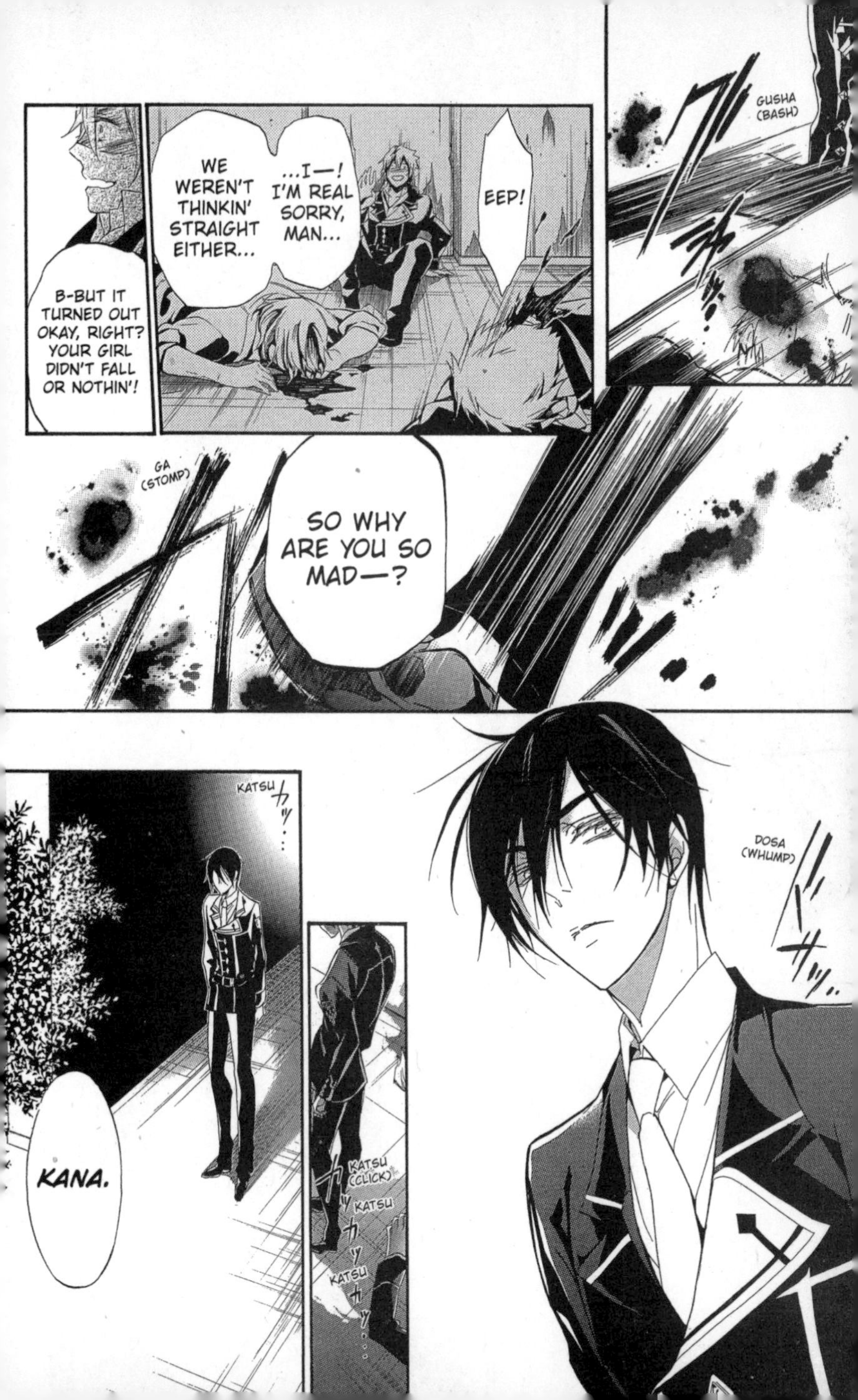
GUSHA (BASH)
EEP!
...I—! I'M REAL SORRY, MAN...
WE WEREN'T THINKIN' STRAIGHT EITHER...
B-BUT IT TURNED OUT OKAY, RIGHT? YOUR GIRL DIDN'T FALL OR NOTHIN'!
SO WHY ARE YOU SO MAD—?
GA (STOMP)
DOSA (WHUMP)
KATSU (CLICK)
KATSU
KATSU
KATSU
KANA.

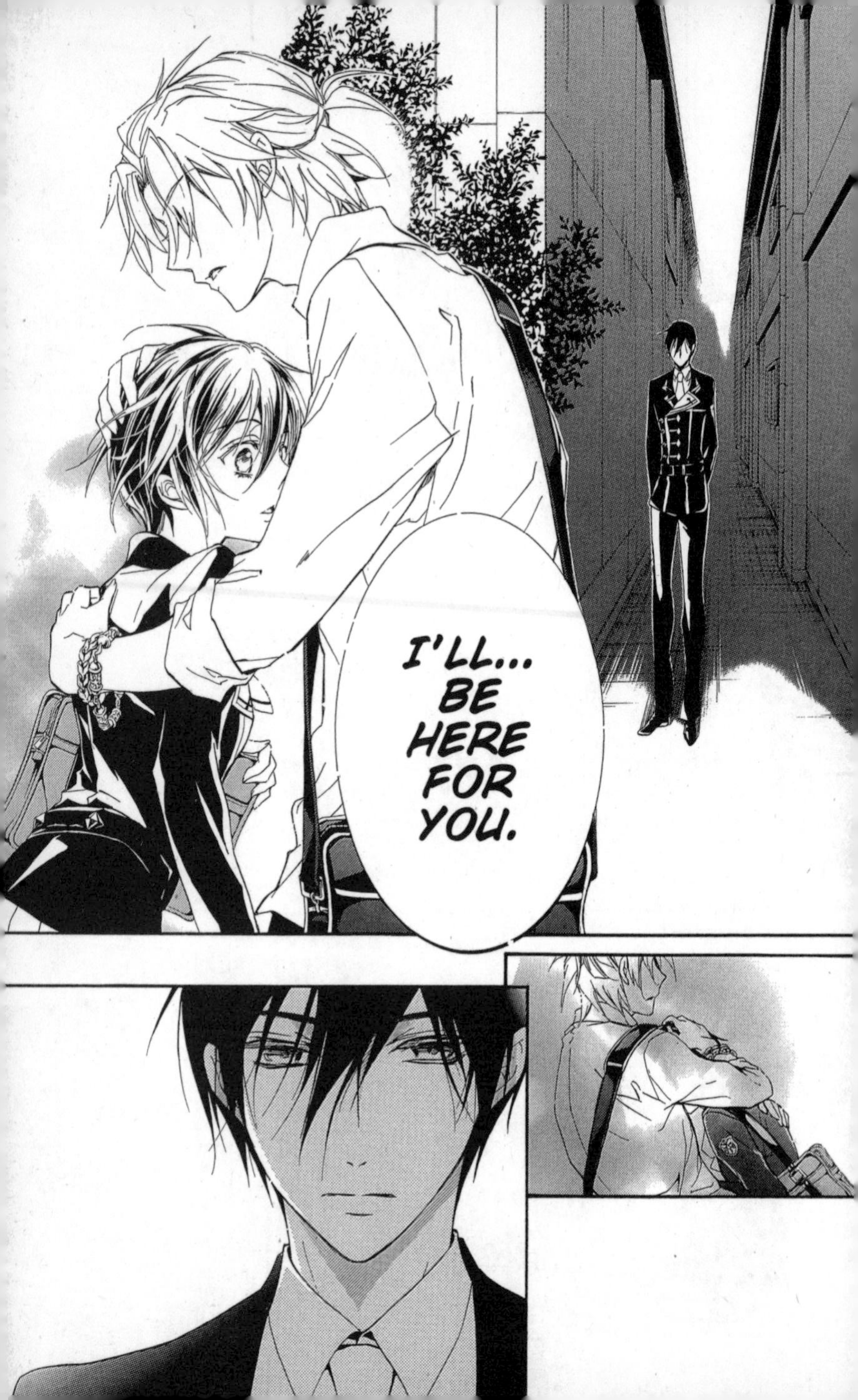
I'LL... BE HERE FOR YOU.

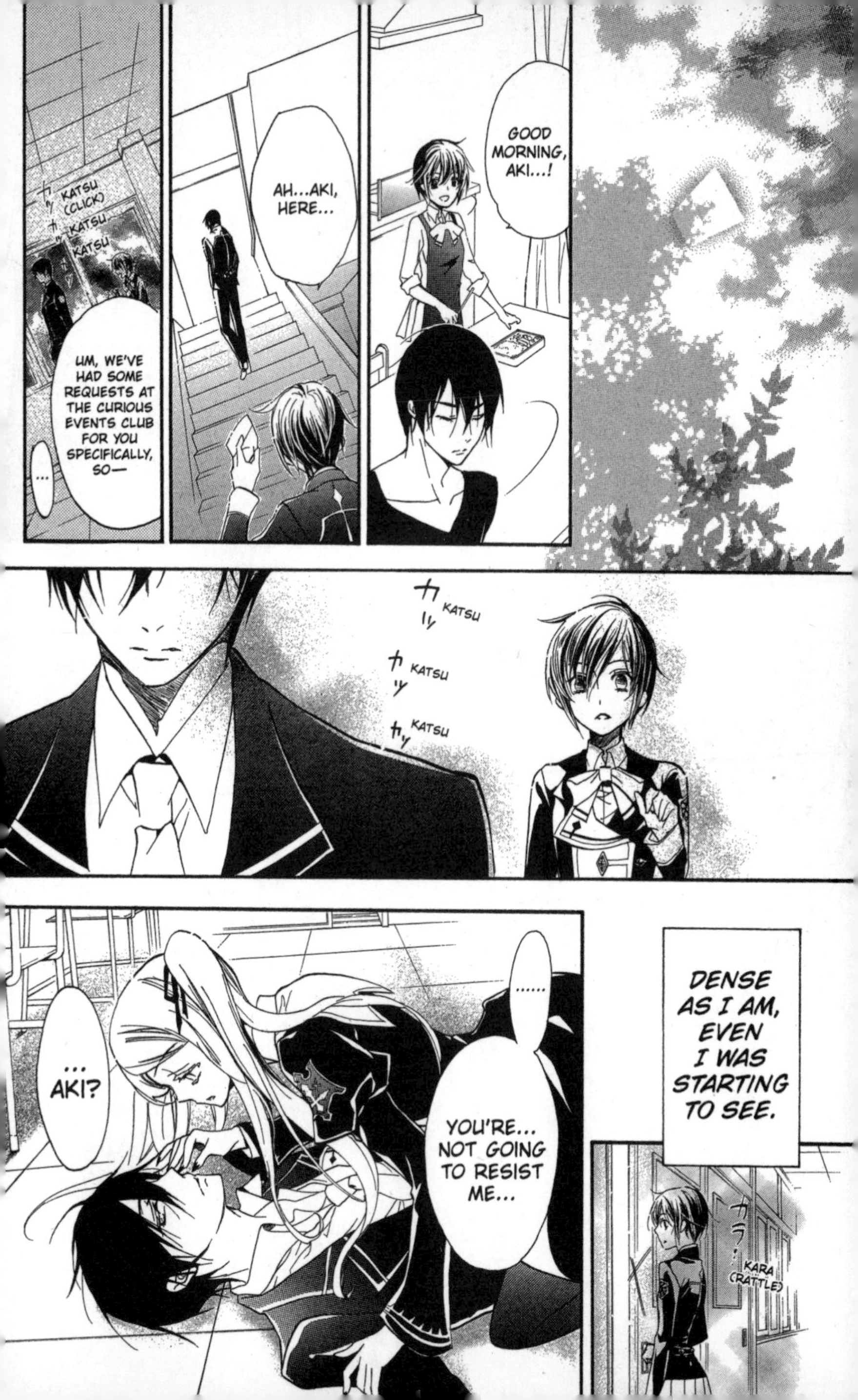
GOOD MORNING, AKI...!
AH...AKI, HERE...
KATSU (CLICK)
KATSU
KATSU
UM, WE'VE HAD SOME REQUESTS AT THE CURIOUS EVENTS CLUB FOR YOU SPECIFICALLY, SO—
...
KATSU
KATSU
KATSU
DENSE AS I AM, EVEN I WAS STARTING TO SEE.
KARA (RATTLE)
......
YOU'RE... NOT GOING TO RESIST ME...
...AKI?

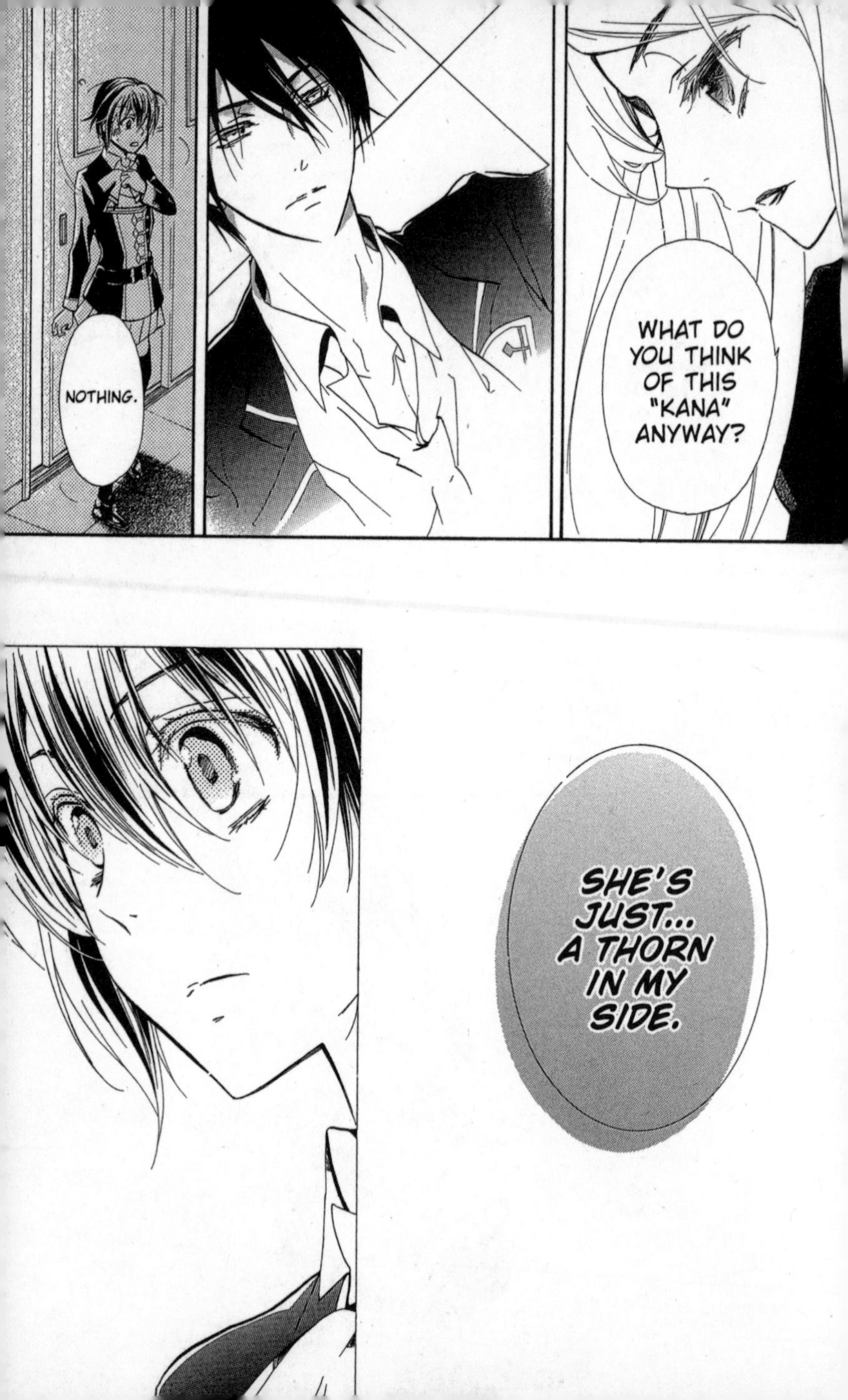
WHAT DO YOU THINK OF THIS "KANA" ANYWAY?
NOTHING.
SHE'S JUST... A THORN IN MY SIDE.

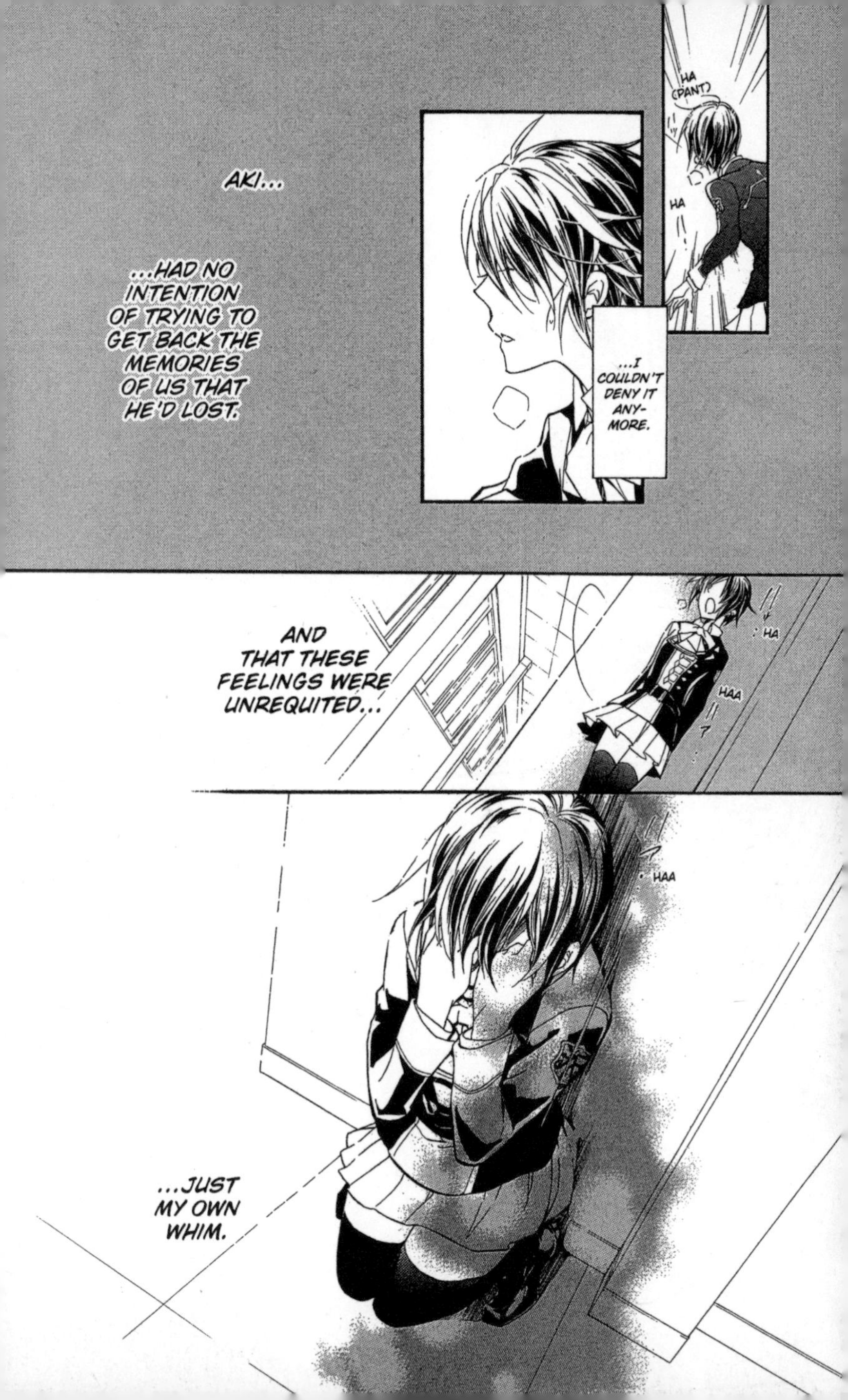
HA (PANT)
HA
...I COULDN'T DENY IT ANYMORE.
AKI...
...HAD NO INTENTION OF TRYING TO GET BACK THE MEMORIES OF US THAT HE'D LOST.
HA
HAA
AND THAT THESE FEELINGS WERE UNREQUITED...
HAA
...JUST MY OWN WHIM.

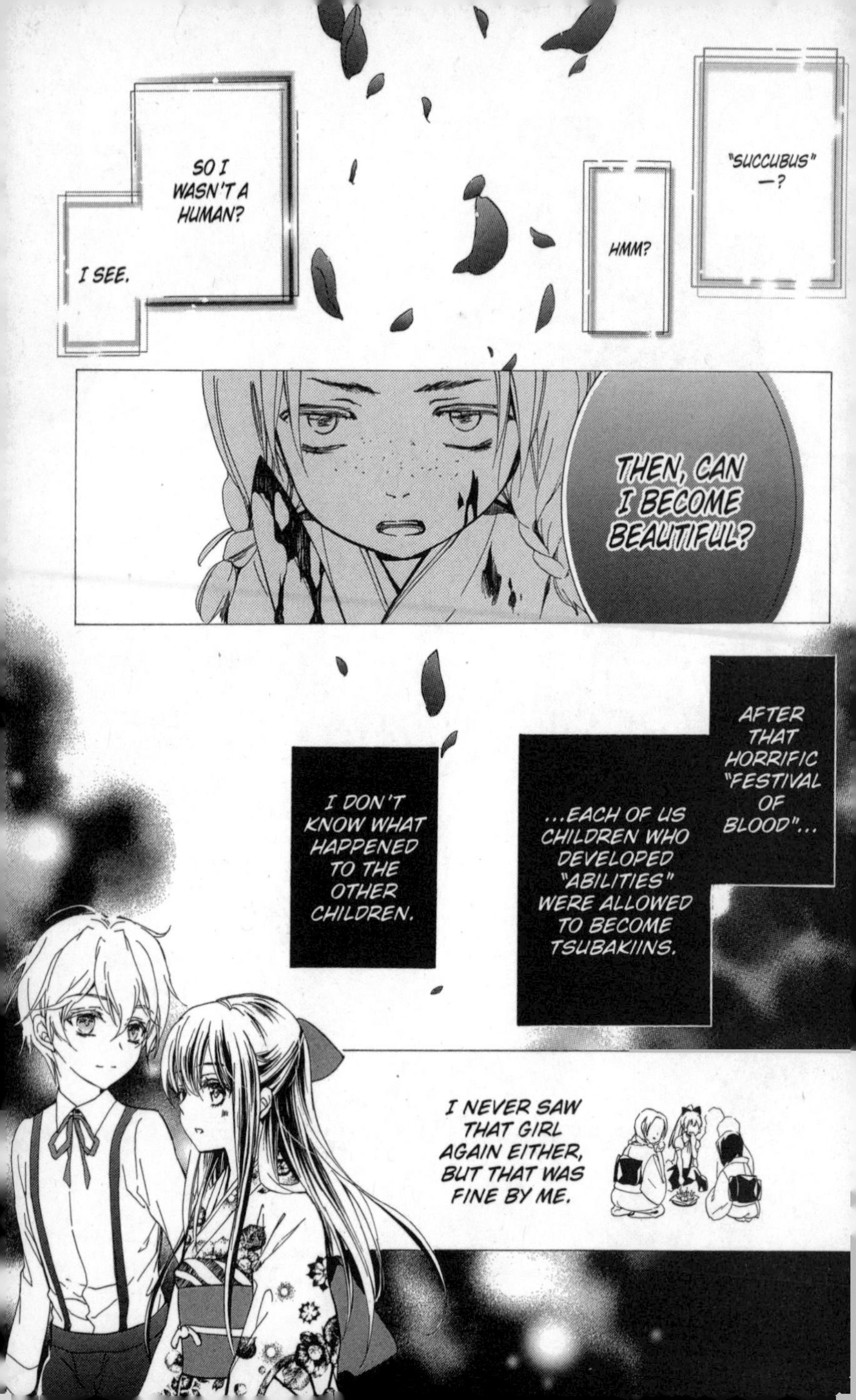
"SUCCUBUS" —?
HMM?
SO I WASN'T A HUMAN?
I SEE.
THEN, CAN I BECOME BEAUTIFUL?
AFTER THAT HORRIFIC "FESTIVAL OF BLOOD"...
...EACH OF US CHILDREN WHO DEVELOPED "ABILITIES" WERE ALLOWED TO BECOME TSUBAKIINS.
I DON'T KNOW WHAT HAPPENED TO THE OTHER CHILDREN.
I NEVER SAW THAT GIRL AGAIN EITHER, BUT THAT WAS FINE BY ME.

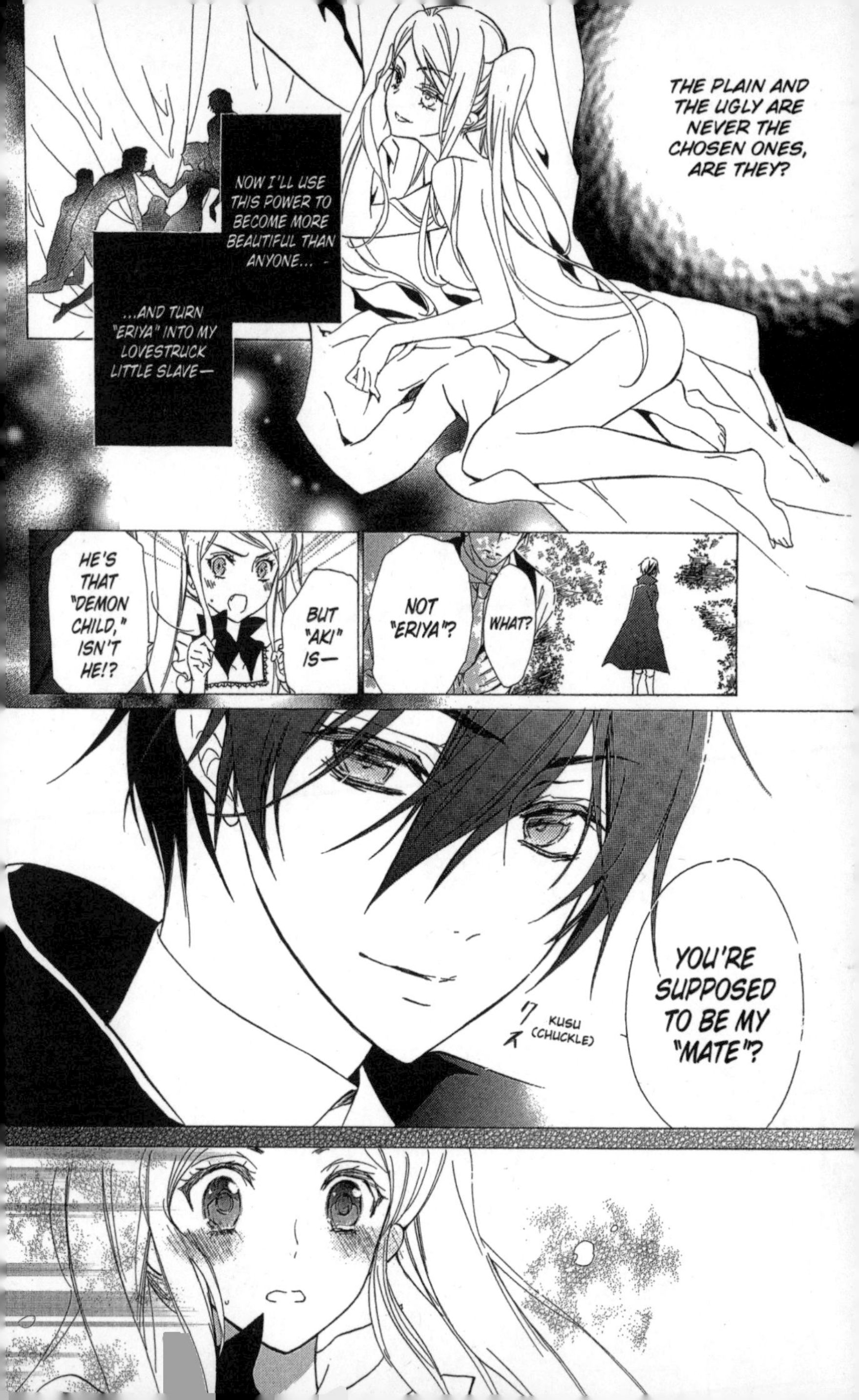
THE PLAIN AND THE UGLY ARE NEVER THE CHOSEN ONES, ARE THEY?
NOW I'LL USE THIS POWER TO BECOME MORE BEAUTIFUL THAN ANYONE... -
...AND TURN "ERIYA" INTO MY LOVESTRUCK LITTLE SLAVE—
WHAT?
NOT "ERIYA"?
BUT "AKI" IS—
HE'S THAT "DEMON CHILD," ISN'T HE!?
YOU'RE SUPPOSED TO BE MY "MATE"?
KUSU (CHUCKLE)

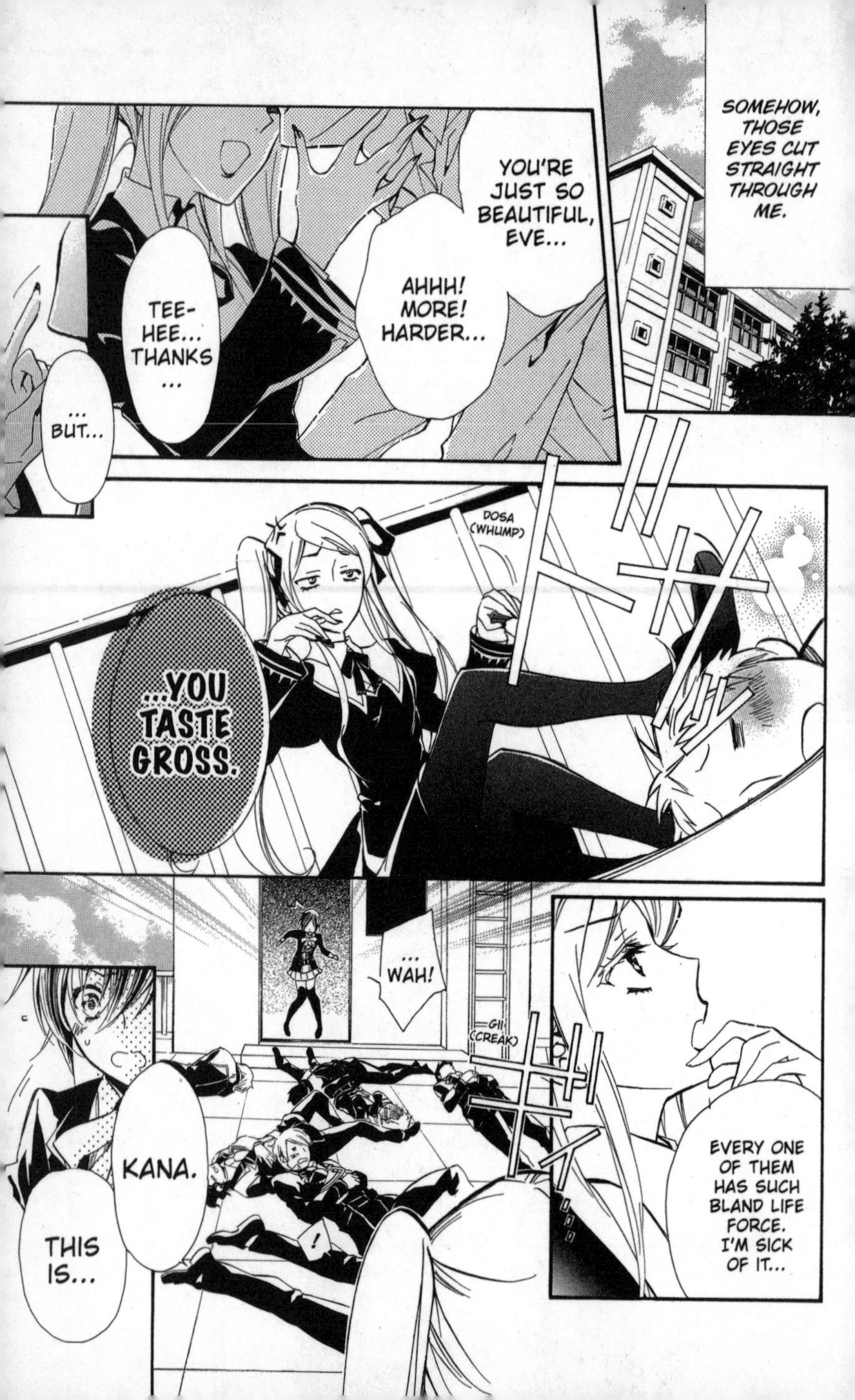
SOMEHOW, THOSE EYES CUT STRAIGHT THROUGH ME.
YOU'RE JUST SO BEAUTIFUL, EVE...
AHHH! MORE! HARDER...
TEE-HEE... THANKS...
...BUT...
DOSA (WHUMP)
...YOU TASTE GROSS.
EVERY ONE OF THEM HAS SUCH BLAND LIFE FORCE. I'M SICK OF IT...
GII (CREAK)
...WAH!
KANA.
THIS IS...

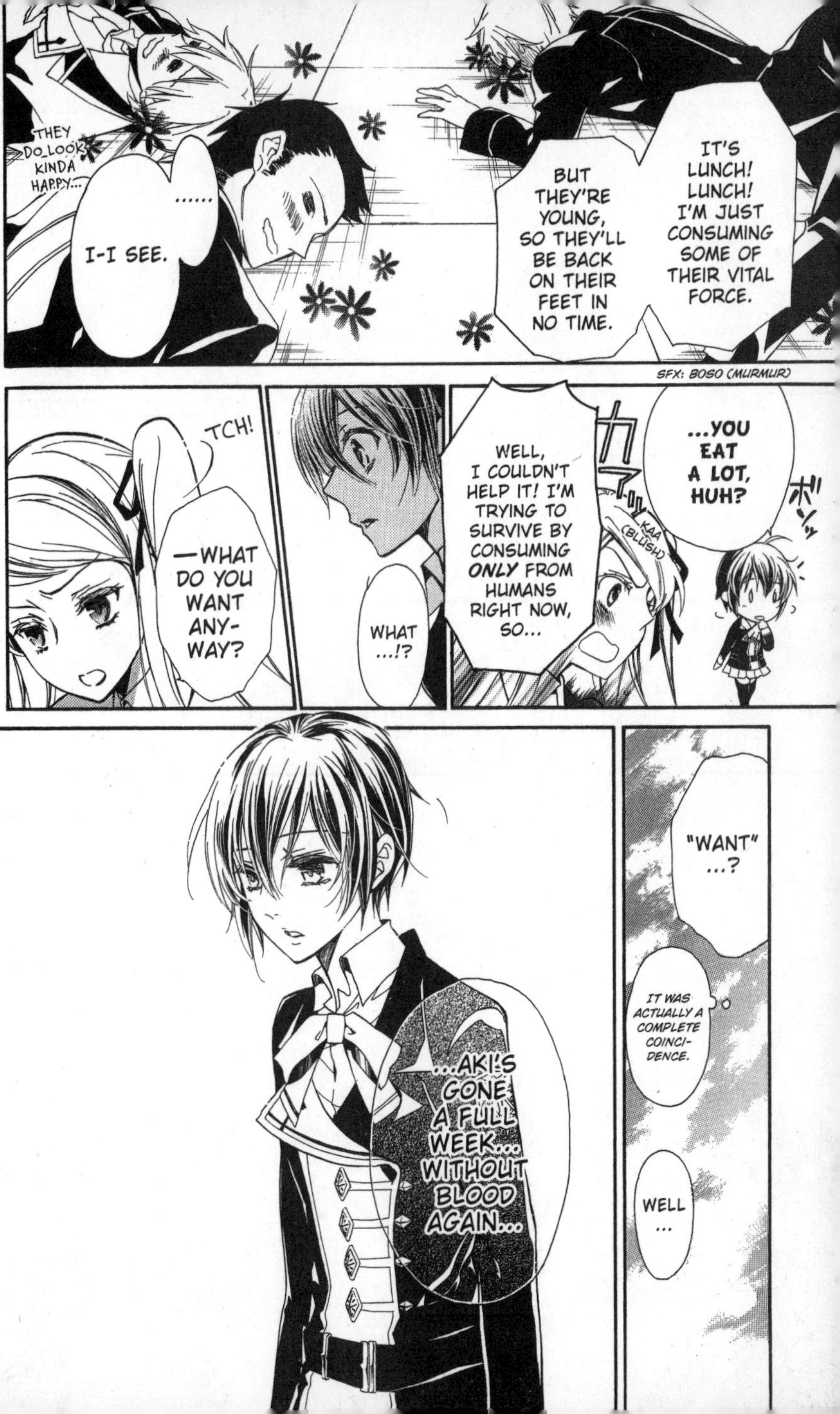
IT'S LUNCH! LUNCH! I'M JUST CONSUMING SOME OF THEIR VITAL FORCE.
BUT THEY'RE YOUNG, SO THEY'LL BE BACK ON THEIR FEET IN NO TIME.
......
I-I SEE.
THEY DO LOOK KINDA HAPPY...
SFX: BOSO (MURMUR)
...YOU EAT A LOT, HUH?
KAA (BLUSH)
WELL, I COULDN'T HELP IT! I'M TRYING TO SURVIVE BY CONSUMING ***ONLY*** FROM HUMANS RIGHT NOW, SO...
WHAT ...!?
TCH!
—WHAT DO YOU WANT ANY-WAY?
"WANT" ...?
IT WAS ACTUALLY A COMPLETE COINCI-DENCE.
WELL ...
...AKI'S GONE A FULL WEEK... WITHOUT BLOOD AGAIN...

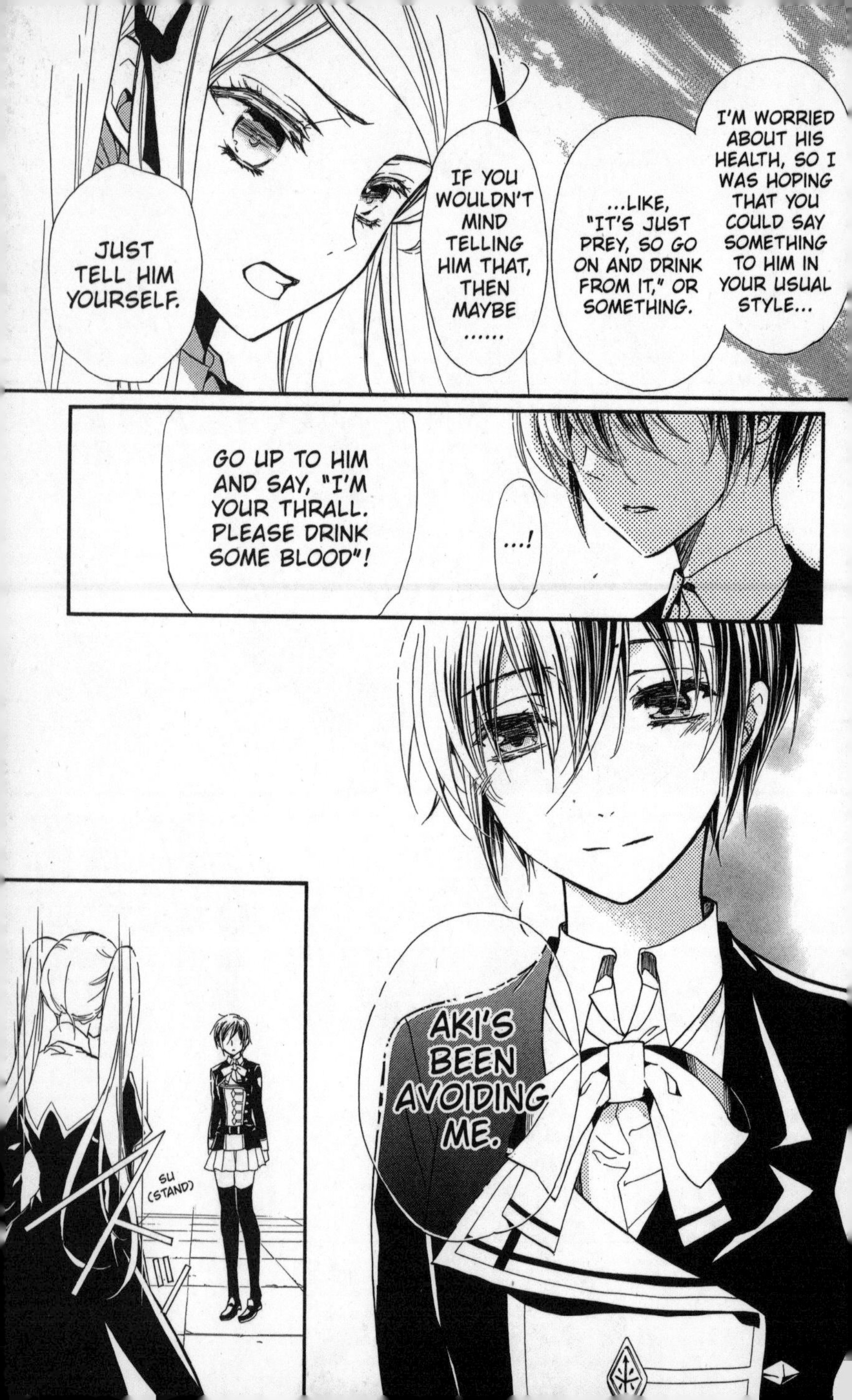
I'M WORRIED ABOUT HIS HEALTH, SO I WAS HOPING THAT YOU COULD SAY SOMETHING TO HIM IN YOUR USUAL STYLE...
...LIKE, "IT'S JUST PREY, SO GO ON AND DRINK FROM IT," OR SOMETHING.
IF YOU WOULDN'T MIND TELLING HIM THAT, THEN MAYBE ......
JUST TELL HIM YOURSELF.
...!
GO UP TO HIM AND SAY, "I'M YOUR THRALL. PLEASE DRINK SOME BLOOD"!
AKI'S BEEN AVOIDING ME.
SU (STAND)

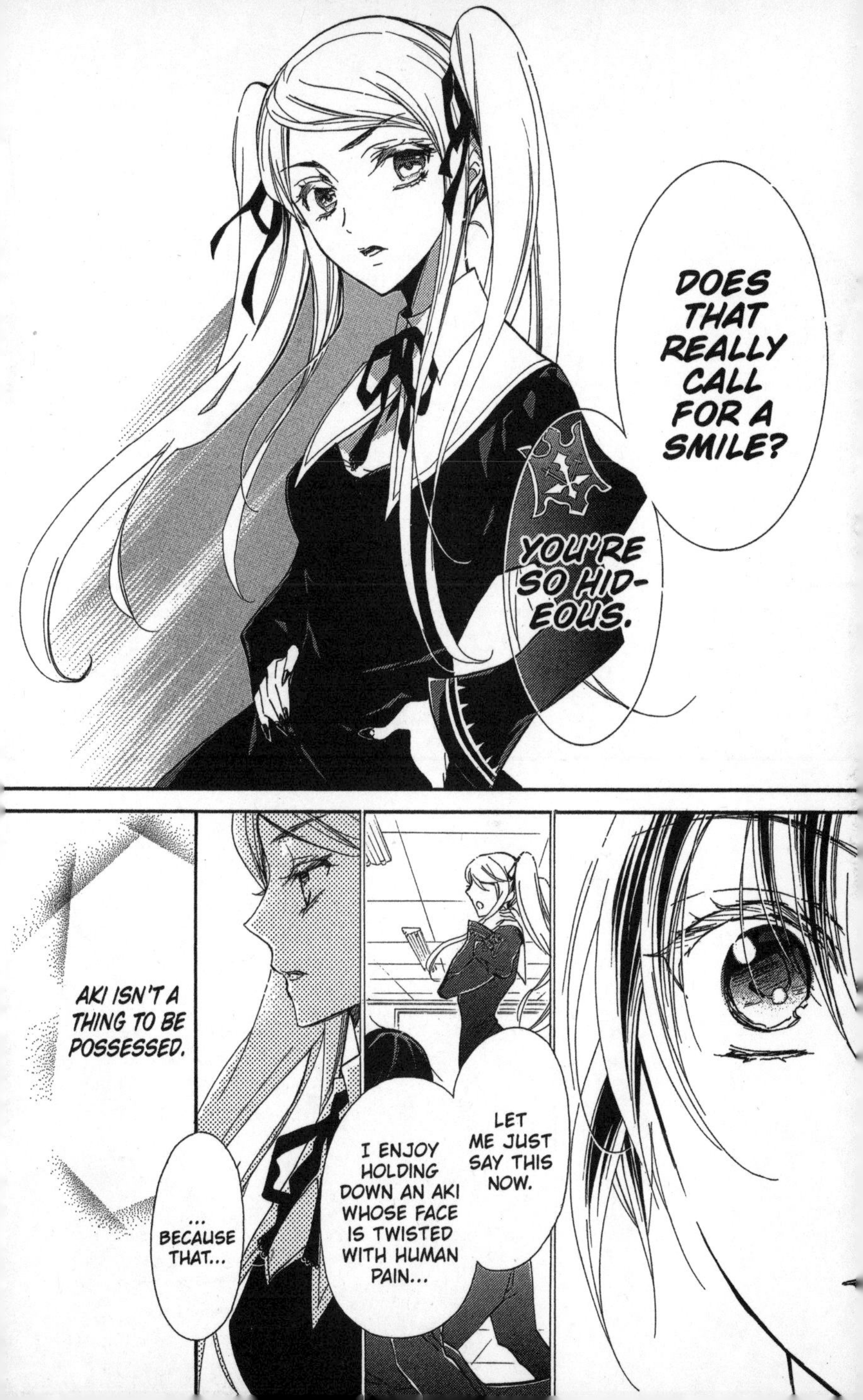
DOES THAT REALLY CALL FOR A SMILE?
YOU'RE SO HID-EOUS.
LET ME JUST SAY THIS NOW.
I ENJOY HOLDING DOWN AN AKI WHOSE FACE IS TWISTED WITH HUMAN PAIN...
...BECAUSE THAT...
AKI ISN'T A THING TO BE POSSESSED.

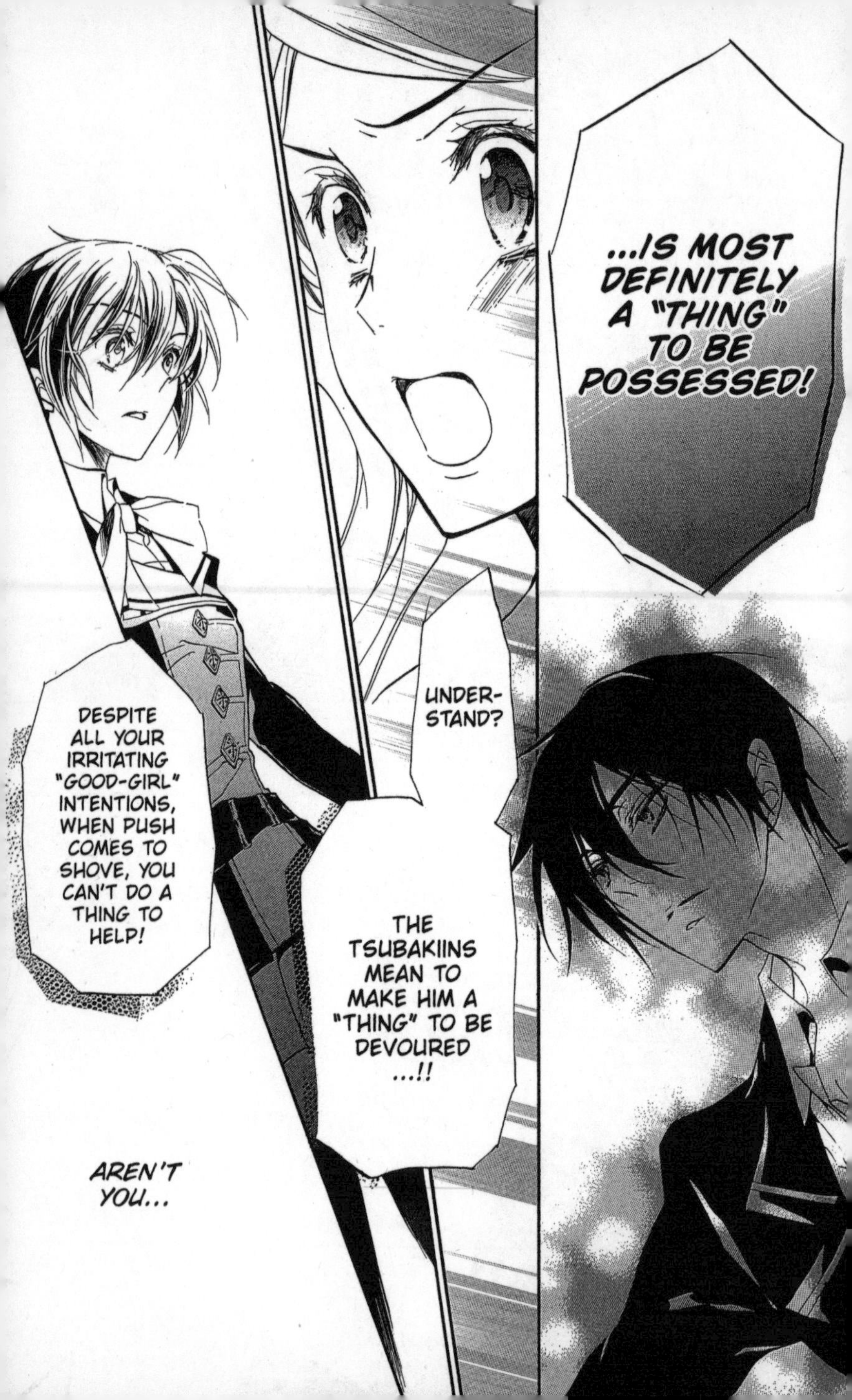
...IS MOST DEFINITELY A "THING" TO BE POSSESSED!
UNDER-STAND?
THE TSUBAKIINS MEAN TO MAKE HIM A "THING" TO BE DEVOURED ...!!
DESPITE ALL YOUR IRRITATING "GOOD-GIRL" INTENTIONS, WHEN PUSH COMES TO SHOVE, YOU CAN'T DO A THING TO HELP!
AREN'T YOU...

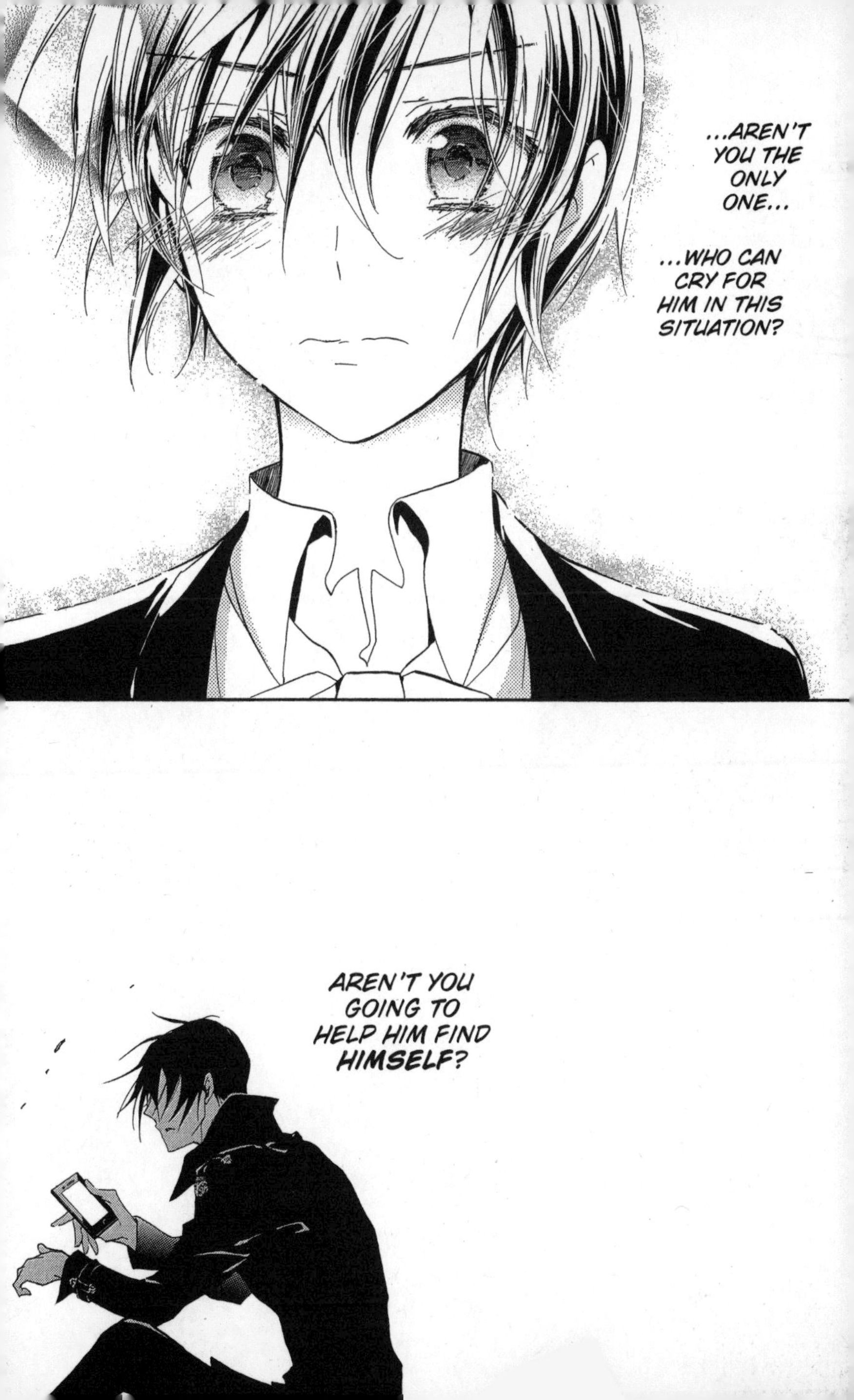
...AREN'T YOU THE ONLY ONE...
...WHO CAN CRY FOR HIM IN THIS SITUATION?
AREN'T YOU GOING TO HELP HIM FIND **HIMSELF**?

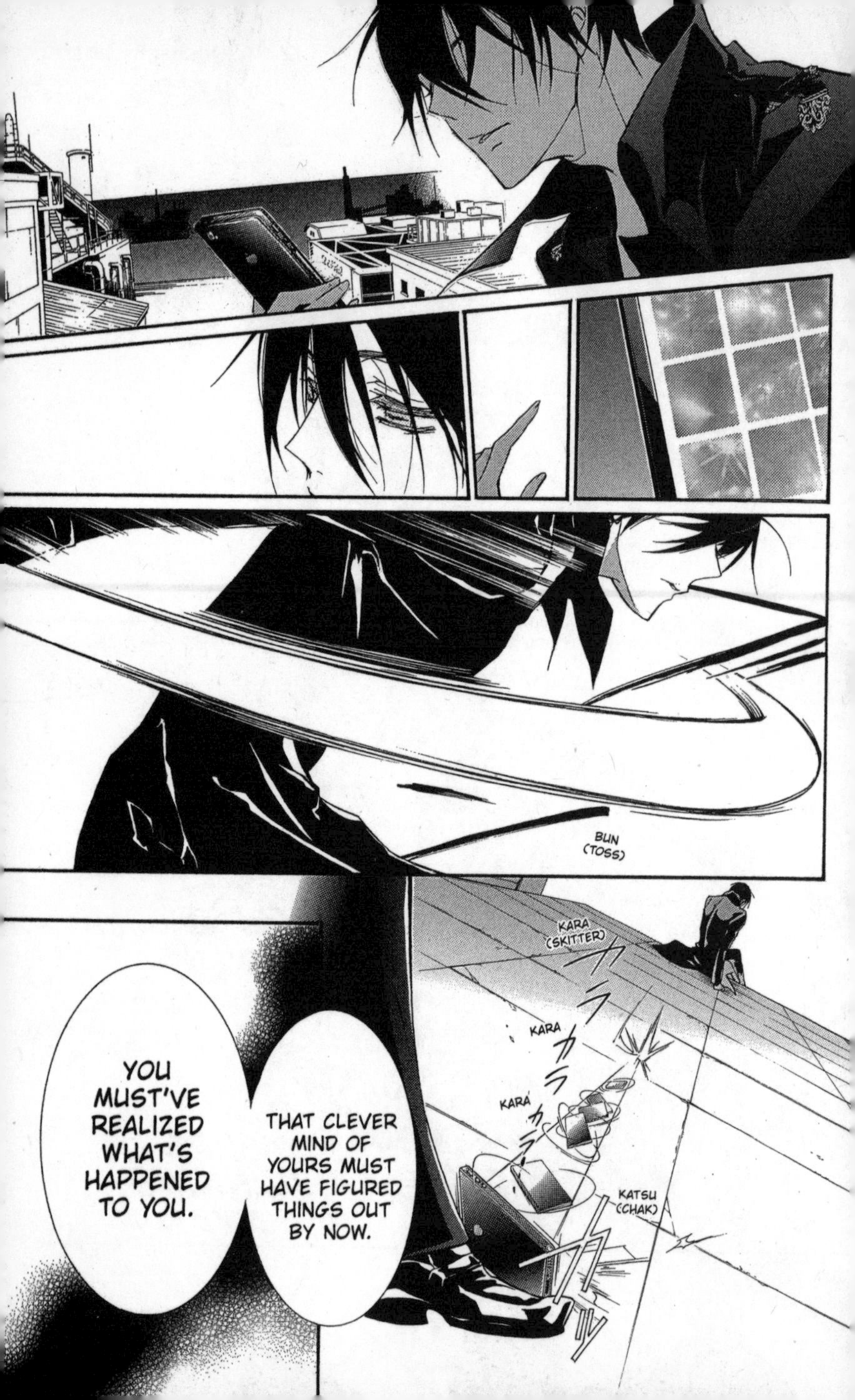
BUN (TOSS)
KARA (SKITTER)
KARA
KARA
KATSU (CHAK)
THAT CLEVER MIND OF YOURS MUST HAVE FIGURED THINGS OUT BY NOW.
YOU MUST'VE REALIZED WHAT'S HAPPENED TO YOU.

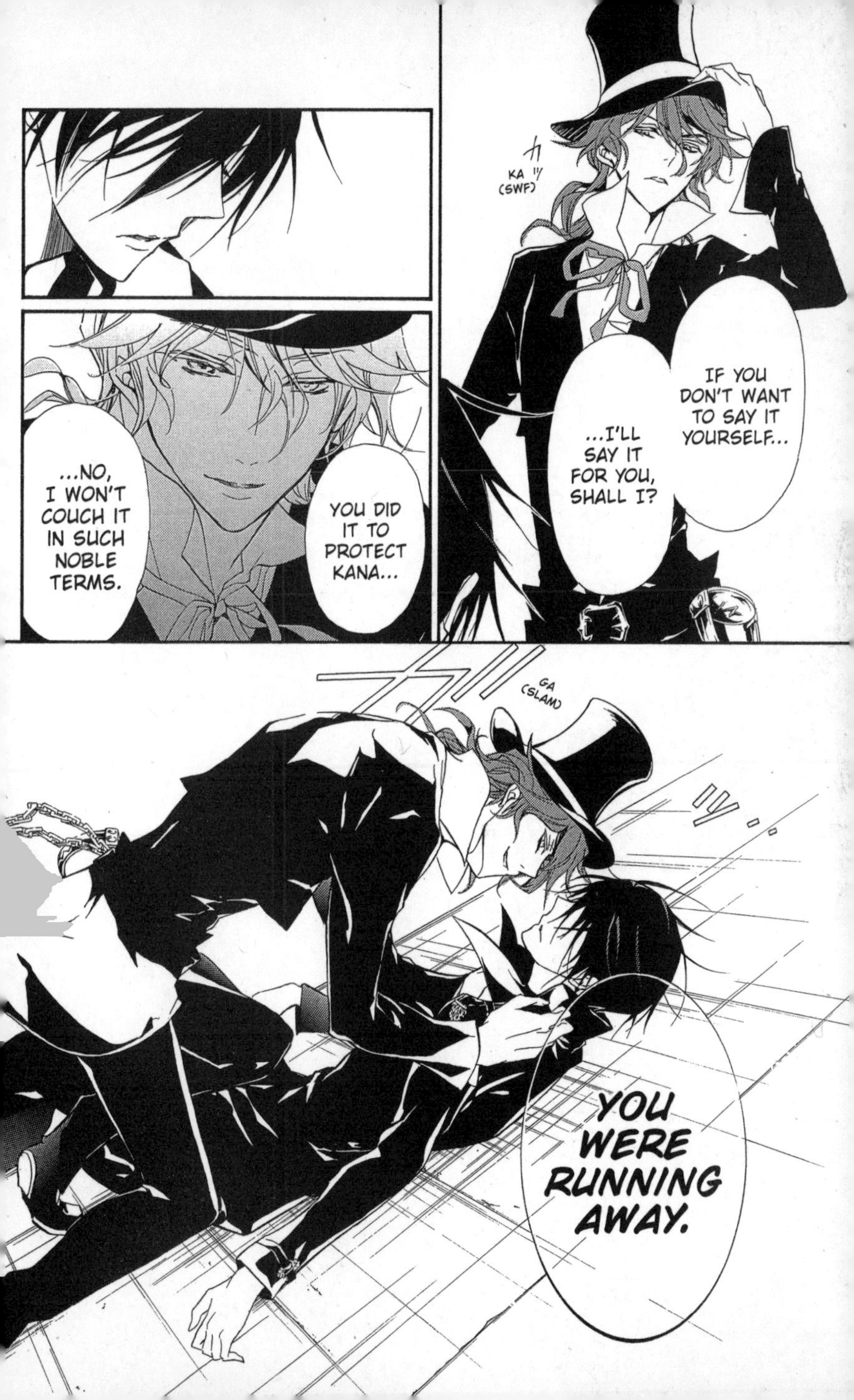
KA (SWF)
IF YOU DON'T WANT TO SAY IT YOURSELF...
...I'LL SAY IT FOR YOU, SHALL I?
YOU DID IT TO PROTECT KANA...
...NO, I WON'T COUCH IT IN SUCH NOBLE TERMS.
GA (SLAM)
YOU WERE RUNNING AWAY.

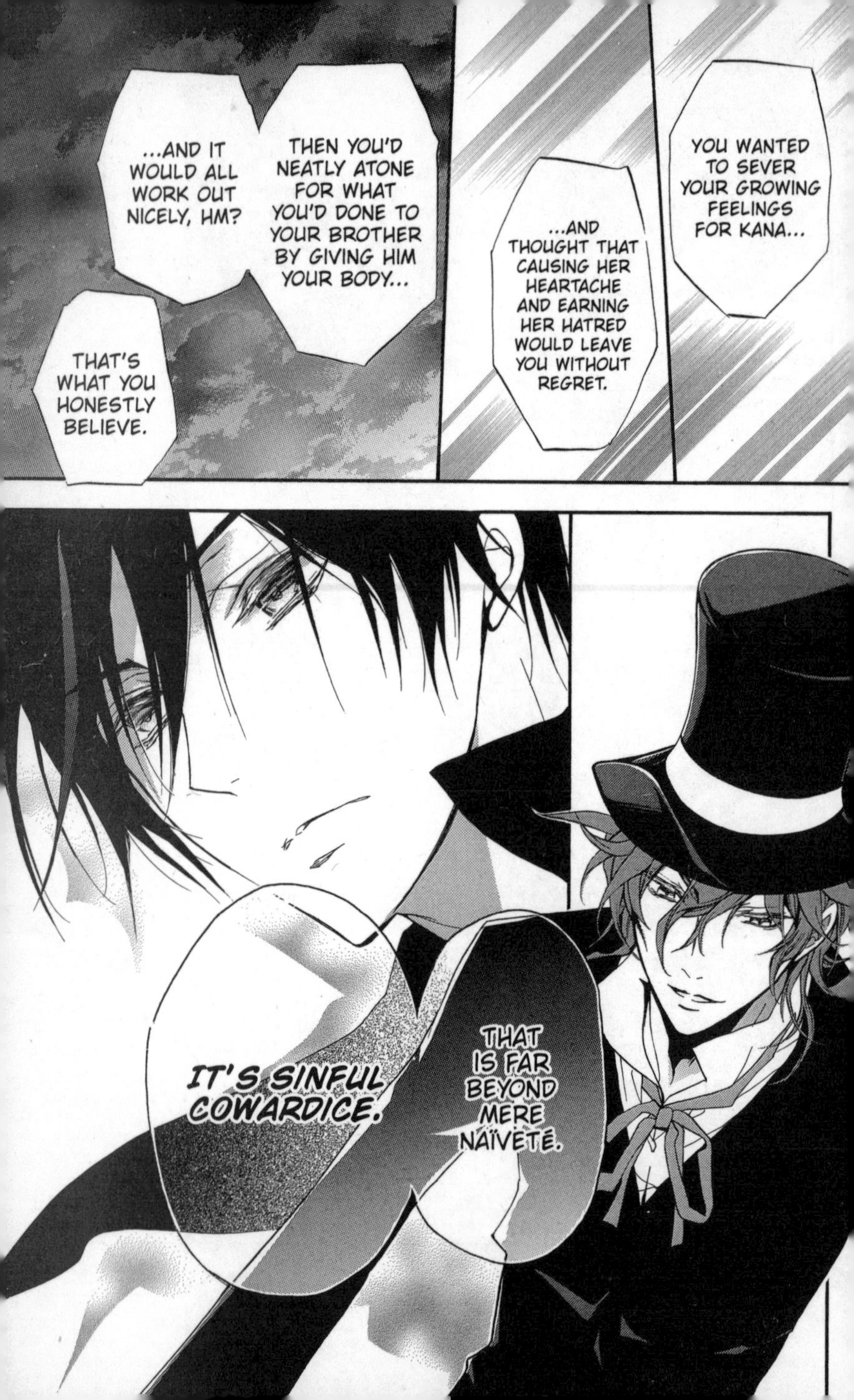
YOU WANTED TO SEVER YOUR GROWING FEELINGS FOR KANA...
...AND THOUGHT THAT CAUSING HER HEARTACHE AND EARNING HER HATRED WOULD LEAVE YOU WITHOUT REGRET.
THEN YOU'D NEATLY ATONE FOR WHAT YOU'D DONE TO YOUR BROTHER BY GIVING HIM YOUR BODY...
...AND IT WOULD ALL WORK OUT NICELY, HM?
THAT'S WHAT YOU HONESTLY BELIEVE.
THAT IS FAR BEYOND MERE NAÏVETÉ.
IT'S SINFUL COWARDICE.

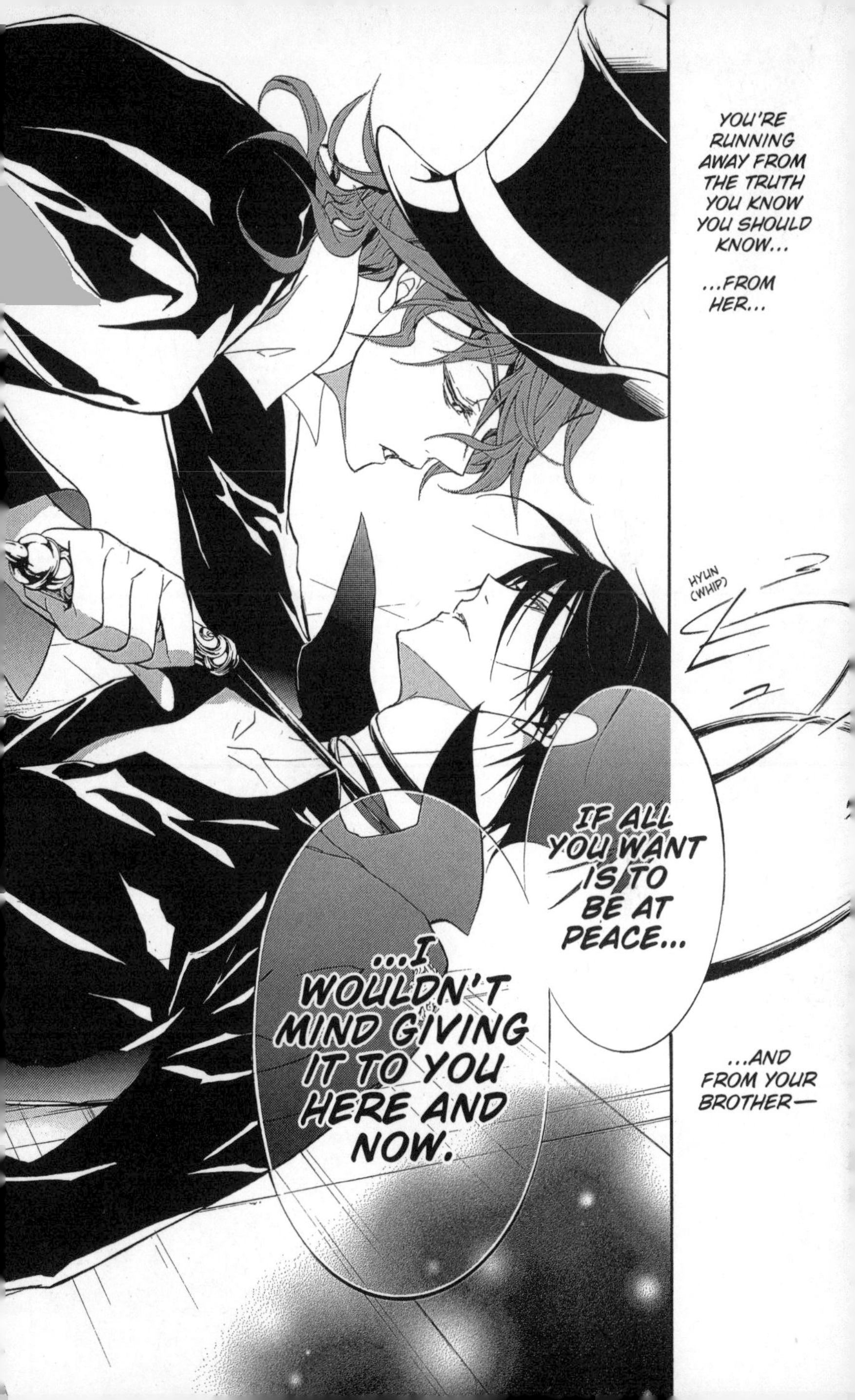
YOU'RE RUNNING AWAY FROM THE TRUTH YOU KNOW YOU SHOULD KNOW...
...FROM HER...
...AND FROM YOUR BROTHER—
HYUN (WHIP)
IF ALL YOU WANT IS TO BE AT PEACE...
...I WOULDN'T MIND GIVING IT TO YOU HERE AND NOW.

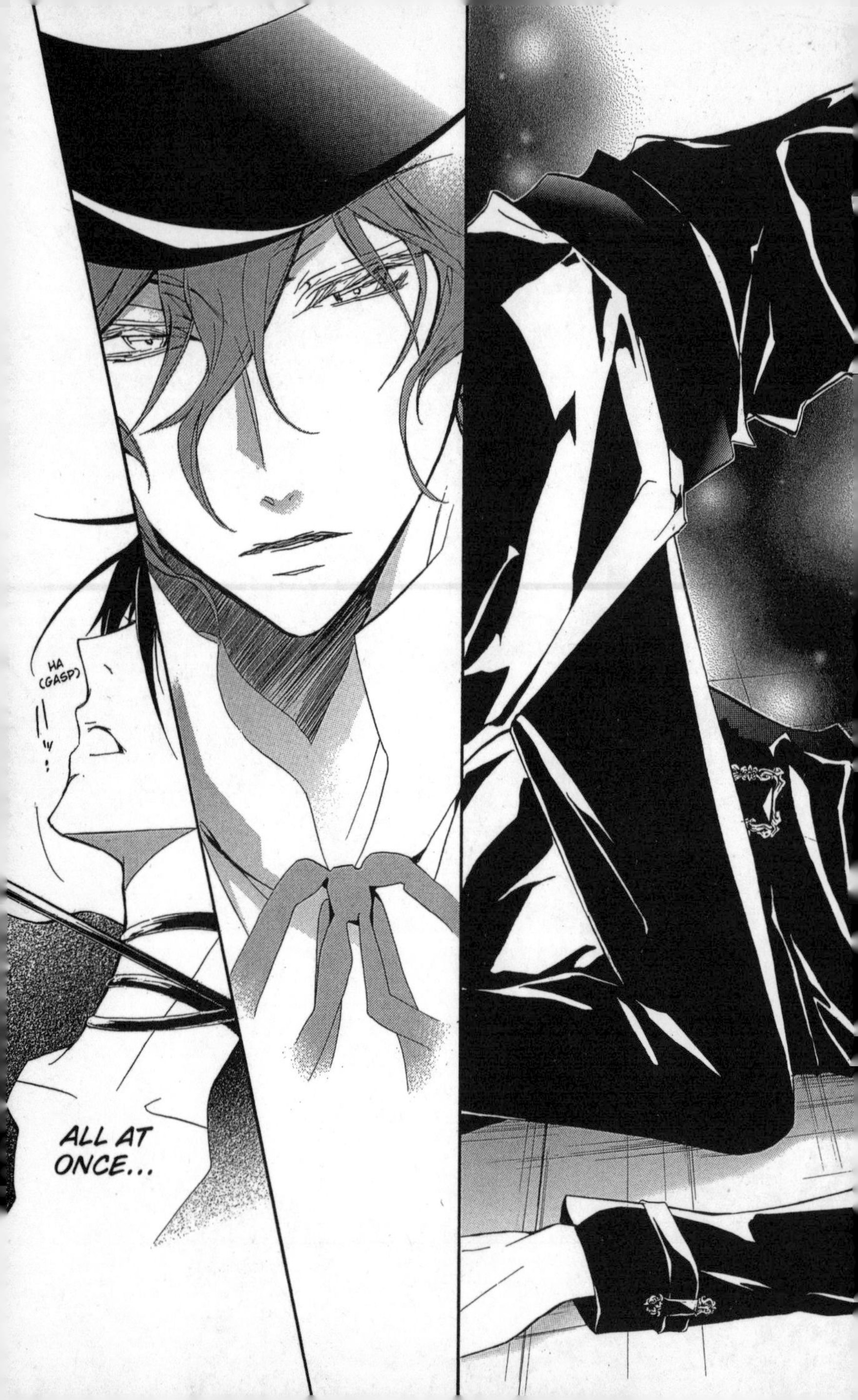
HA (GASP)
ALL AT ONCE...

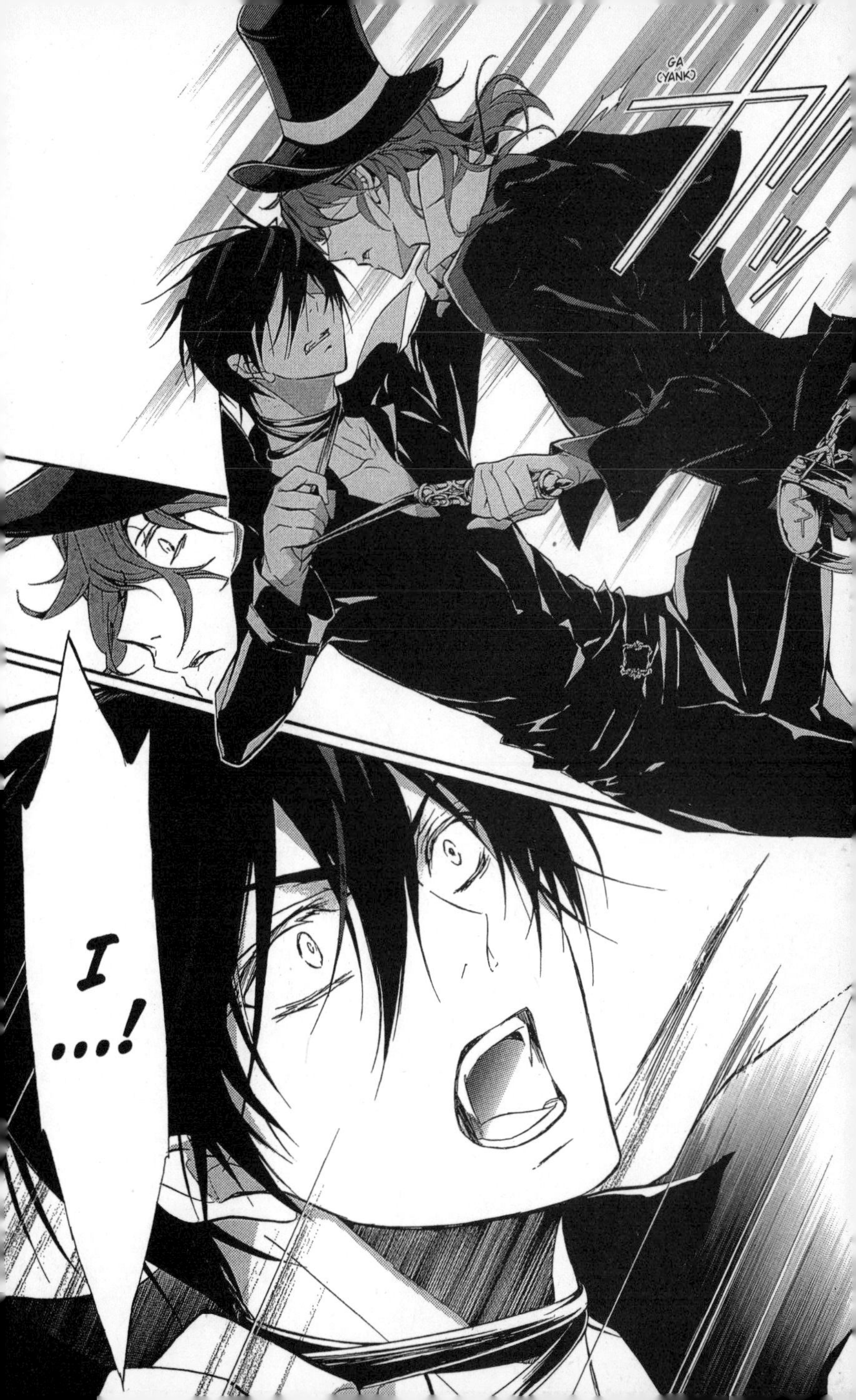
GA
(YANK)
I ...!

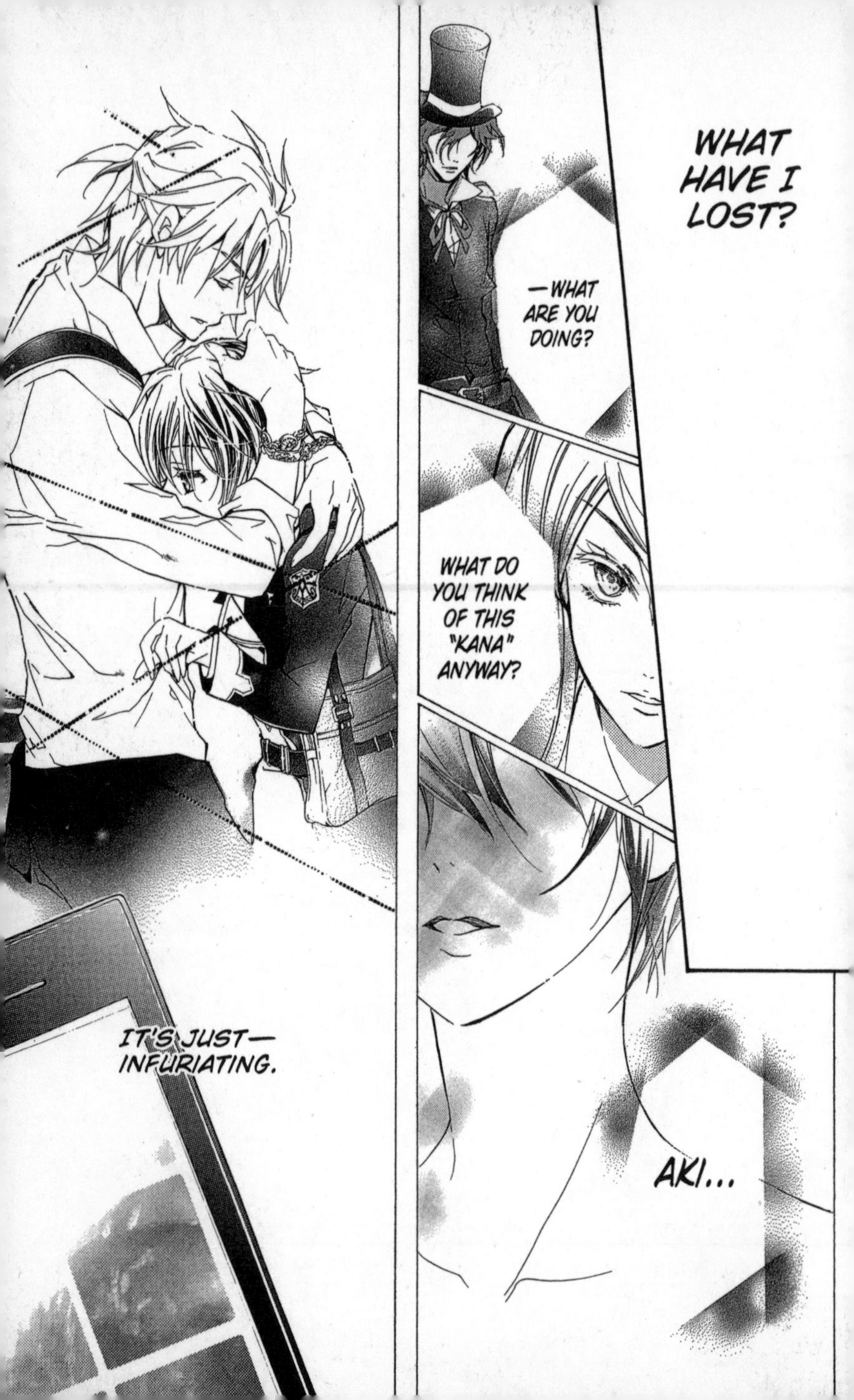
WHAT HAVE I LOST?
—WHAT ARE YOU DOING?
WHAT DO YOU THINK OF THIS "KANA" ANYWAY?
AKI...
IT'S JUST— INFURIATING.

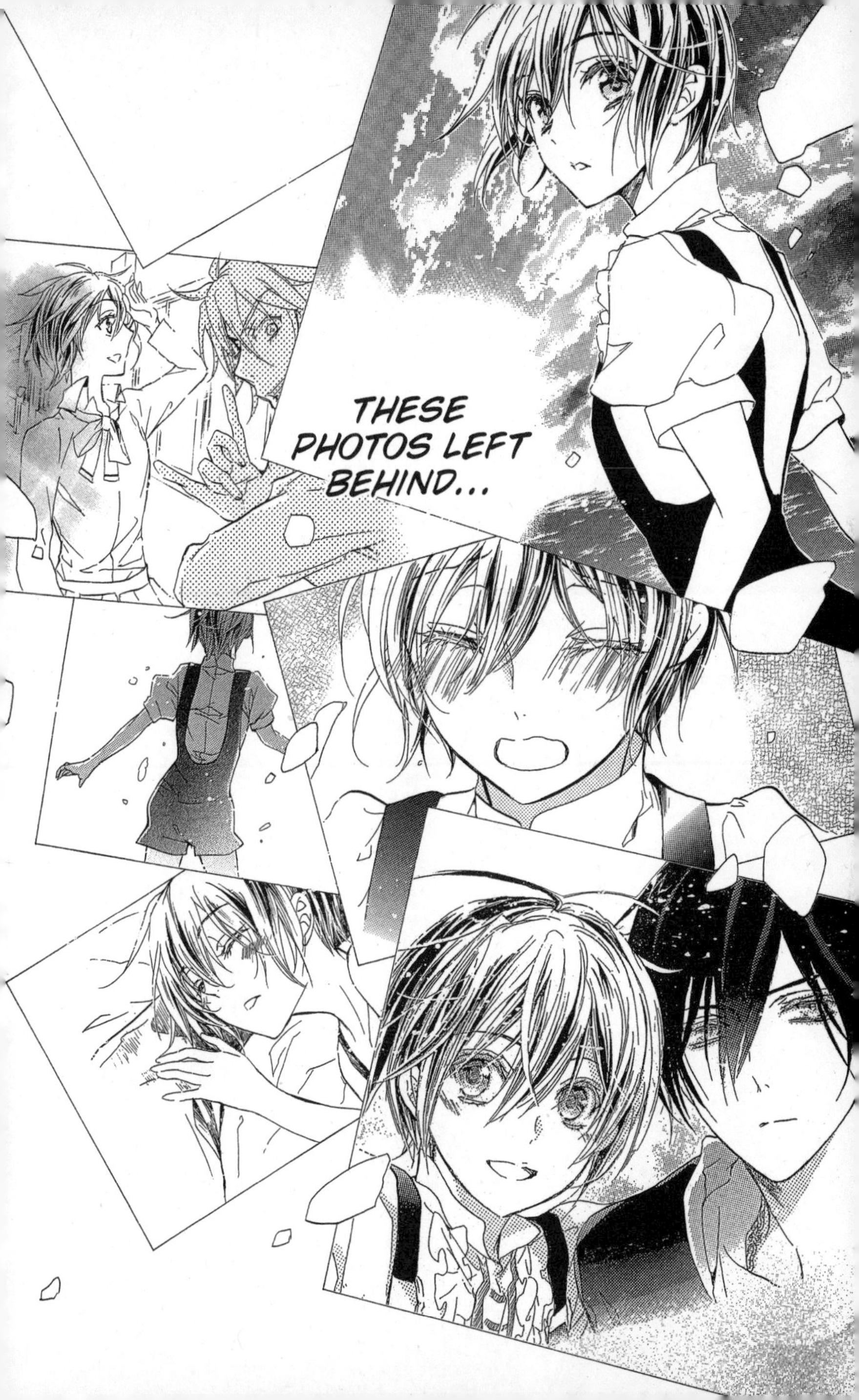
THESE PHOTOS LEFT BEHIND...

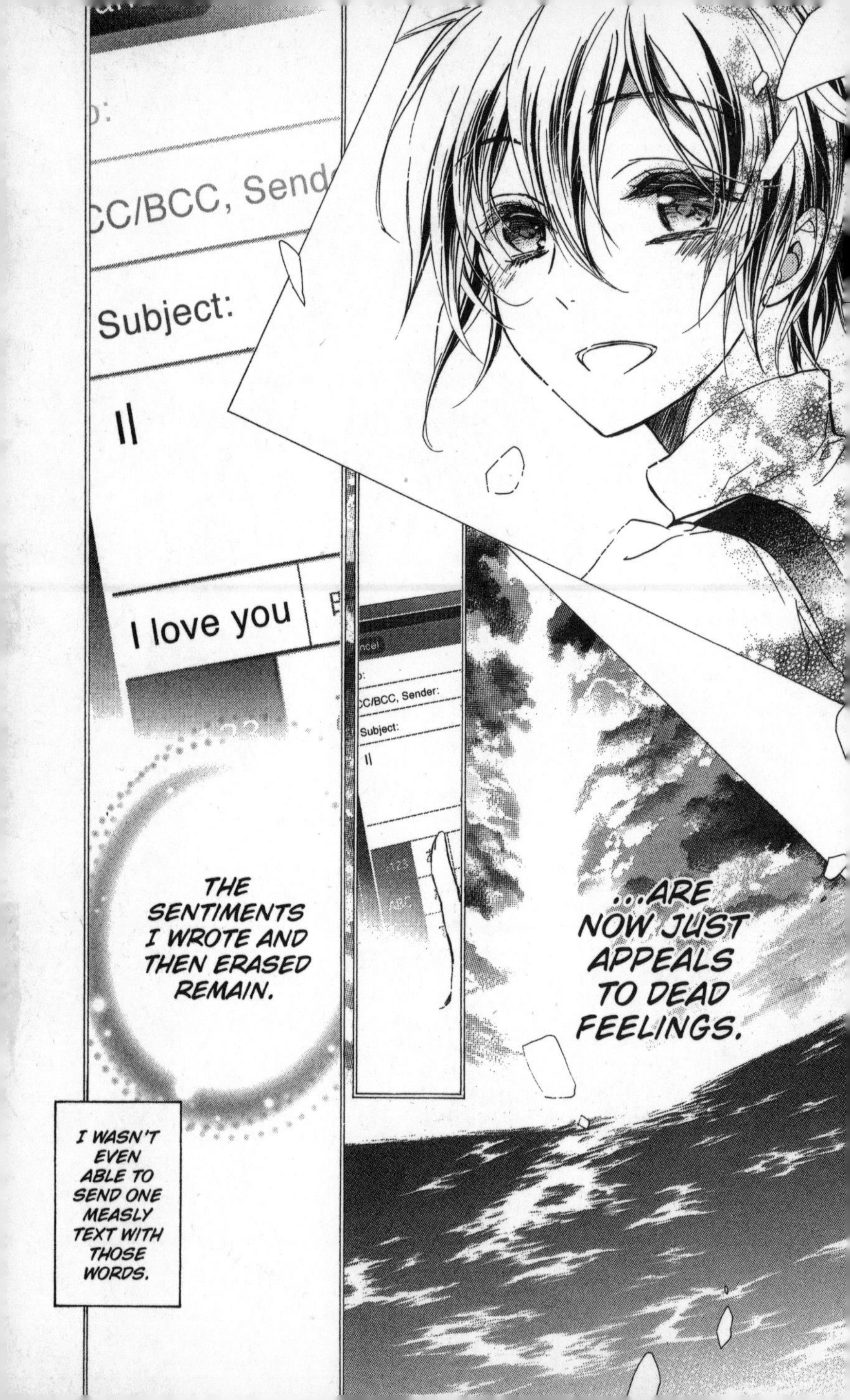
...ARE NOW JUST APPEALS TO DEAD FEELINGS.
CC/BCC, Sender:
Subject:
CC/BCC, Send
Subject:
I love you
THE SENTIMENTS I WROTE AND THEN ERASED REMAIN.
I WASN'T EVEN ABLE TO SEND ONE MEASLY TEXT WITH THOSE WORDS.

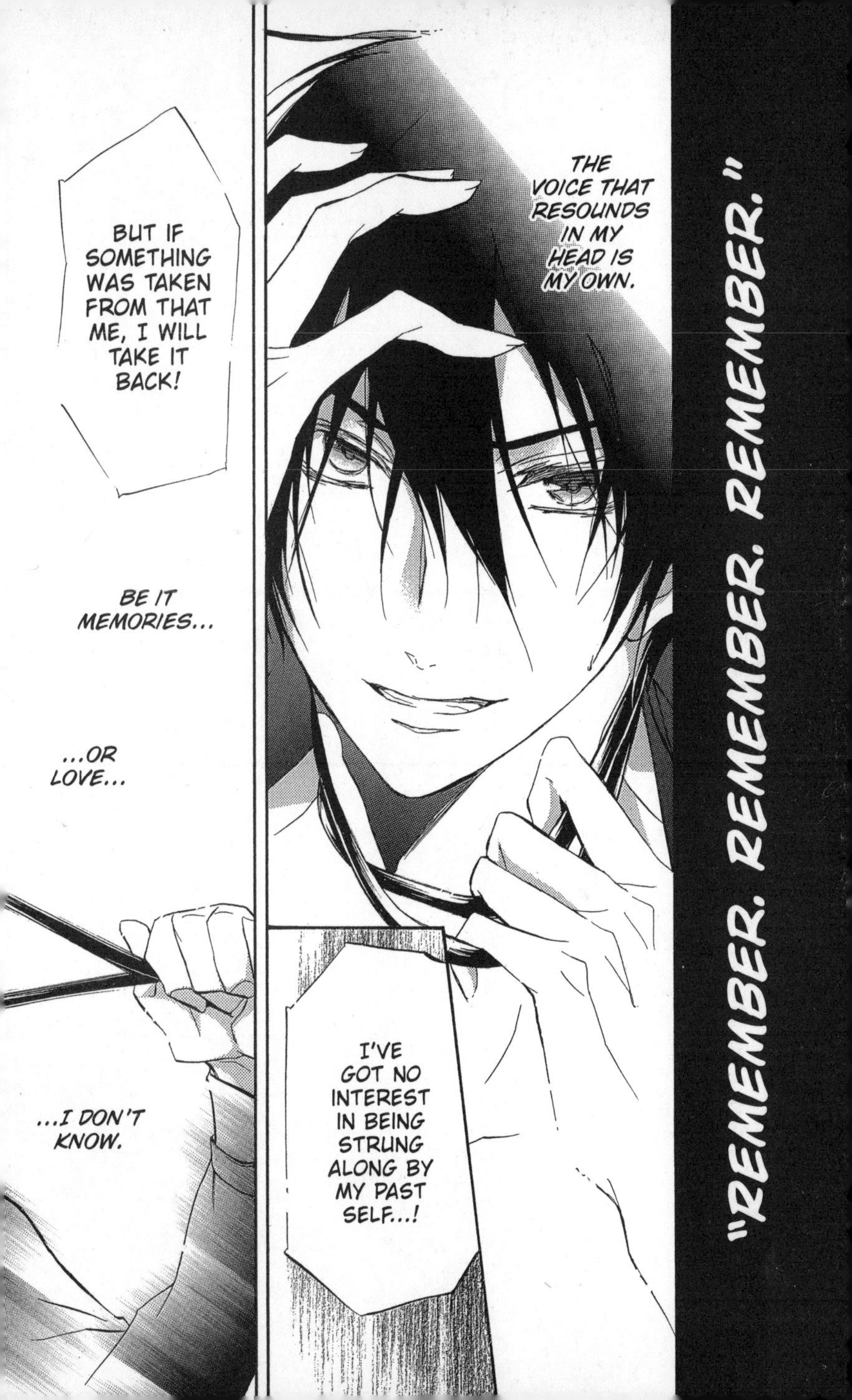
"REMEMBER. REMEMBER. REMEMBER."
THE VOICE THAT RESOUNDS IN MY HEAD IS MY OWN.
I'VE GOT NO INTEREST IN BEING STRUNG ALONG BY MY PAST SELF...!
BUT IF SOMETHING WAS TAKEN FROM THAT ME, I WILL TAKE IT BACK!
BE IT MEMORIES...
...OR LOVE...
...I DON'T KNOW.

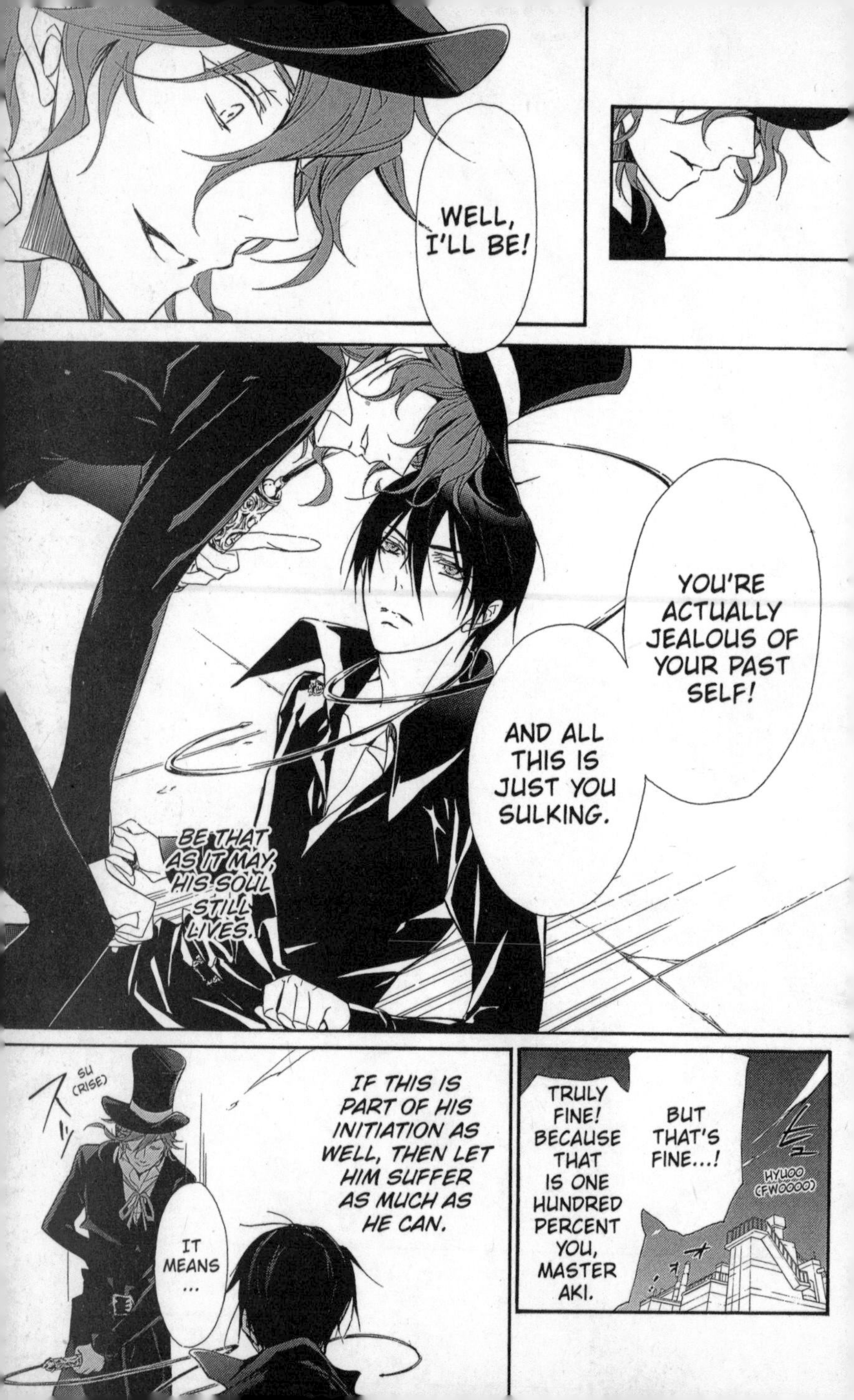
WELL, I'LL BE!
YOU'RE ACTUALLY JEALOUS OF YOUR PAST SELF!
AND ALL THIS IS JUST YOU SULKING.
BE THAT AS IT MAY, HIS SOUL STILL LIVES.
BUT THAT'S FINE...!
TRULY FINE! BECAUSE THAT IS ONE HUNDRED PERCENT YOU, MASTER AKI.
HYUOO (FWOOOO)
IF THIS IS PART OF HIS INITIATION AS WELL, THEN LET HIM SUFFER AS MUCH AS HE CAN.
SU (RISE)
IT MEANS ...

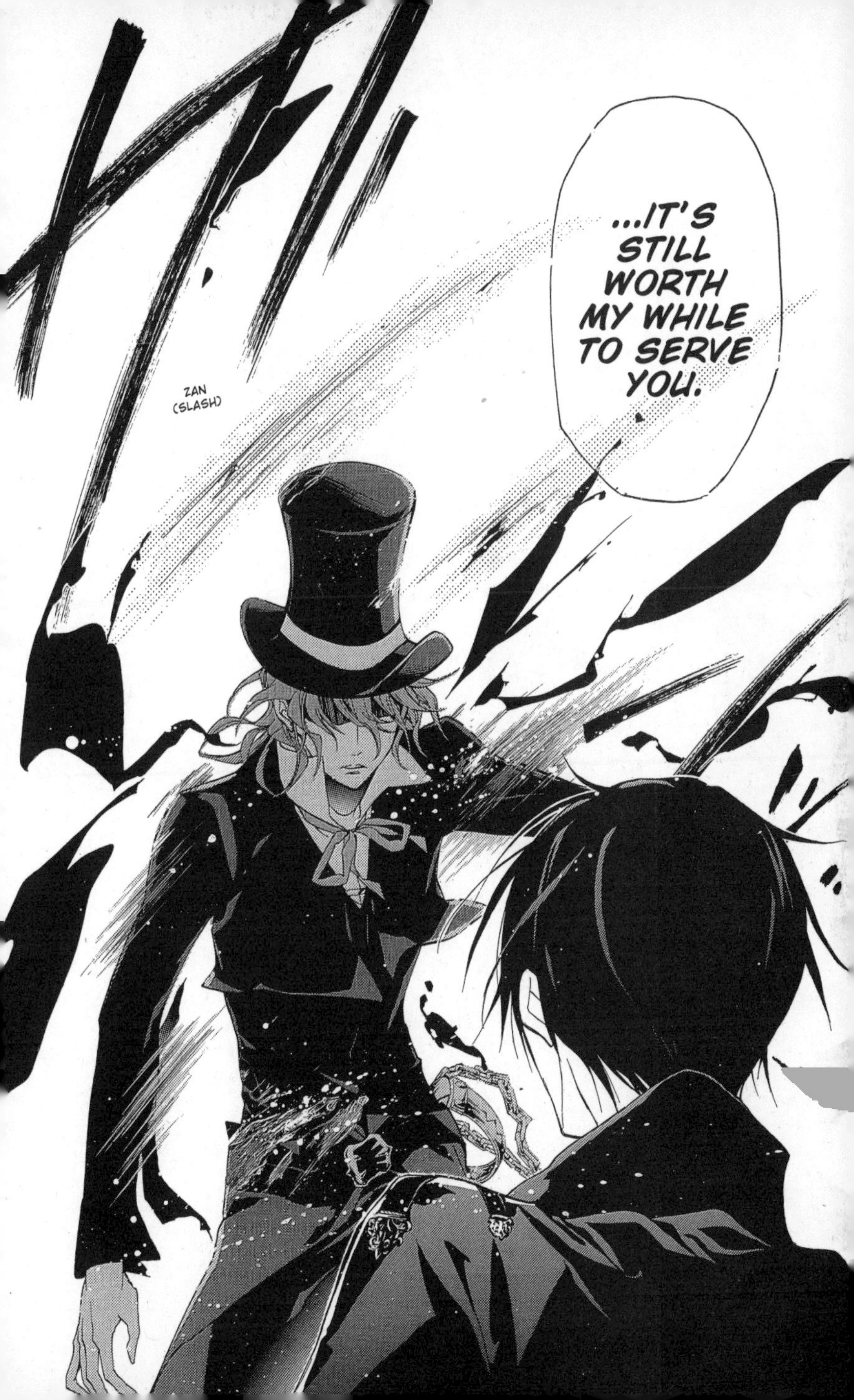
...IT'S STILL WORTH MY WHILE TO SERVE YOU.
ZAN (SLASH)

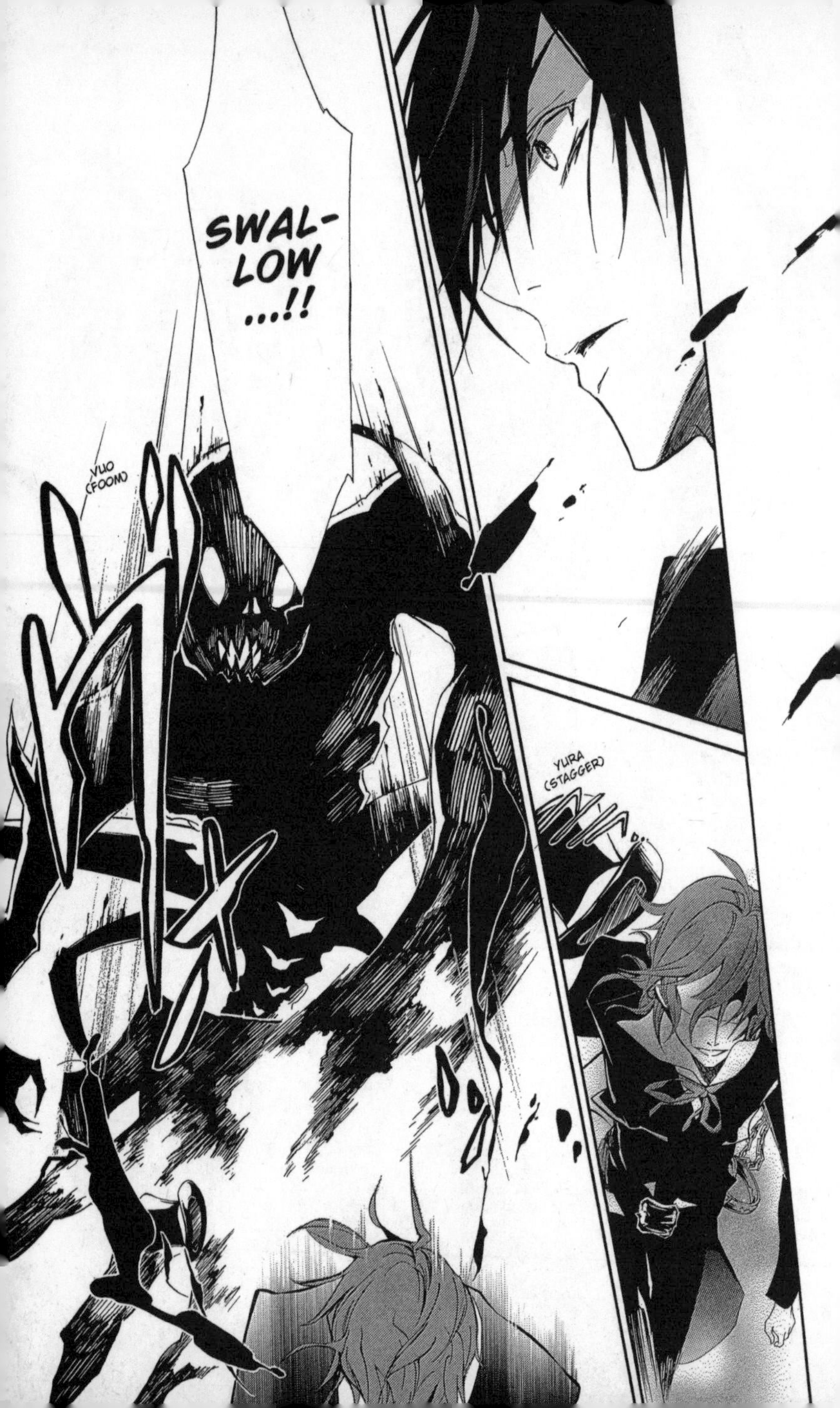
SWAL-
LOW
...!!
VUO
(FOOM)
YURA
(STAGGER)

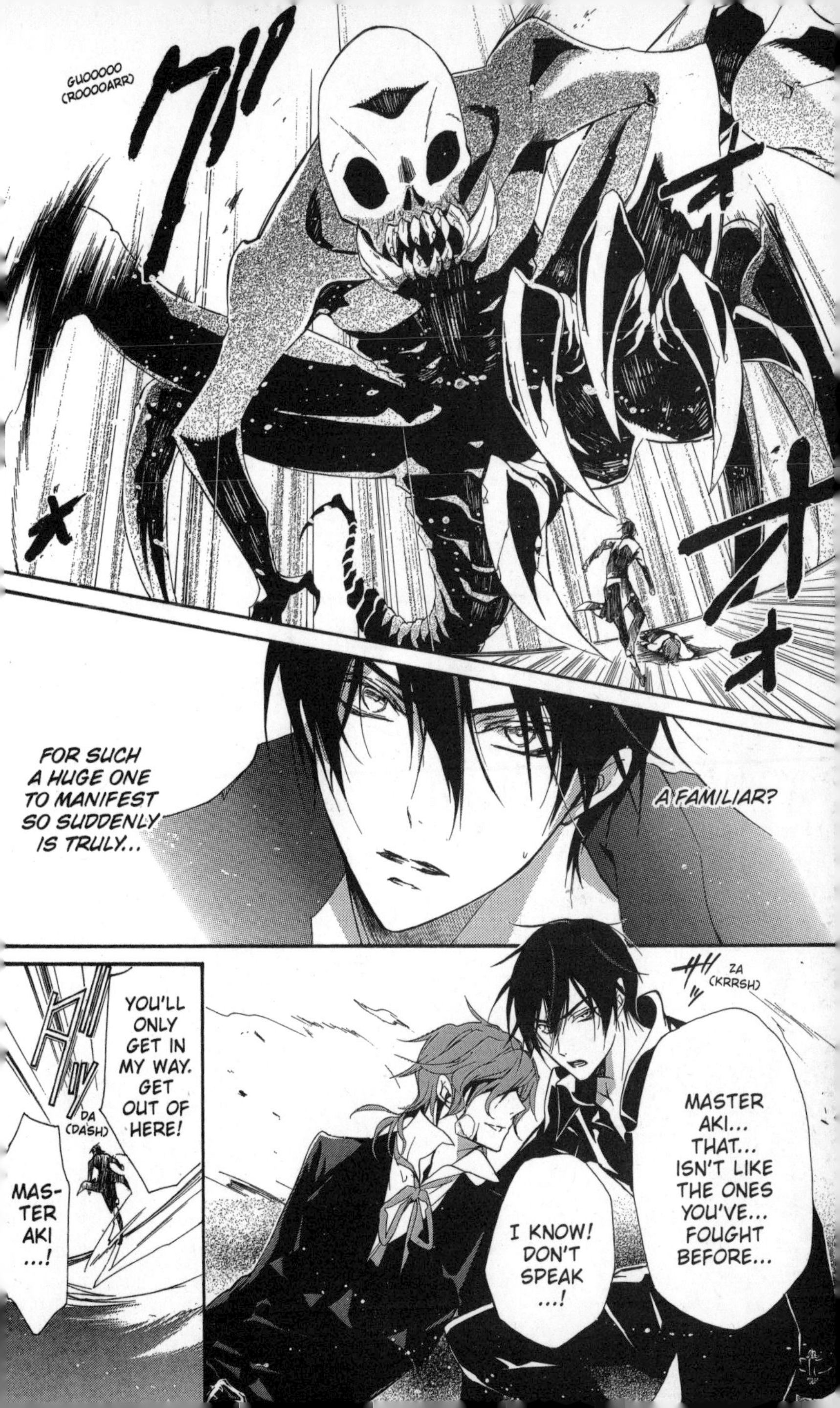
GUOOOOO (ROOOOARR)
A FAMILIAR?
FOR SUCH A HUGE ONE TO MANIFEST SO SUDDENLY IS TRULY...
ZA (KRRSH)
MASTER AKI... THAT... ISN'T LIKE THE ONES YOU'VE... FOUGHT BEFORE...
I KNOW! DON'T SPEAK ...!
YOU'LL ONLY GET IN MY WAY. GET OUT OF HERE!
DA (DASH)
MAS-TER AKI ...!

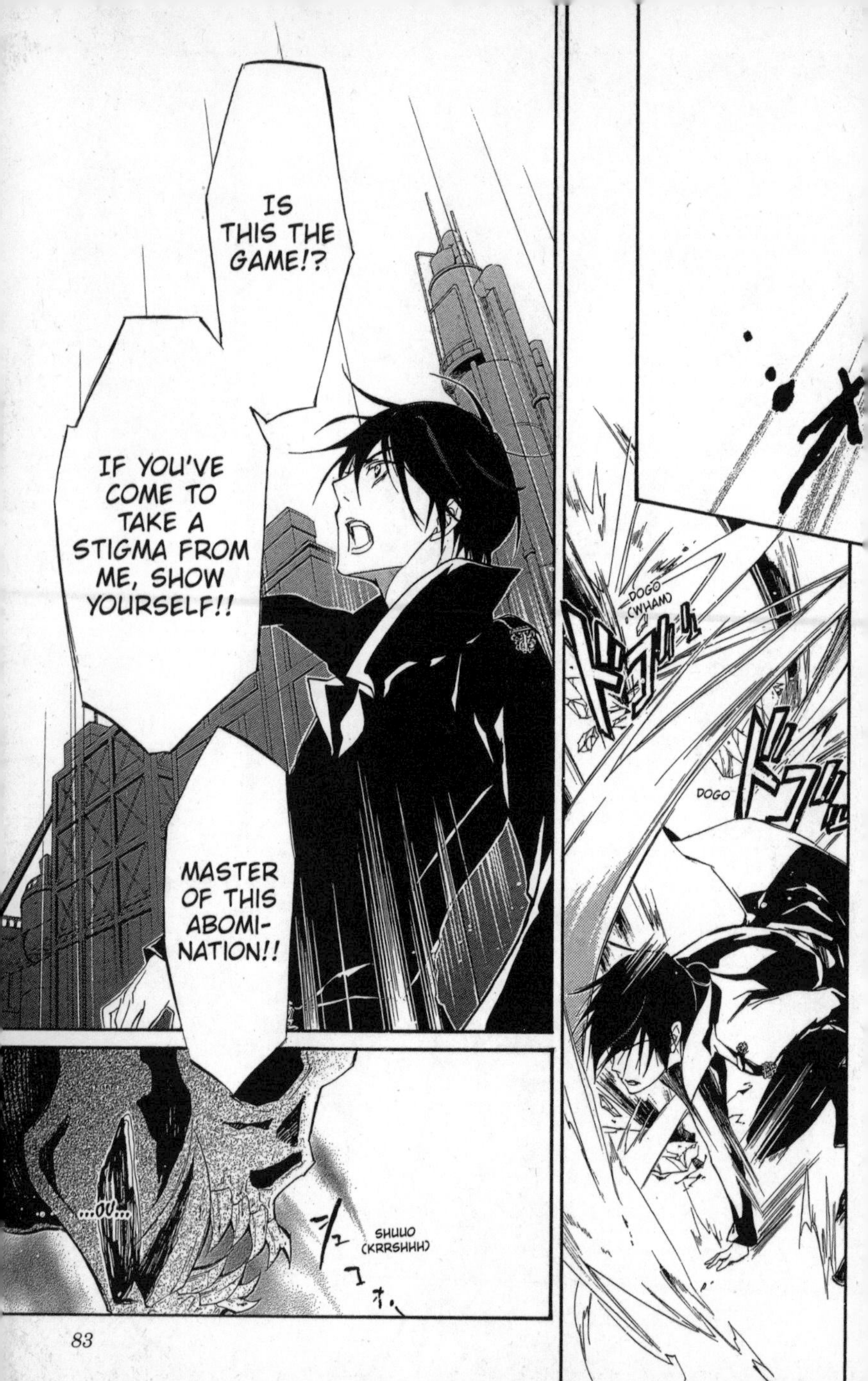
DOGO (WHAM)
DOGO
IS THIS THE GAME!?
IF YOU'VE COME TO TAKE A STIGMA FROM ME, SHOW YOURSELF!!
MASTER OF THIS ABOMI-NATION!!
...OU...
SHUUO (KRRSHHH)

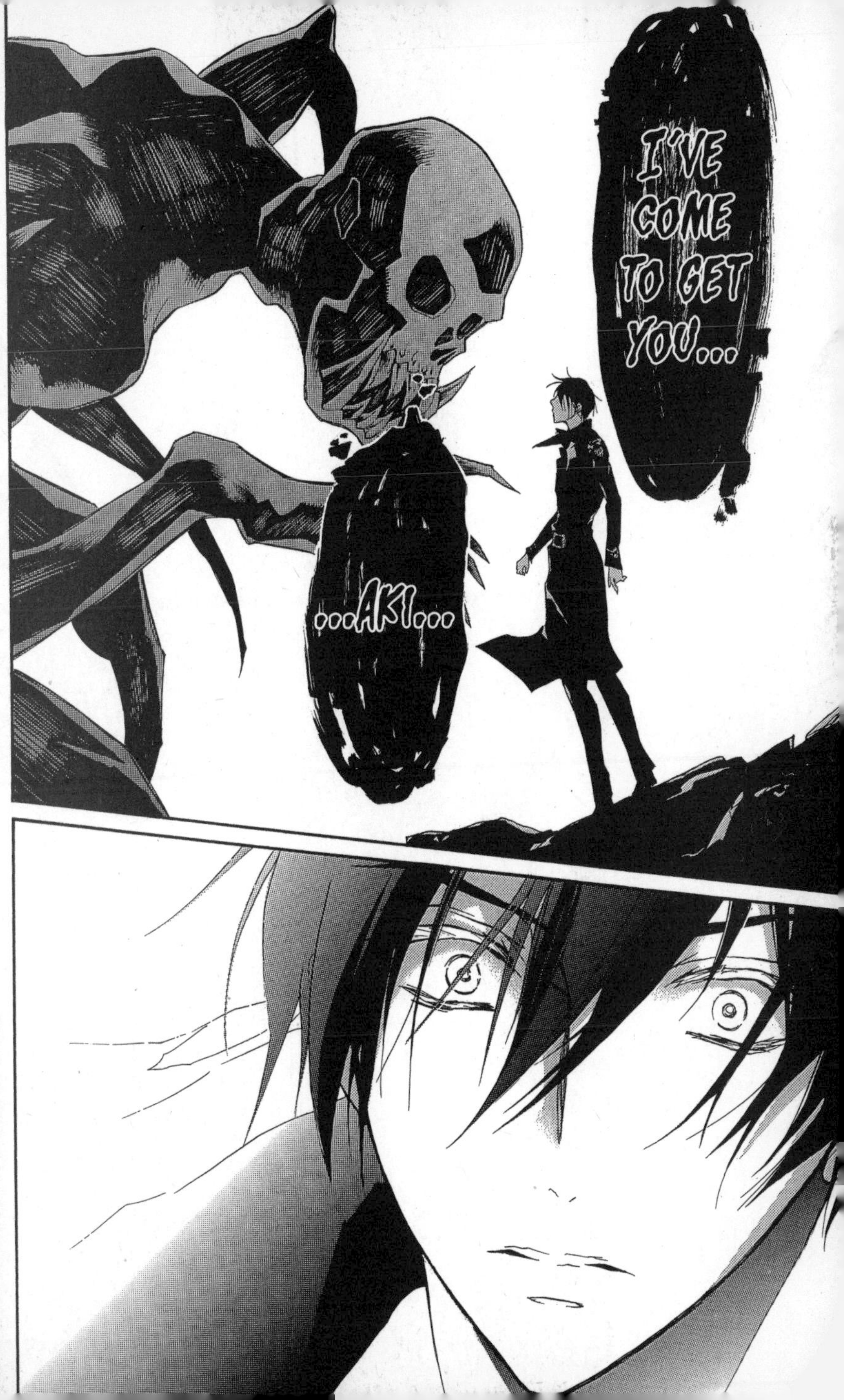
I'VE COME TO GET YOU...
...AKI...

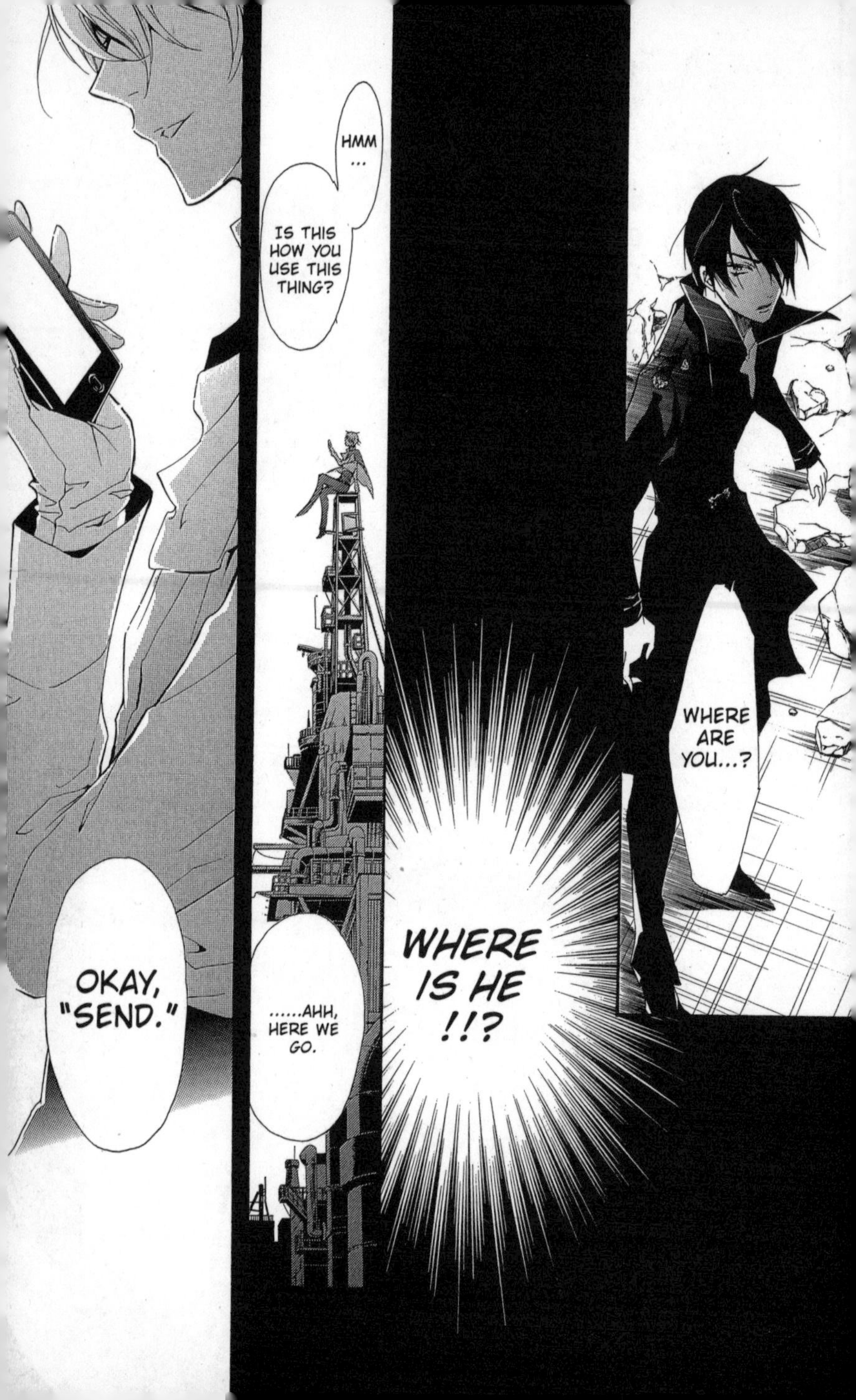
WHERE ARE YOU...?
WHERE IS HE !!?
HMM ...
IS THIS HOW YOU USE THIS THING?
......AHH, HERE WE GO.
OKAY, "SEND."

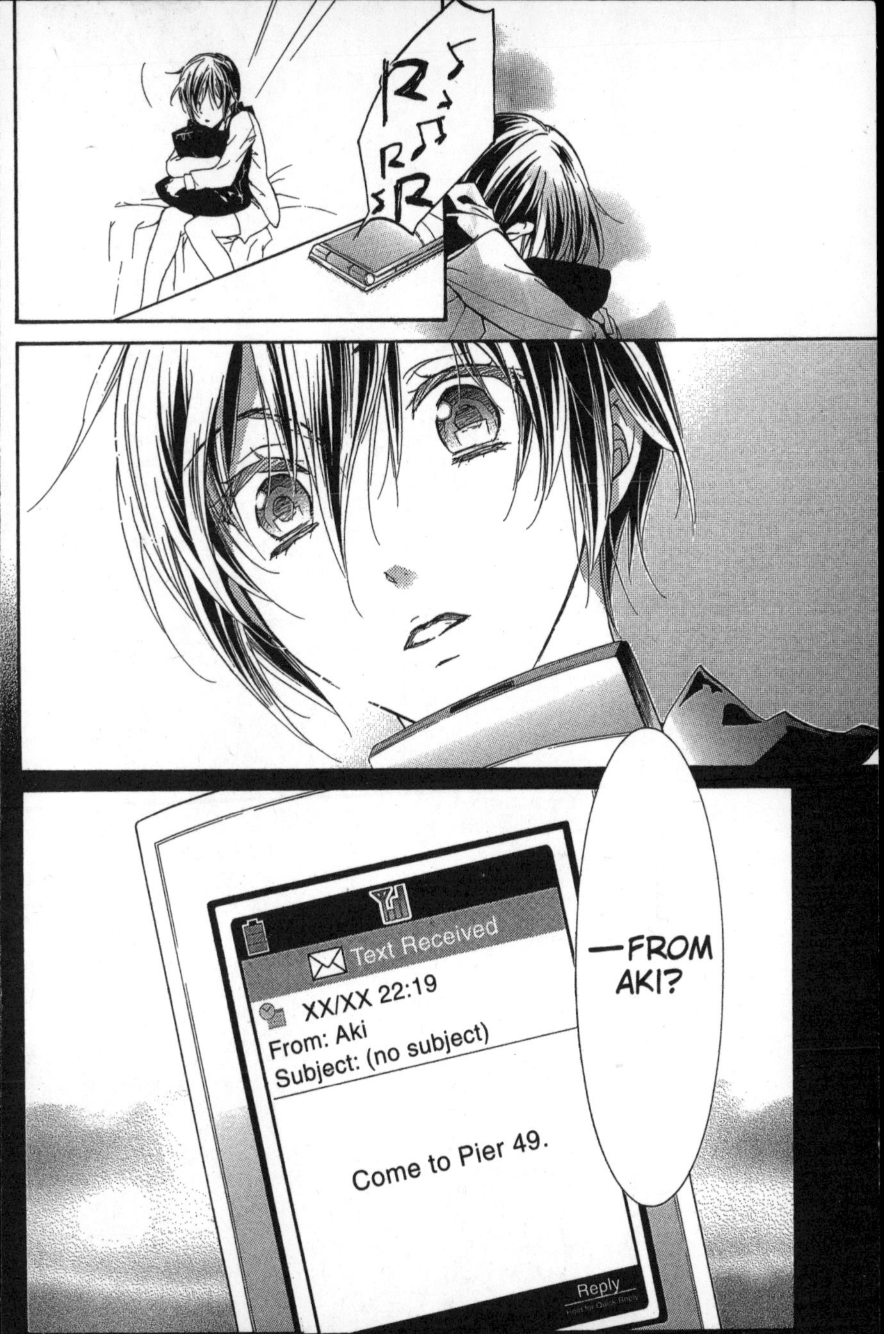
R R R
—FROM AKI?
Text Received
XX/XX 22:19
From: Aki
Subject: (no subject)
Come to Pier 49.
Reply

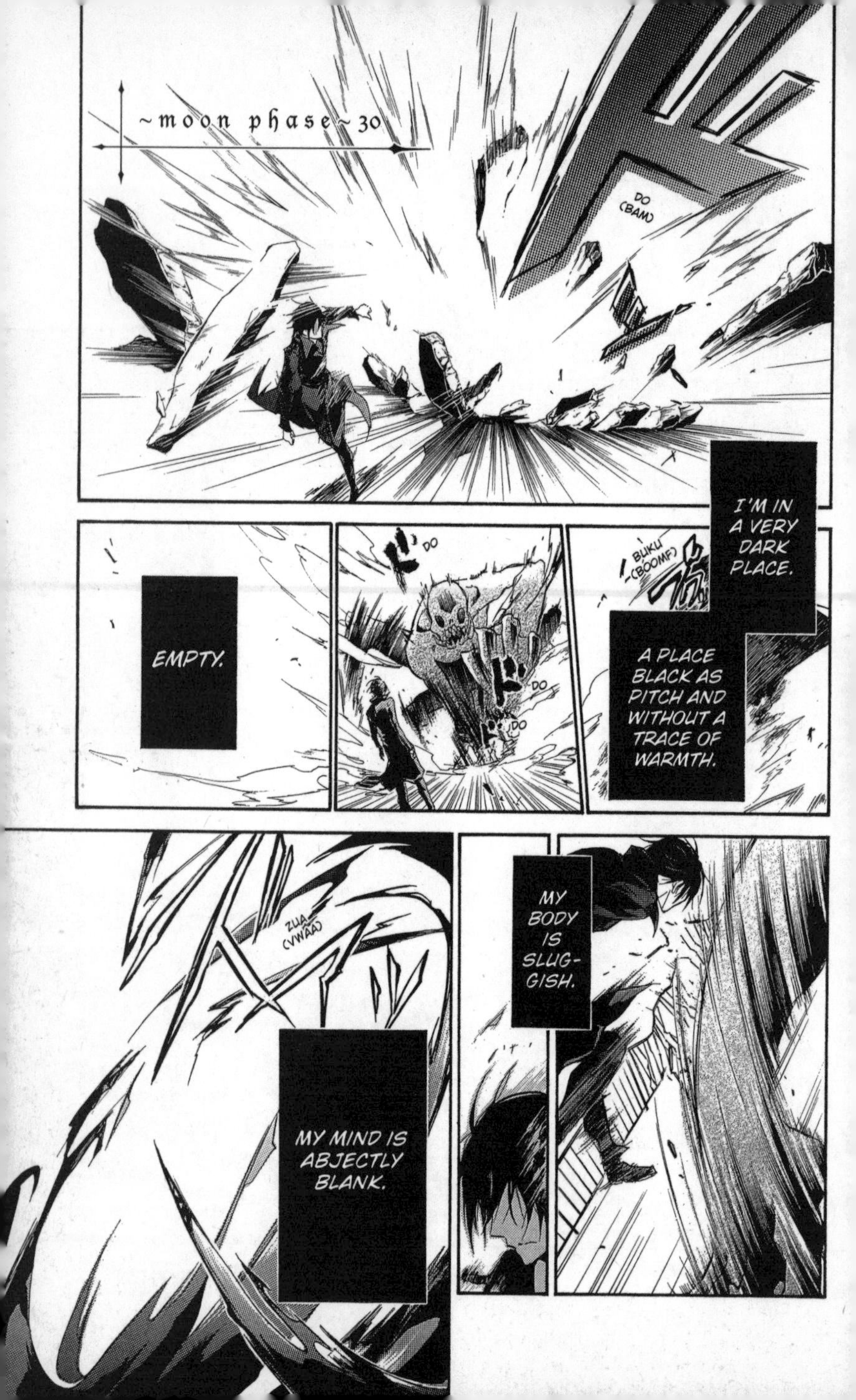
~moon phase~30
DO (BAM)
I'M IN A VERY DARK PLACE.
BUKU (BOOMF)
A PLACE BLACK AS PITCH AND WITHOUT A TRACE OF WARMTH.
DO
DO
DO
EMPTY.
MY BODY IS SLUG-GISH.
ZUA (VWAA)
MY MIND IS ABJECTLY BLANK.

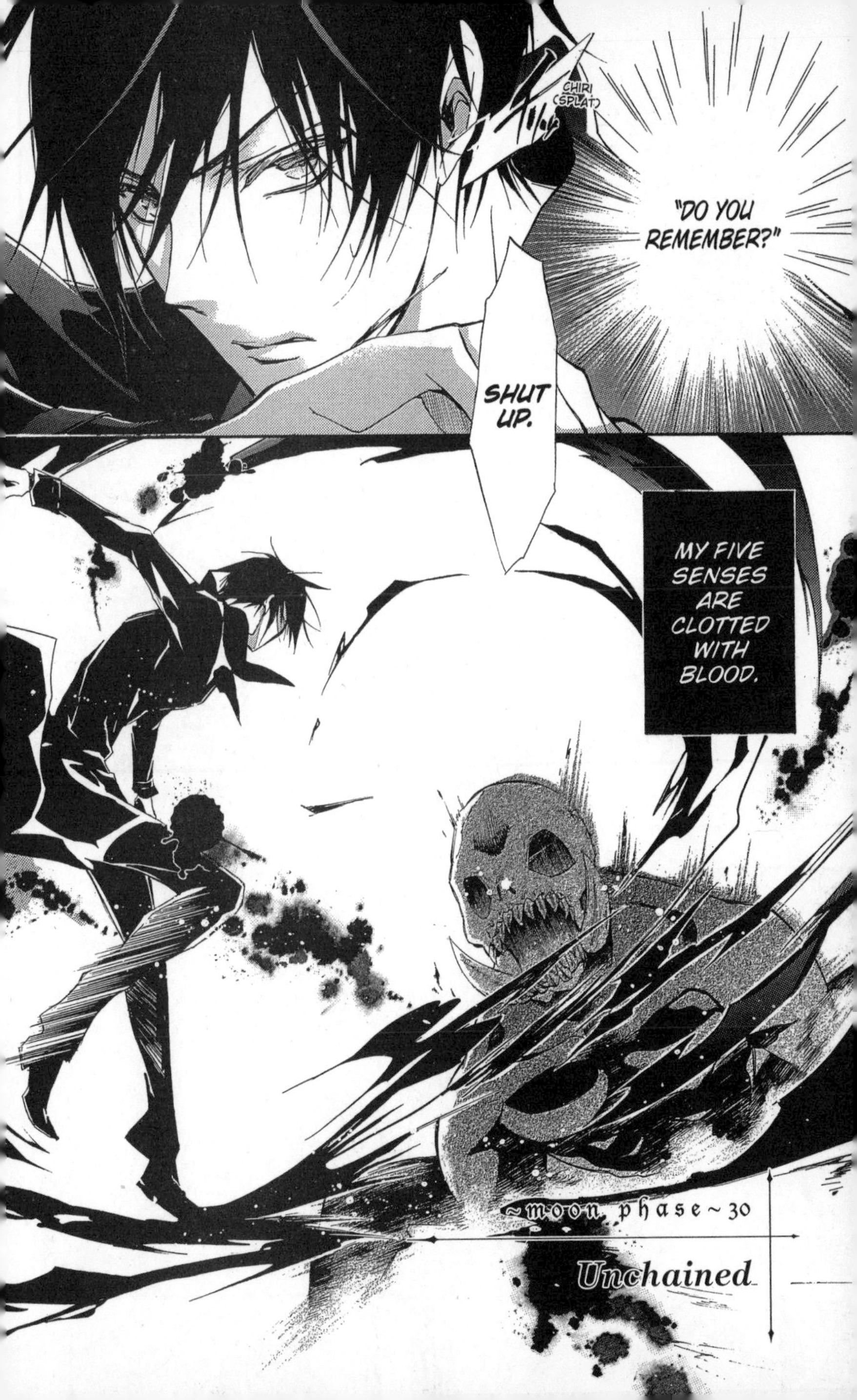
CHIRI (SPLAT)
"DO YOU REMEMBER?"
SHUT UP.
MY FIVE SENSES ARE CLOTTED WITH BLOOD.
~moon phase~ 30
Unchained

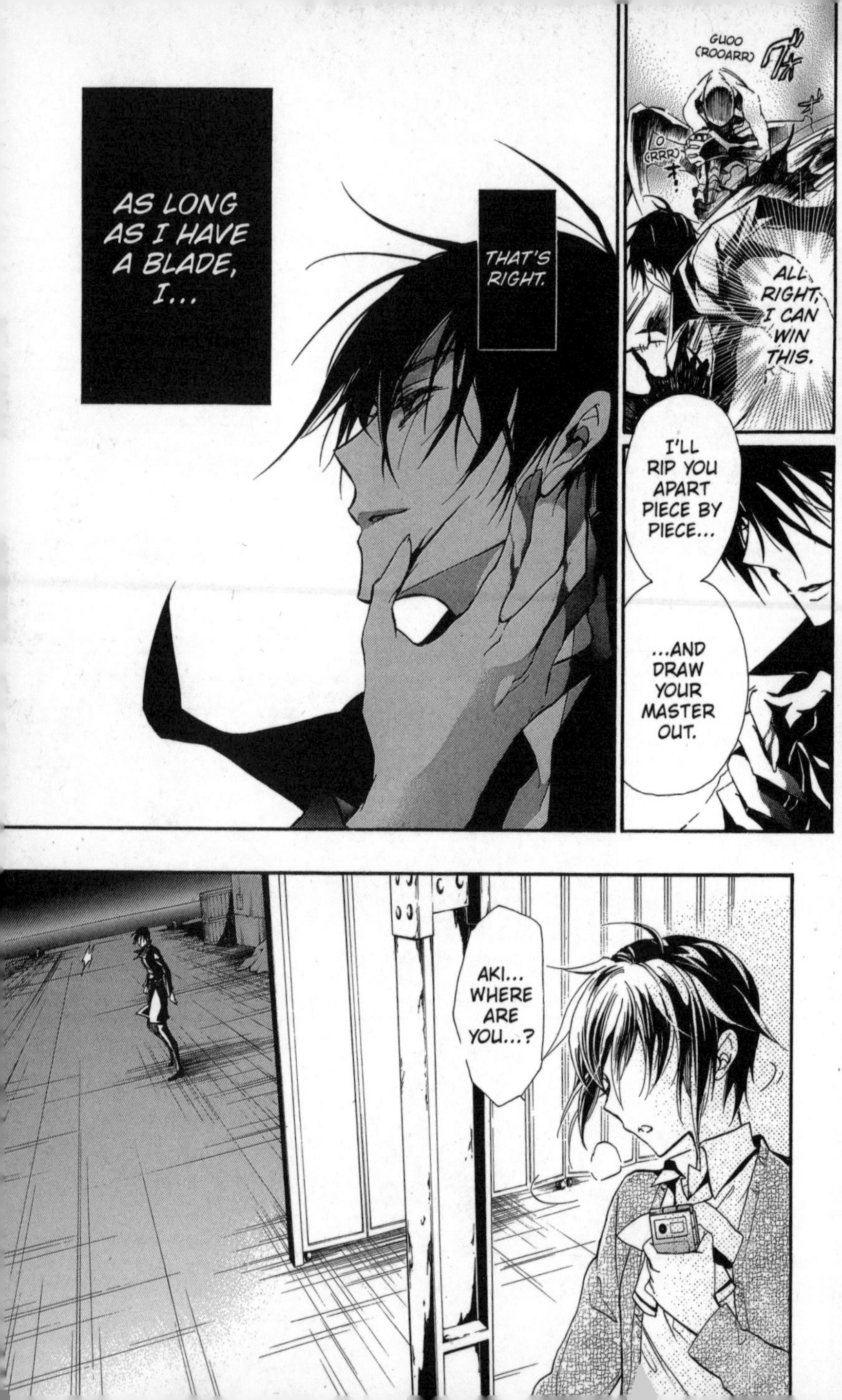
GUOO (ROOARR)
O (RRR)
ALL RIGHT, I CAN WIN THIS.
I'LL RIP YOU APART PIECE BY PIECE...
...AND DRAW YOUR MASTER OUT.
THAT'S RIGHT.
AS LONG AS I HAVE A BLADE, I...
AKI... WHERE ARE YOU...?

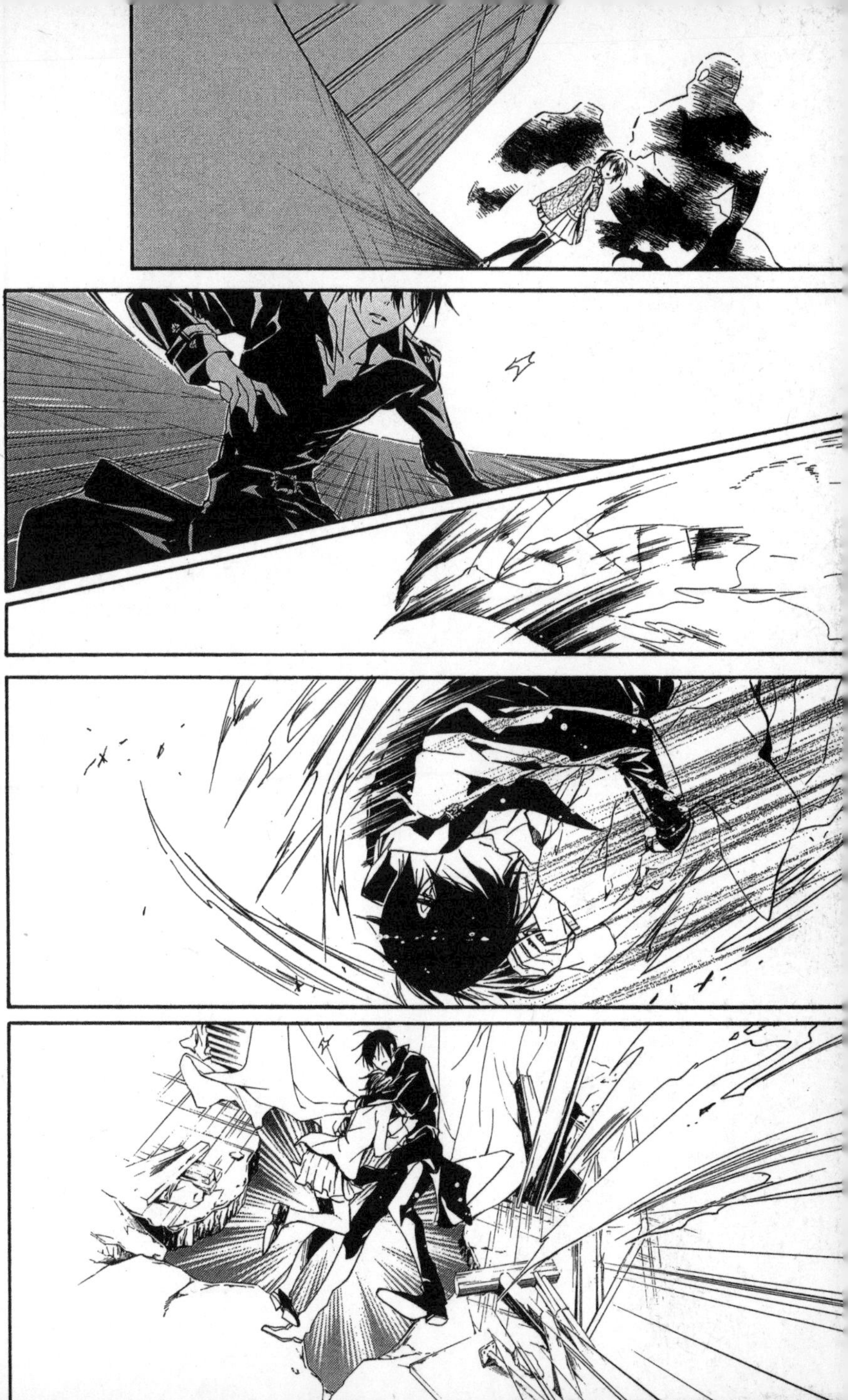

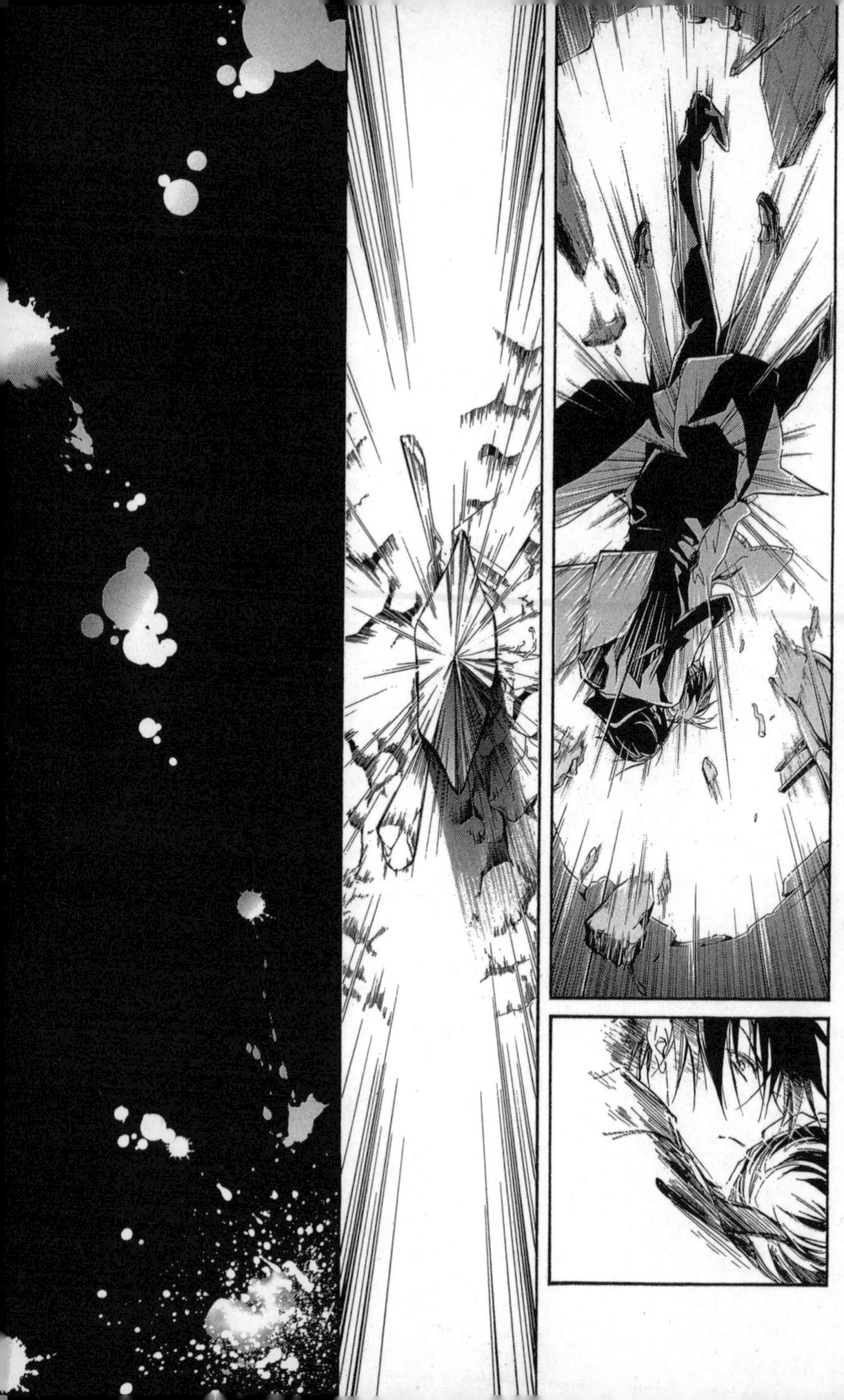

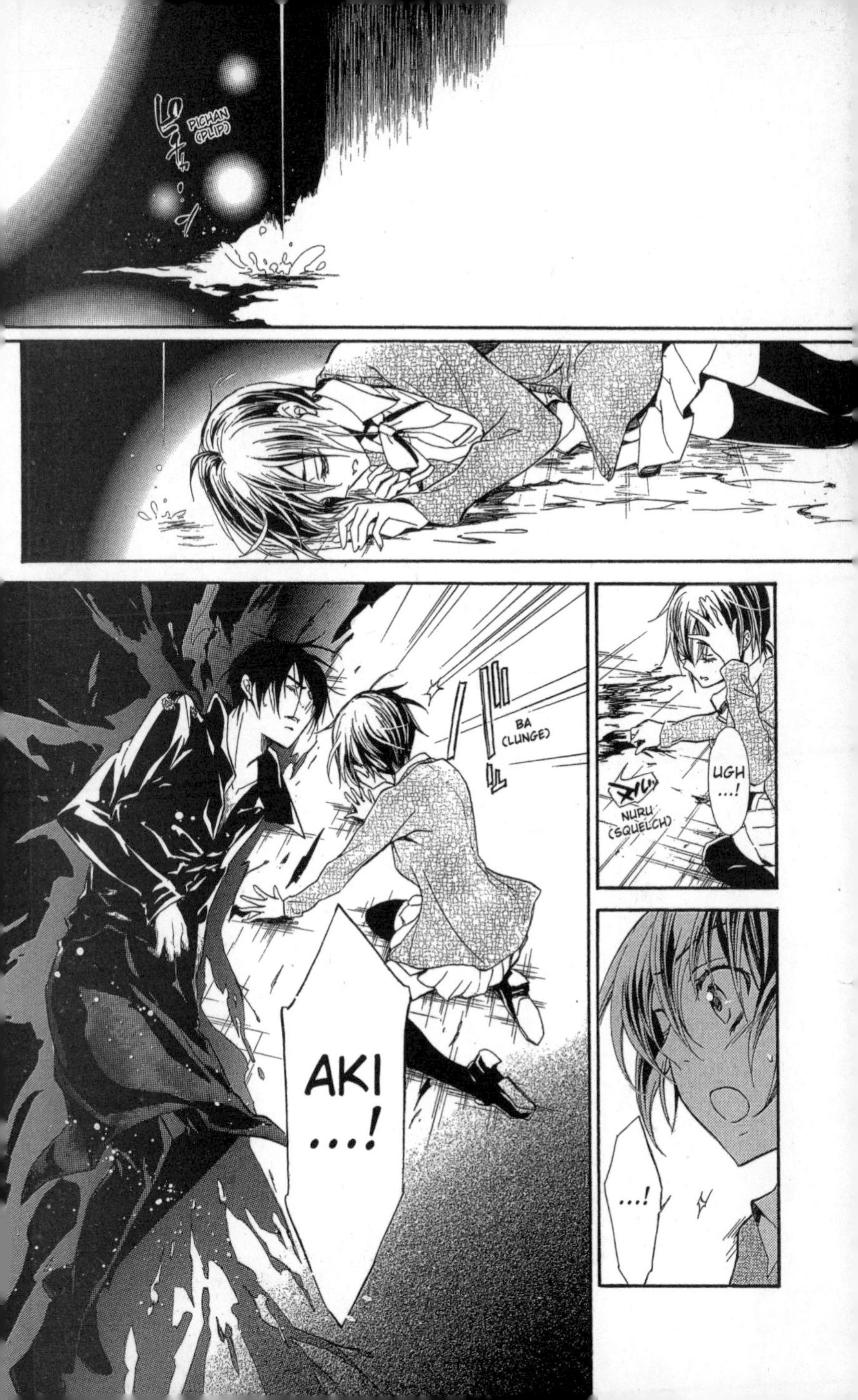
PICHAN (PLIP)
NURU (SQUELCH)
UGH ...!
BA (LUNGE)
AKI ...!
...!

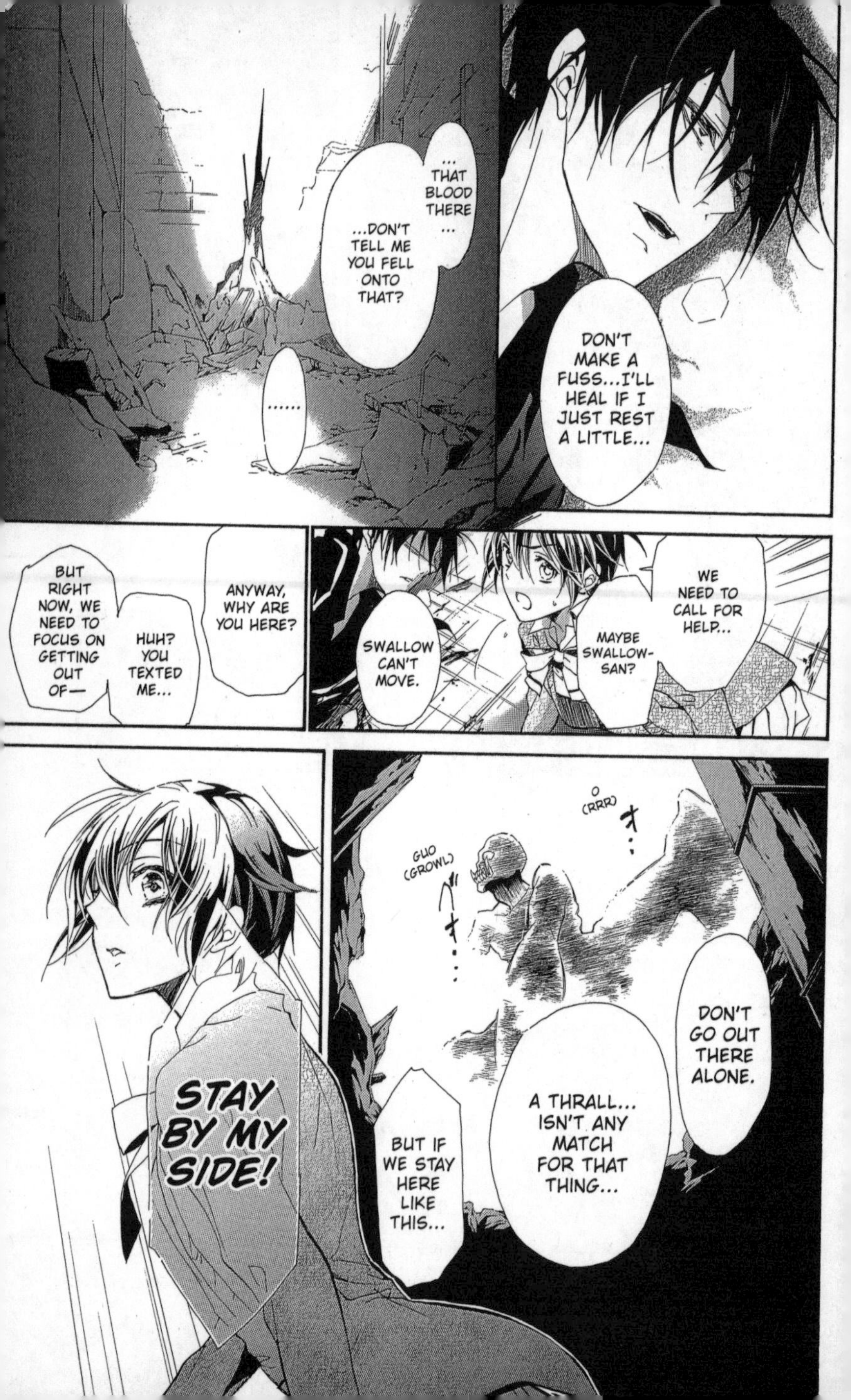
DON'T MAKE A FUSS...I'LL HEAL IF I JUST REST A LITTLE...
...THAT BLOOD THERE...
...DON'T TELL ME YOU FELL ONTO THAT?
......
WE NEED TO CALL FOR HELP...
MAYBE SWALLOW-SAN?
SWALLOW CAN'T MOVE.
ANYWAY, WHY ARE YOU HERE?
HUH? YOU TEXTED ME...
BUT RIGHT NOW, WE NEED TO FOCUS ON GETTING OUT OF—
O (RRR)
GUO (GROWL)
DON'T GO OUT THERE ALONE.
A THRALL... ISN'T ANY MATCH FOR THAT THING...
BUT IF WE STAY HERE LIKE THIS...
STAY BY MY SIDE!

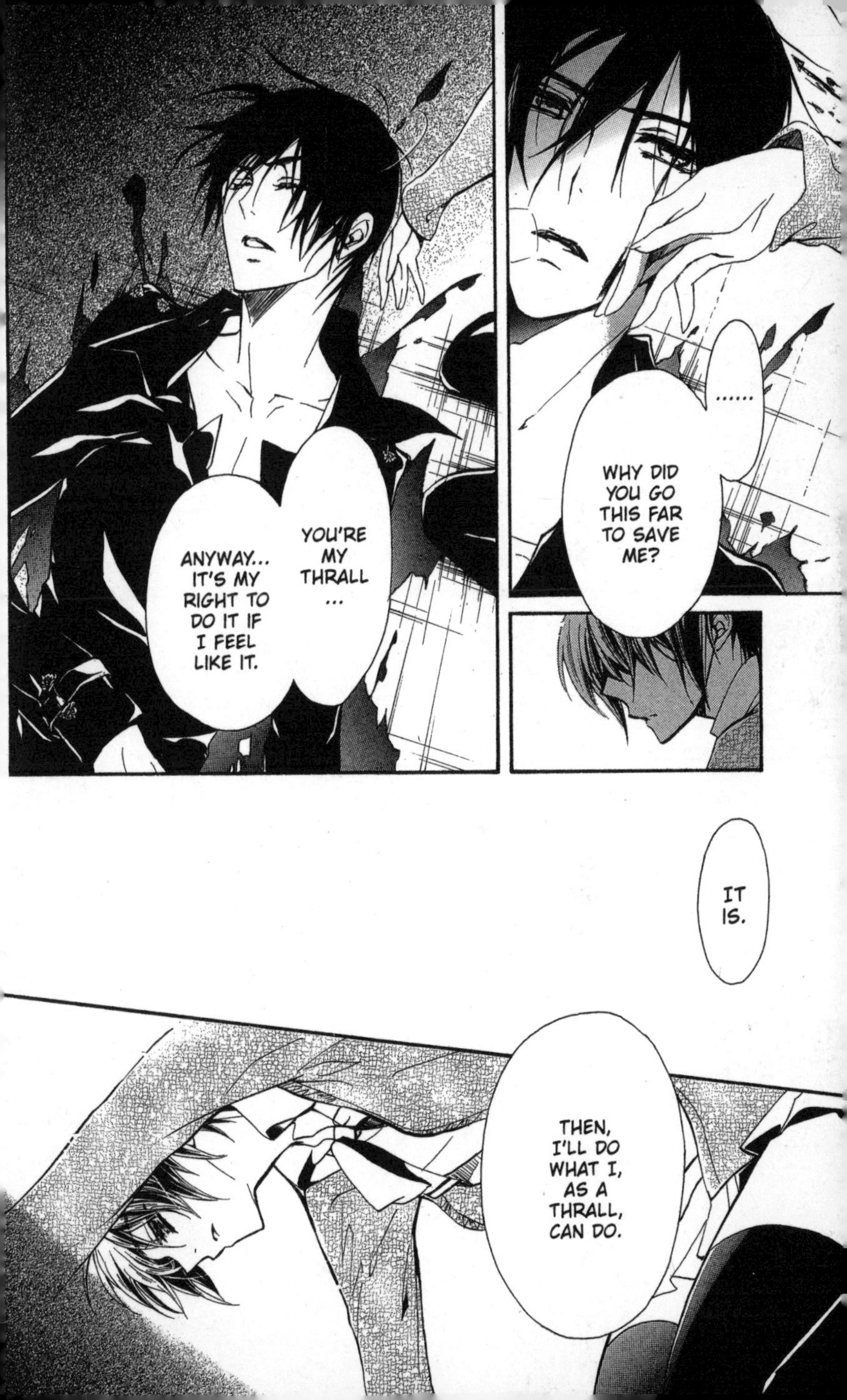
......
WHY DID YOU GO THIS FAR TO SAVE ME?
YOU'RE MY THRALL...
ANYWAY... IT'S MY RIGHT TO DO IT IF I FEEL LIKE IT.
IT IS.
THEN, I'LL DO WHAT I, AS A THRALL, CAN DO.

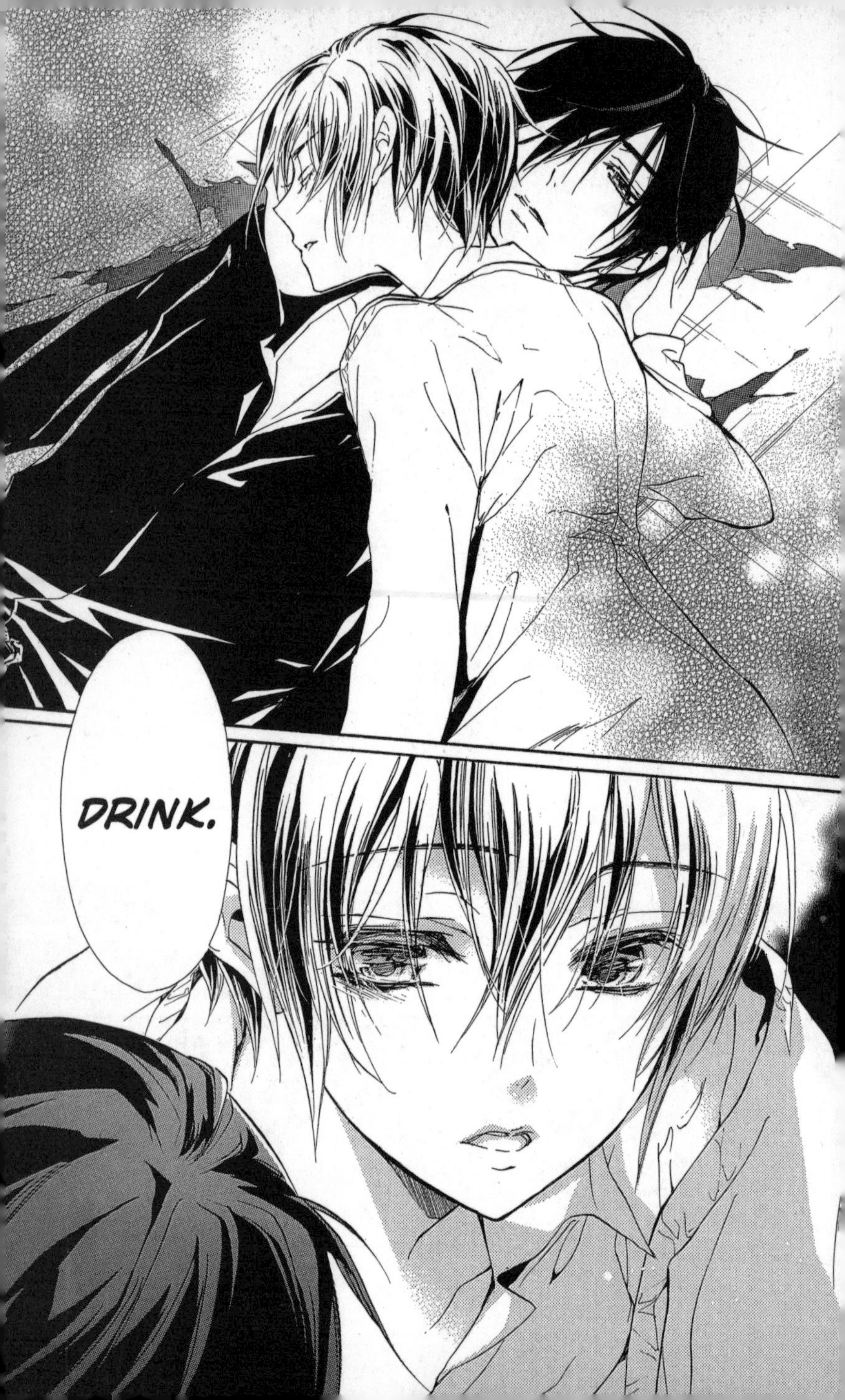
DRINK.

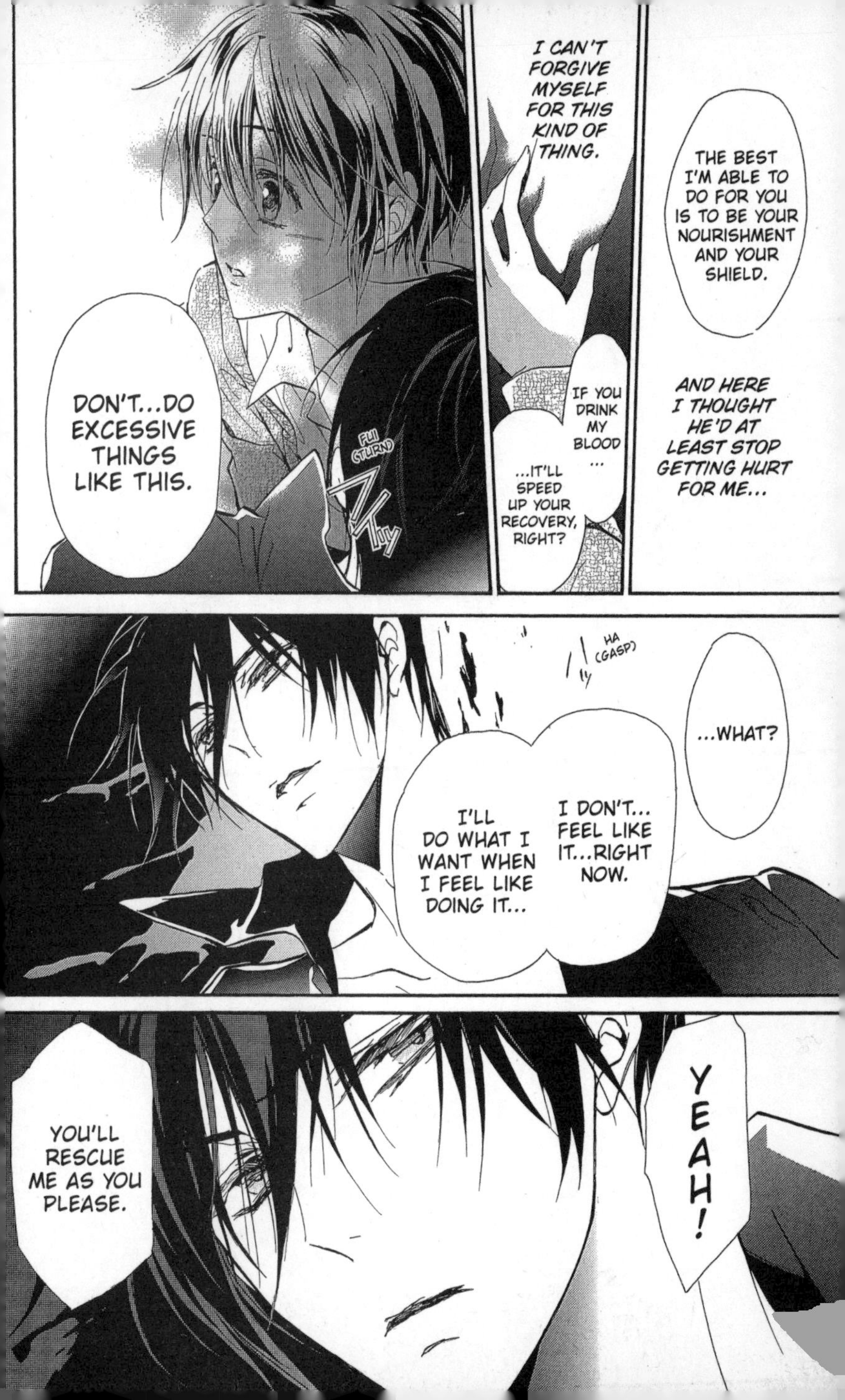
THE BEST I'M ABLE TO DO FOR YOU IS TO BE YOUR NOURISHMENT AND YOUR SHIELD.
AND HERE I THOUGHT HE'D AT LEAST STOP GETTING HURT FOR ME...
I CAN'T FORGIVE MYSELF FOR THIS KIND OF THING.
IF YOU DRINK MY BLOOD...
...IT'LL SPEED UP YOUR RECOVERY, RIGHT?
FUI (TURN)
DON'T...DO EXCESSIVE THINGS LIKE THIS.
HA (GASP)
...WHAT?
I DON'T... FEEL LIKE IT...RIGHT NOW.
I'LL DO WHAT I WANT WHEN I FEEL LIKE DOING IT...
YEAH!
YOU'LL RESCUE ME AS YOU PLEASE.

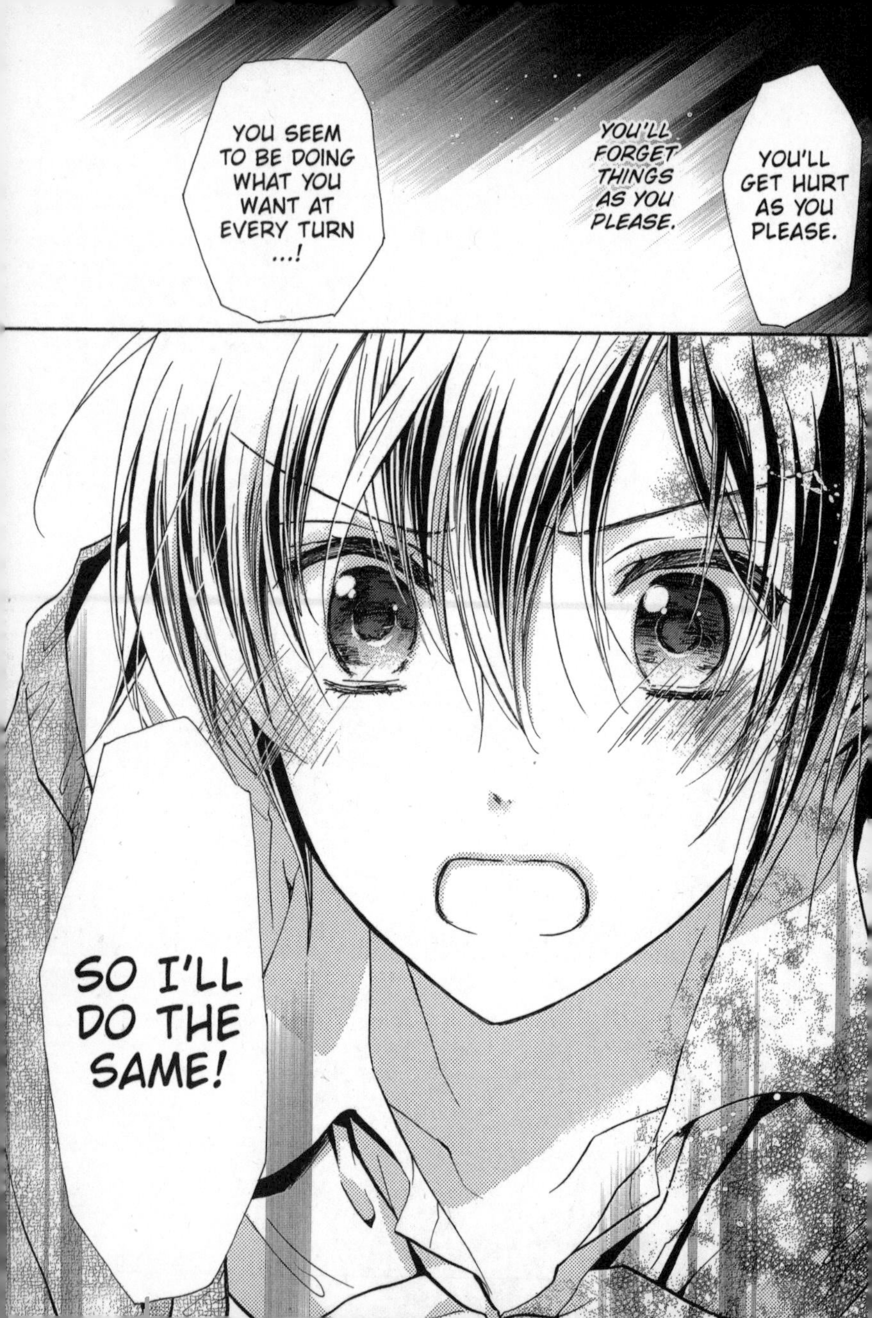
YOU'LL GET HURT AS YOU PLEASE.
YOU'LL FORGET THINGS AS YOU PLEASE.
YOU SEEM TO BE DOING WHAT YOU WANT AT EVERY TURN ...!
SO I'LL DO THE SAME!

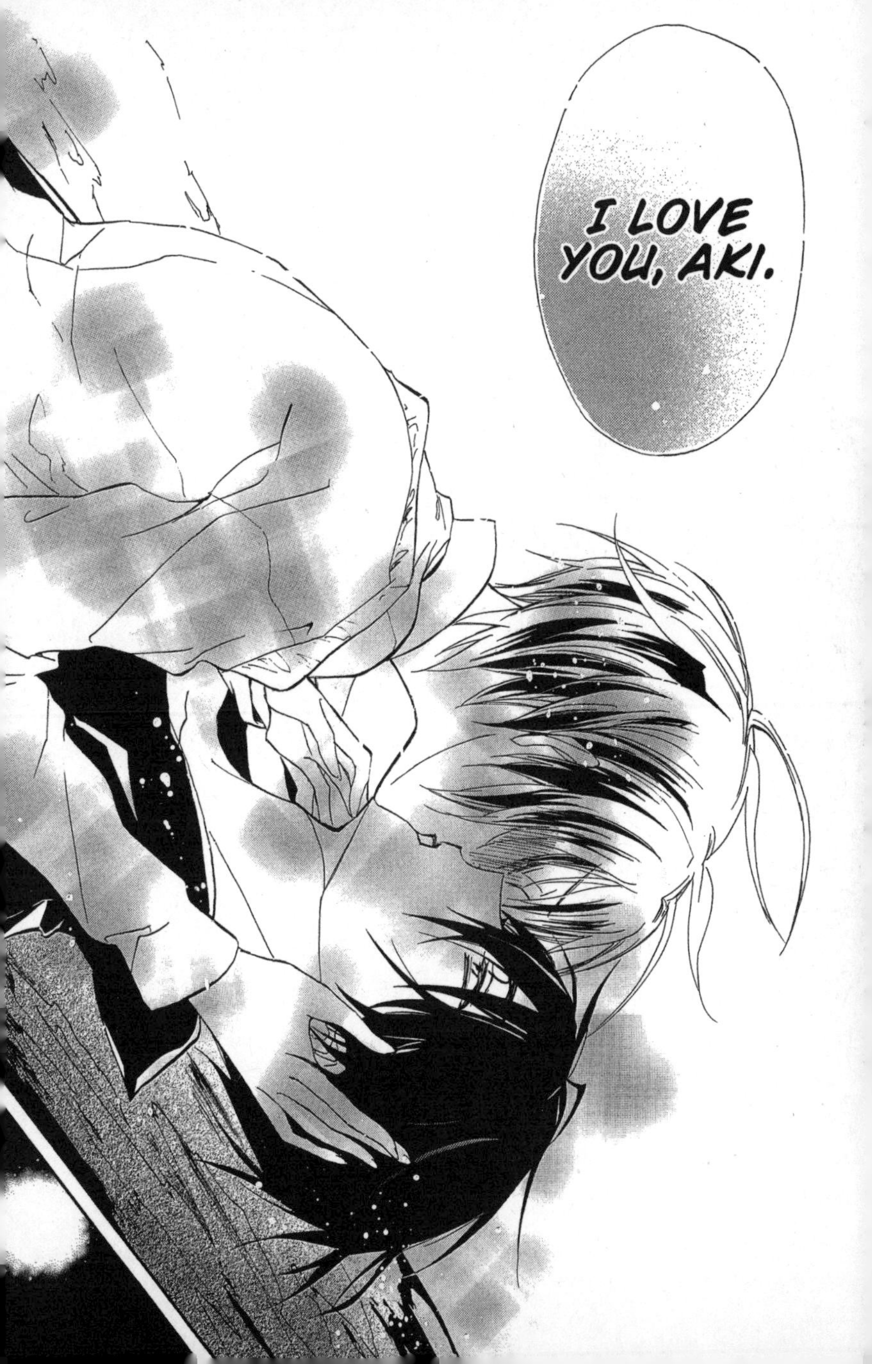
I LOVE YOU, AKI.

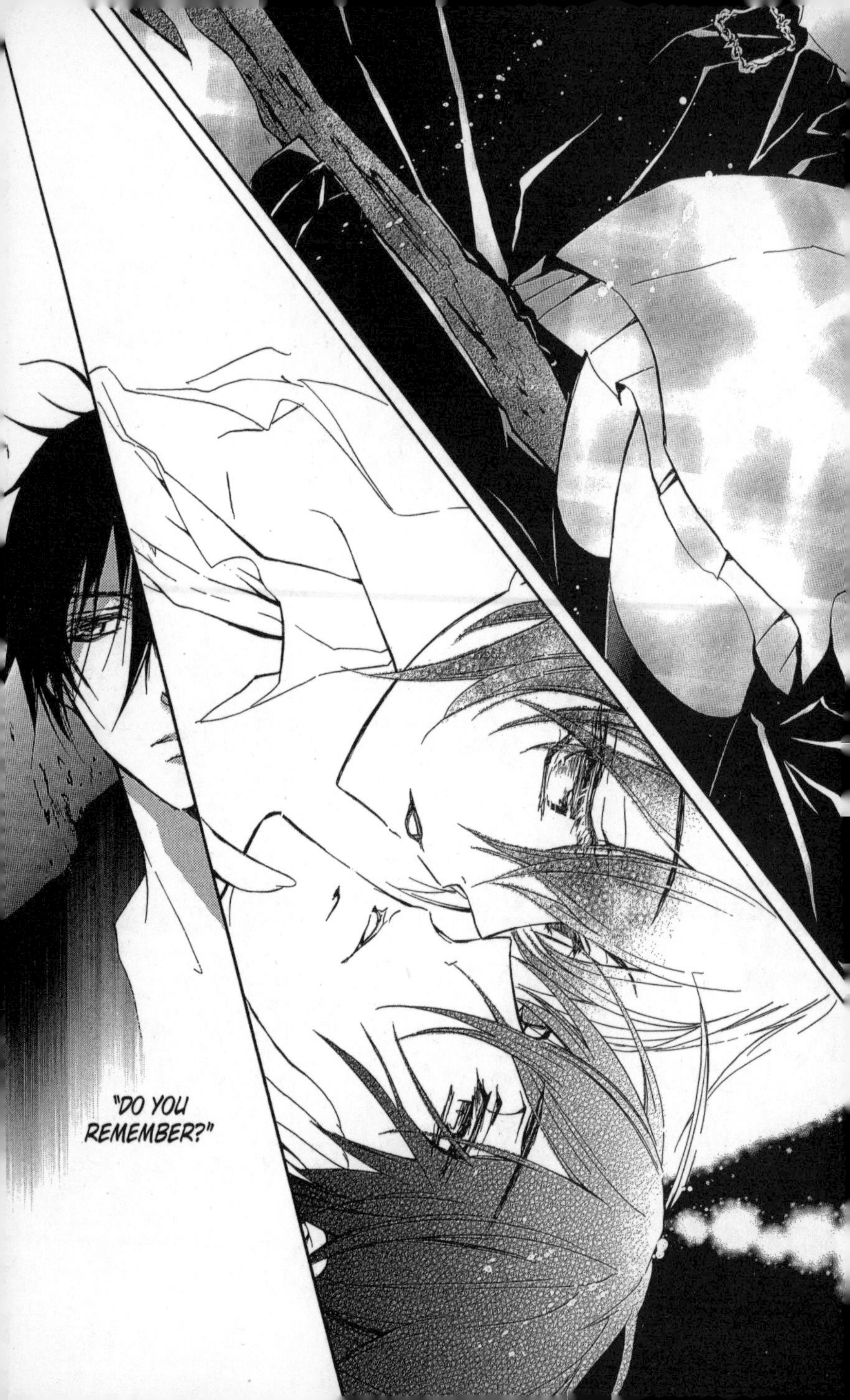
"DO YOU REMEMBER?"

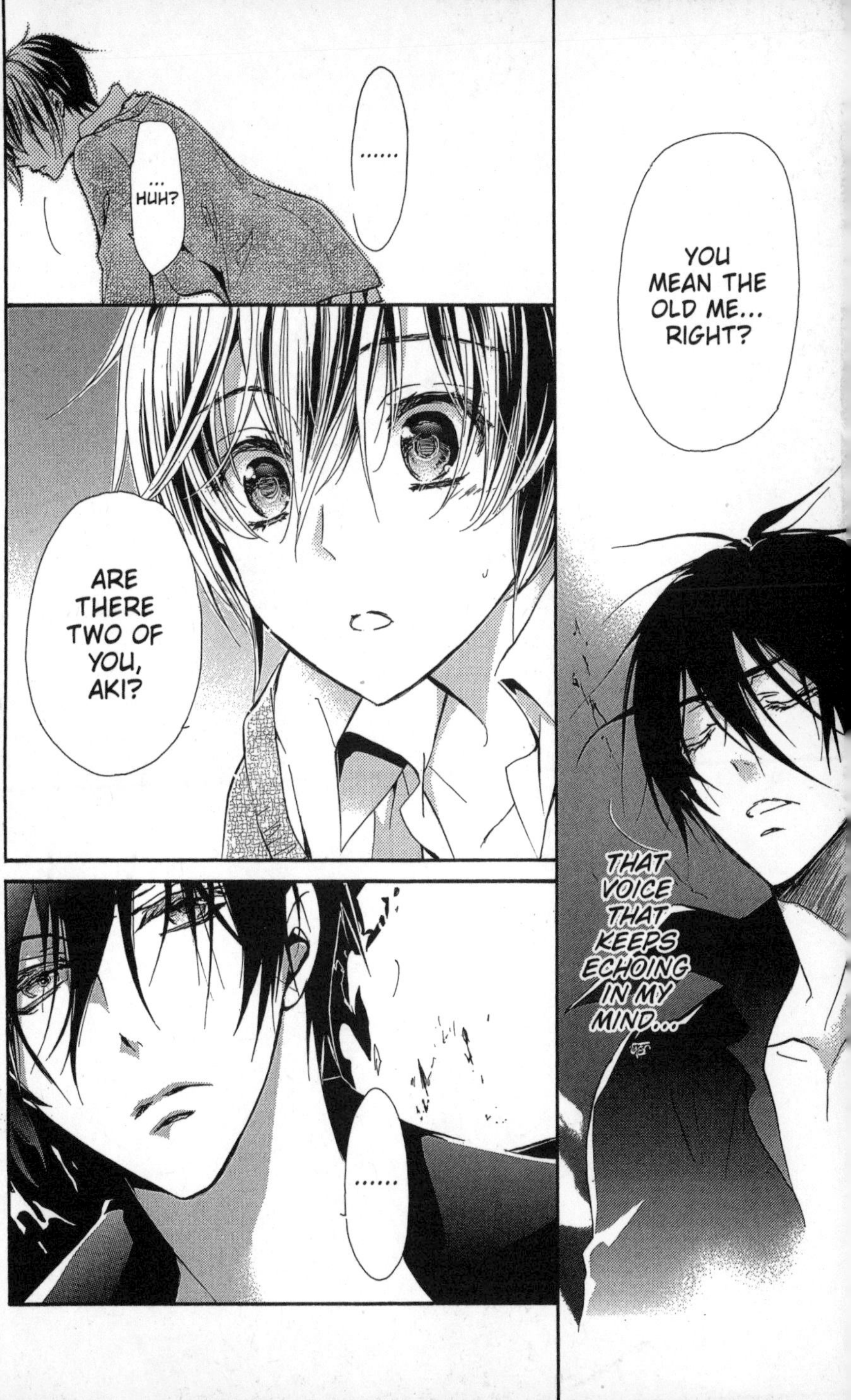
YOU MEAN THE OLD ME... RIGHT?
THAT VOICE THAT KEEPS ECHOING IN MY MIND...
......
... HUH?
ARE THERE TWO OF YOU, AKI?
......

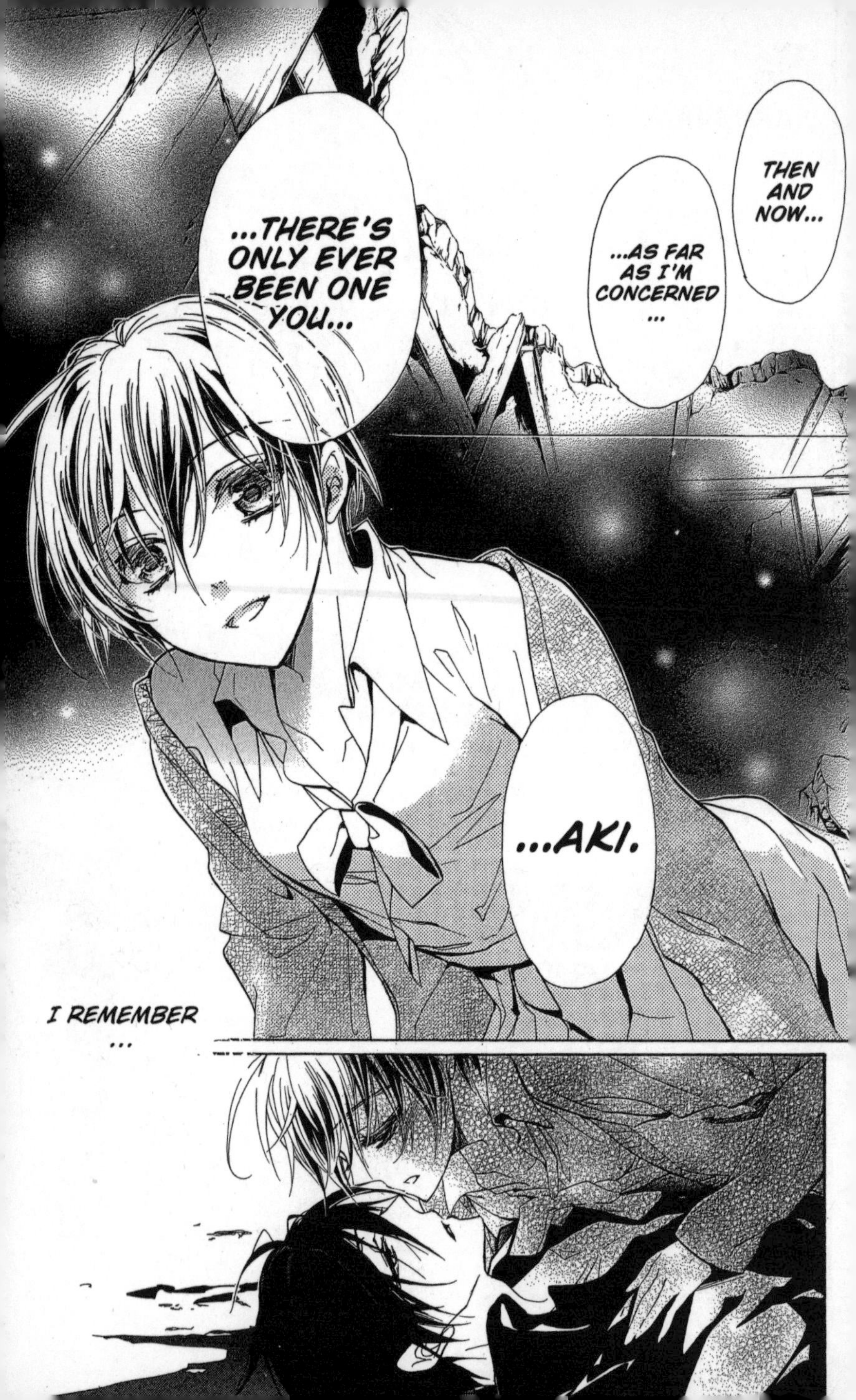
THEN AND NOW...
...AS FAR AS I'M CONCERNED...
...THERE'S ONLY EVER BEEN ONE YOU...
...AKI.
I REMEMBER...

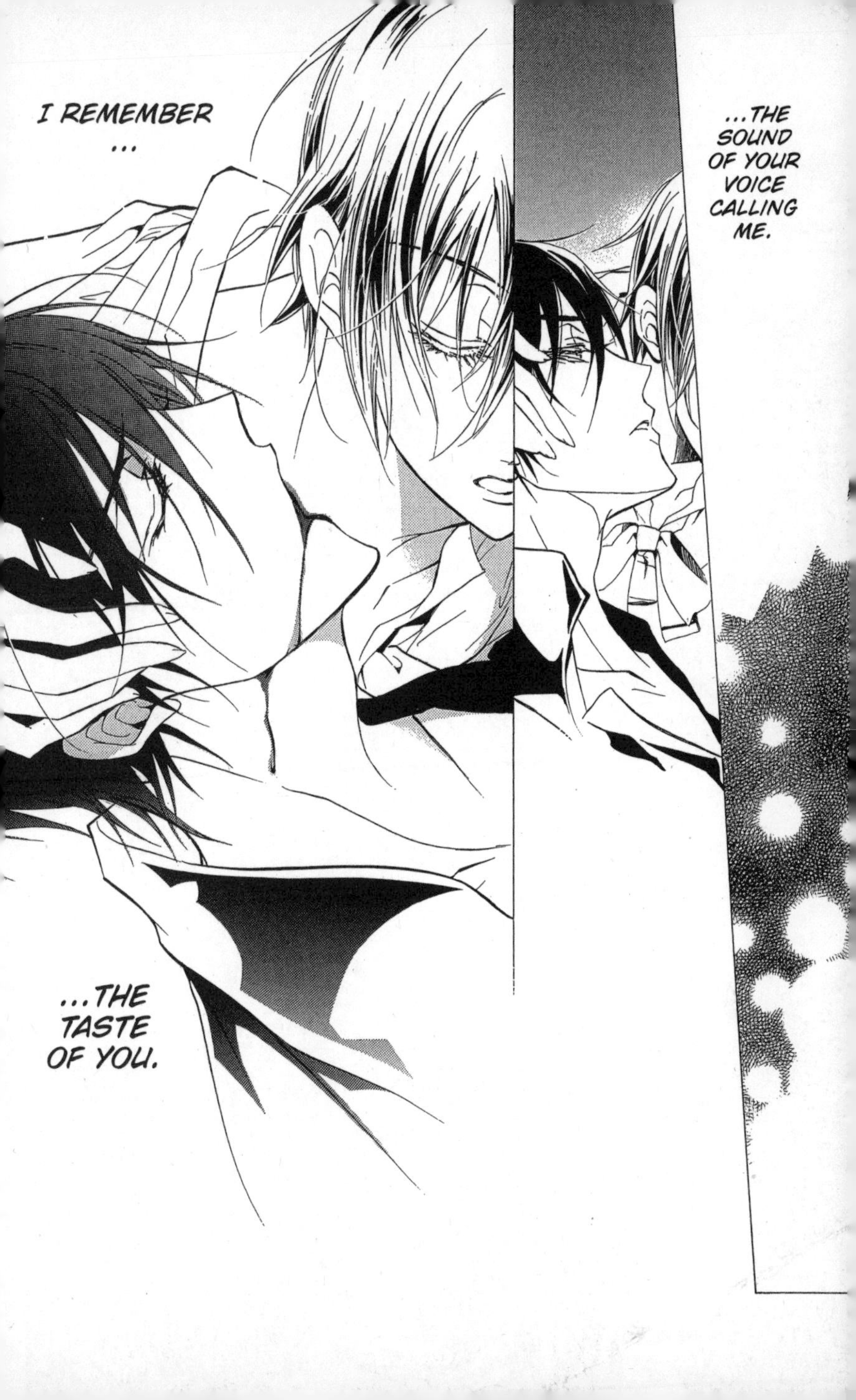
I REMEMBER ...
...THE SOUND OF YOUR VOICE CALLING ME.
...THE TASTE OF YOU.

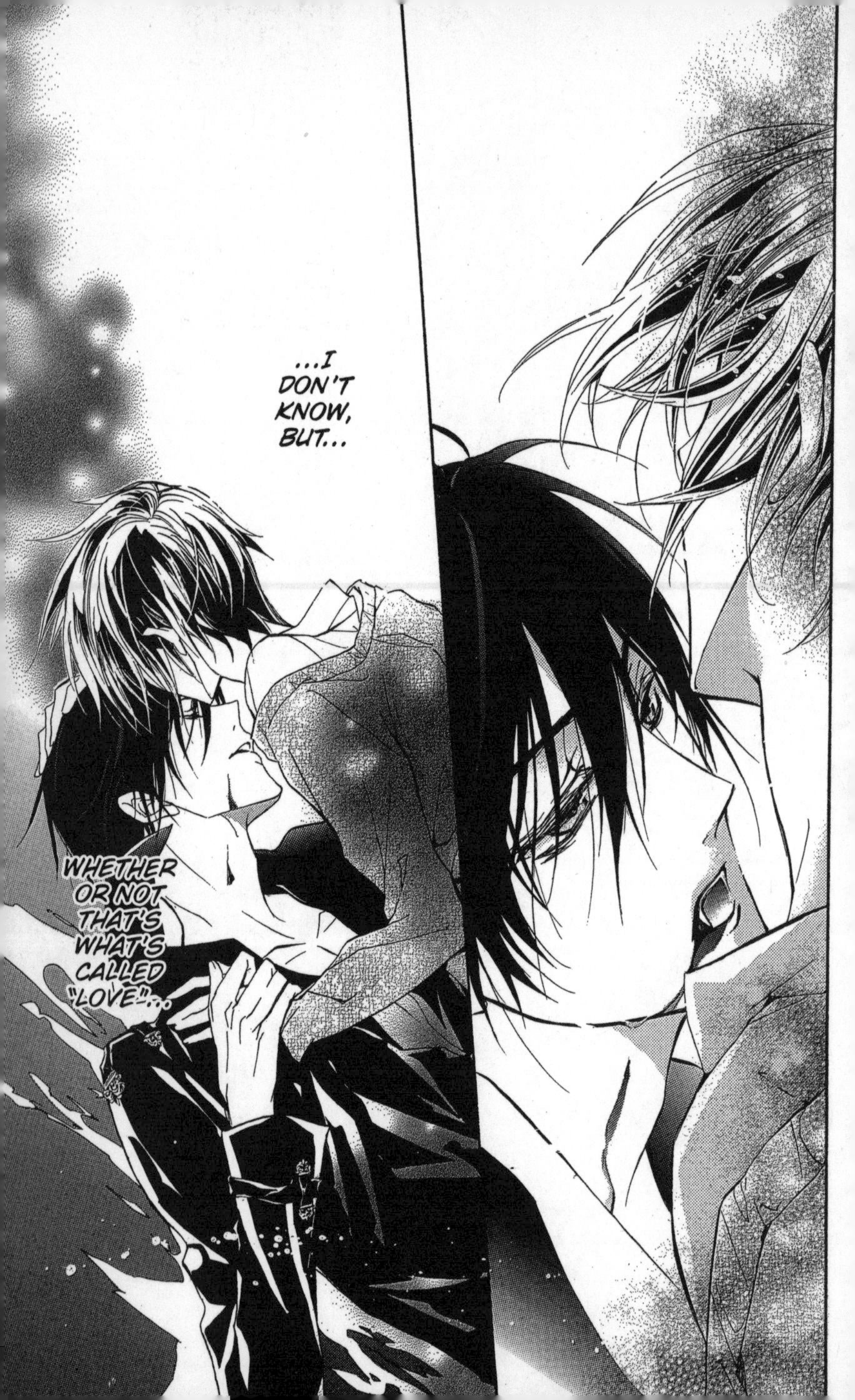
...I DON'T KNOW, BUT...
WHETHER OR NOT THAT'S WHAT'S CALLED "LOVE"...

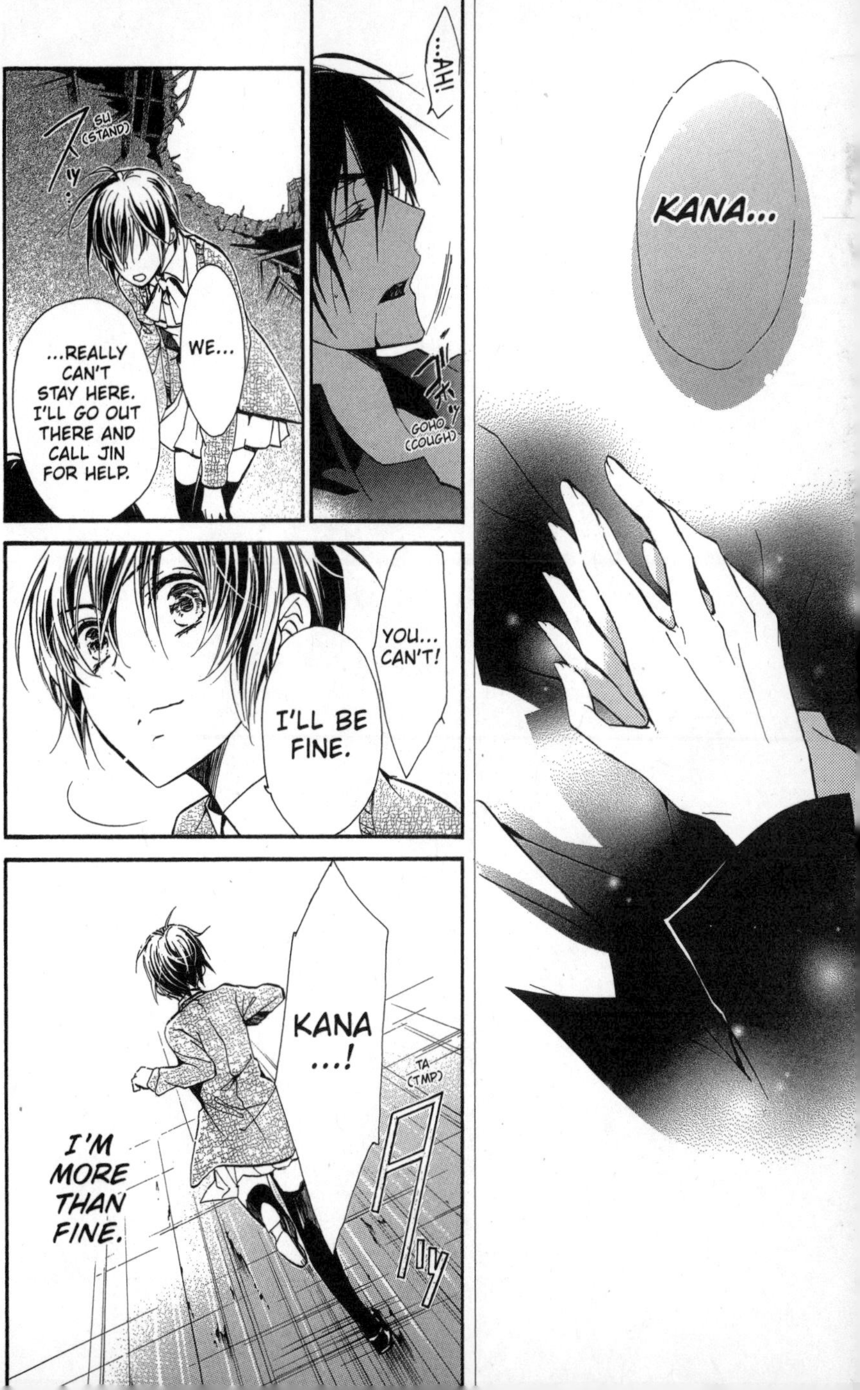
KANA...
...AH!
GOHO (COUGH)
SU (STAND)
WE...
...REALLY CAN'T STAY HERE. I'LL GO OUT THERE AND CALL JIN FOR HELP.
YOU... CAN'T!
I'LL BE FINE.
KANA ...!
TA (TMP)
I'M MORE THAN FINE.

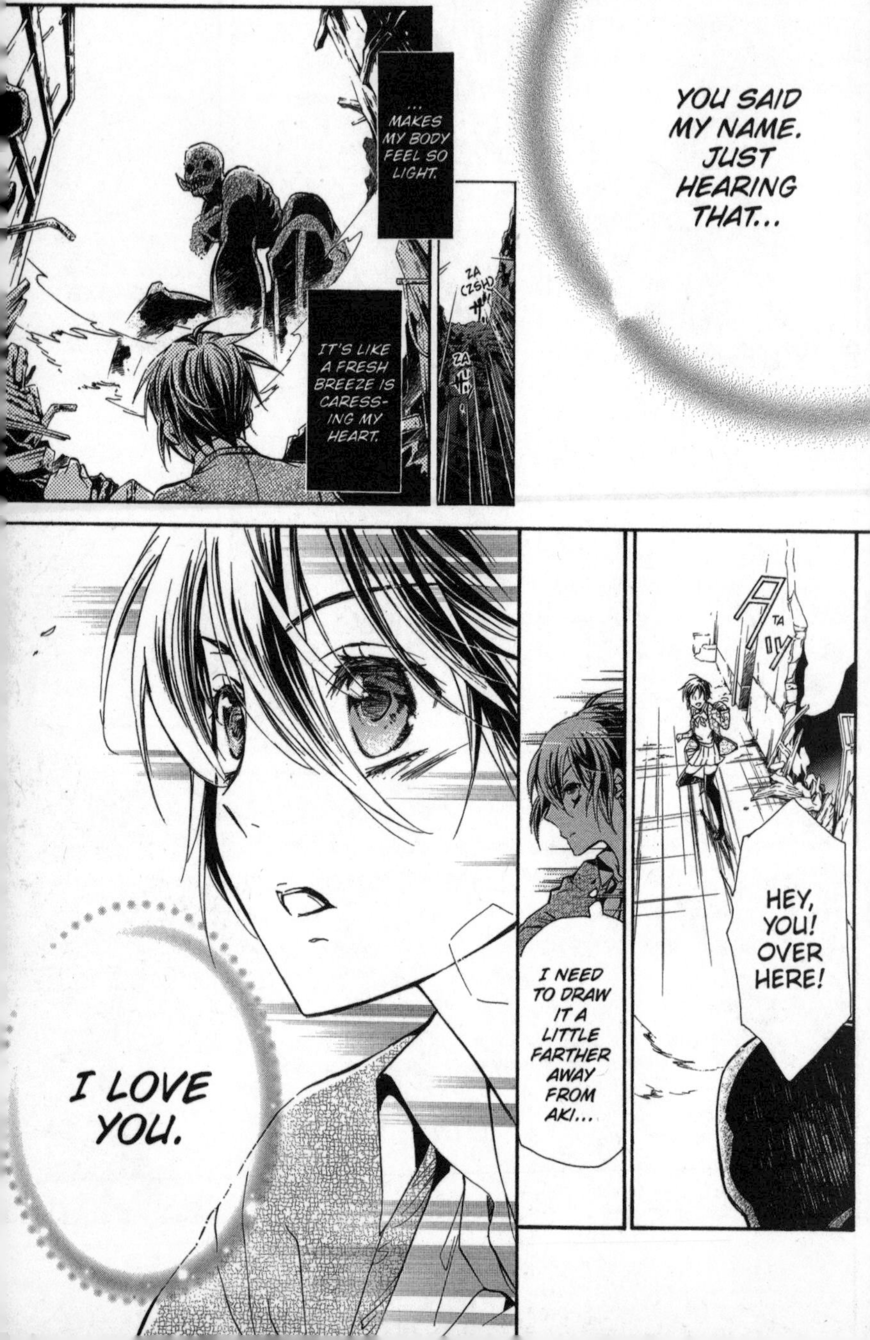
YOU SAID MY NAME. JUST HEARING THAT...
...MAKES MY BODY FEEL SO LIGHT.
ZA (ZSH)
ZA
IT'S LIKE A FRESH BREEZE IS CARESS-ING MY HEART.
TA
HEY, YOU! OVER HERE!
I NEED TO DRAW IT A LITTLE FARTHER AWAY FROM AKI...
I LOVE YOU.

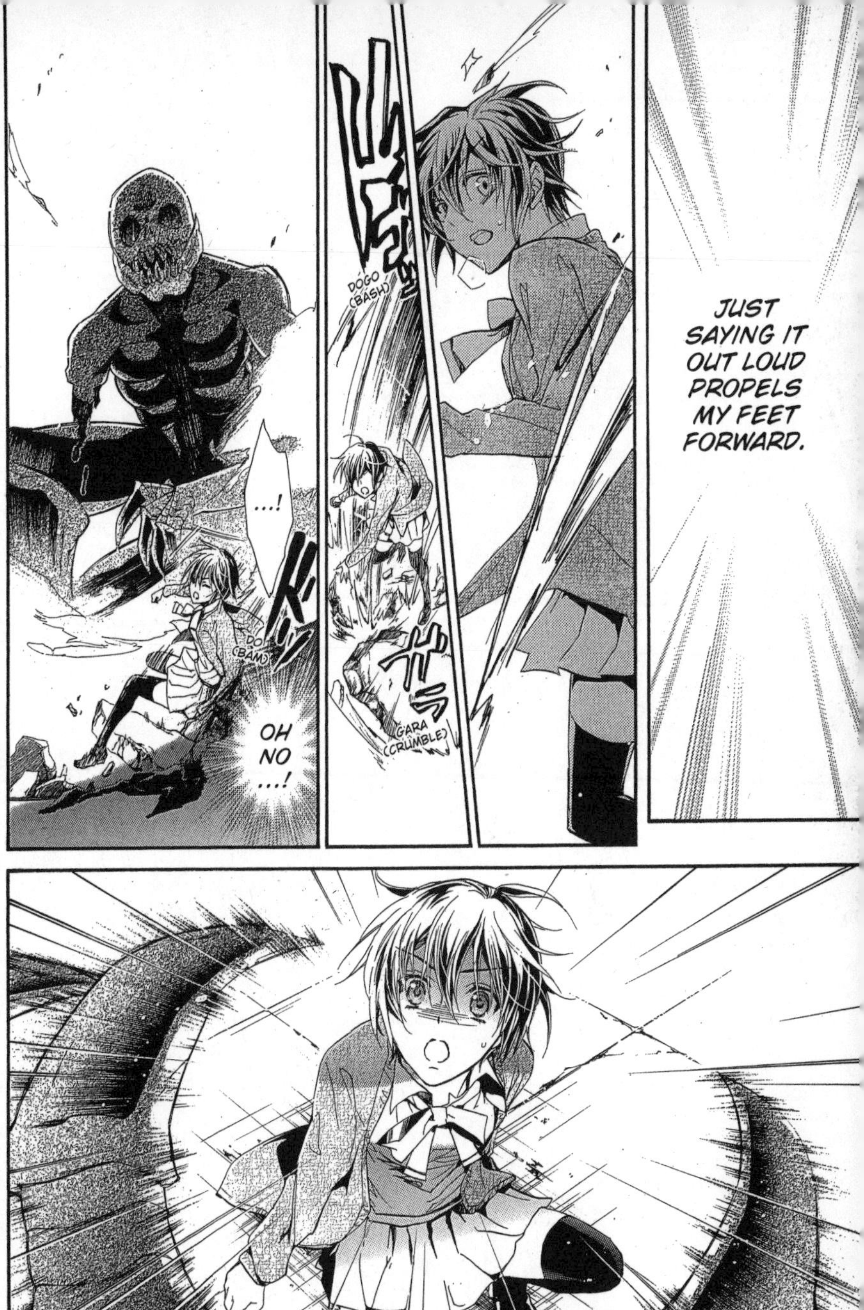
JUST SAYING IT OUT LOUD PROPELS MY FEET FORWARD.
DOGO (BASH)
GARA (CRUMBLE)
...!
DO (BAM)
OH NO ...!

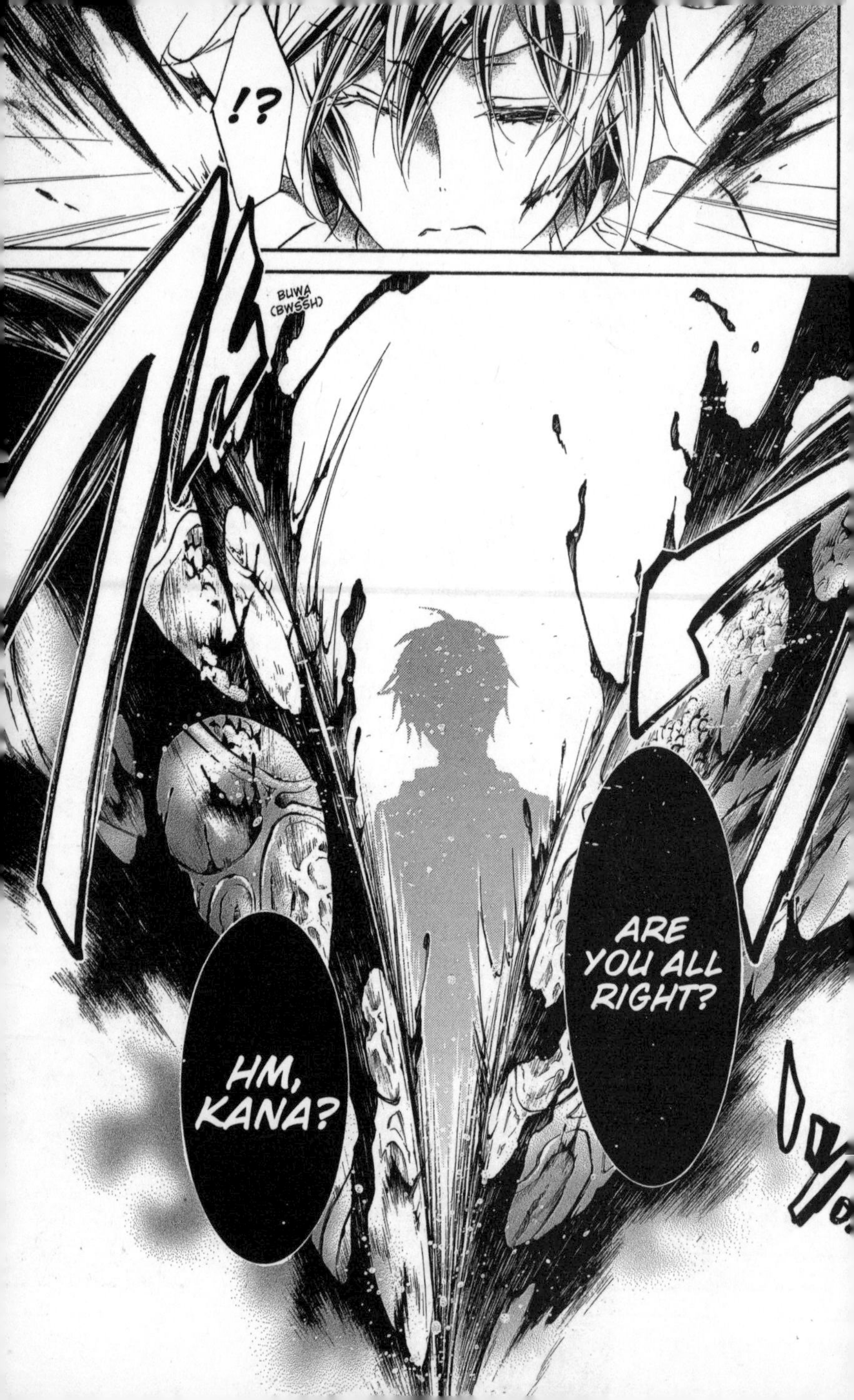
!?
BUWA (BWSSH)
ARE YOU ALL RIGHT?
HM, KANA?

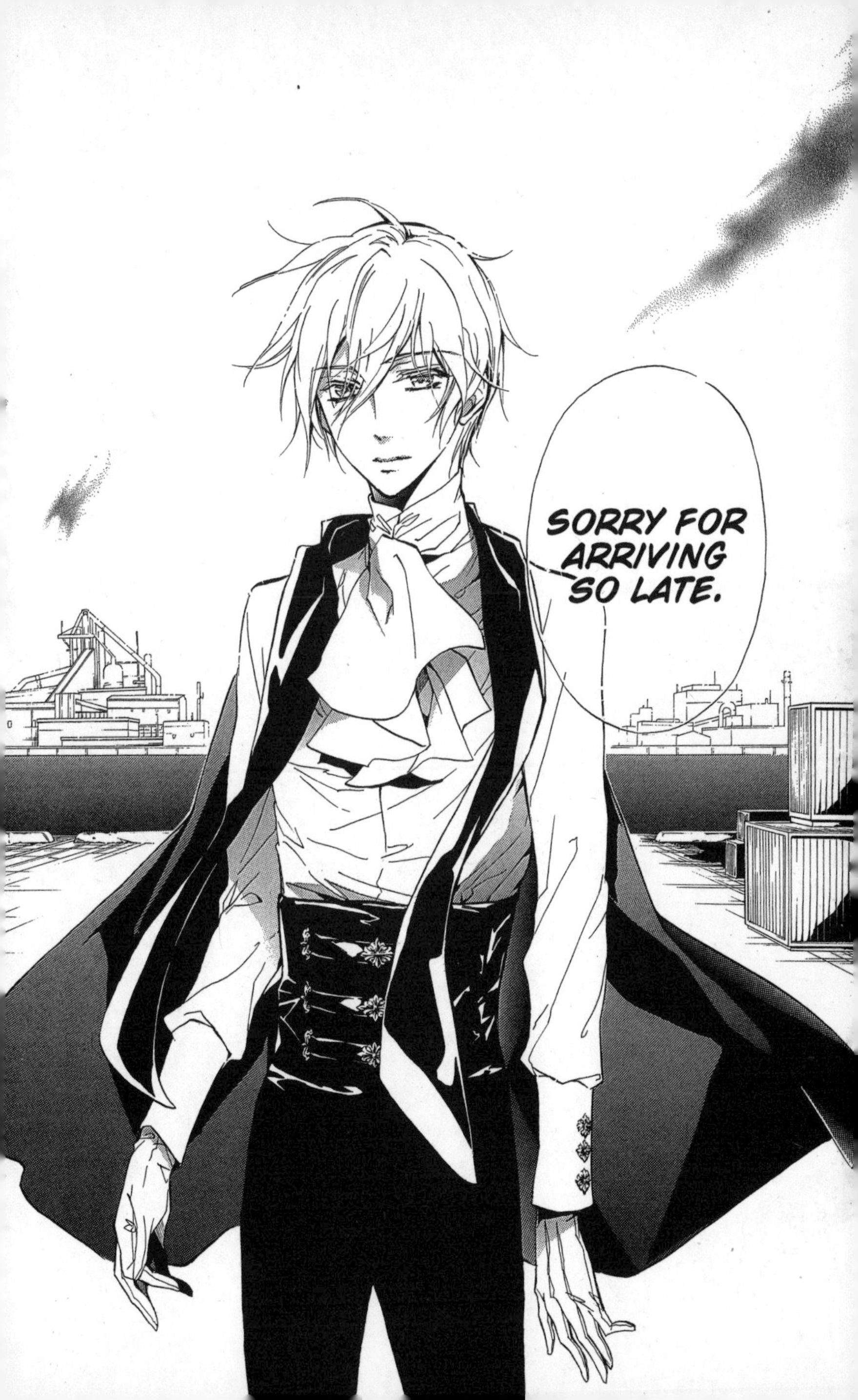
SORRY FOR ARRIVING SO LATE.

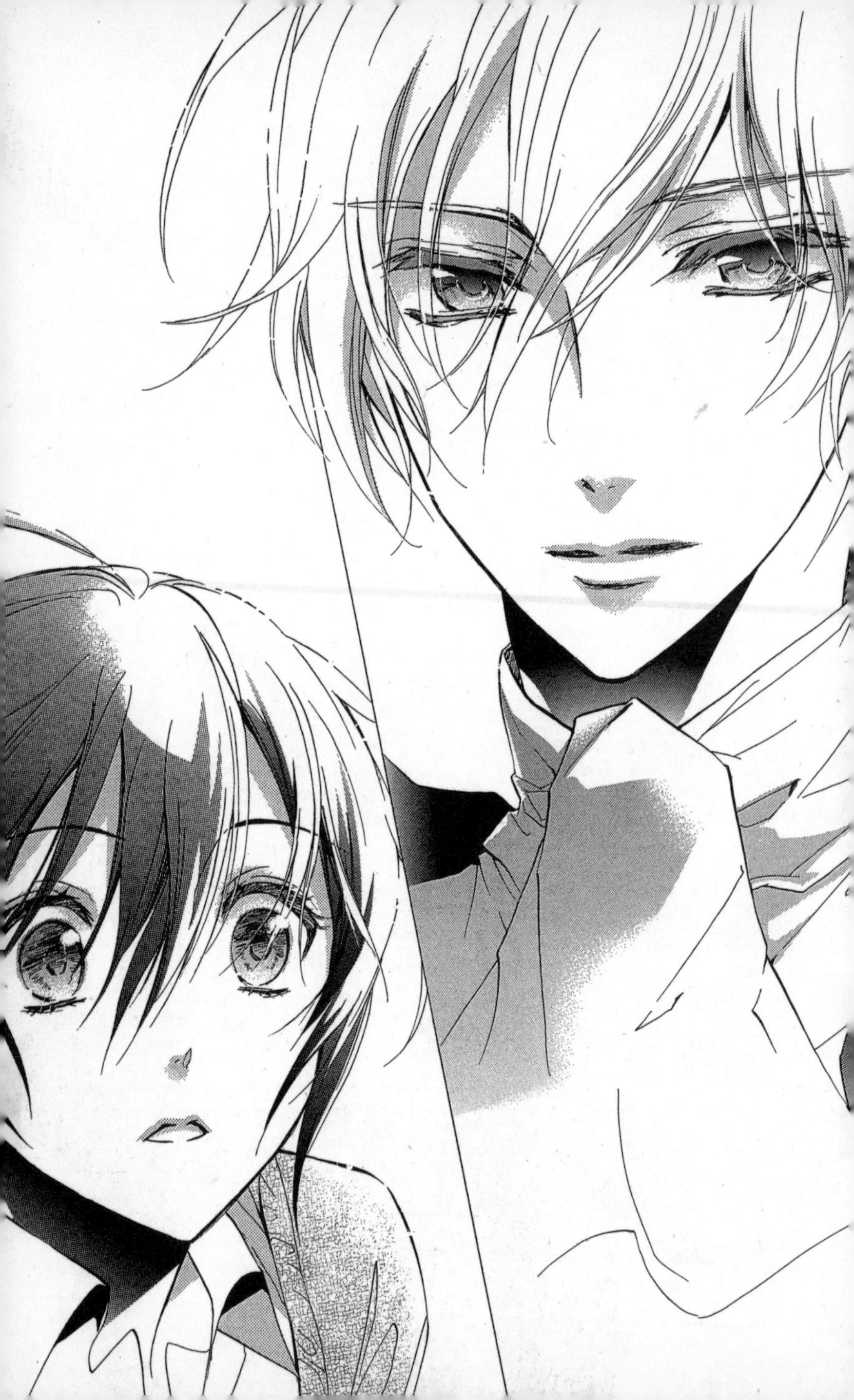

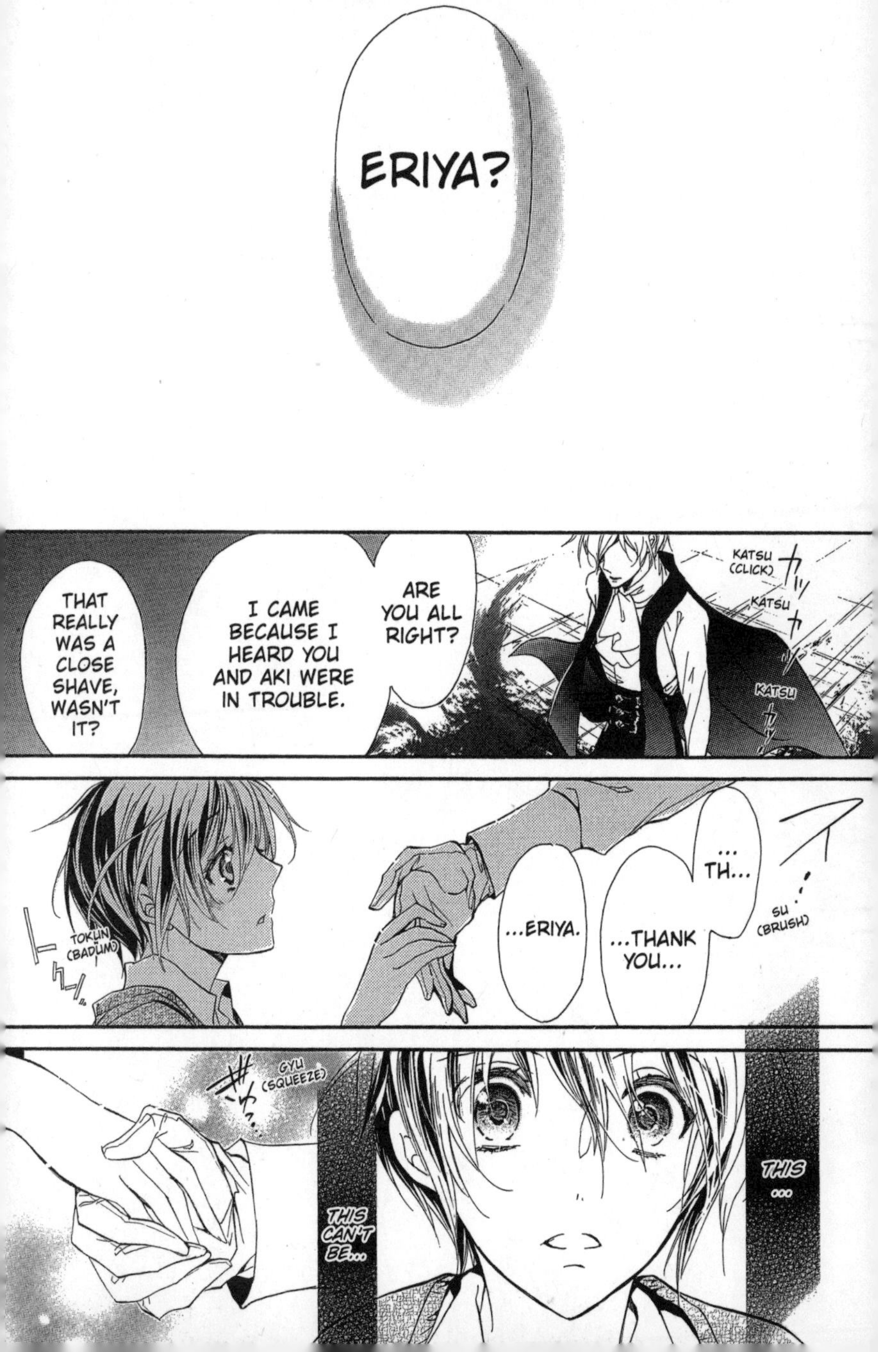
ERIYA?
KATSU (CLICK)
KATSU
KATSU
ARE YOU ALL RIGHT?
I CAME BECAUSE I HEARD YOU AND AKI WERE IN TROUBLE.
THAT REALLY WAS A CLOSE SHAVE, WASN'T IT?
SU (BRUSH)
... TH...
...THANK YOU...
...ERIYA.
TOKUN (BADUM)
THIS ...
THIS CAN'T BE...
GYU (SQUEEZE)

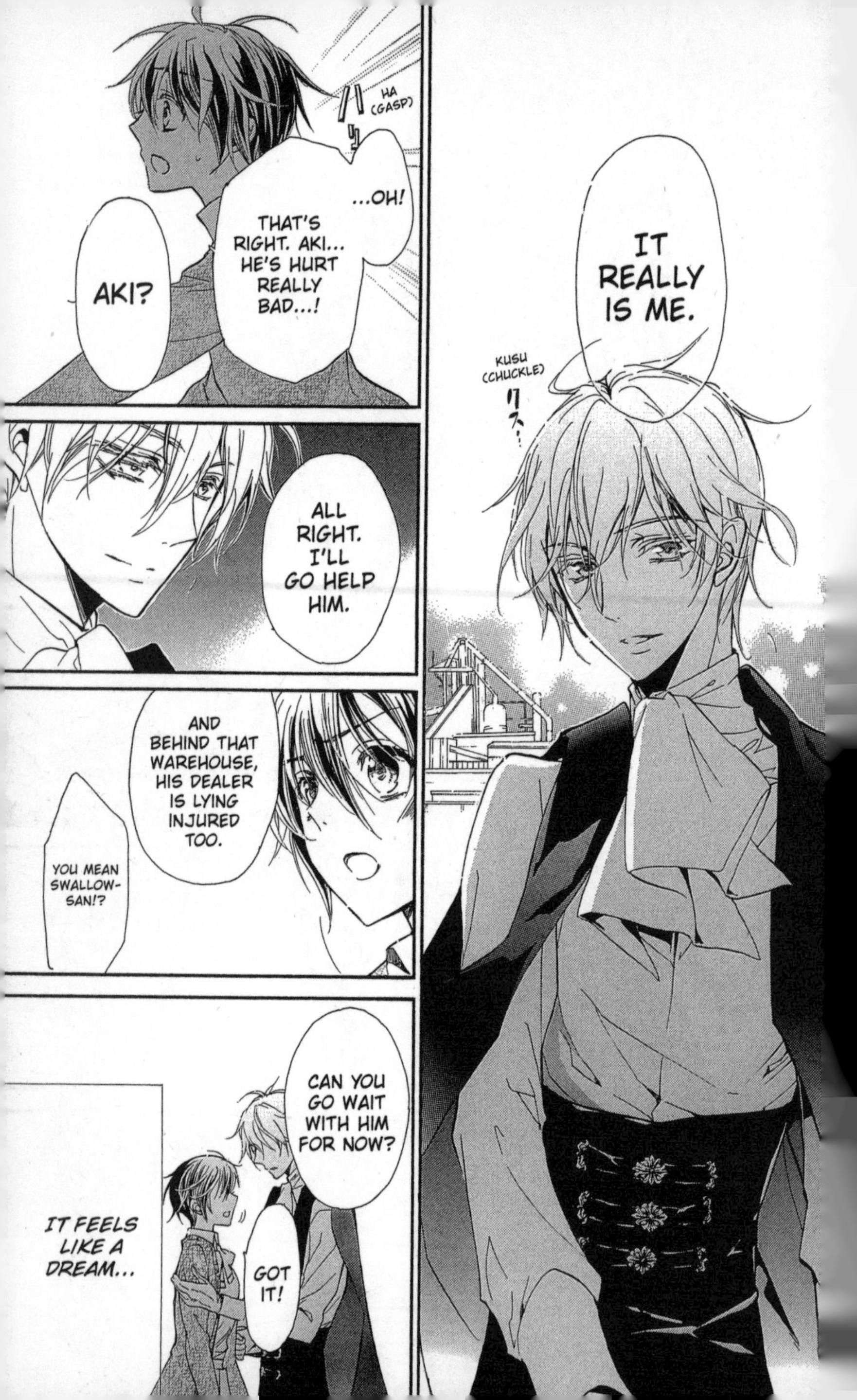
IT REALLY IS ME.
KUSU (CHUCKLE)
HA (GASP)
...OH! THAT'S RIGHT. AKI... HE'S HURT REALLY BAD...!
AKI?
ALL RIGHT. I'LL GO HELP HIM.
AND BEHIND THAT WAREHOUSE, HIS DEALER IS LYING INJURED TOO.
YOU MEAN SWALLOW-SAN!?
CAN YOU GO WAIT WITH HIM FOR NOW?
GOT IT!
IT FEELS LIKE A DREAM...

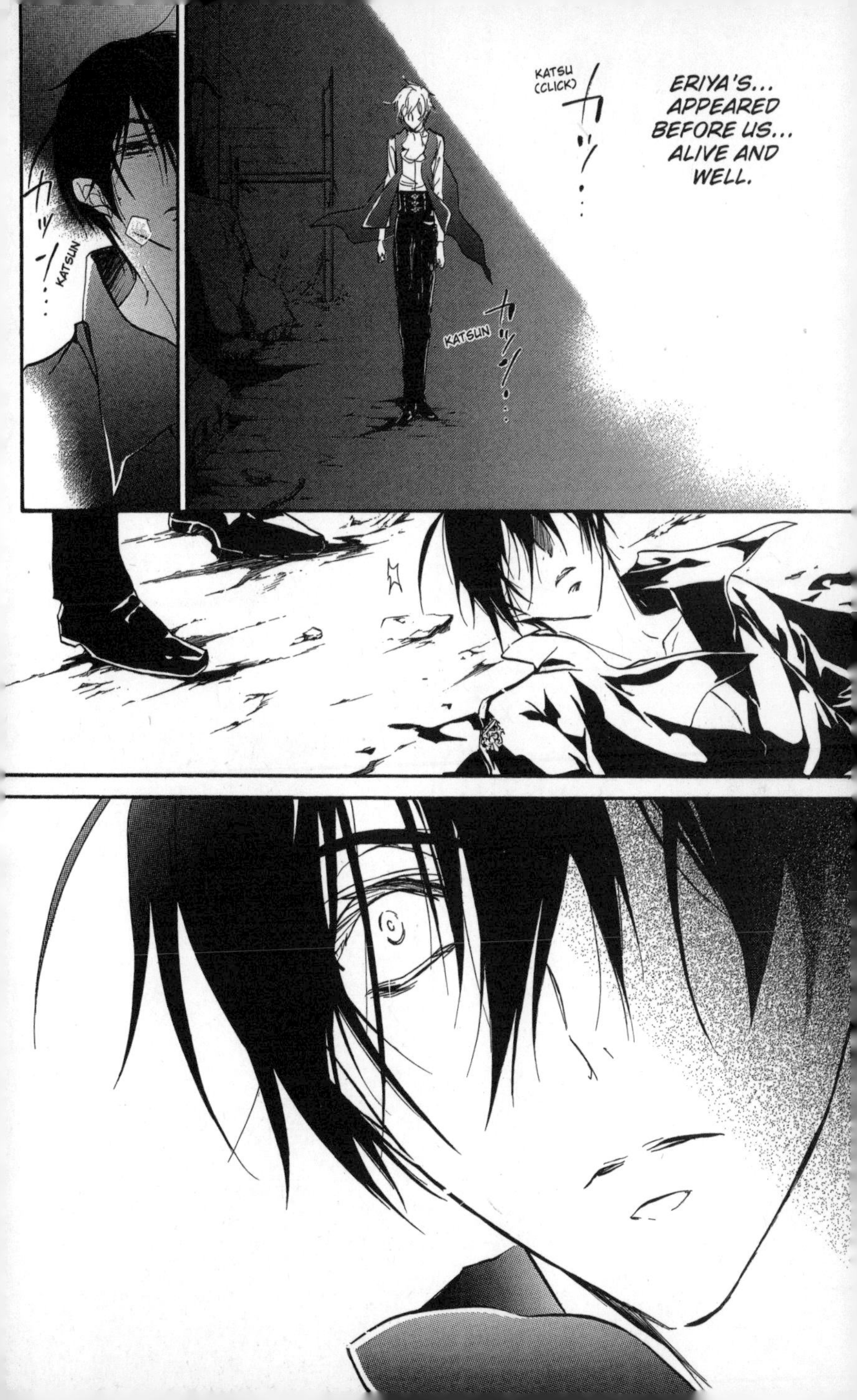
KATSU (CLICK)
ERIYA'S... APPEARED BEFORE US... ALIVE AND WELL.
KATSUN
KATSUN

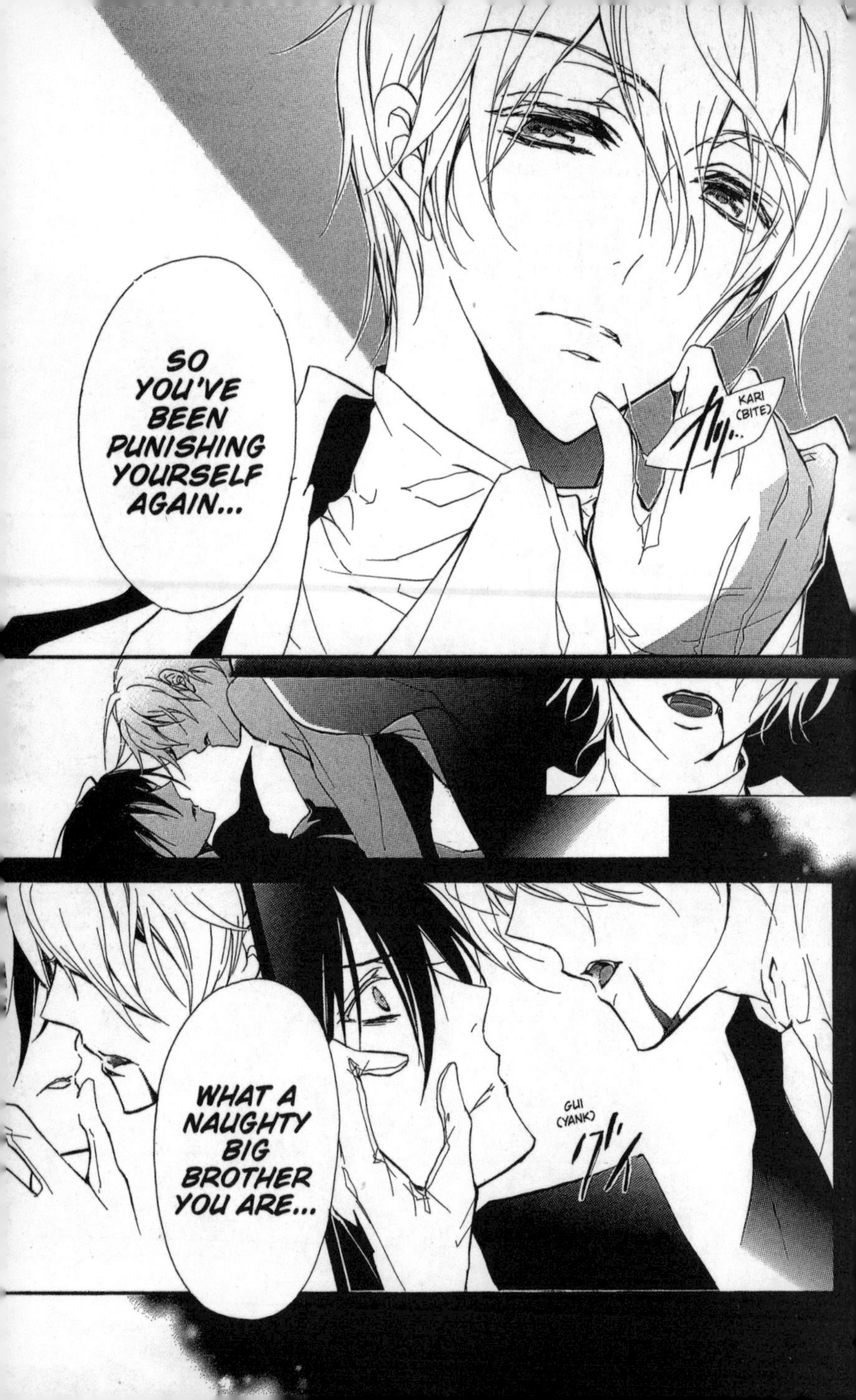
SO YOU'VE BEEN PUNISHING YOURSELF AGAIN...
KARI (BITE)
GUI (YANK)
WHAT A NAUGHTY BIG BROTHER YOU ARE...

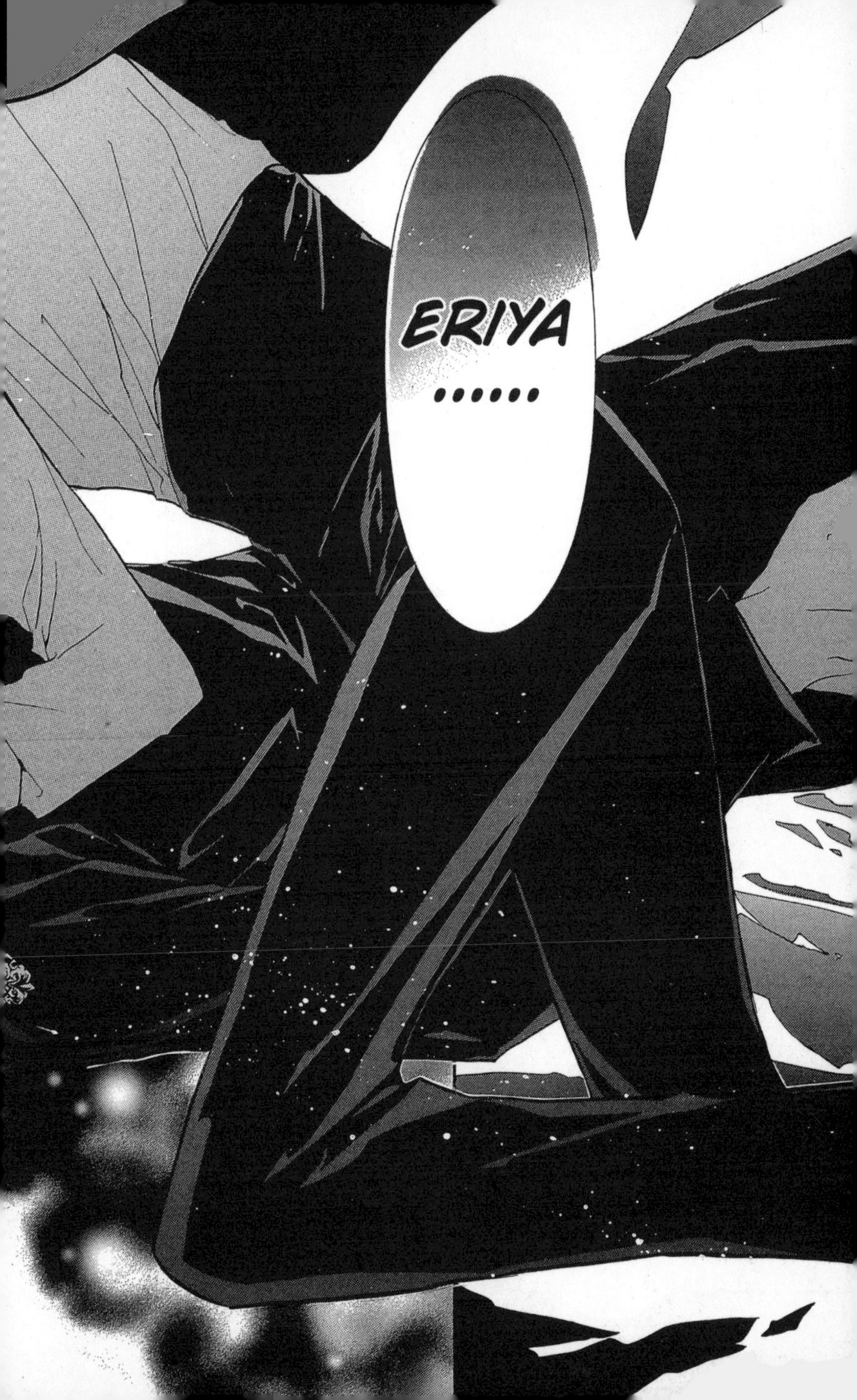
ERIYA ......

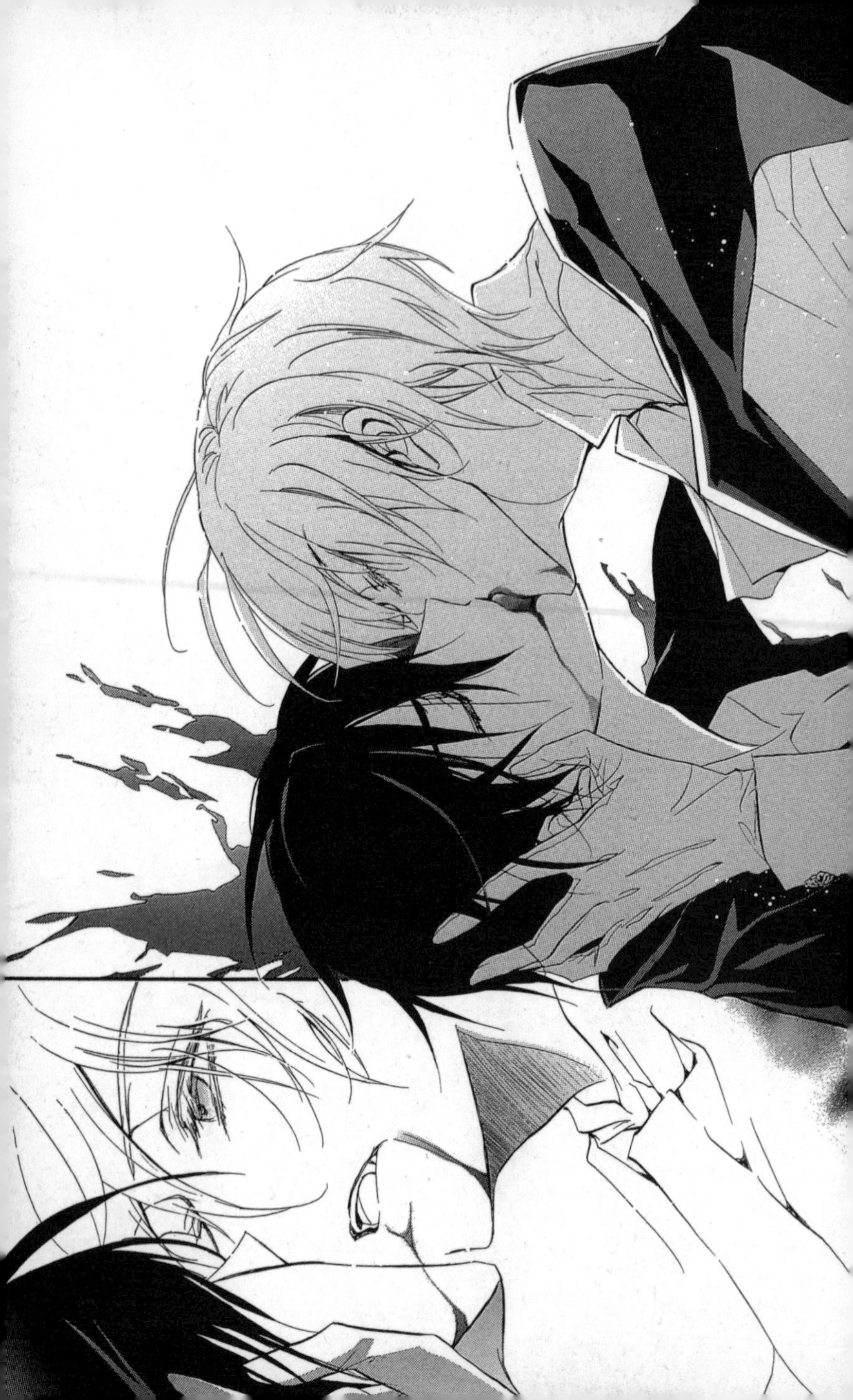

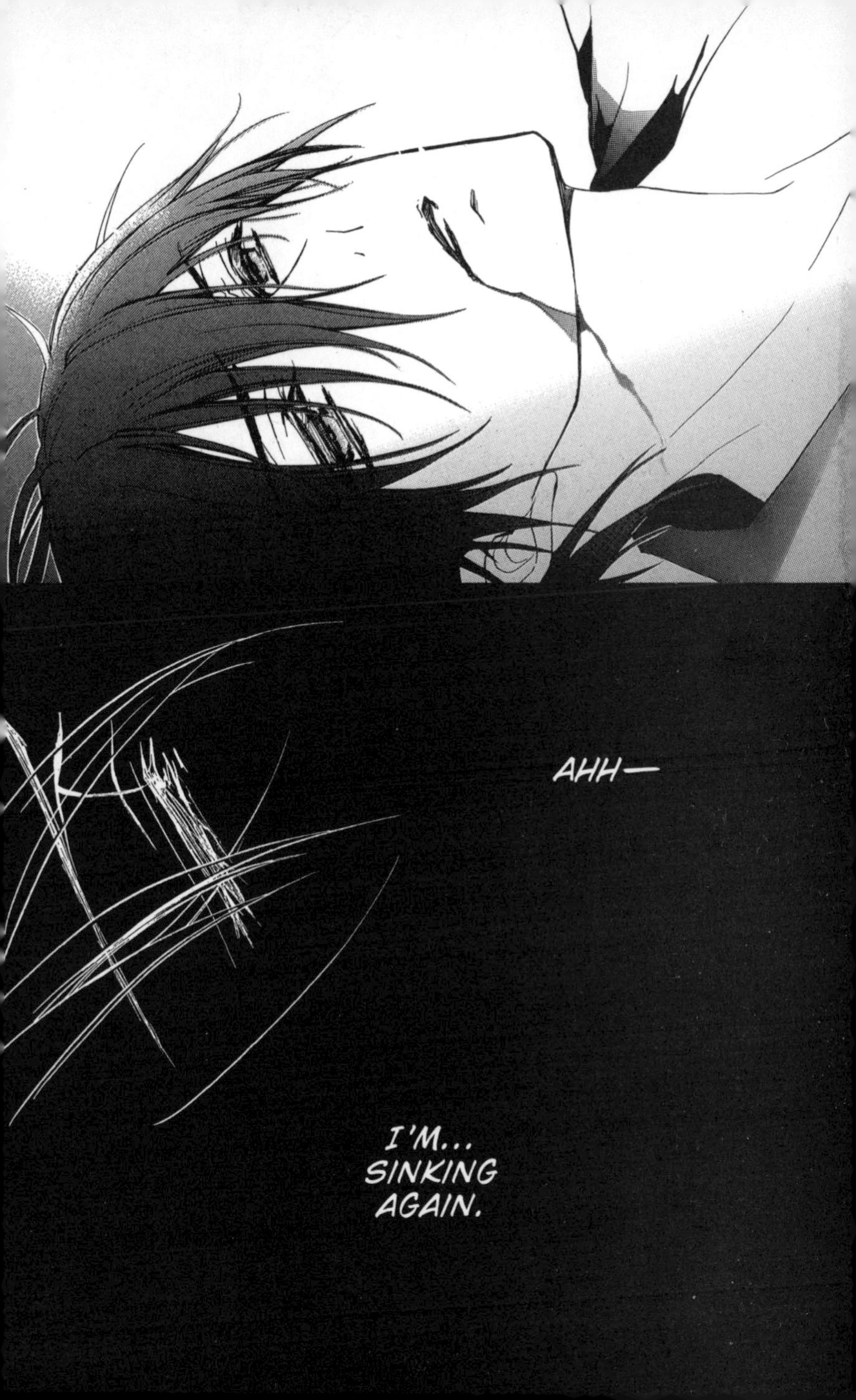
AHH—
I'M... SINKING AGAIN.

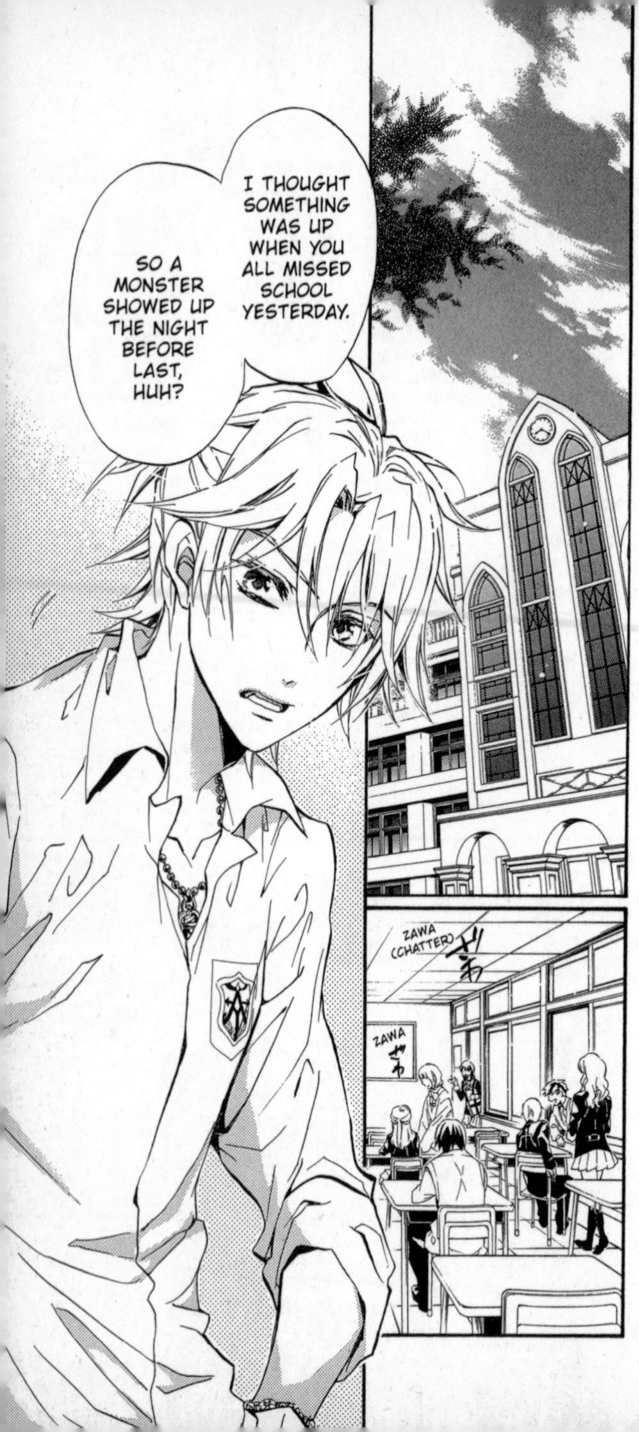
ZAWA (CHATTER)
ZAWA
I THOUGHT SOMETHING WAS UP WHEN YOU ALL MISSED SCHOOL YESTERDAY.
SO A MONSTER SHOWED UP THE NIGHT BEFORE LAST, HUH?

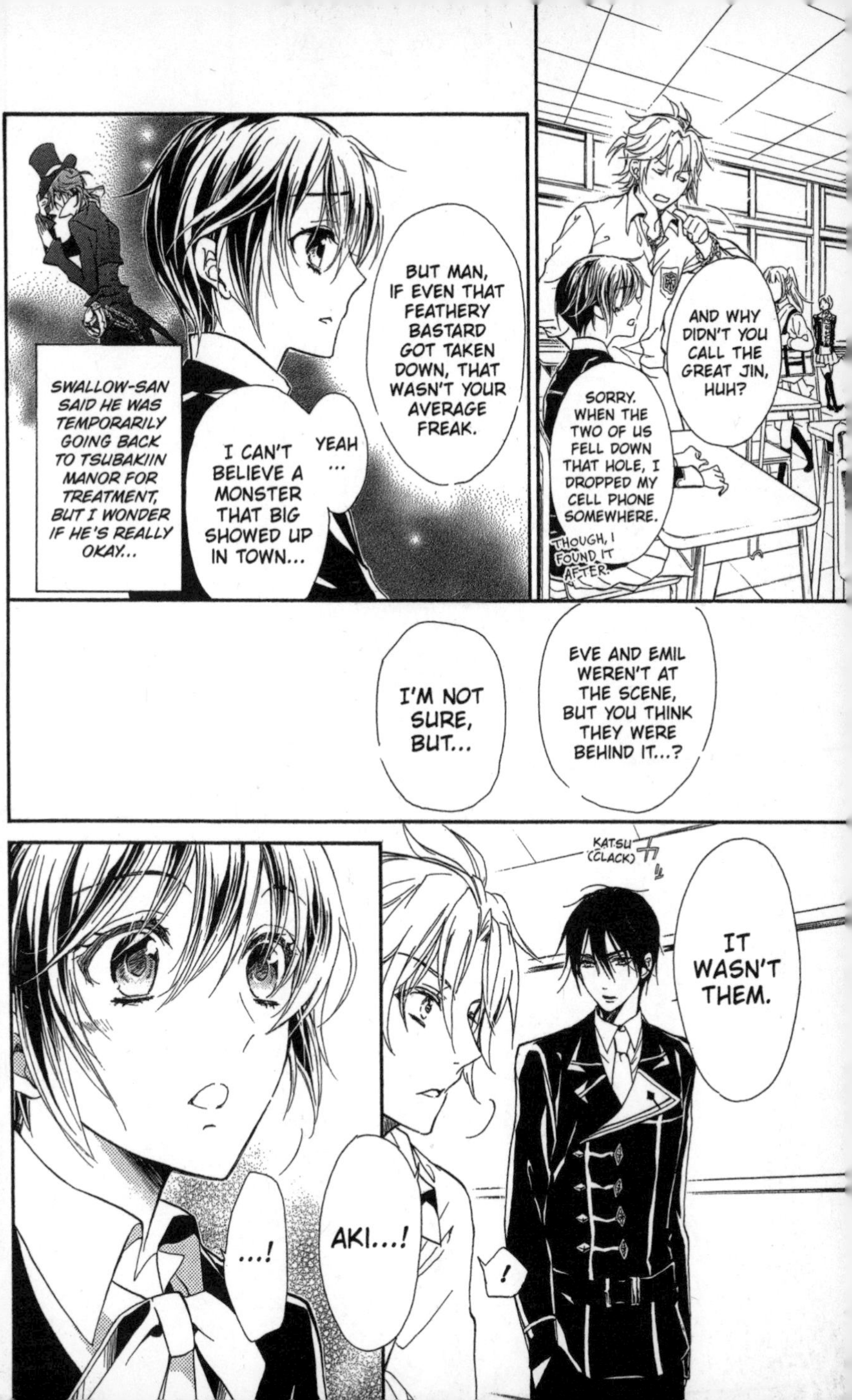
AND WHY DIDN'T YOU CALL THE GREAT JIN, HUH?
SORRY. WHEN THE TWO OF US FELL DOWN THAT HOLE, I DROPPED MY CELL PHONE SOMEWHERE.
THOUGH, I FOUND IT AFTER.
BUT MAN, IF EVEN THAT FEATHERY BASTARD GOT TAKEN DOWN, THAT WASN'T YOUR AVERAGE FREAK.
YEAH ...
I CAN'T BELIEVE A MONSTER THAT BIG SHOWED UP IN TOWN...
SWALLOW-SAN SAID HE WAS TEMPORARILY GOING BACK TO TSUBAKIIN MANOR FOR TREATMENT, BUT I WONDER IF HE'S REALLY OKAY...
EVE AND EMIL WEREN'T AT THE SCENE, BUT YOU THINK THEY WERE BEHIND IT...?
I'M NOT SURE, BUT...
KATSU (CLACK)
IT WASN'T THEM.
!
AKI...!
...!

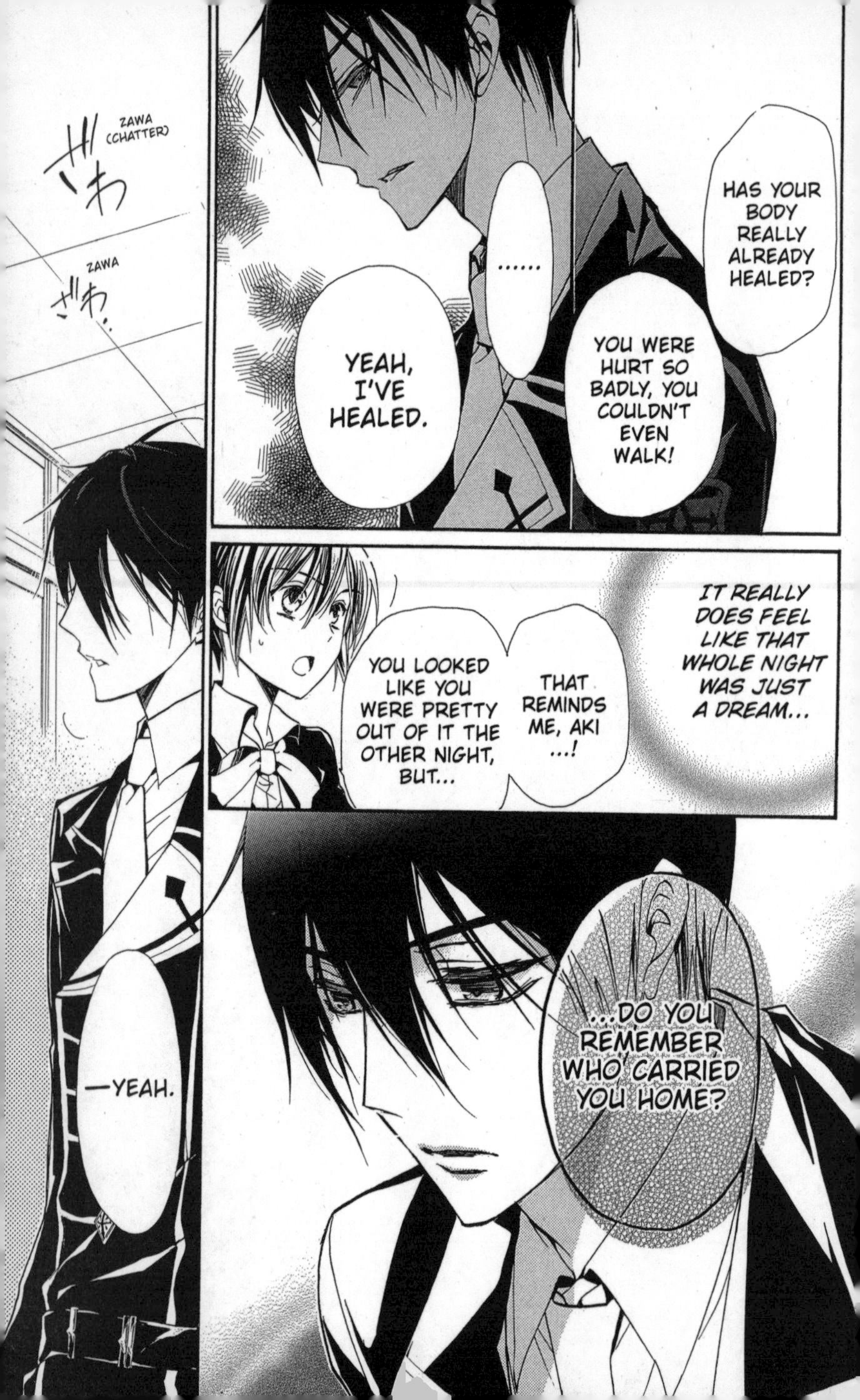
HAS YOUR BODY REALLY ALREADY HEALED?
YOU WERE HURT SO BADLY, YOU COULDN'T EVEN WALK!
......
YEAH, I'VE HEALED.
IT REALLY DOES FEEL LIKE THAT WHOLE NIGHT WAS JUST A DREAM...
THAT REMINDS ME, AKI ...!
YOU LOOKED LIKE YOU WERE PRETTY OUT OF IT THE OTHER NIGHT, BUT...
...DO YOU REMEMBER WHO CARRIED YOU HOME?
ざわ
ZAWA (CHATTER)
ざわ...
ZAWA
—YEAH.

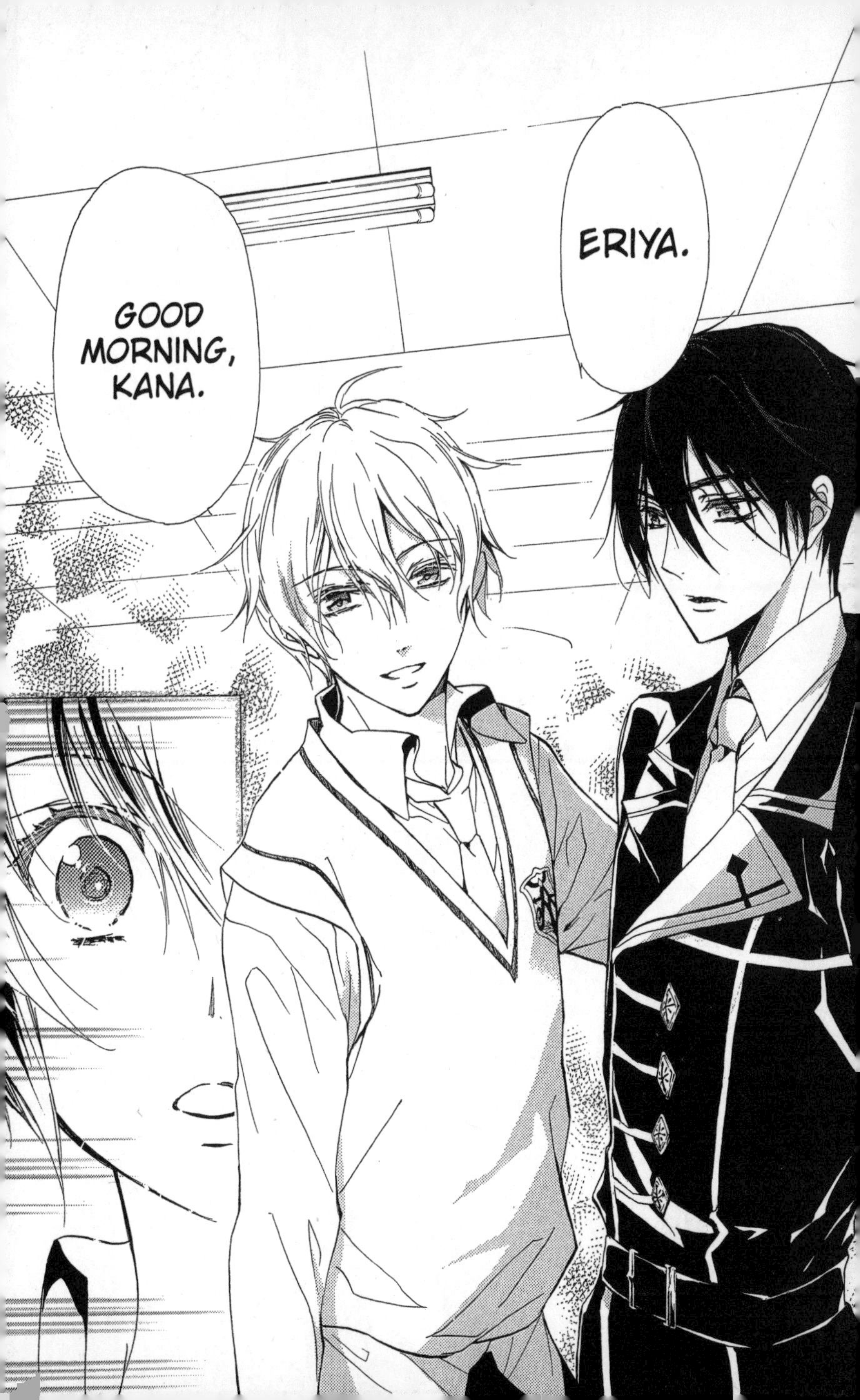
ERIYA.
GOOD MORNING, KANA.

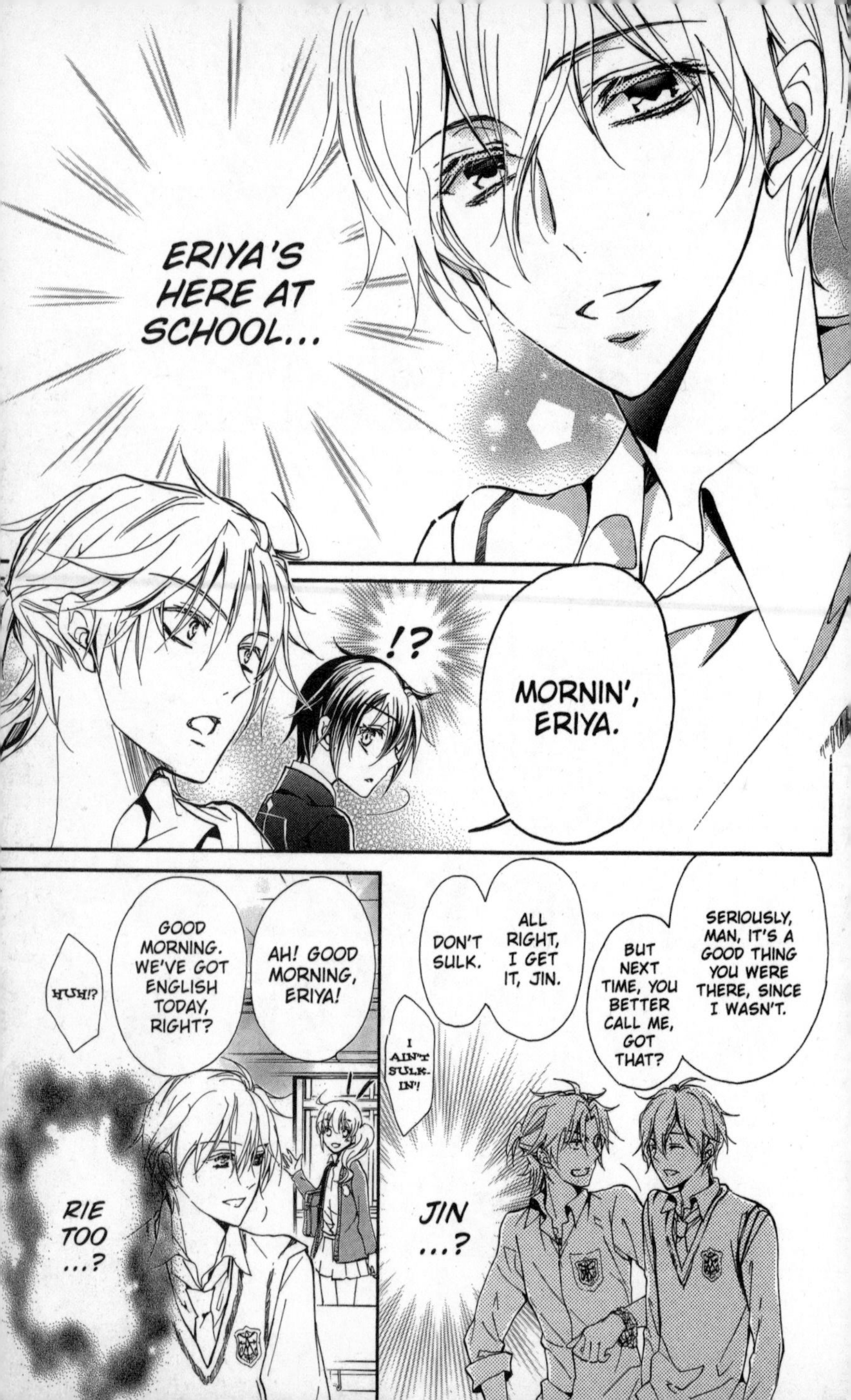
ERIYA'S HERE AT SCHOOL...
MORNIN', ERIYA.
!?
SERIOUSLY, MAN, IT'S A GOOD THING YOU WERE THERE, SINCE I WASN'T.
BUT NEXT TIME, YOU BETTER CALL ME, GOT THAT?
ALL RIGHT, I GET IT, JIN.
DON'T SULK.
I AIN'T SULKIN'!
JIN ...?
AH! GOOD MORNING, ERIYA!
GOOD MORNING. WE'VE GOT ENGLISH TODAY, RIGHT?
HUH!?
RIE TOO ...?

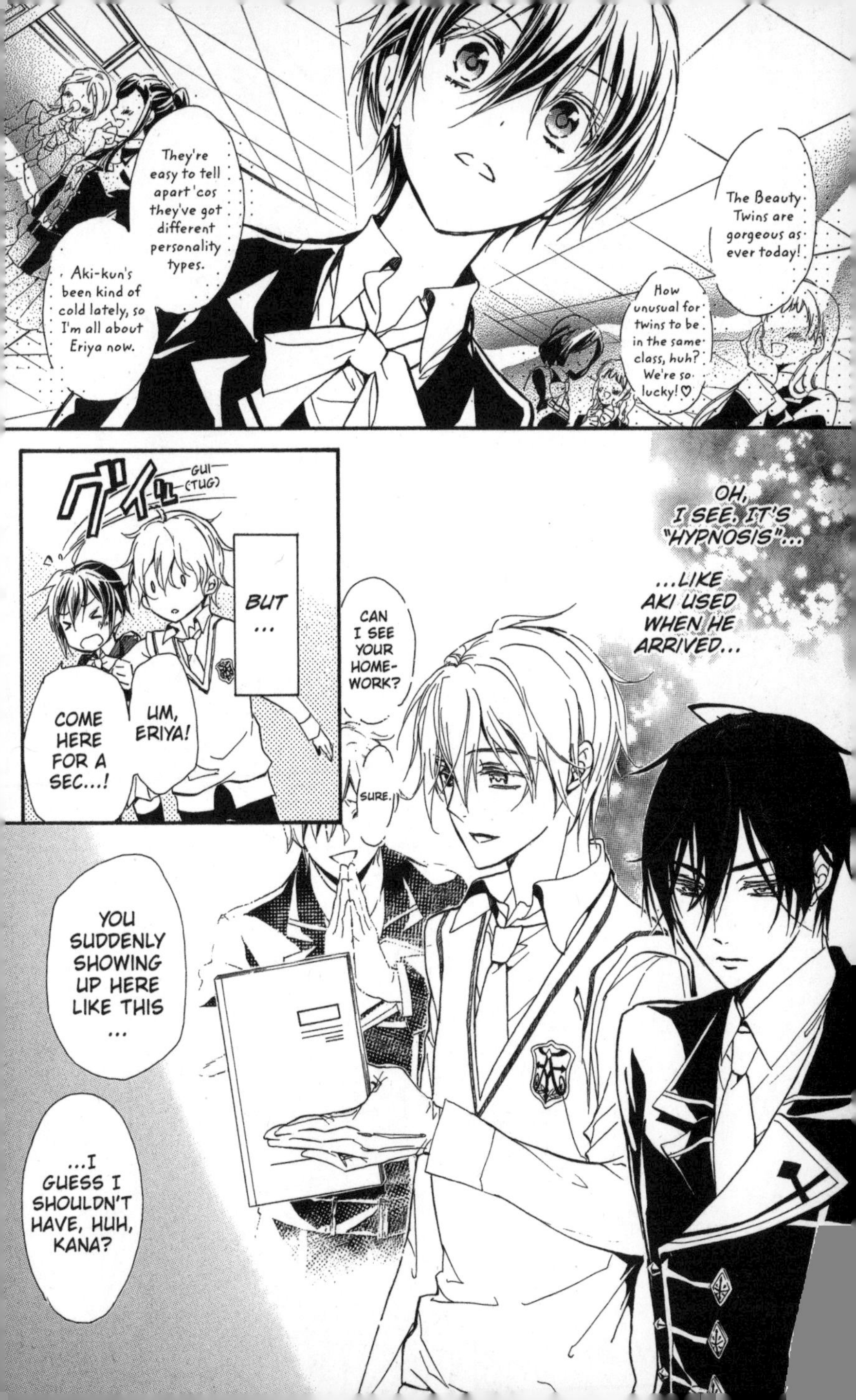
The Beauty Twins are gorgeous as ever today!
How unusual for twins to be in the same class, huh? We're so lucky! ♡
They're easy to tell apart 'cos they've got different personality types.
Aki-kun's been kind of cold lately, so I'm all about Eriya now.
OH, I SEE. IT'S "HYPNOSIS"...
...LIKE AKI USED WHEN HE ARRIVED...
CAN I SEE YOUR HOMEWORK?
SURE.
GUI (TUG)
BUT...
UM, ERIYA!
COME HERE FOR A SEC...!
YOU SUDDENLY SHOWING UP HERE LIKE THIS...
...I GUESS I SHOULDN'T HAVE, HUH, KANA?

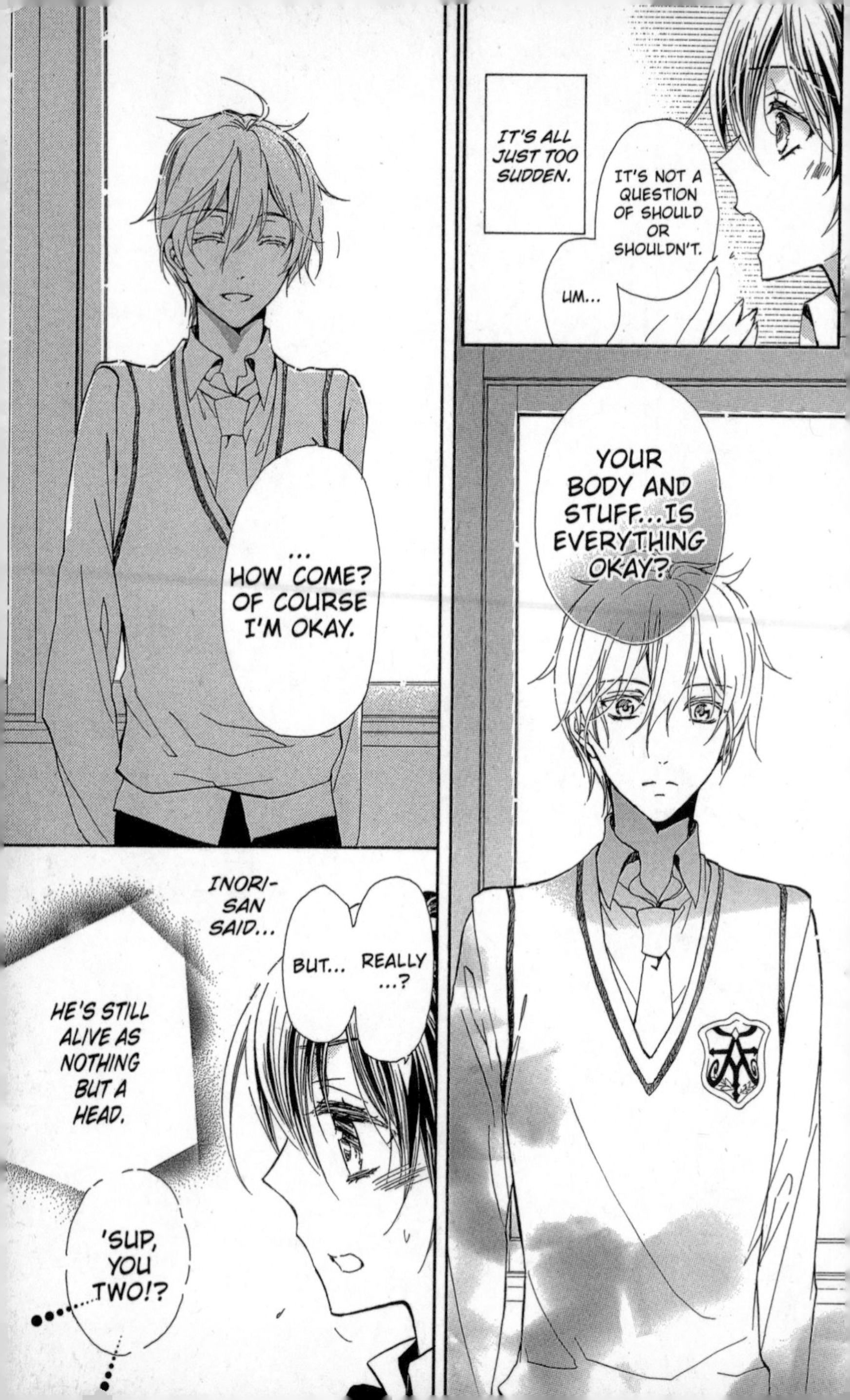
IT'S NOT A QUESTION OF SHOULD OR SHOULDN'T.
UM...
IT'S ALL JUST TOO SUDDEN.
YOUR BODY AND STUFF...IS EVERYTHING OKAY?
... HOW COME? OF COURSE I'M OKAY.
INORI-SAN SAID...
BUT... REALLY ...?
HE'S STILL ALIVE AS NOTHING BUT A HEAD.
'SUP, YOU TWO!?

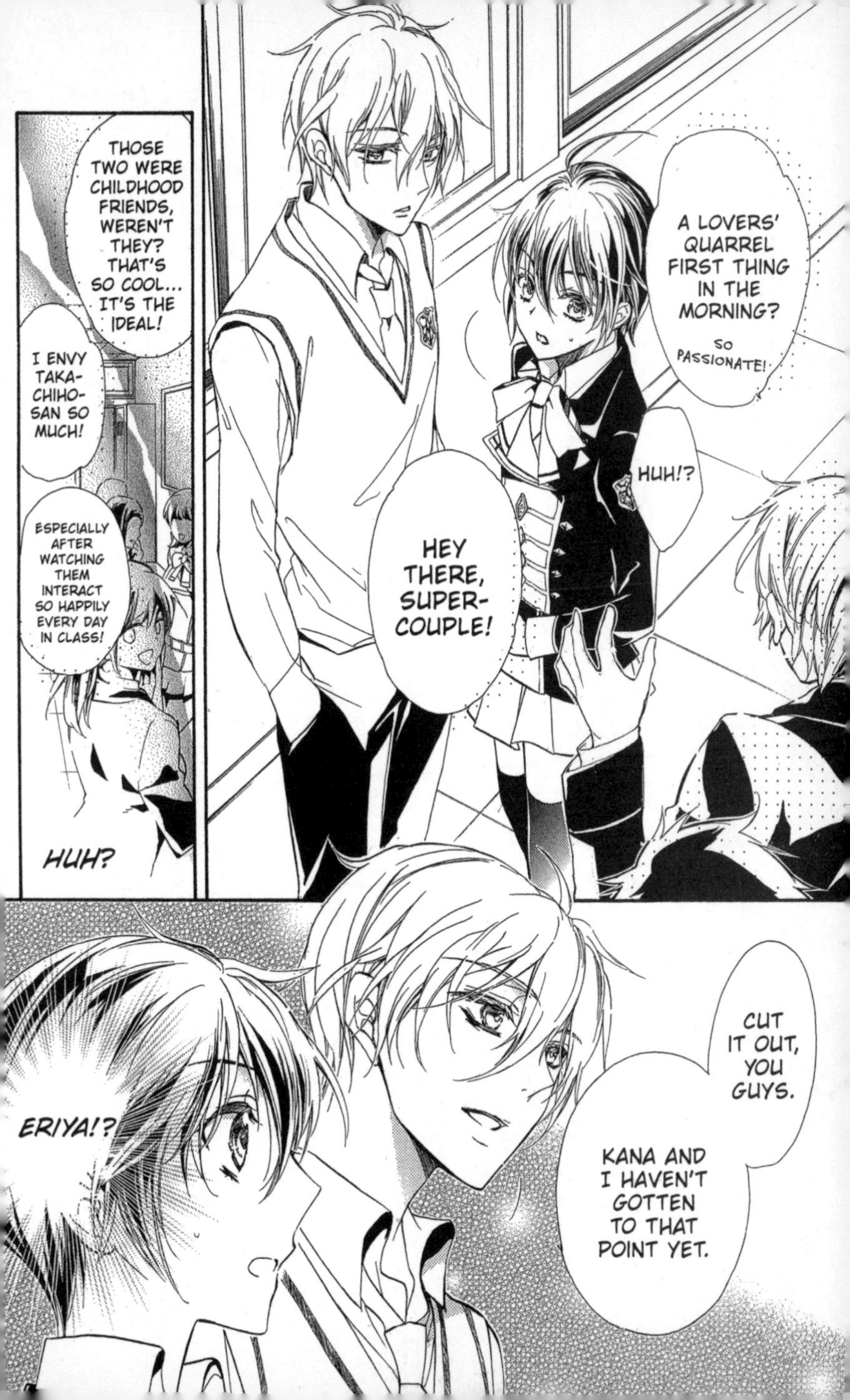
A LOVERS' QUARREL FIRST THING IN THE MORNING?
SO PASSIONATE!
HUH!?
HEY THERE, SUPER-COUPLE!
THOSE TWO WERE CHILDHOOD FRIENDS, WEREN'T THEY? THAT'S SO COOL... IT'S THE IDEAL!
I ENVY TAKA-CHIHO-SAN SO MUCH!
ESPECIALLY AFTER WATCHING THEM INTERACT SO HAPPILY EVERY DAY IN CLASS!
HUH?
CUT IT OUT, YOU GUYS.
KANA AND I HAVEN'T GOTTEN TO THAT POINT YET.
ERIYA!?

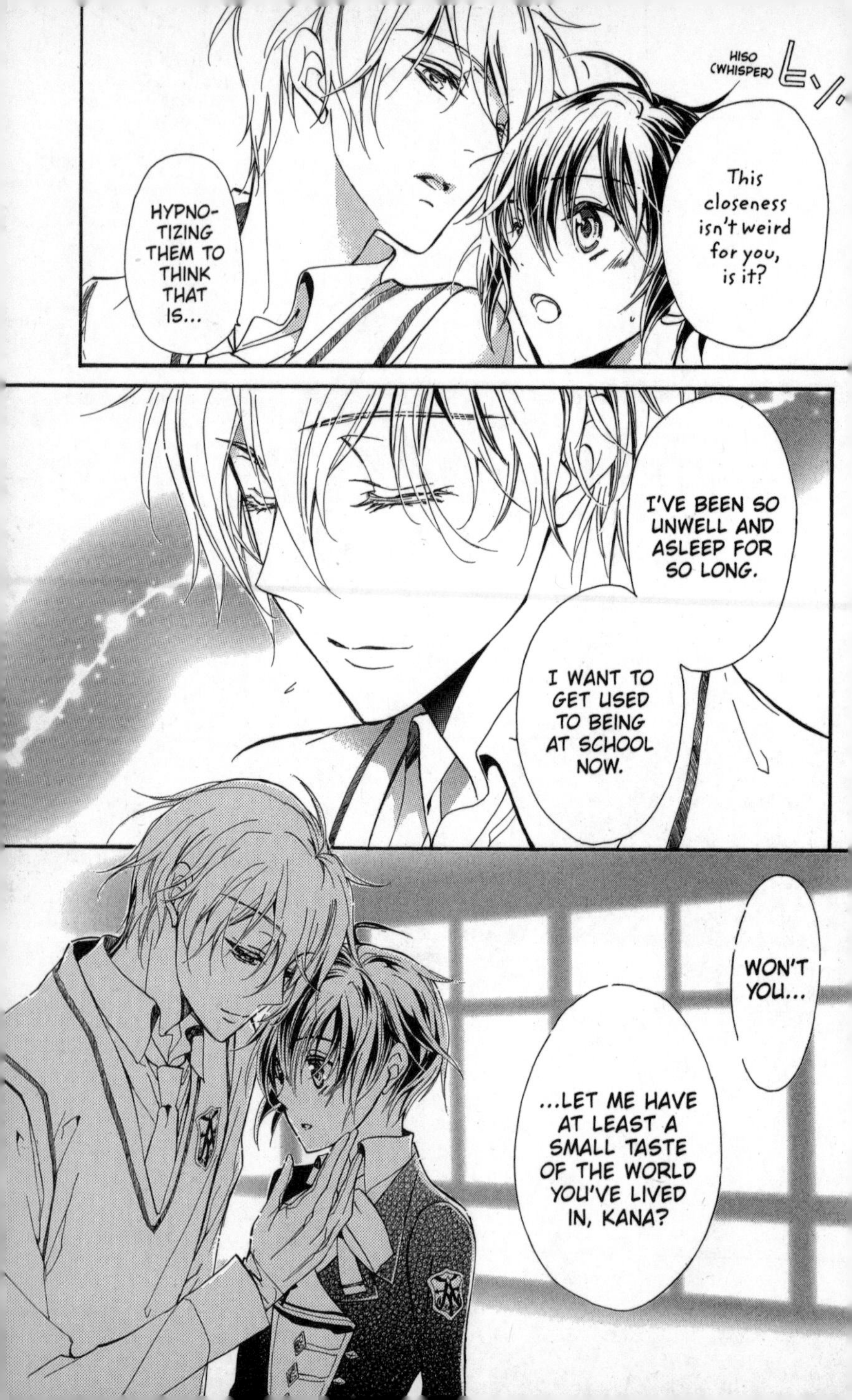
HISO (WHISPER)
This closeness isn't weird for you, is it?
HYPNO-TIZING THEM TO THINK THAT IS...
I'VE BEEN SO UNWELL AND ASLEEP FOR SO LONG.
I WANT TO GET USED TO BEING AT SCHOOL NOW.
WON'T YOU...
...LET ME HAVE AT LEAST A SMALL TASTE OF THE WORLD YOU'VE LIVED IN, KANA?

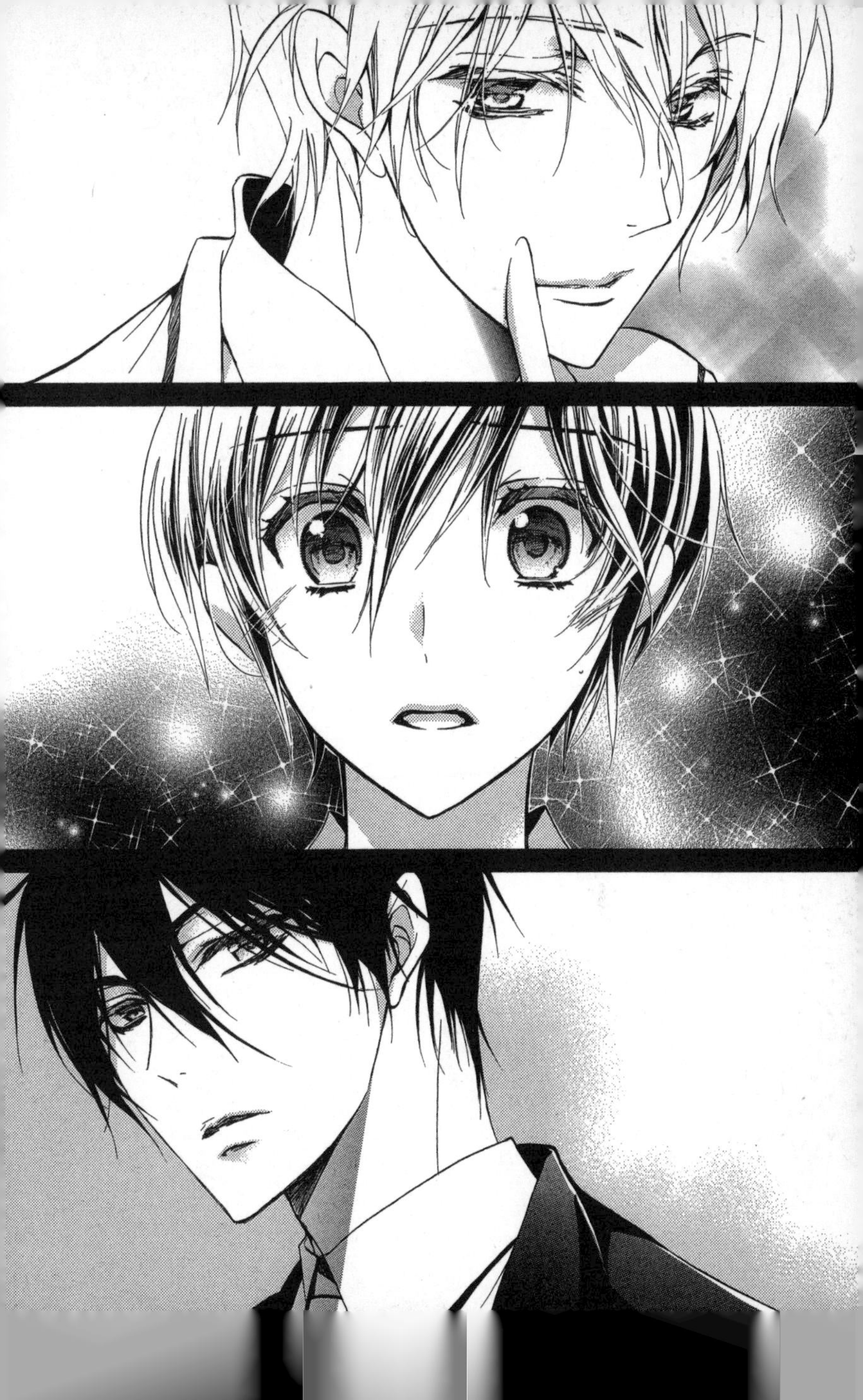

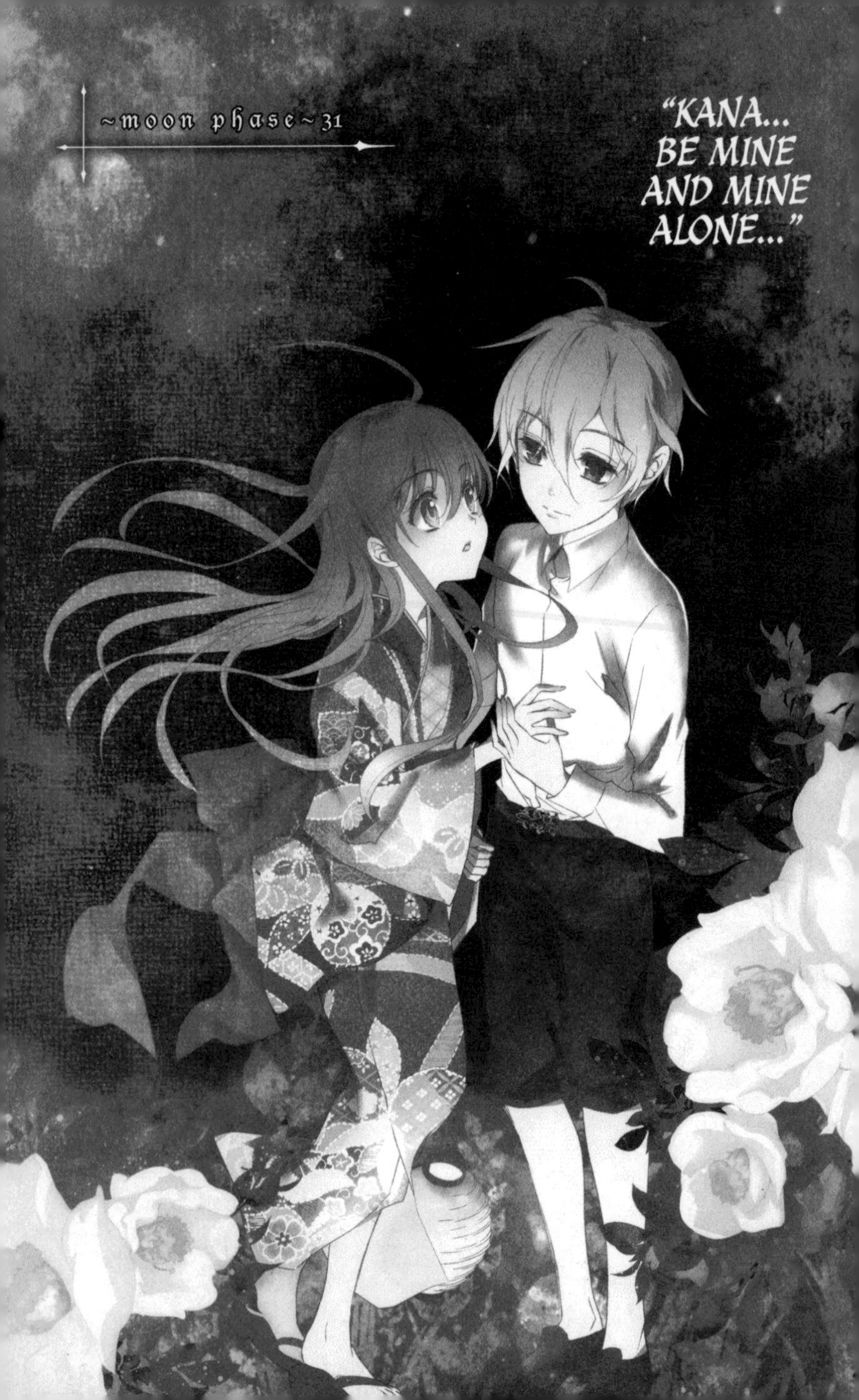
~moon phase~31
"KANA... BE MINE AND MINE ALONE..."

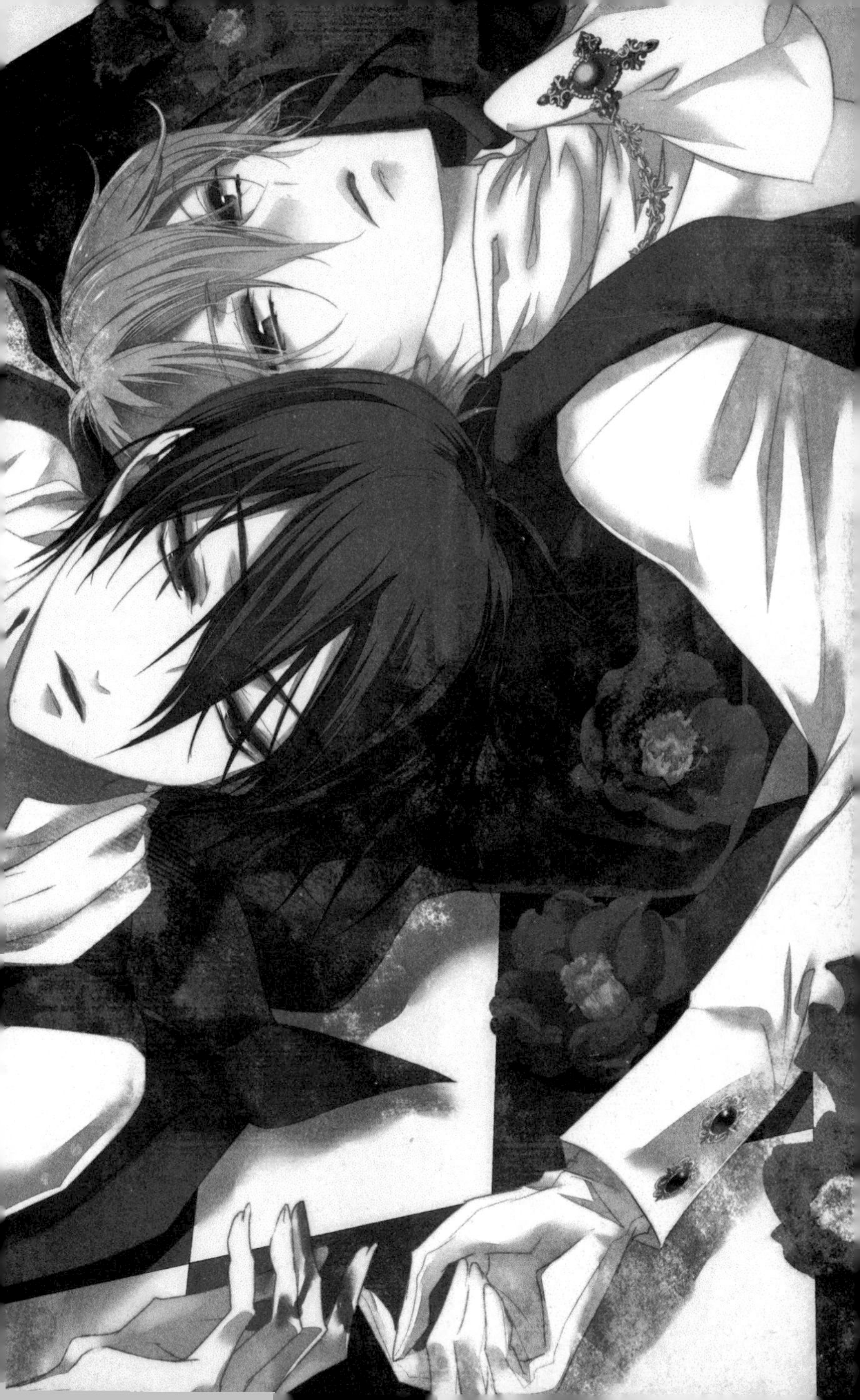

~moon phase~31

A Campus Game of Tag

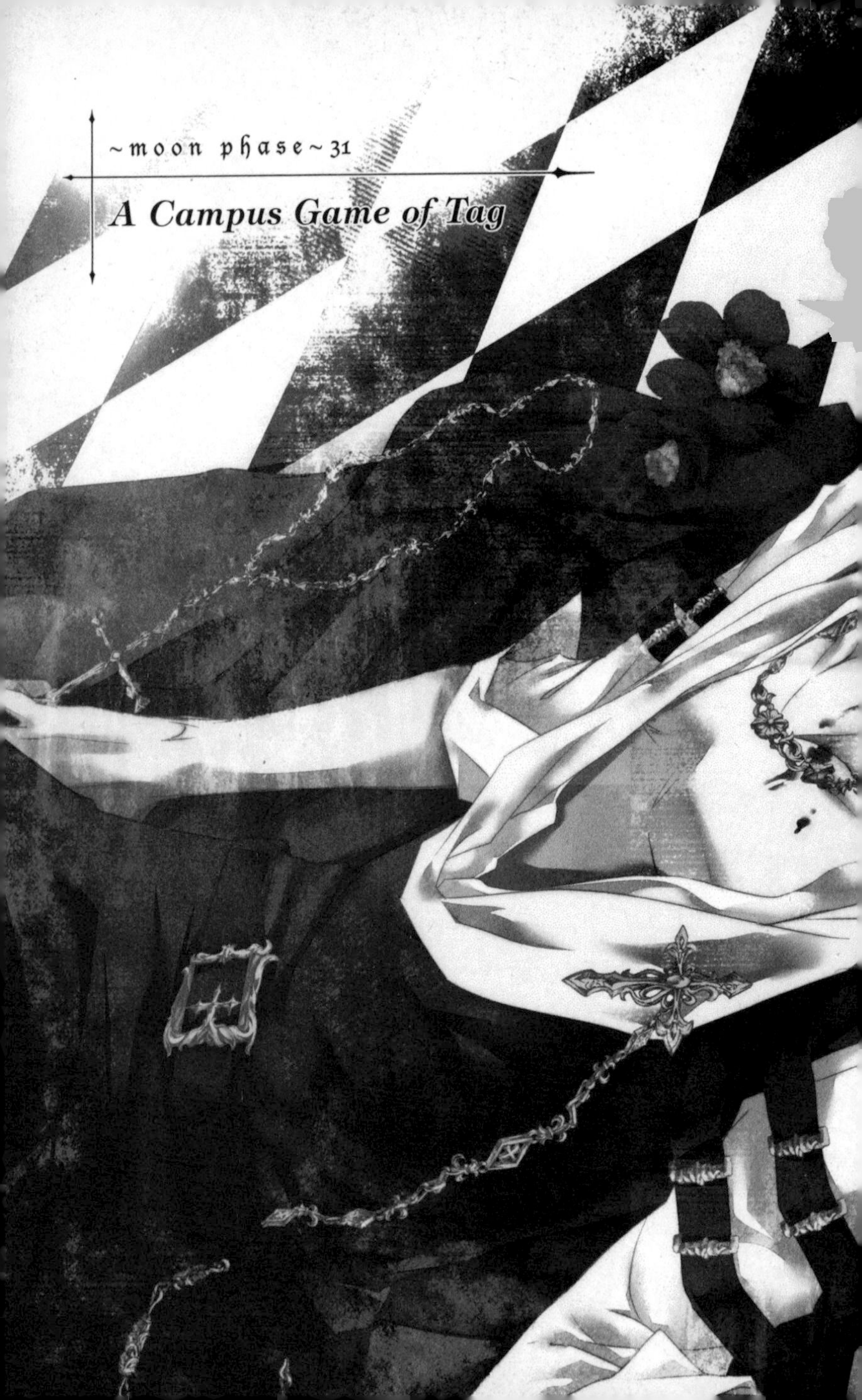

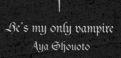

He's my only vampire
Aya Shouoto

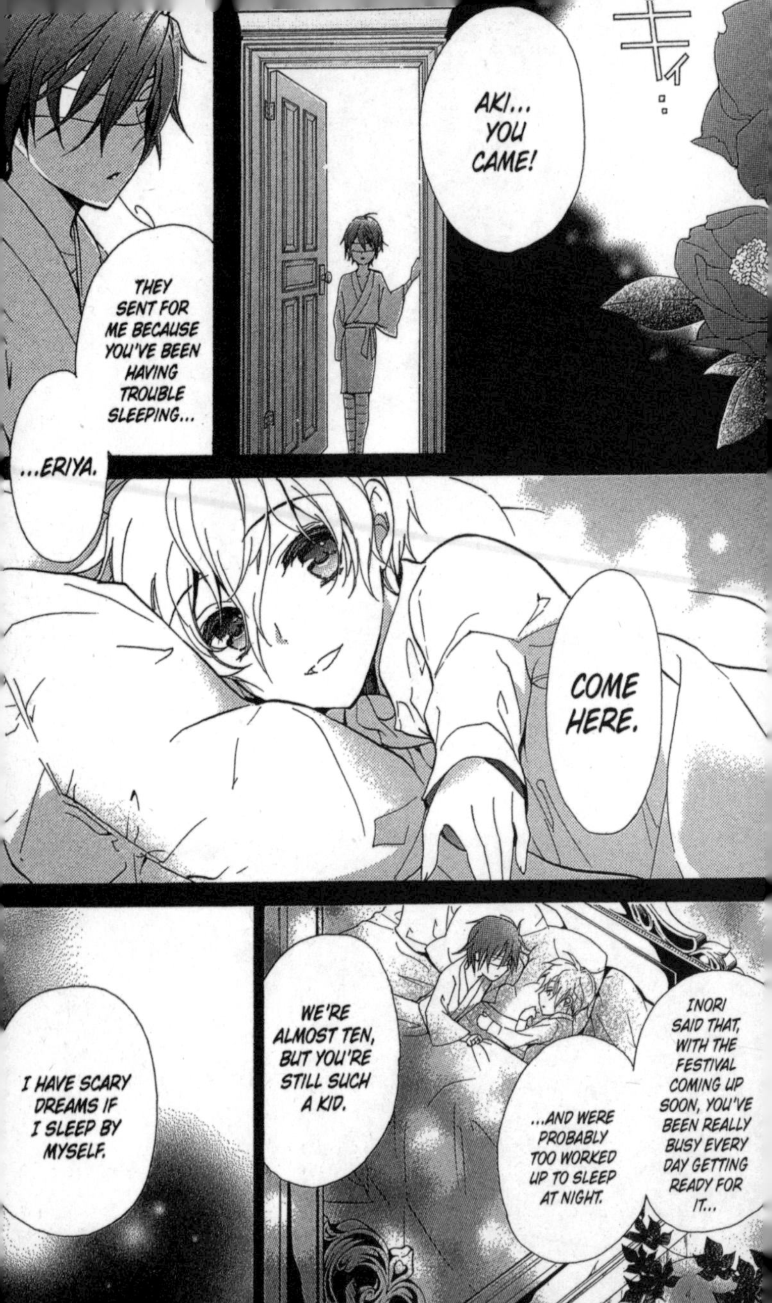

キィ…
AKI... YOU CAME!
THEY SENT FOR ME BECAUSE YOU'VE BEEN HAVING TROUBLE SLEEPING...
...ERIYA.
COME HERE.
INORI SAID THAT, WITH THE FESTIVAL COMING UP SOON, YOU'VE BEEN REALLY BUSY EVERY DAY GETTING READY FOR IT...
...AND WERE PROBABLY TOO WORKED UP TO SLEEP AT NIGHT.
WE'RE ALMOST TEN, BUT YOU'RE STILL SUCH A KID.
I HAVE SCARY DREAMS IF I SLEEP BY MYSELF.

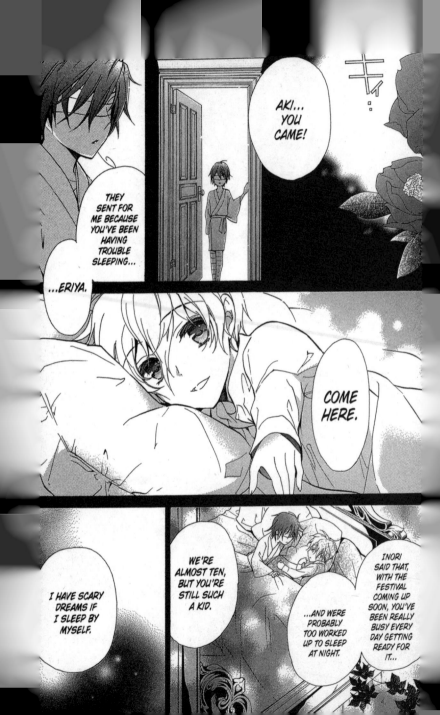

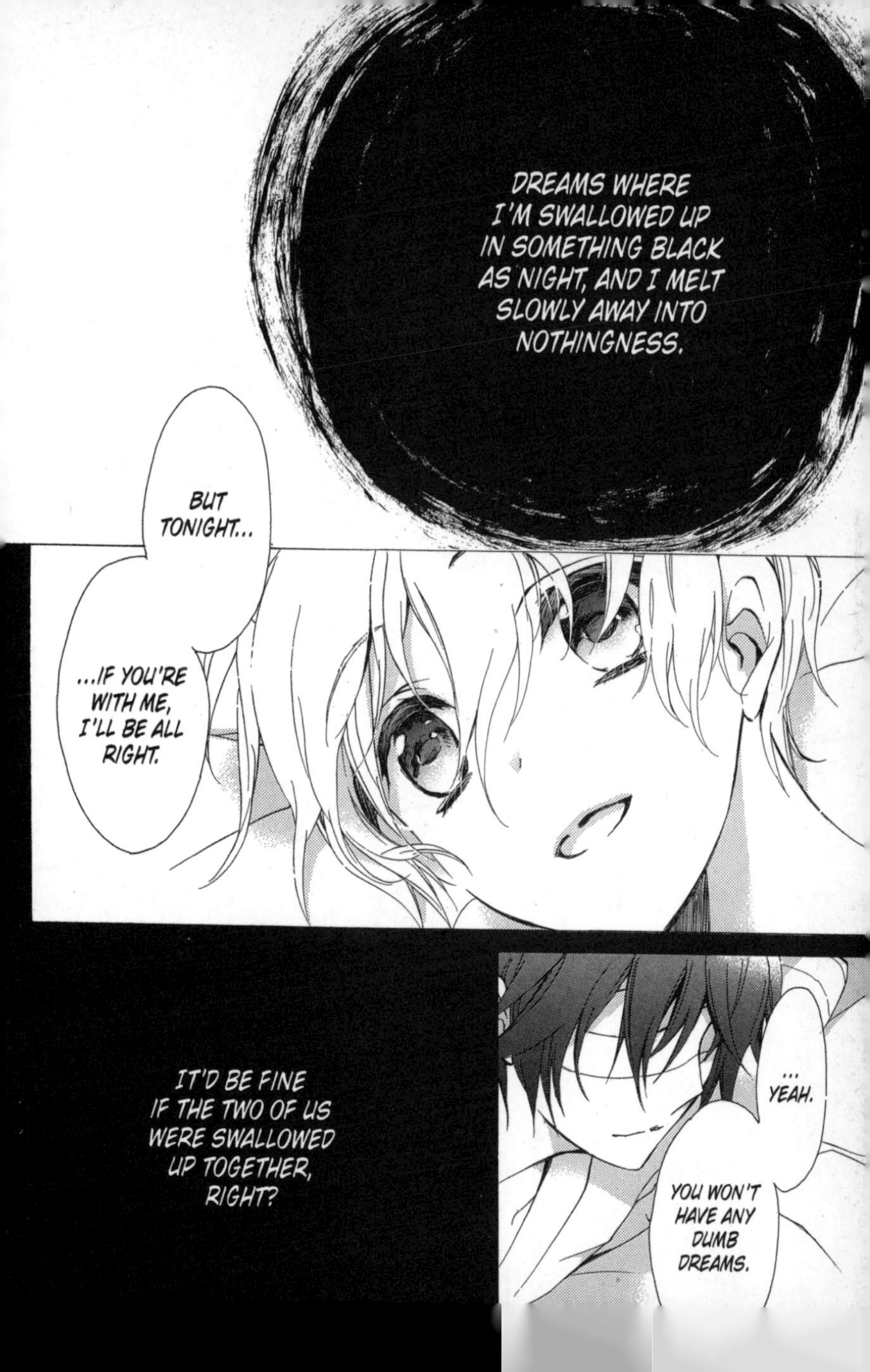
DREAMS WHERE I'M SWALLOWED UP IN SOMETHING BLACK AS NIGHT, AND I MELT SLOWLY AWAY INTO NOTHINGNESS.
BUT TONIGHT...
...IF YOU'RE WITH ME, I'LL BE ALL RIGHT.
...YEAH.
YOU WON'T HAVE ANY DUMB DREAMS.
IT'D BE FINE IF THE TWO OF US WERE SWALLOWED UP TOGETHER, RIGHT?

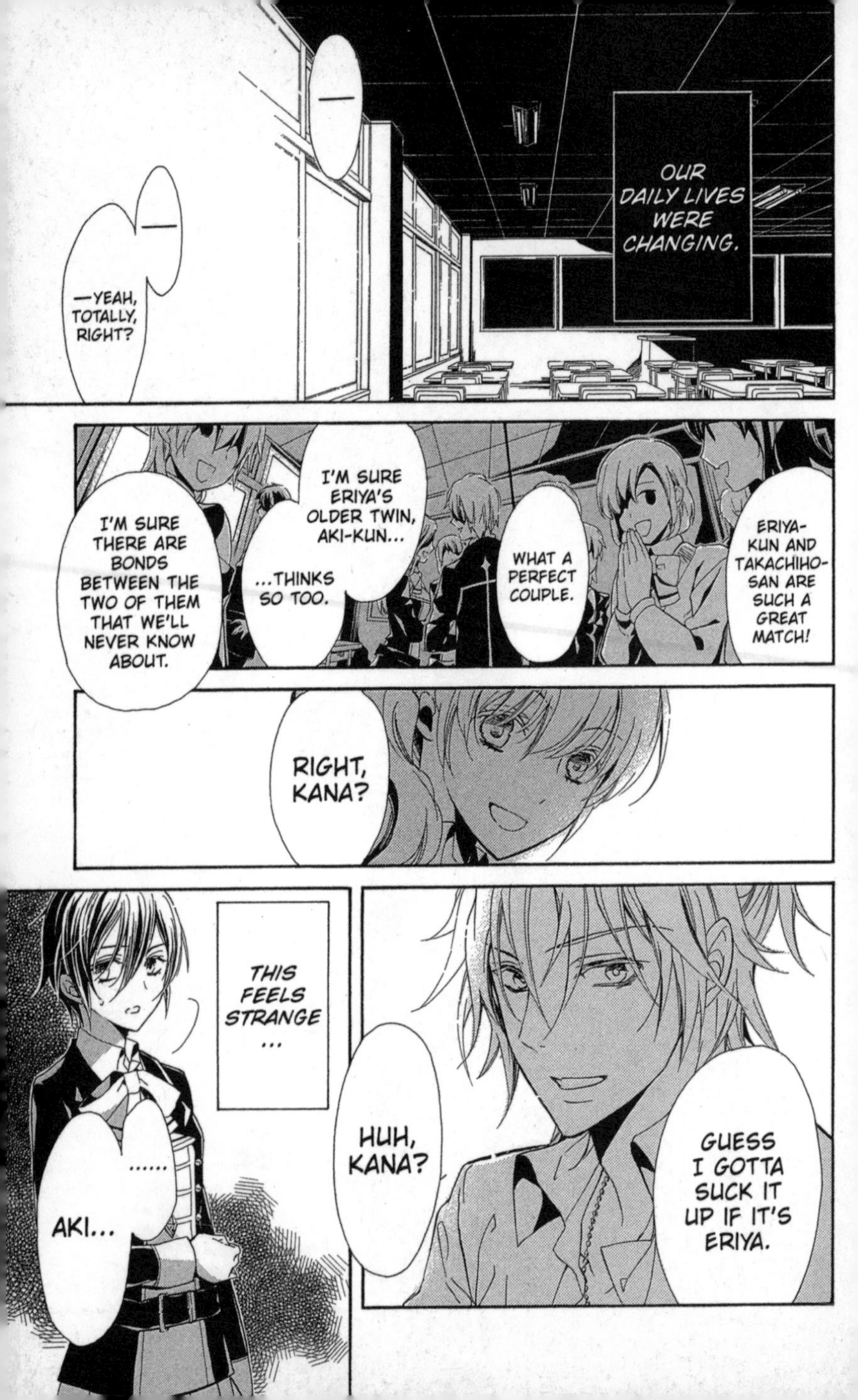
OUR DAILY LIVES WERE CHANGING.
—
—
—YEAH, TOTALLY, RIGHT?
ERIYA-KUN AND TAKACHIHO-SAN ARE SUCH A GREAT MATCH!
WHAT A PERFECT COUPLE.
I'M SURE ERIYA'S OLDER TWIN, AKI-KUN...
...THINKS SO TOO.
I'M SURE THERE ARE BONDS BETWEEN THE TWO OF THEM THAT WE'LL NEVER KNOW ABOUT.
RIGHT, KANA?
GUESS I GOTTA SUCK IT UP IF IT'S ERIYA.
HUH, KANA?
THIS FEELS STRANGE...
......
AKI...

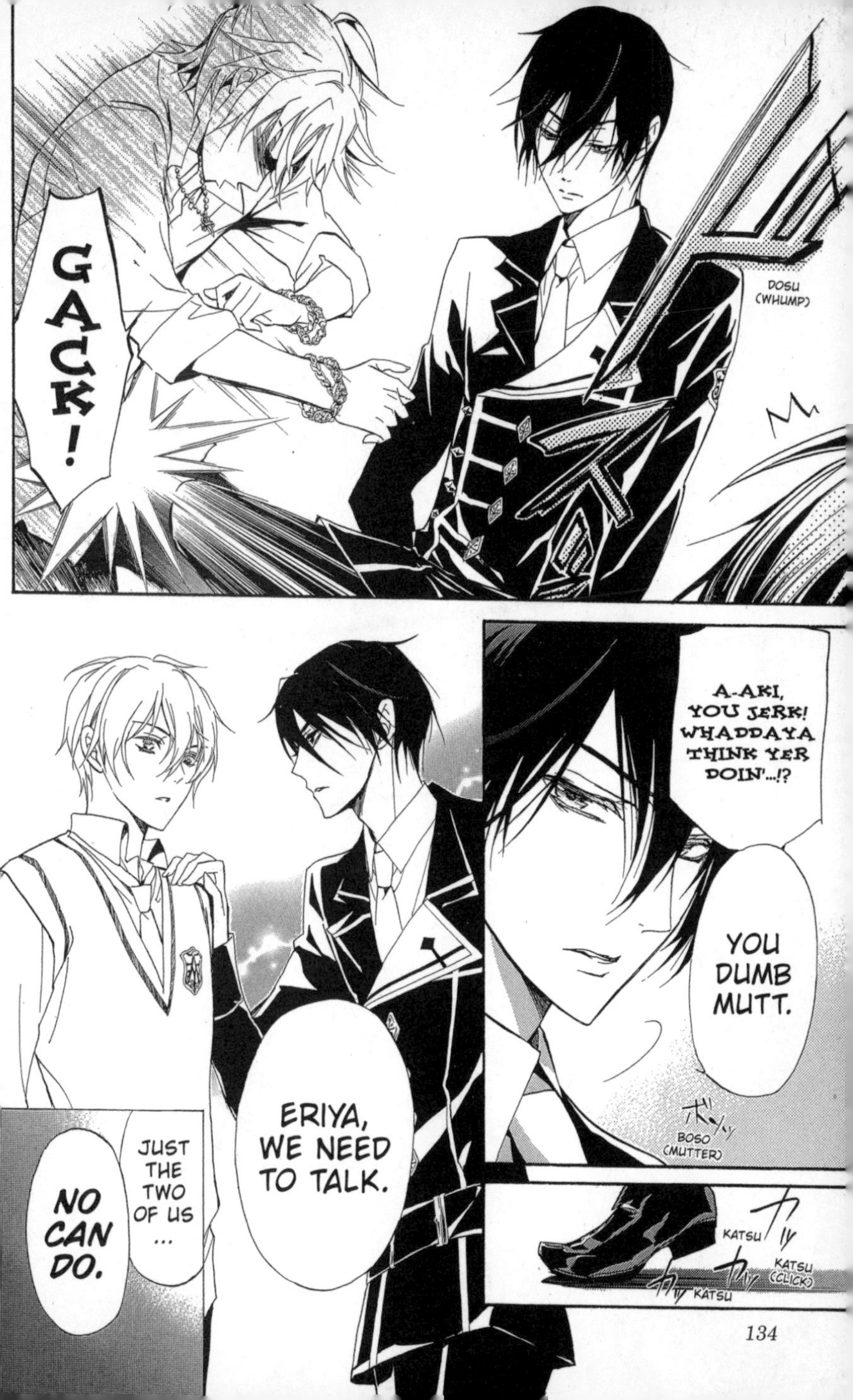
DOSU (WHUMP)
GACK!
A-AKI, YOU JERK! WHADDAYA THINK YER DOIN'...!?
YOU DUMB MUTT.
ボソ
BOSO (MUTTER)
カッ
KATSU
カッ
KATSU (CLICK)
カッ
KATSU
ERIYA, WE NEED TO TALK.
JUST THE TWO OF US...
NO CAN DO.

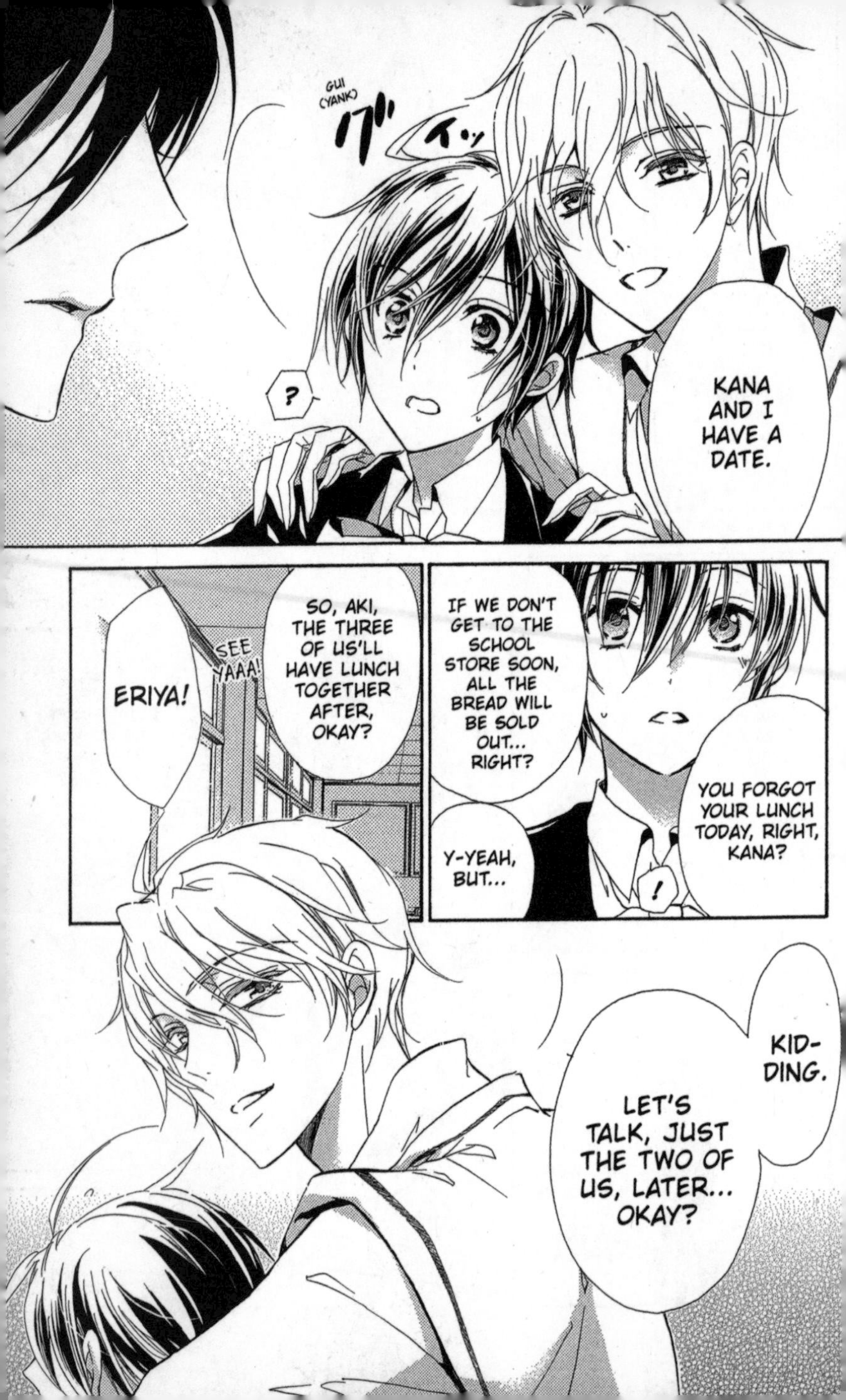
KANA AND I HAVE A DATE.
GUI (YANK)
?
IF WE DON'T GET TO THE SCHOOL STORE SOON, ALL THE BREAD WILL BE SOLD OUT... RIGHT?
YOU FORGOT YOUR LUNCH TODAY, RIGHT, KANA?
!
Y-YEAH, BUT...
SO, AKI, THE THREE OF US'LL HAVE LUNCH TOGETHER AFTER, OKAY?
SEE YAAA!
ERIYA!
KID-DING.
LET'S TALK, JUST THE TWO OF US, LATER... OKAY?

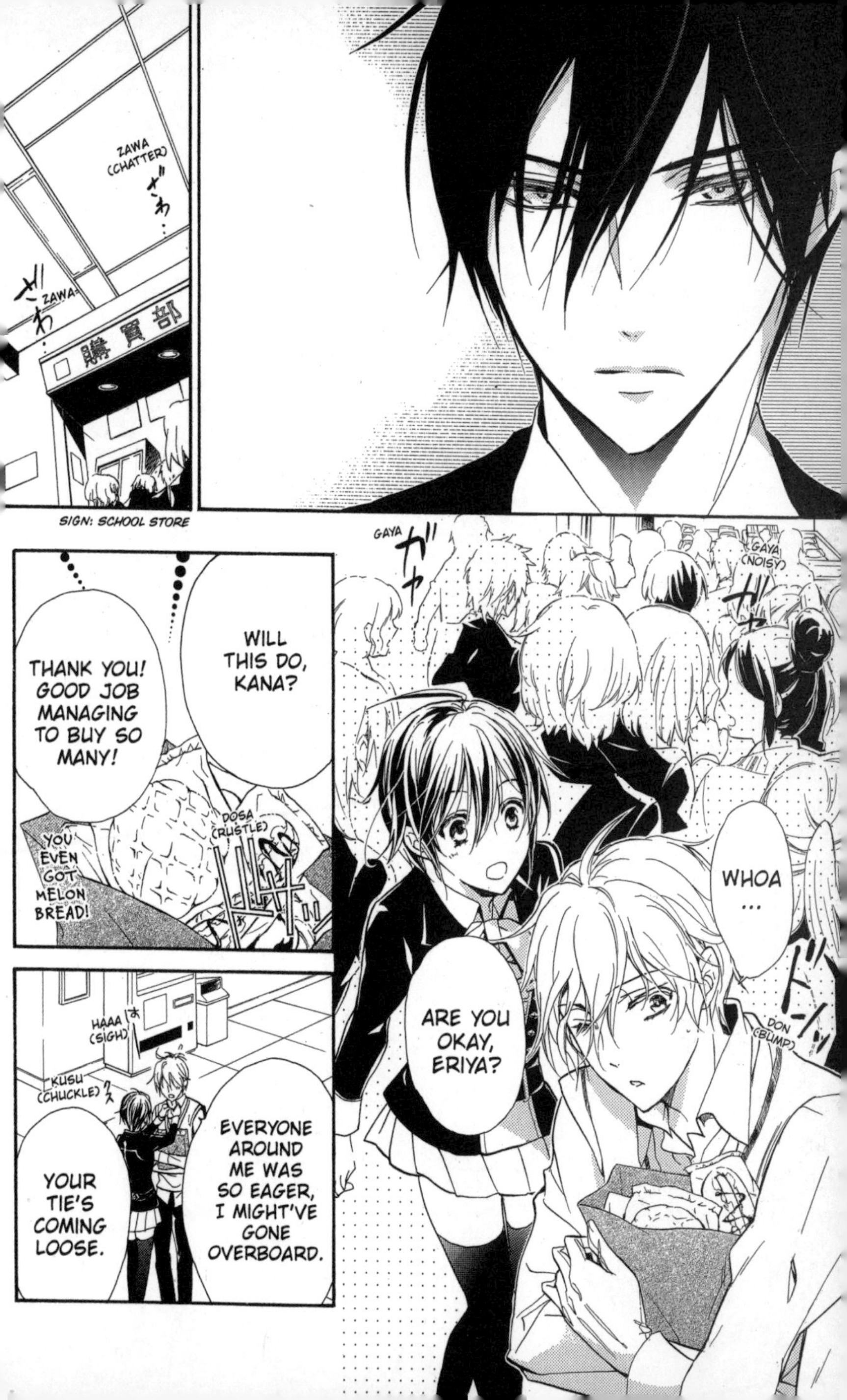
ZAWA (CHATTER)
ざわ…
ざわ
ZAWA
購買部
SIGN: SCHOOL STORE
GAYA
ガヤ
GAYA (NOISY)
WHOA ...
DON (BUMP)
ARE YOU OKAY, ERIYA?
WILL THIS DO, KANA?
THANK YOU! GOOD JOB MANAGING TO BUY SO MANY!
DOSA (RUSTLE)
YOU EVEN GOT MELON BREAD!
EVERYONE AROUND ME WAS SO EAGER, I MIGHT'VE GONE OVERBOARD.
HAAA (SIGH)
KUSU (CHUCKLE)
YOUR TIE'S COMING LOOSE.

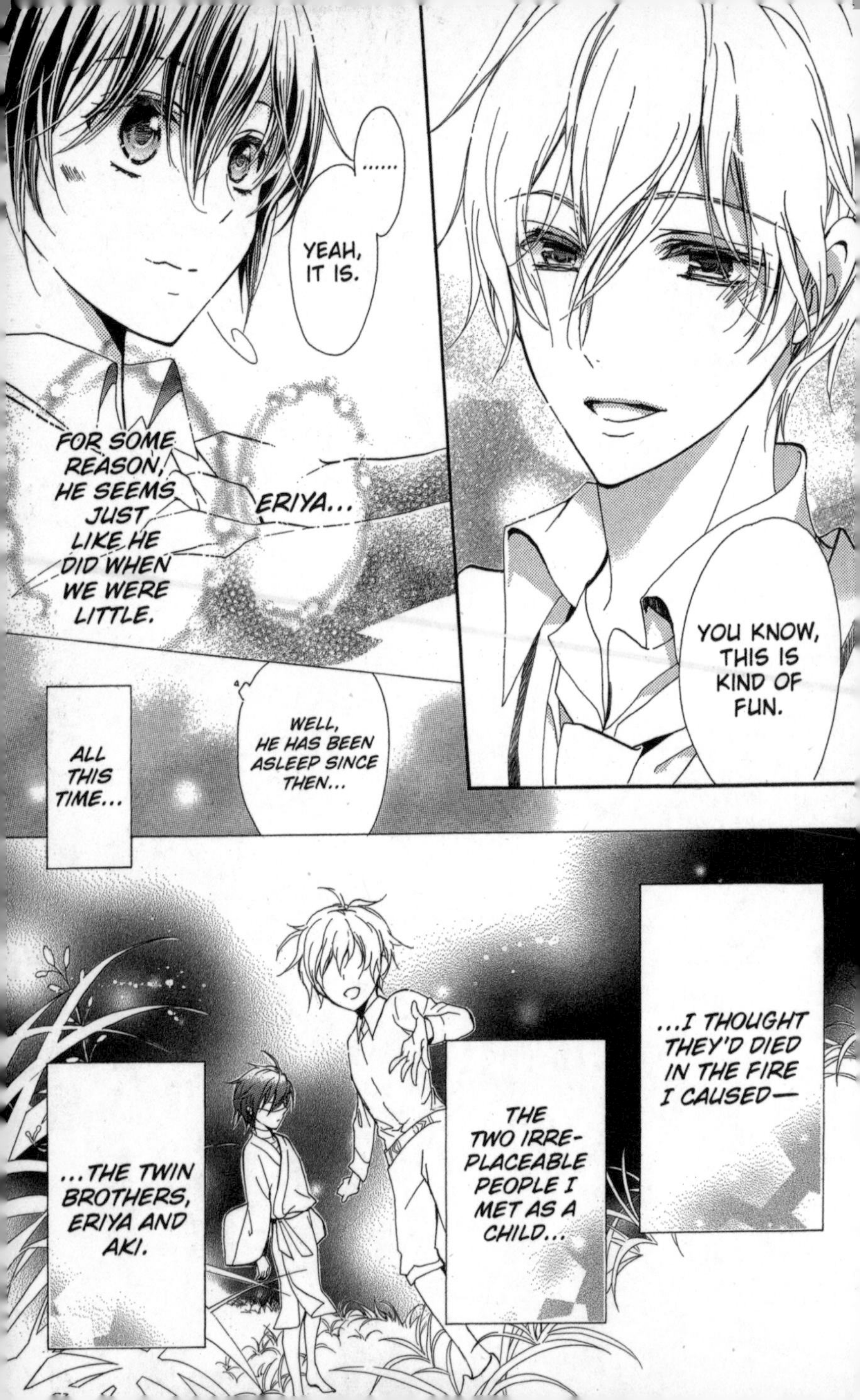
YOU KNOW, THIS IS KIND OF FUN.
......
YEAH, IT IS.
FOR SOME REASON, HE SEEMS JUST LIKE HE DID WHEN WE WERE LITTLE.
ERIYA...
WELL, HE HAS BEEN ASLEEP SINCE THEN...
ALL THIS TIME...
...I THOUGHT THEY'D DIED IN THE FIRE I CAUSED—
THE TWO IRRE-PLACEABLE PEOPLE I MET AS A CHILD...
...THE TWIN BROTHERS, ERIYA AND AKI.

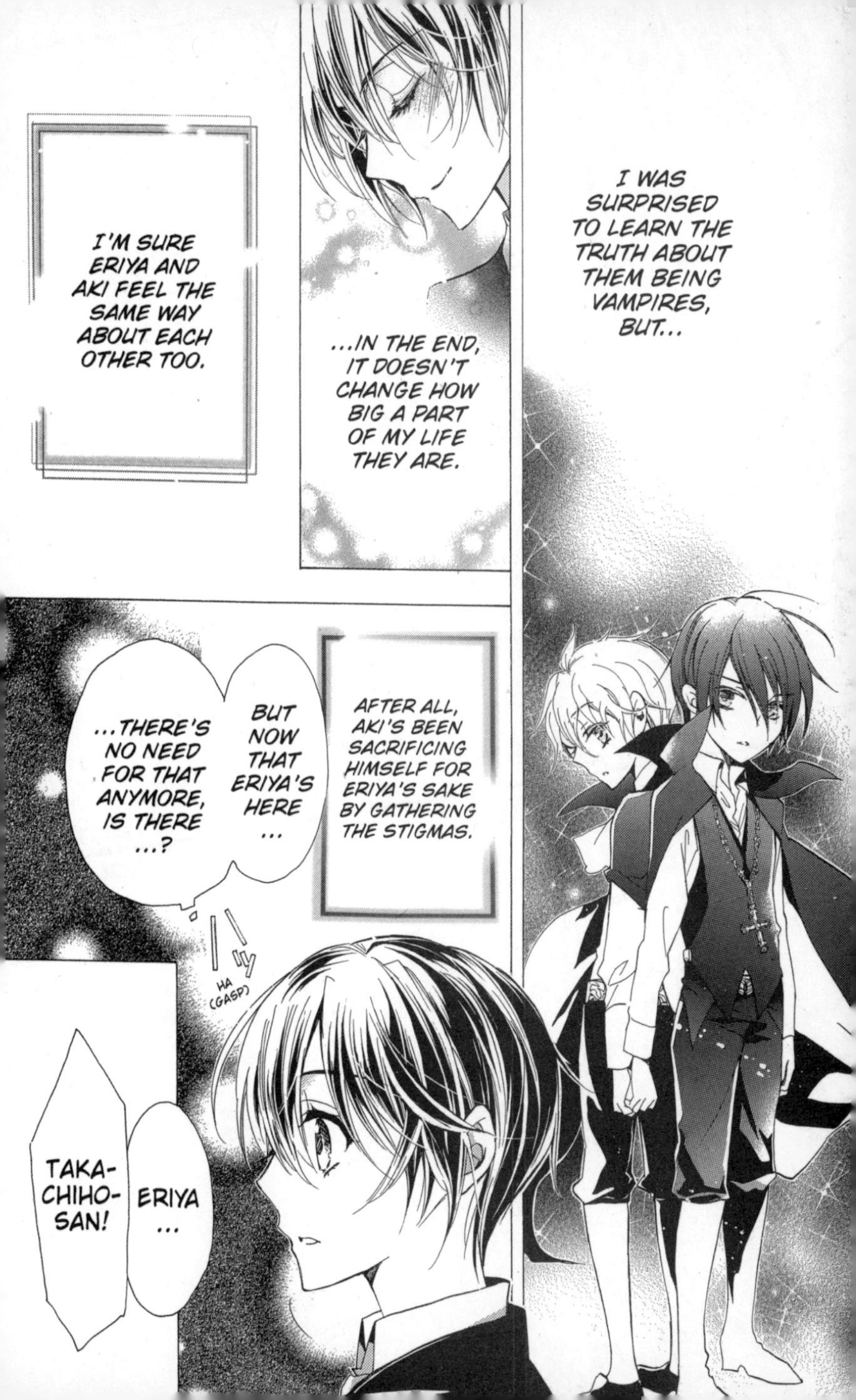
I WAS SURPRISED TO LEARN THE TRUTH ABOUT THEM BEING VAMPIRES, BUT...
...IN THE END, IT DOESN'T CHANGE HOW BIG A PART OF MY LIFE THEY ARE.
I'M SURE ERIYA AND AKI FEEL THE SAME WAY ABOUT EACH OTHER TOO.
AFTER ALL, AKI'S BEEN SACRIFICING HIMSELF FOR ERIYA'S SAKE BY GATHERING THE STIGMAS.
BUT NOW THAT ERIYA'S HERE ...
...THERE'S NO NEED FOR THAT ANYMORE, IS THERE ...?
HA (GASP)
ERIYA ...
TAKA-CHIHO-SAN!

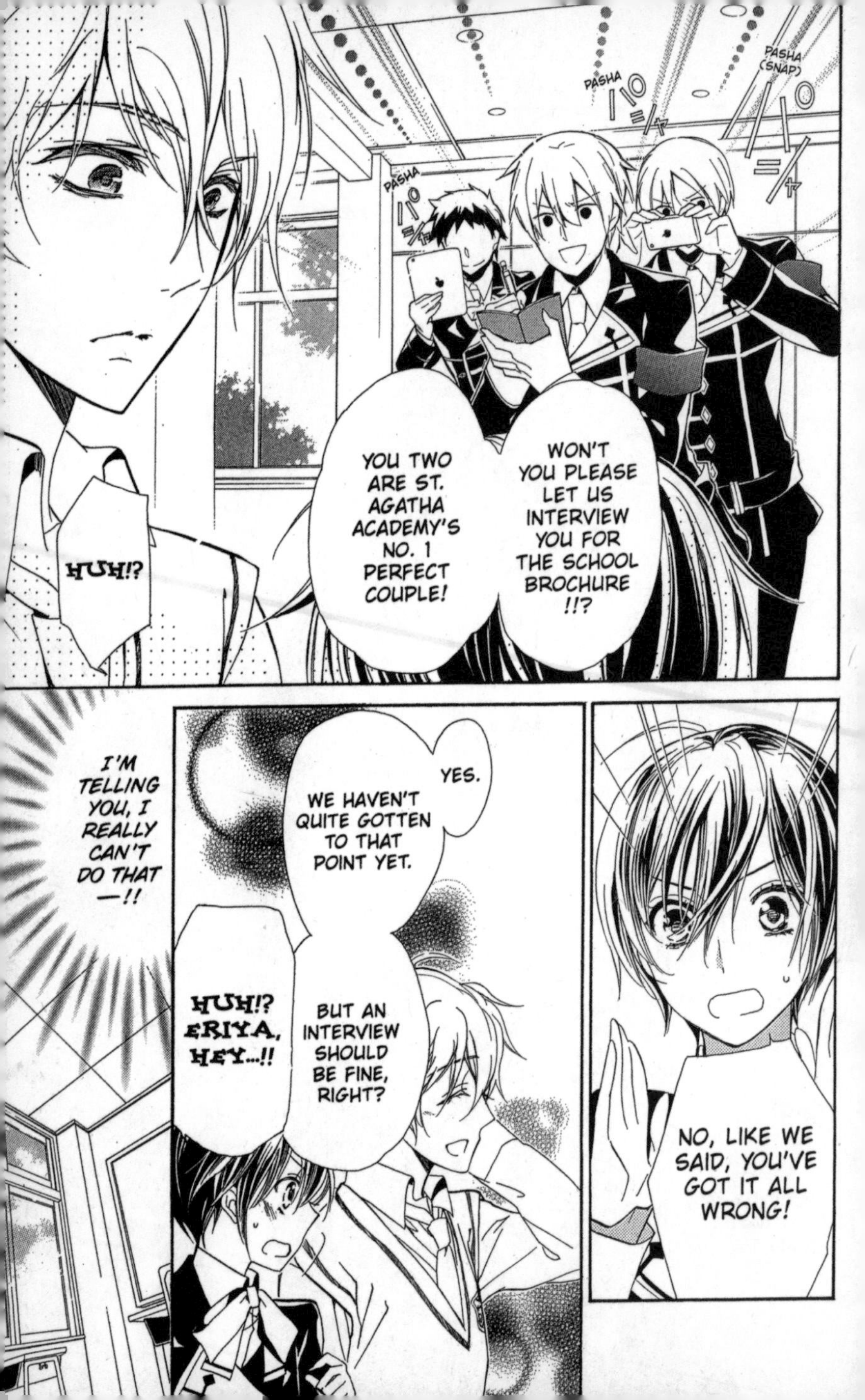
PASHA (SNAP)
PASHA
PASHA
WON'T YOU PLEASE LET US INTERVIEW YOU FOR THE SCHOOL BROCHURE !!?
YOU TWO ARE ST. AGATHA ACADEMY'S NO. 1 PERFECT COUPLE!
HUH!?
NO, LIKE WE SAID, YOU'VE GOT IT ALL WRONG!
YES.
WE HAVEN'T QUITE GOTTEN TO THAT POINT YET.
BUT AN INTERVIEW SHOULD BE FINE, RIGHT?
HUH!? ERIYA, HEY...!!
I'M TELLING YOU, I REALLY CAN'T DO THAT—!!

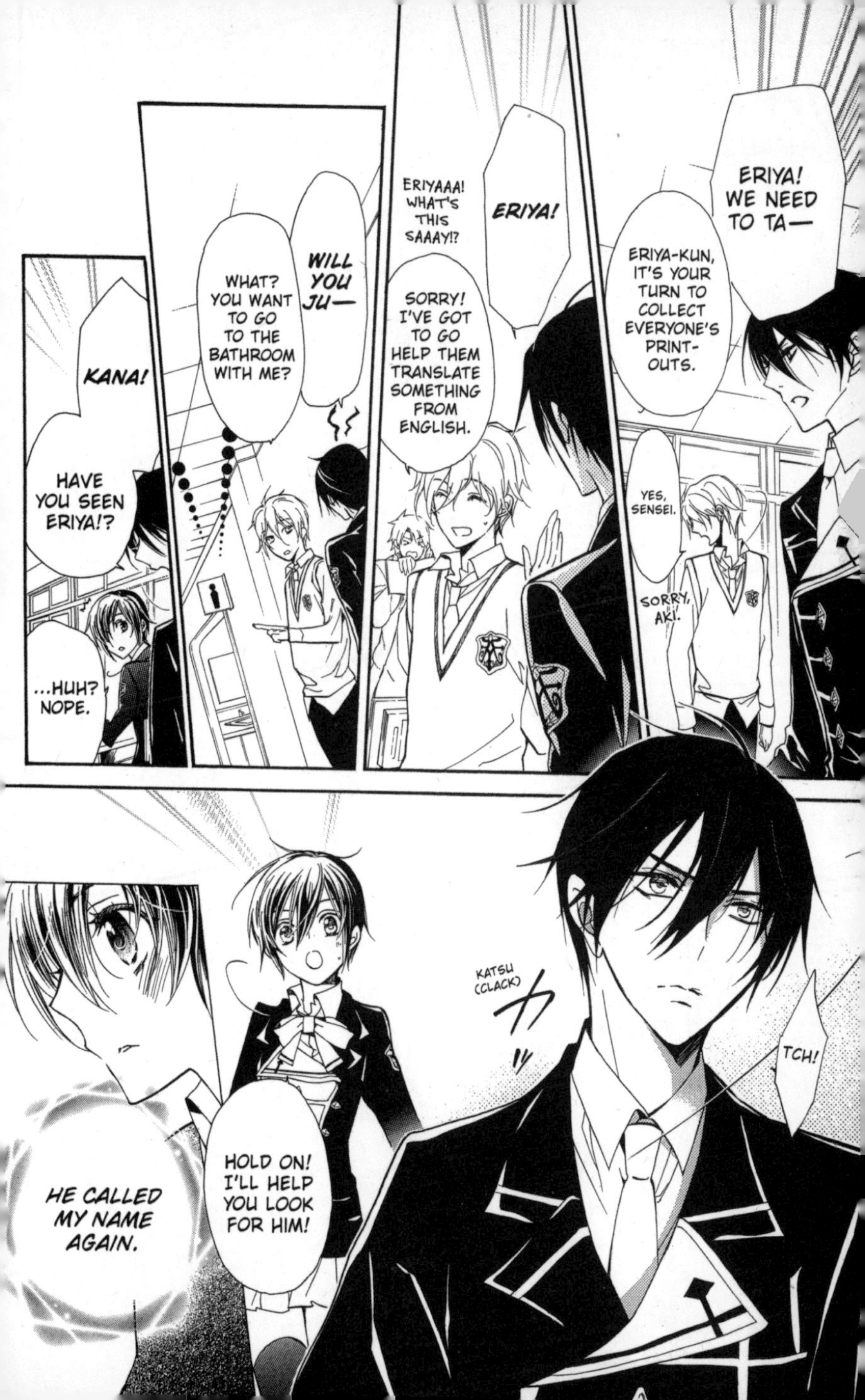
ERIYA! WE NEED TO TA—
ERIYA-KUN, IT'S YOUR TURN TO COLLECT EVERYONE'S PRINT-OUTS.
YES, SENSEI.
SORRY, AKI.
ERIYA!
ERIYAAA! WHAT'S THIS SAAAY!?
SORRY! I'VE GOT TO GO HELP THEM TRANSLATE SOMETHING FROM ENGLISH.
WILL YOU JU—
WHAT? YOU WANT TO GO TO THE BATHROOM WITH ME?
KANA!
HAVE YOU SEEN ERIYA!?
...HUH? NOPE.
TCH!
KATSU (CLACK)
HOLD ON! I'LL HELP YOU LOOK FOR HIM!
HE CALLED MY NAME AGAIN.

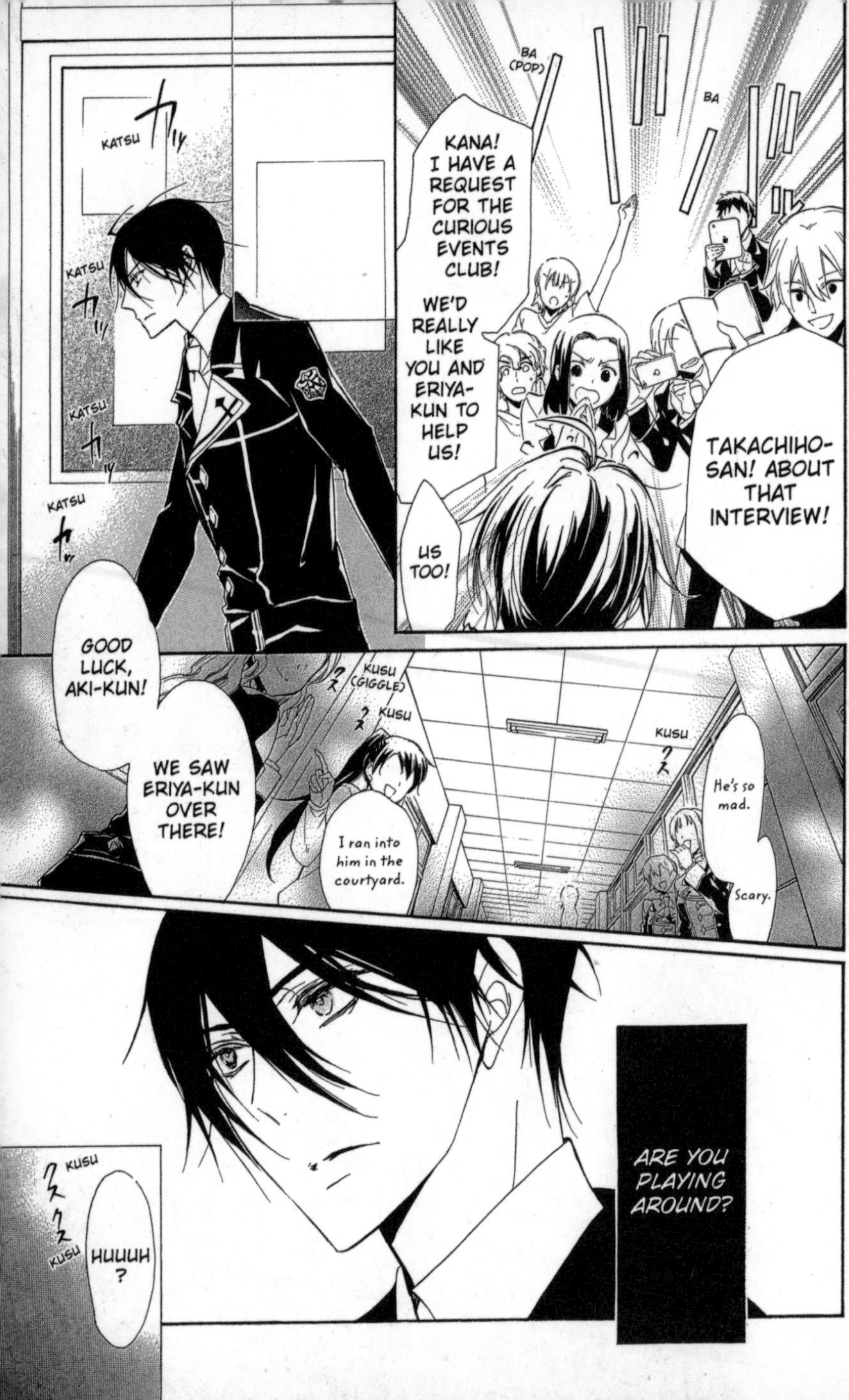
BA
BA (POP)
KANA! I HAVE A REQUEST FOR THE CURIOUS EVENTS CLUB!
TAKACHIHO-SAN! ABOUT THAT INTERVIEW!
WE'D REALLY LIKE YOU AND ERIYA-KUN TO HELP US!
US TOO!
KATSU
KATSU
KATSU
KATSU
He's so mad.
Scary.
KUSU
KUSU (GIGGLE)
KUSU
I ran into him in the courtyard.
WE SAW ERIYA-KUN OVER THERE!
GOOD LUCK, AKI-KUN!
ARE YOU PLAYING AROUND?
KUSU
KUSU
HUUUH?

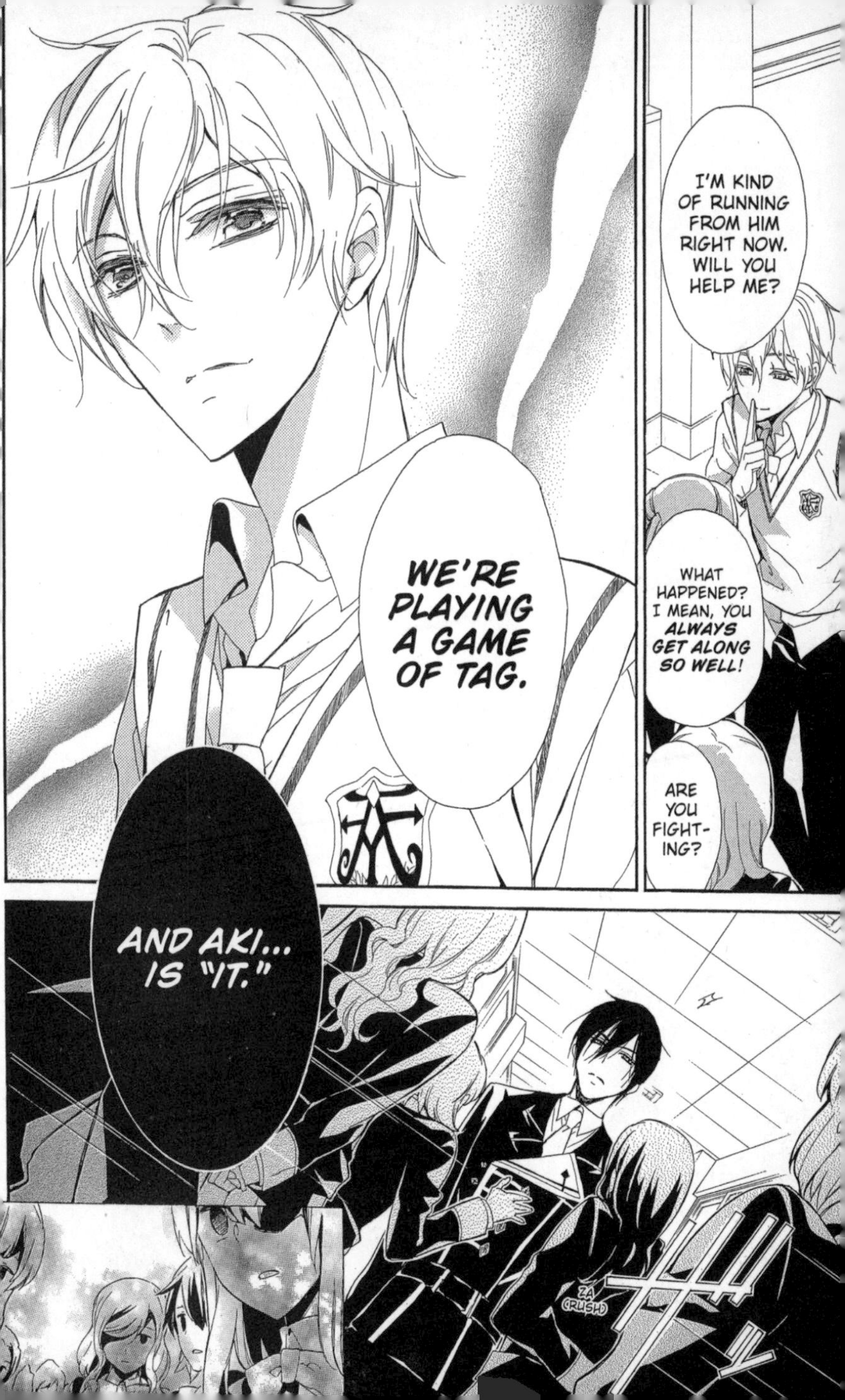
I'M KIND OF RUNNING FROM HIM RIGHT NOW. WILL YOU HELP ME?
WHAT HAPPENED? I MEAN, YOU ALWAYS GET ALONG SO WELL!
ARE YOU FIGHT-ING?
WE'RE PLAYING A GAME OF TAG.
AND AKI... IS "IT."
ZA (RUSH)

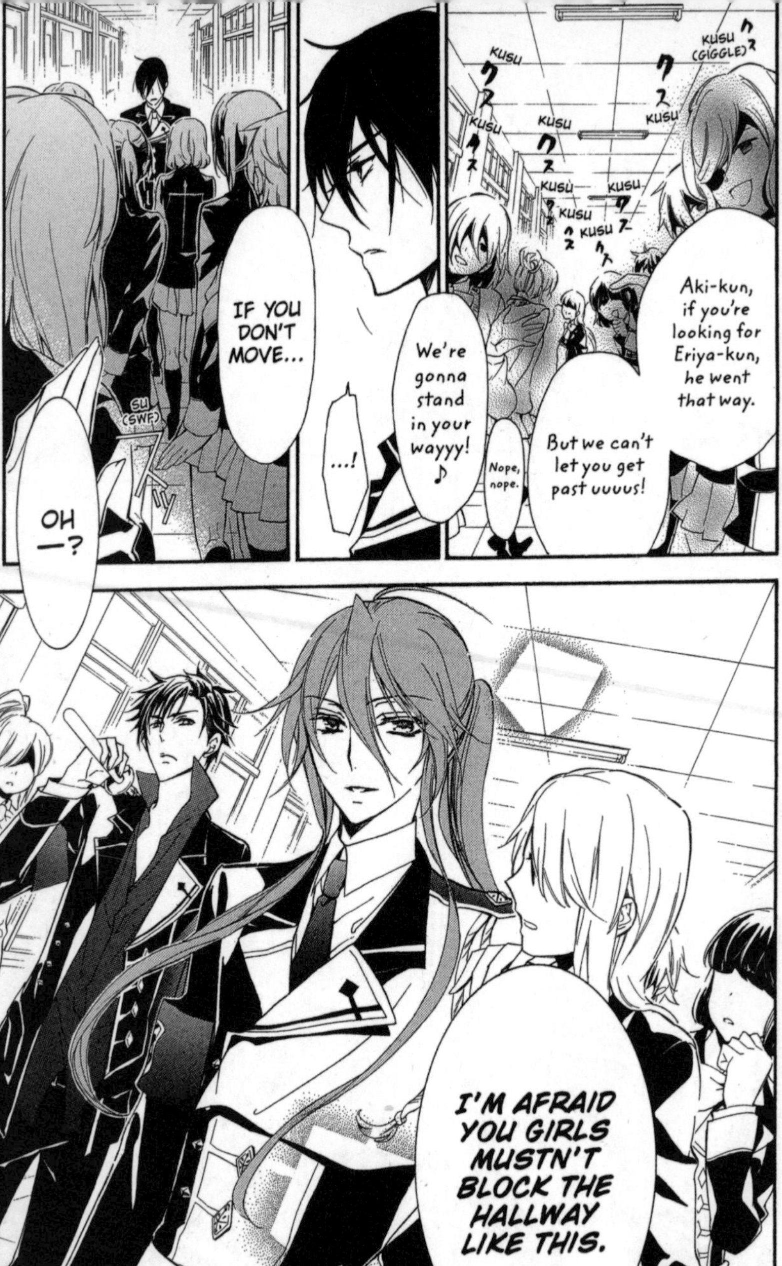
KUSU (GIGGLE)
KUSU
KUSU
KUSU
KUSU
KUSU
KUSU
KUSU
KUSU
Aki-kun, if you're looking for Eriya-kun, he went that way.
But we can't let you get past uuuus!
Nope, nope.
We're gonna stand in your wayyy! ♪
...!
IF YOU DON'T MOVE...
SU (SWF)
OH—?
I'M AFRAID YOU GIRLS MUSTN'T BLOCK THE HALLWAY LIKE THIS.

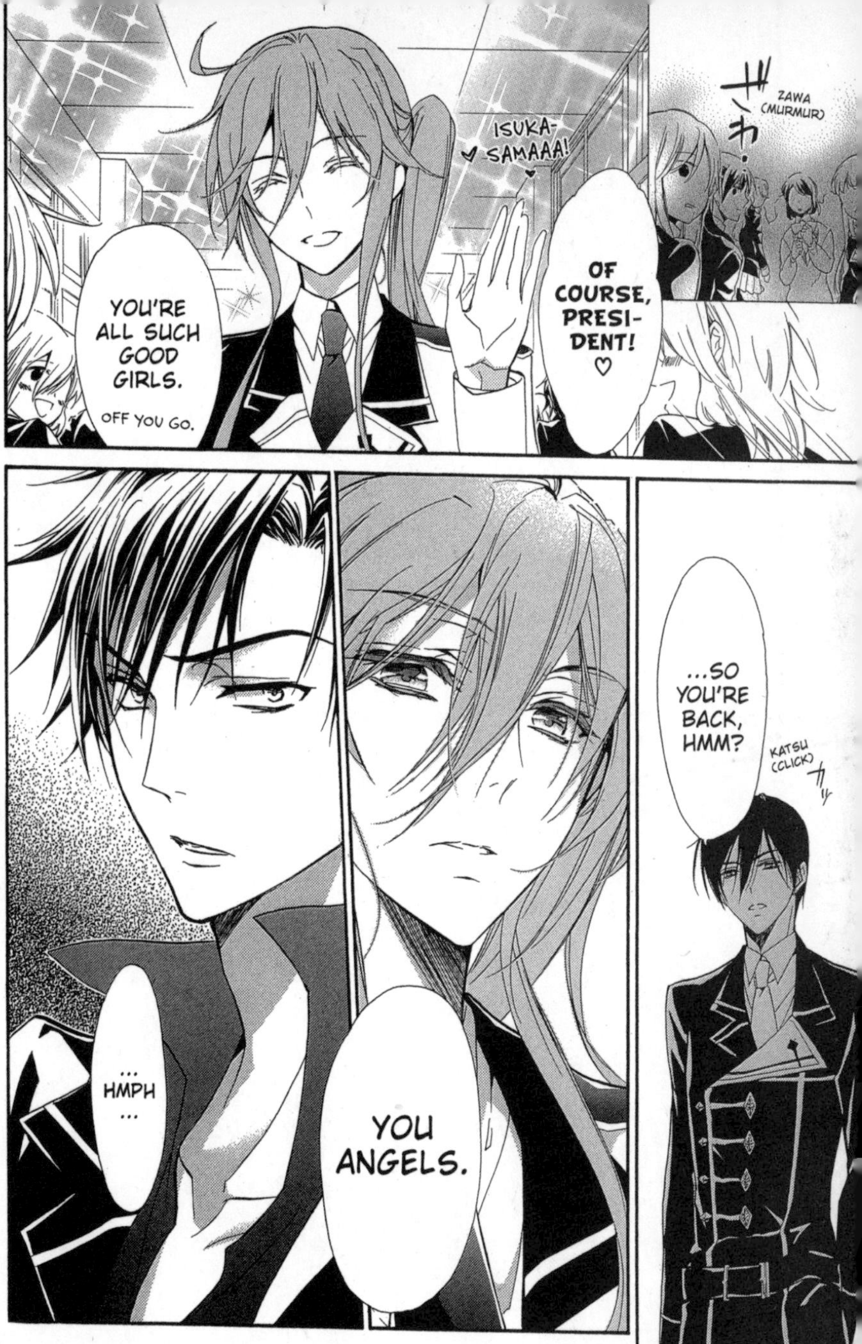
ZAWA (MURMUR)
ISUKA-SAMAAA!
OF COURSE, PRESI-DENT! ♡
YOU'RE ALL SUCH GOOD GIRLS.
OFF YOU GO.
...SO YOU'RE BACK, HMM?
KATSU (CLICK)
YOU ANGELS.
...HMPH...

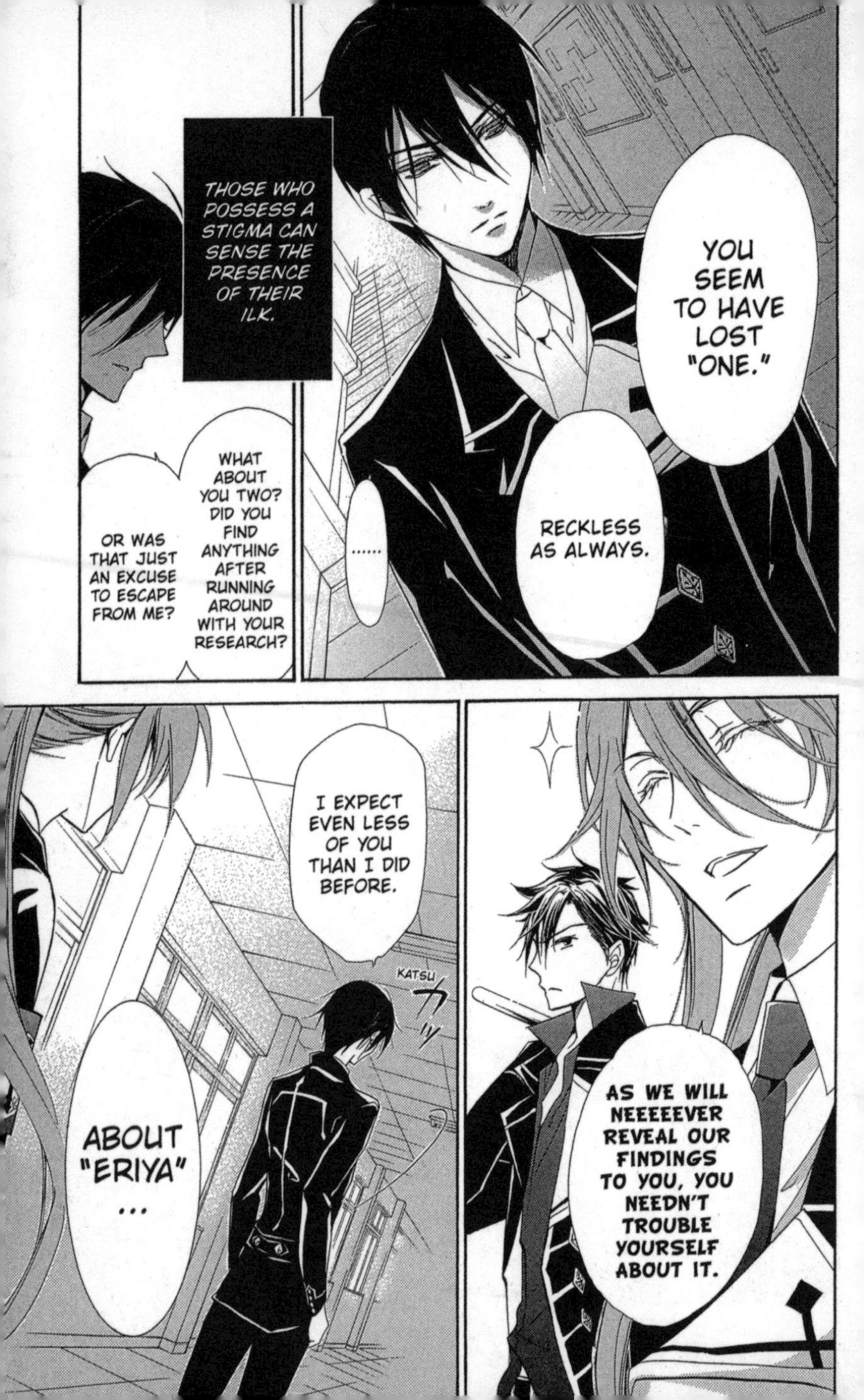

THOSE WHO POSSESS A STIGMA CAN SENSE THE PRESENCE OF THEIR ILK.
YOU SEEM TO HAVE LOST "ONE."
RECKLESS AS ALWAYS.
......
WHAT ABOUT YOU TWO? DID YOU FIND ANYTHING AFTER RUNNING AROUND WITH YOUR RESEARCH?
OR WAS THAT JUST AN EXCUSE TO ESCAPE FROM ME?
AS WE WILL NEEEEEVER REVEAL OUR FINDINGS TO YOU, YOU NEEDN'T TROUBLE YOURSELF ABOUT IT.
I EXPECT EVEN LESS OF YOU THAN I DID BEFORE.
KATSU
ABOUT "ERIYA" ...

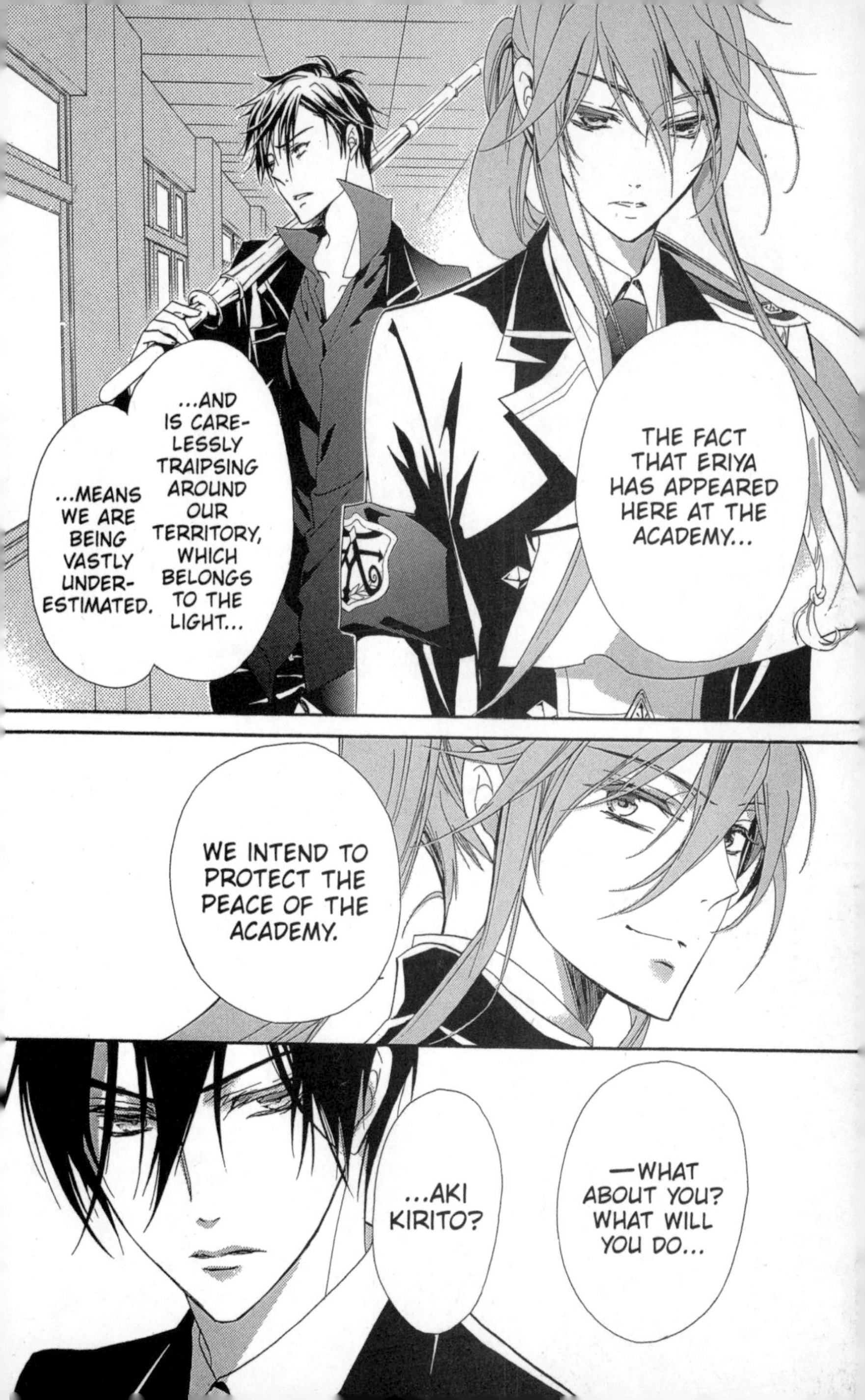
THE FACT THAT ERIYA HAS APPEARED HERE AT THE ACADEMY...
...AND IS CARE-LESSLY TRAIPSING AROUND OUR TERRITORY, WHICH BELONGS TO THE LIGHT...
...MEANS WE ARE BEING VASTLY UNDER-ESTIMATED.
WE INTEND TO PROTECT THE PEACE OF THE ACADEMY.
—WHAT ABOUT YOU? WHAT WILL YOU DO...
...AKI KIRITO?

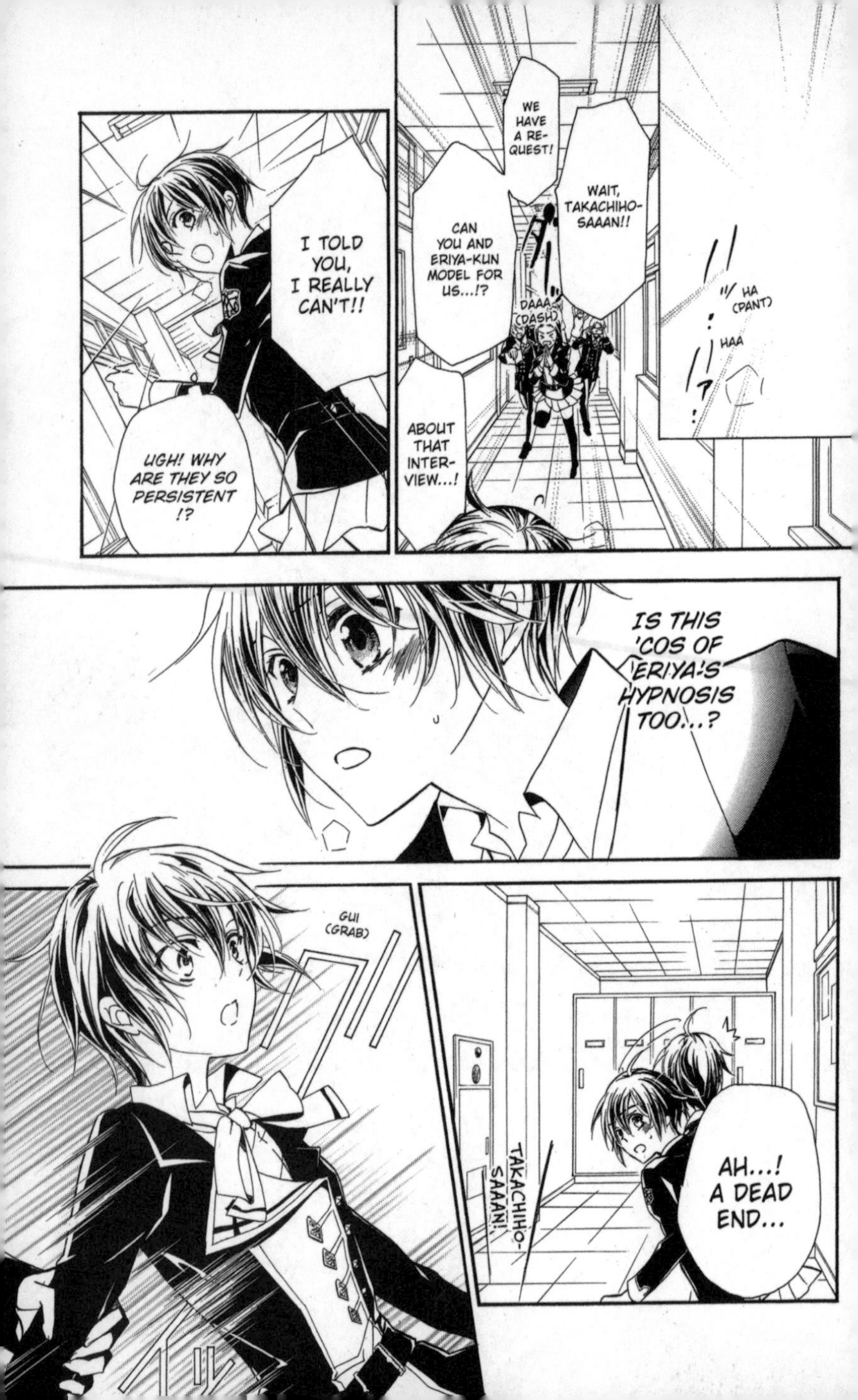
HA (PANT)
HAA
WAIT, TAKACHIHO-SAAAN!!
WE HAVE A RE-QUEST!
CAN YOU AND ERIYA-KUN MODEL FOR US...!?
DAAA (DASH)
ABOUT THAT INTER-VIEW...!
I TOLD YOU, I REALLY CAN'T!!
UGH! WHY ARE THEY SO PERSISTENT!?
IS THIS 'COS OF ERIYA'S HYPNOSIS TOO...?
TAKACHIHO-SAAAN!
AH...! A DEAD END...
GUI (GRAB)

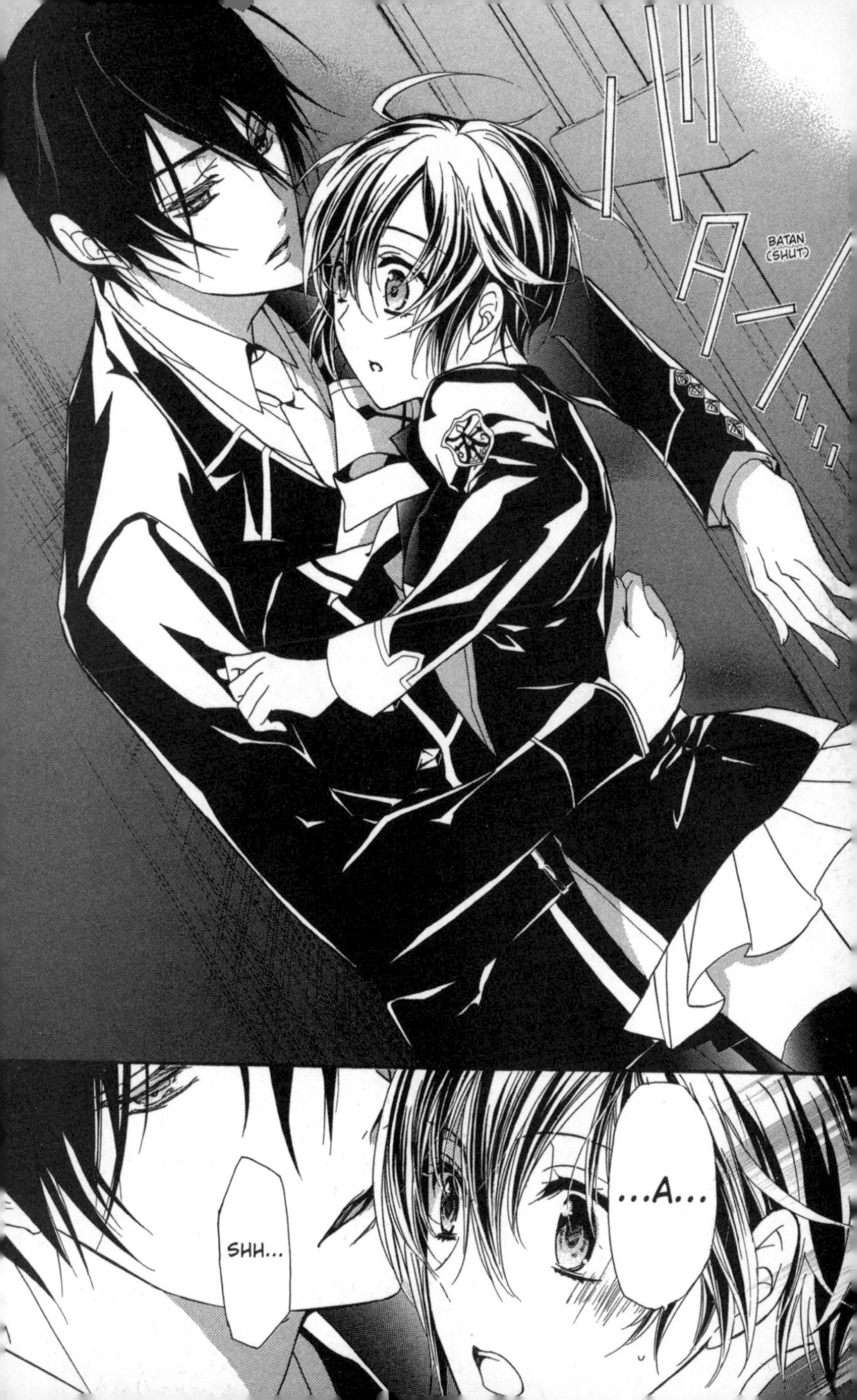
BATAN (SHUT)
...A...
SHH...

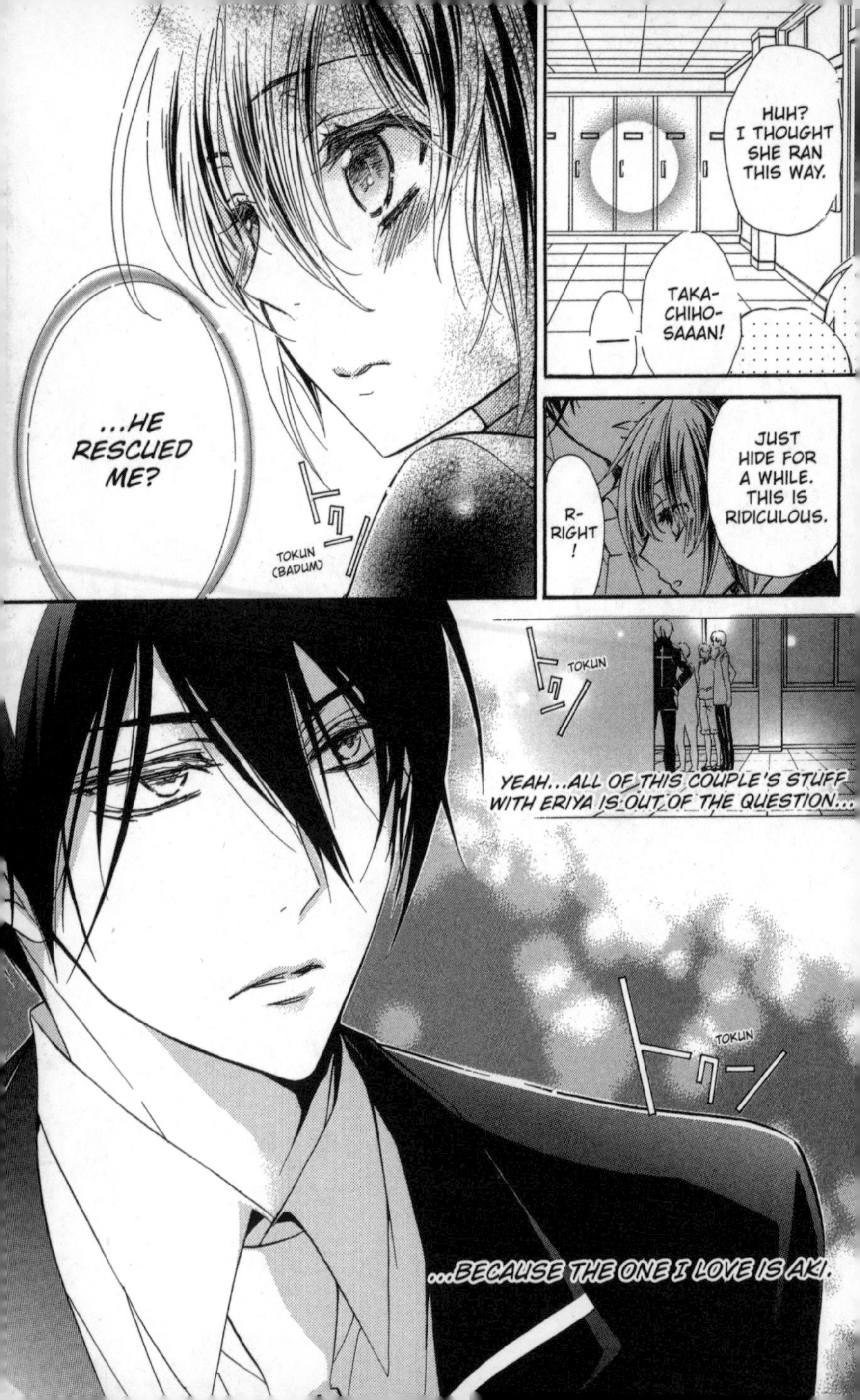
HUH? I THOUGHT SHE RAN THIS WAY.
TAKA-CHIHO-SAAAN!
JUST HIDE FOR A WHILE. THIS IS RIDICULOUS.
R-RIGHT!
...HE RESCUED ME?
TOKUN (BADUM)
TOKUN
YEAH...ALL OF THIS COUPLE'S STUFF WITH ERIYA IS OUT OF THE QUESTION...
TOKUN
...BECAUSE THE ONE I LOVE IS AKI.

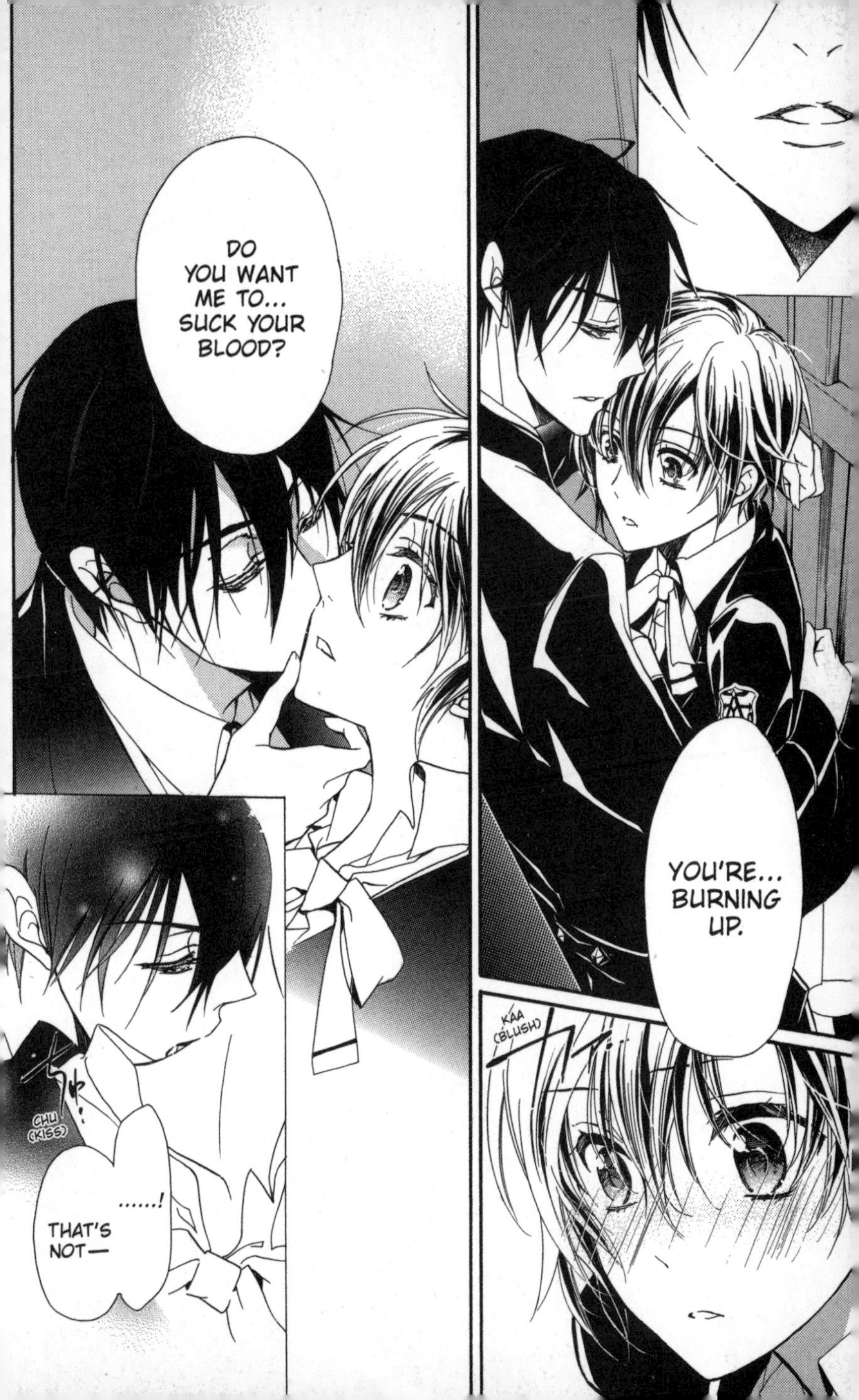
YOU'RE... BURNING UP.
KAA (BLUSH)
DO YOU WANT ME TO... SUCK YOUR BLOOD?
CHU (KISS)
......! THAT'S NOT—

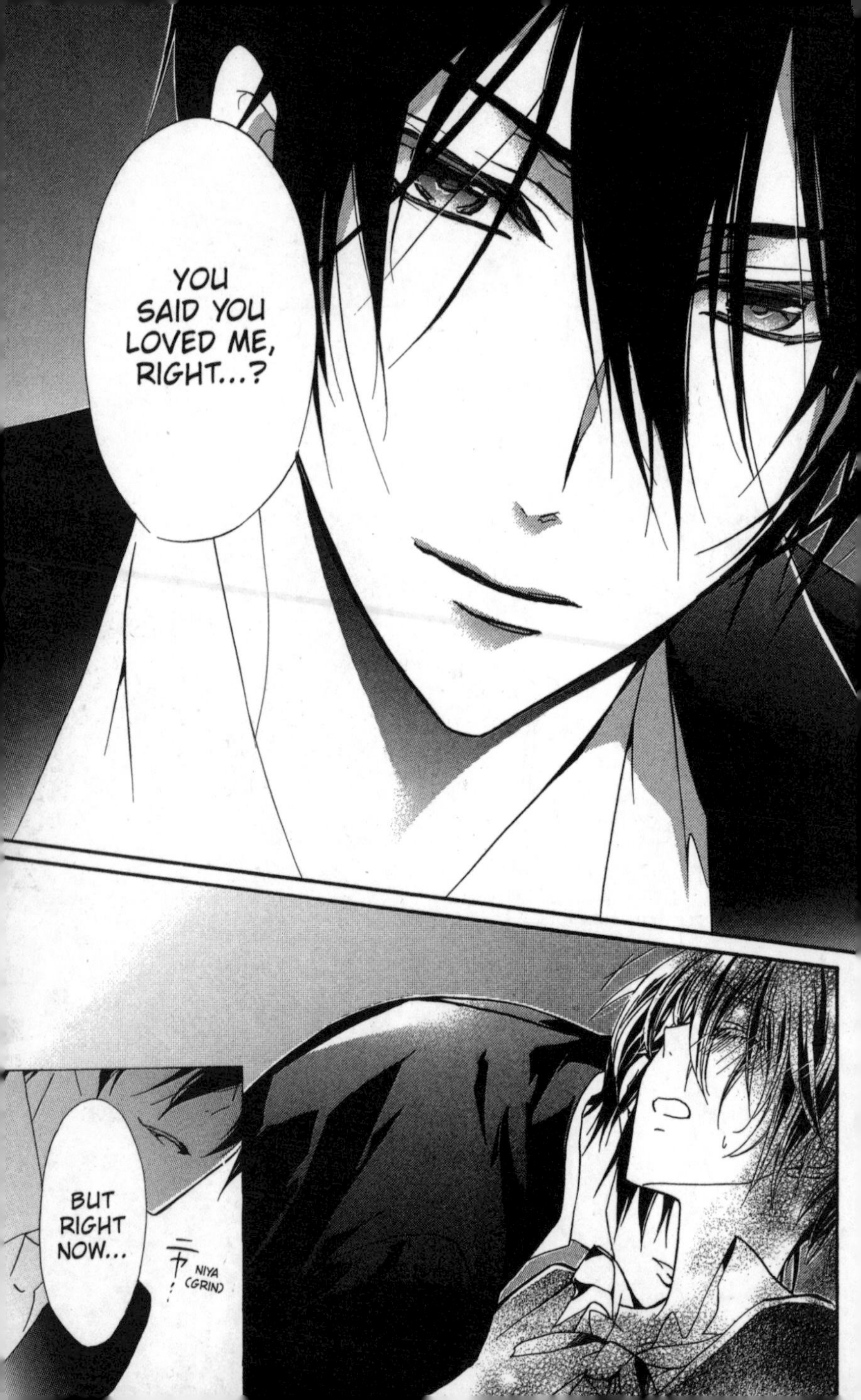
YOU SAID YOU LOVED ME, RIGHT...?
BUT RIGHT NOW...
NIYA (GRIN)

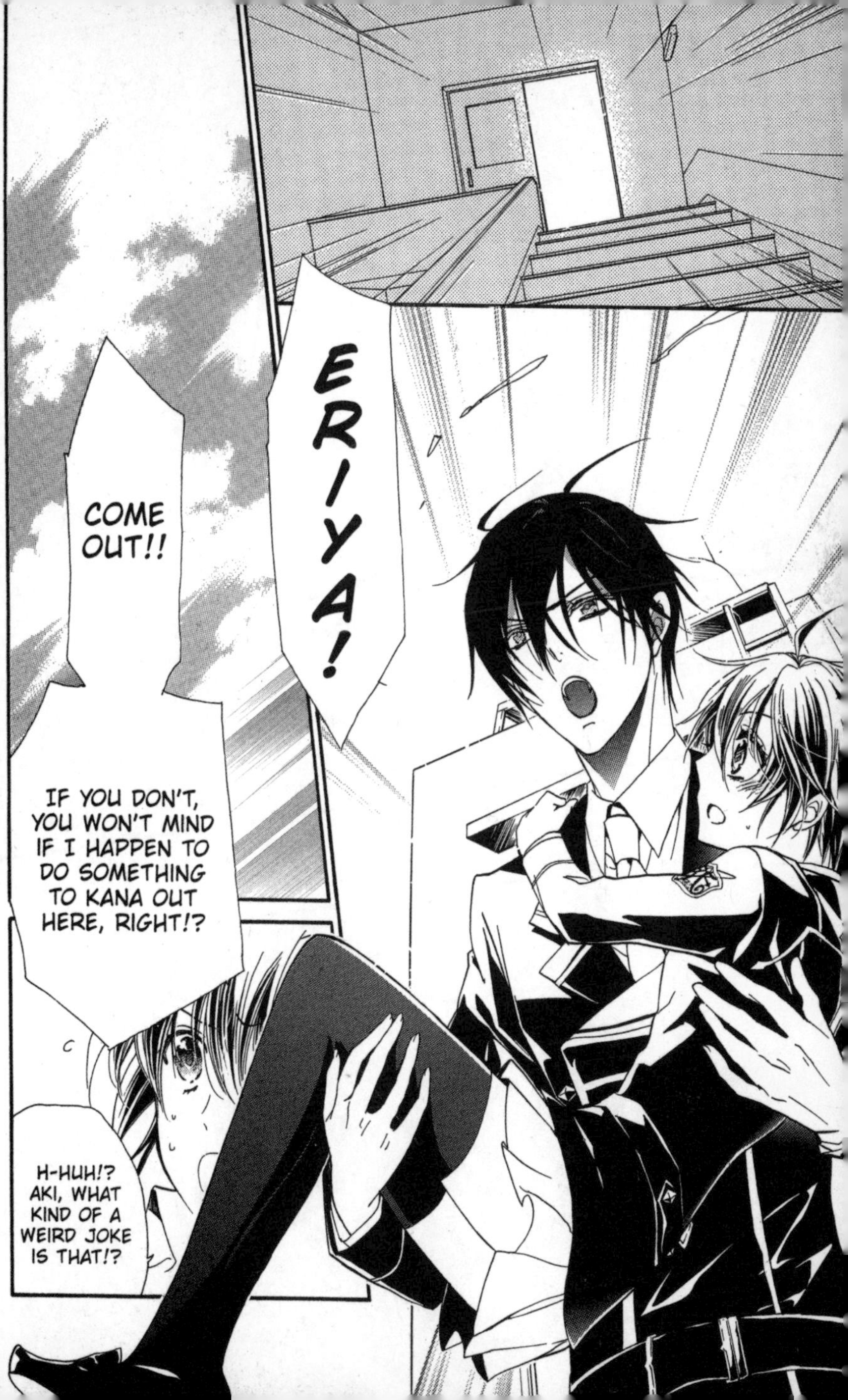
ERIYA!
COME OUT!!
IF YOU DON'T, YOU WON'T MIND IF I HAPPEN TO DO SOMETHING TO KANA OUT HERE, RIGHT!?
H-HUH!? AKI, WHAT KIND OF A WEIRD JOKE IS THAT!?

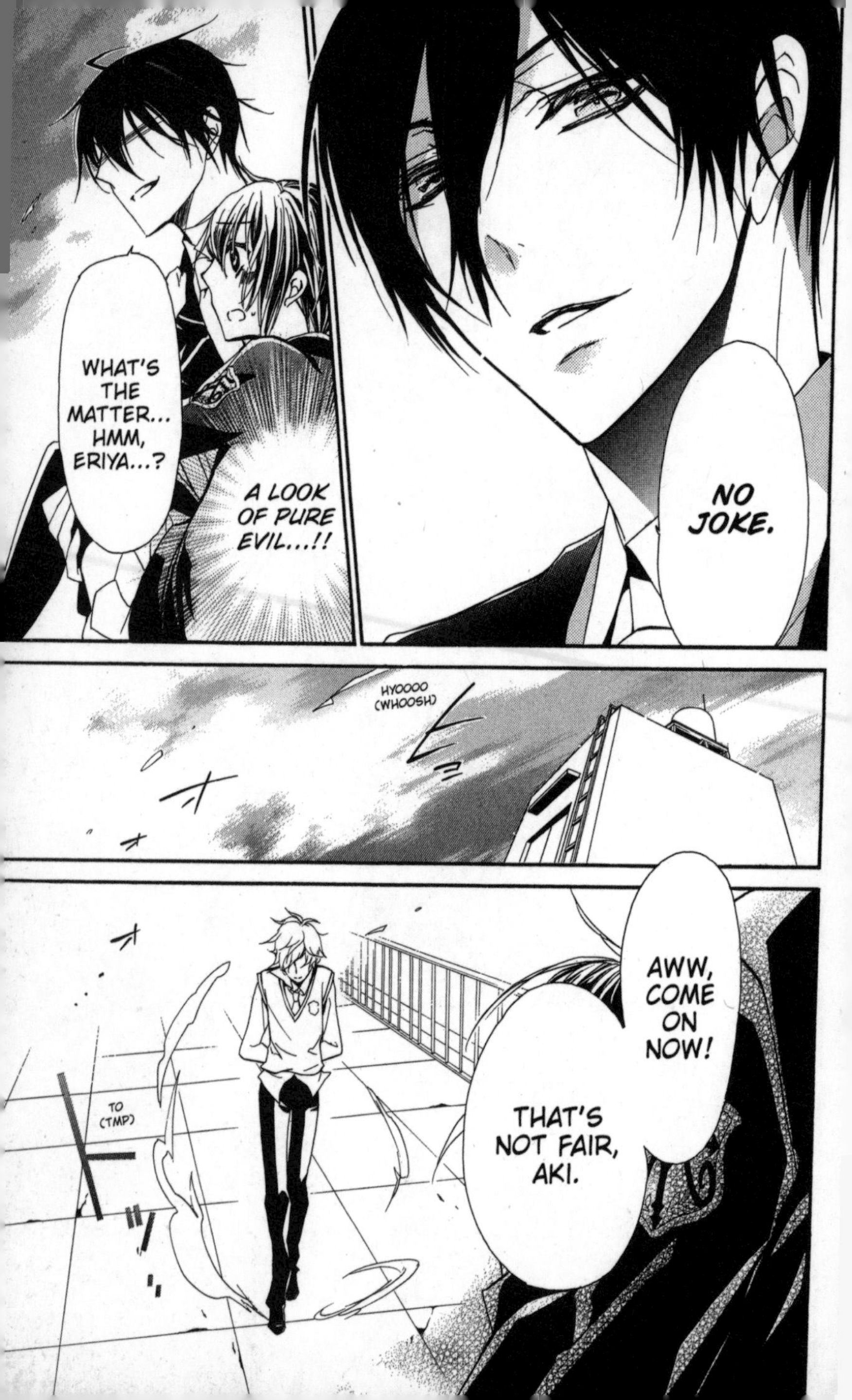
NO JOKE.
WHAT'S THE MATTER... HMM, ERIYA...?
A LOOK OF PURE EVIL...!!
HYOOOO (WHOOSH)
AWW, COME ON NOW!
THAT'S NOT FAIR, AKI.
TO (TMP)

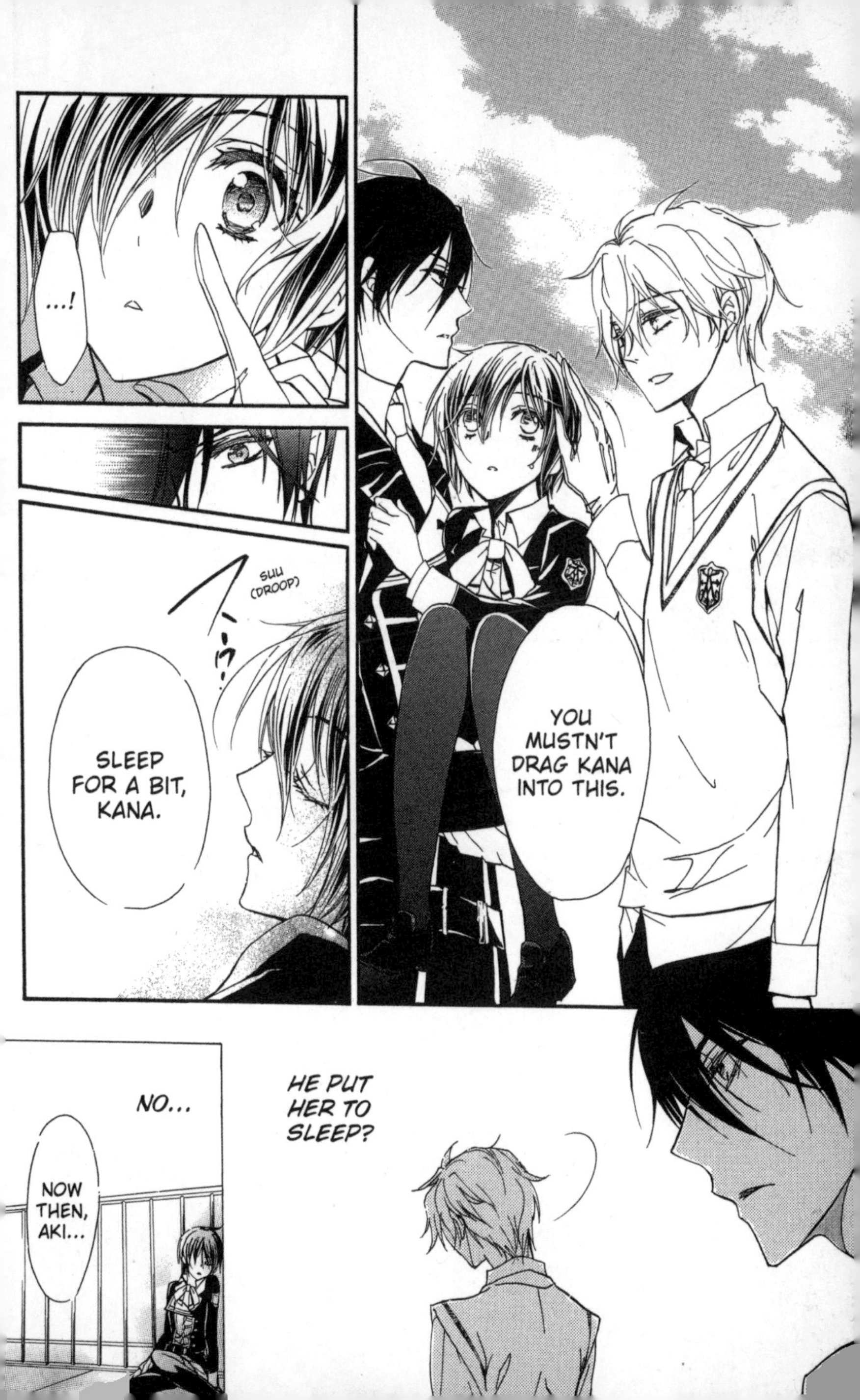
YOU MUSTN'T DRAG KANA INTO THIS.
...!
SUU (DROOP)
SLEEP FOR A BIT, KANA.
HE PUT HER TO SLEEP?
NO...
NOW THEN, AKI...

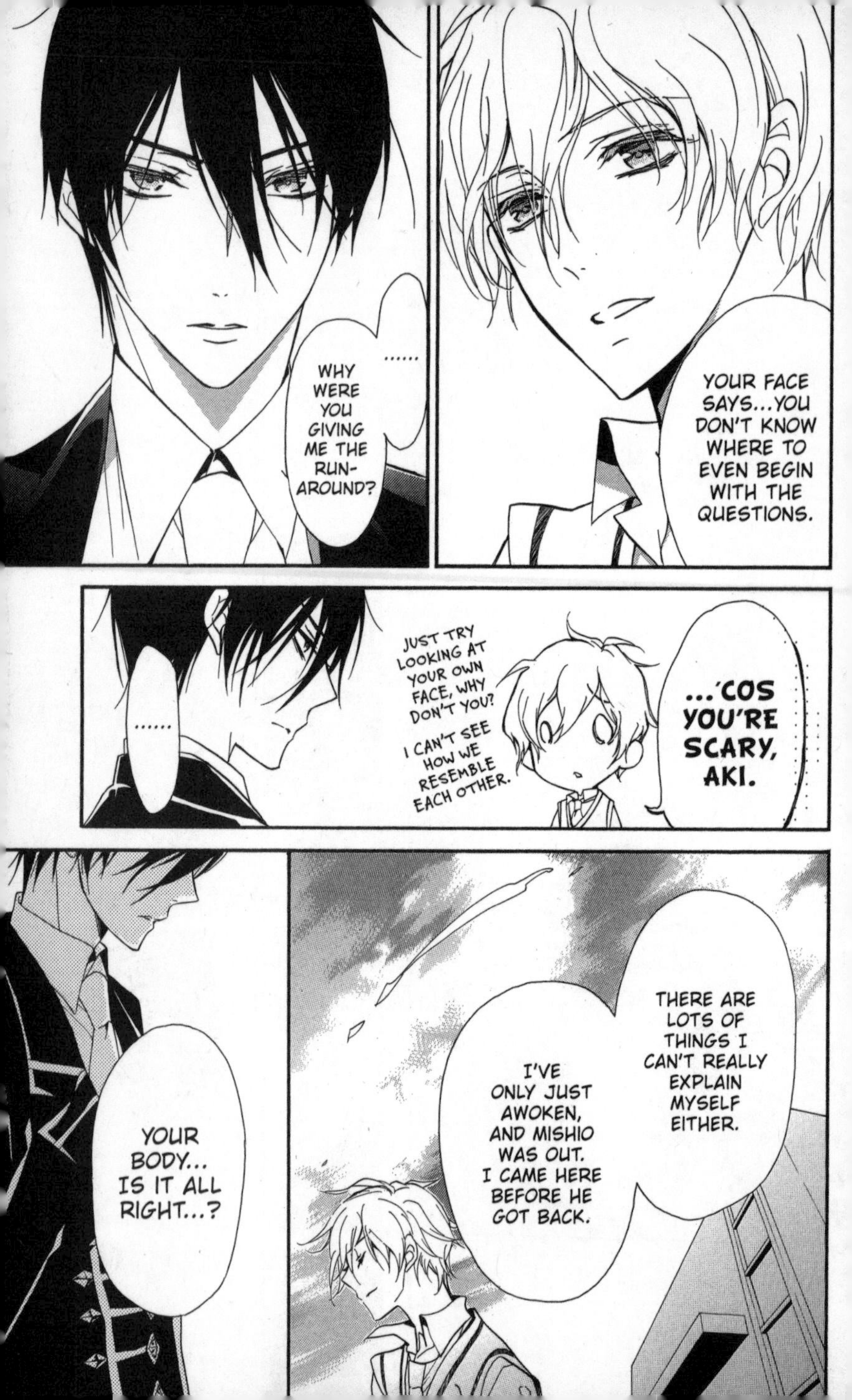
YOUR FACE SAYS...YOU DON'T KNOW WHERE TO EVEN BEGIN WITH THE QUESTIONS.
......
WHY WERE YOU GIVING ME THE RUN-AROUND?
...'COS YOU'RE SCARY, AKI.
JUST TRY LOOKING AT YOUR OWN FACE, WHY DON'T YOU?
I CAN'T SEE HOW WE RESEMBLE EACH OTHER.
......
THERE ARE LOTS OF THINGS I CAN'T REALLY EXPLAIN MYSELF EITHER.
I'VE ONLY JUST AWOKEN, AND MISHIO WAS OUT. I CAME HERE BEFORE HE GOT BACK.
YOUR BODY... IS IT ALL RIGHT...?

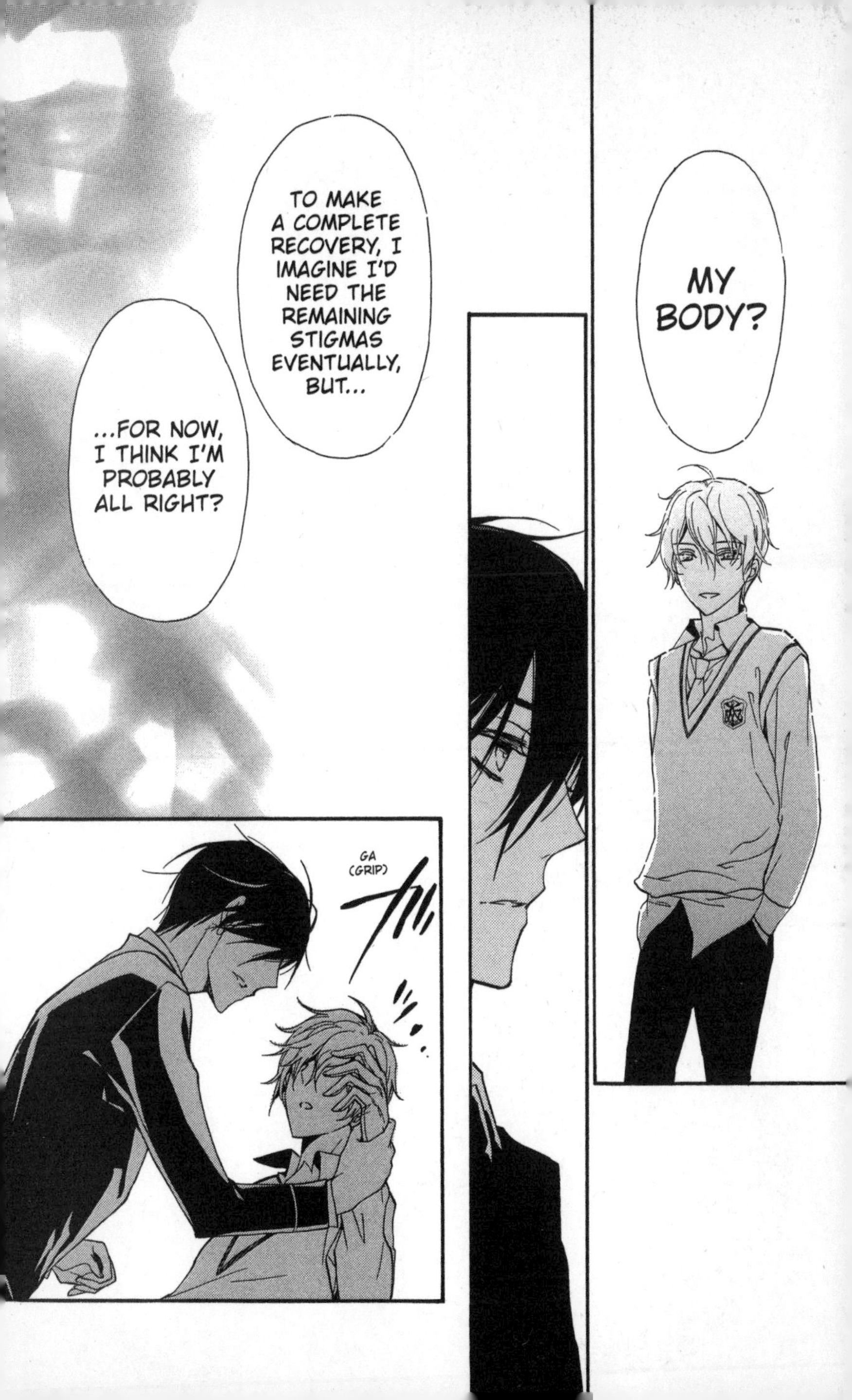
MY BODY?
TO MAKE A COMPLETE RECOVERY, I IMAGINE I'D NEED THE REMAINING STIGMAS EVENTUALLY, BUT...
...FOR NOW, I THINK I'M PROBABLY ALL RIGHT?
GA (GRIP)

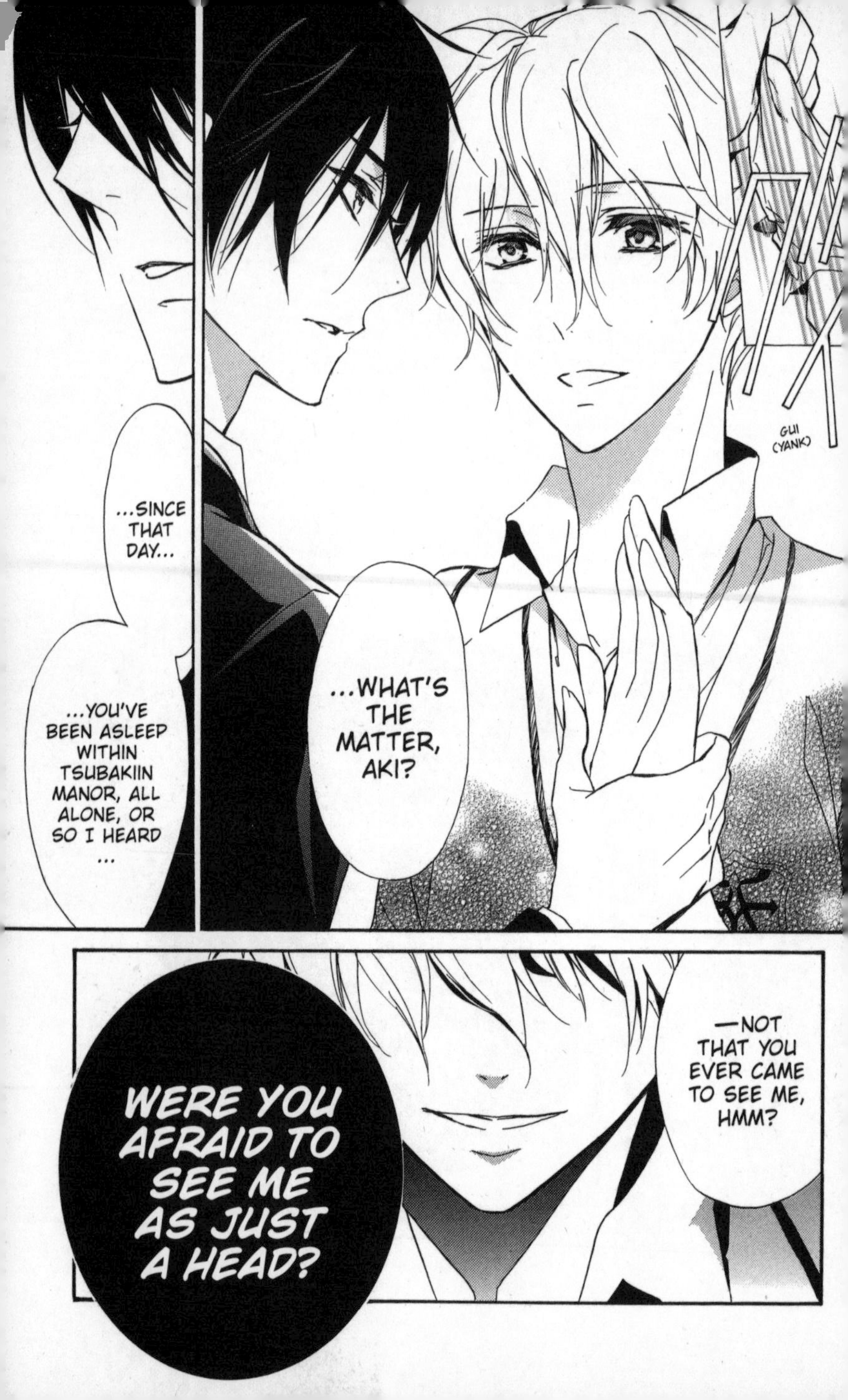
GUI (YANK)
...WHAT'S THE MATTER, AKI?
...SINCE THAT DAY...
...YOU'VE BEEN ASLEEP WITHIN TSUBAKIIN MANOR, ALL ALONE, OR SO I HEARD ...
—NOT THAT YOU EVER CAME TO SEE ME, HMM?
WERE YOU AFRAID TO SEE ME AS JUST A HEAD?

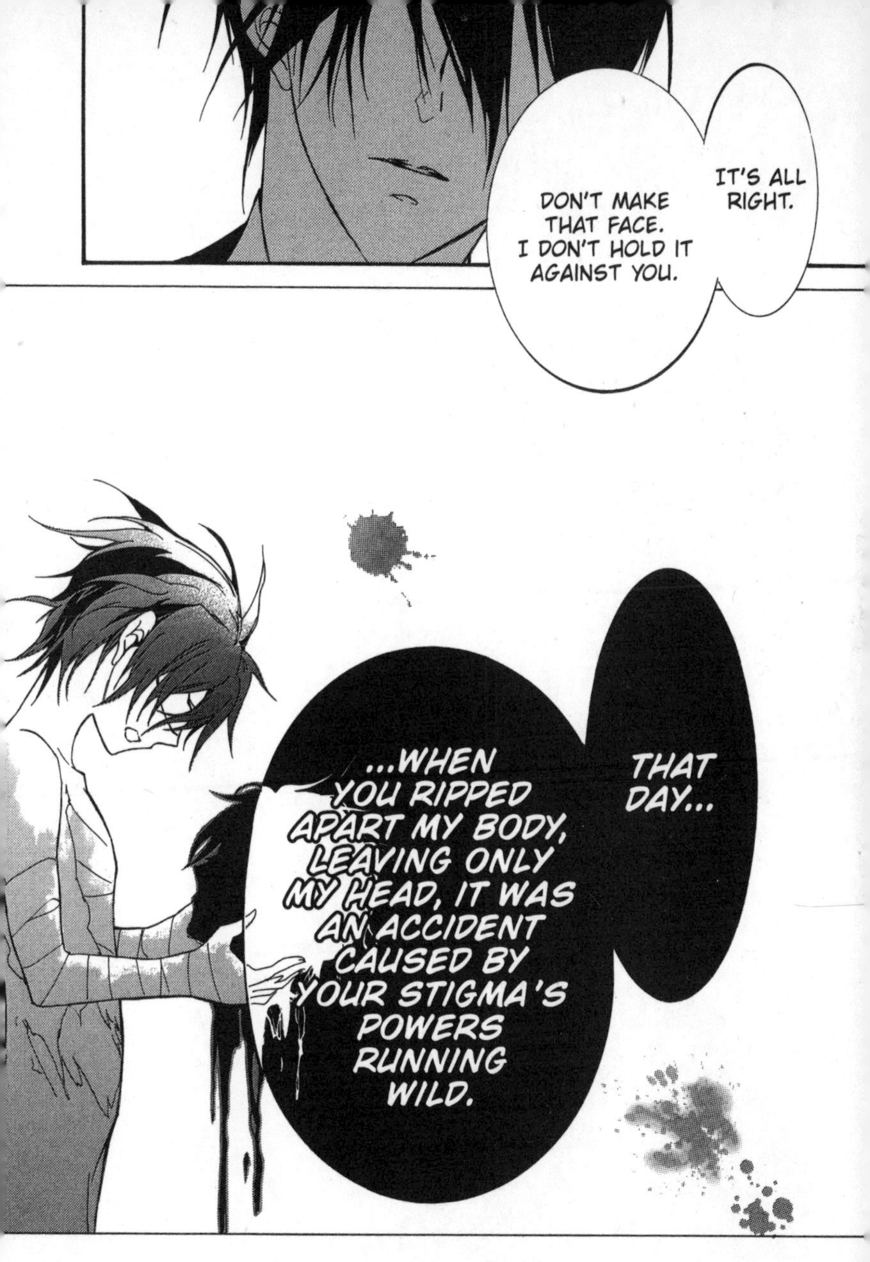
IT'S ALL RIGHT.
DON'T MAKE THAT FACE. I DON'T HOLD IT AGAINST YOU.
THAT DAY...
...WHEN YOU RIPPED APART MY BODY, LEAVING ONLY MY HEAD, IT WAS AN ACCIDENT CAUSED BY YOUR STIGMA'S POWERS RUNNING WILD.

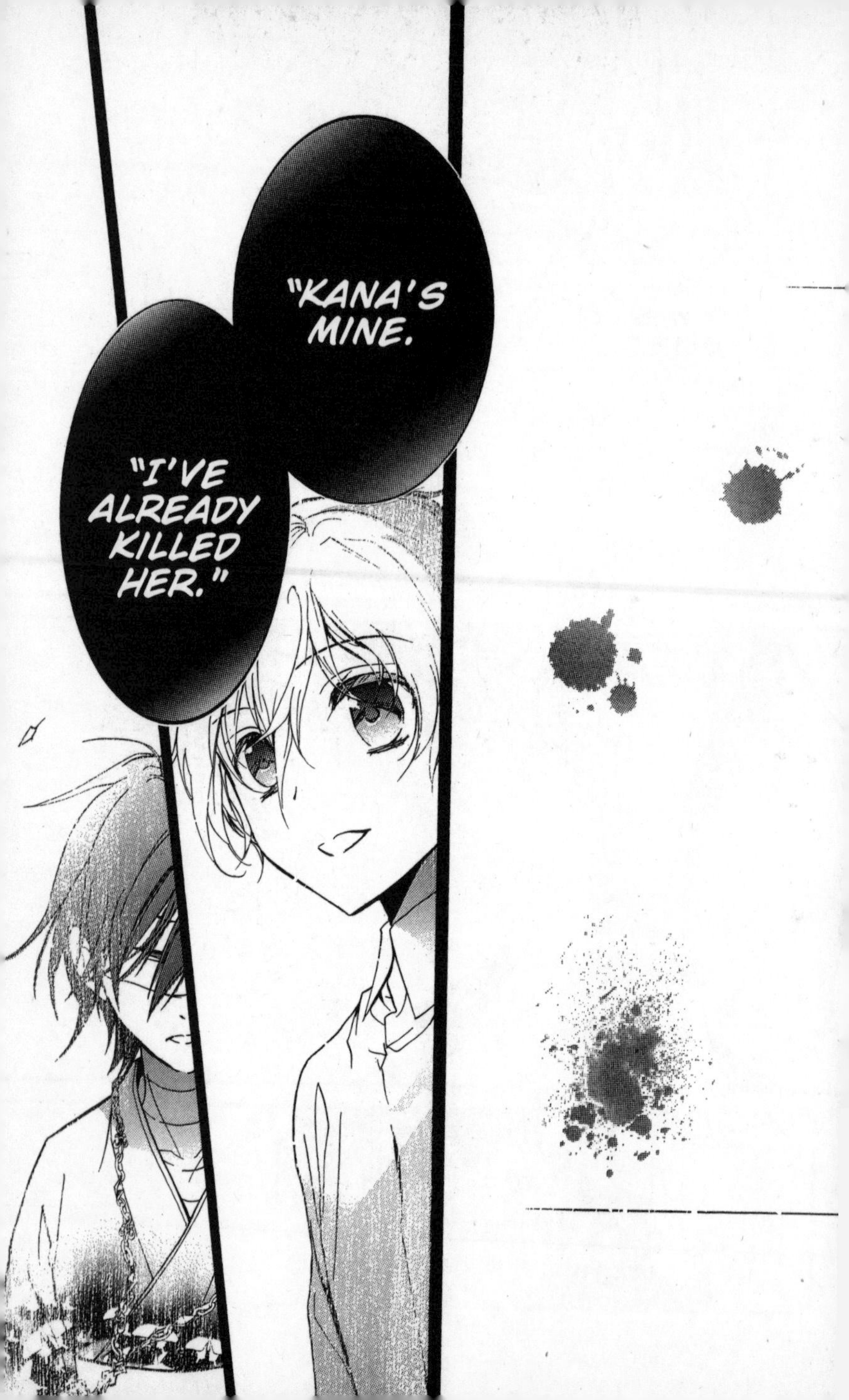
"KANA'S MINE.
"I'VE ALREADY KILLED HER."

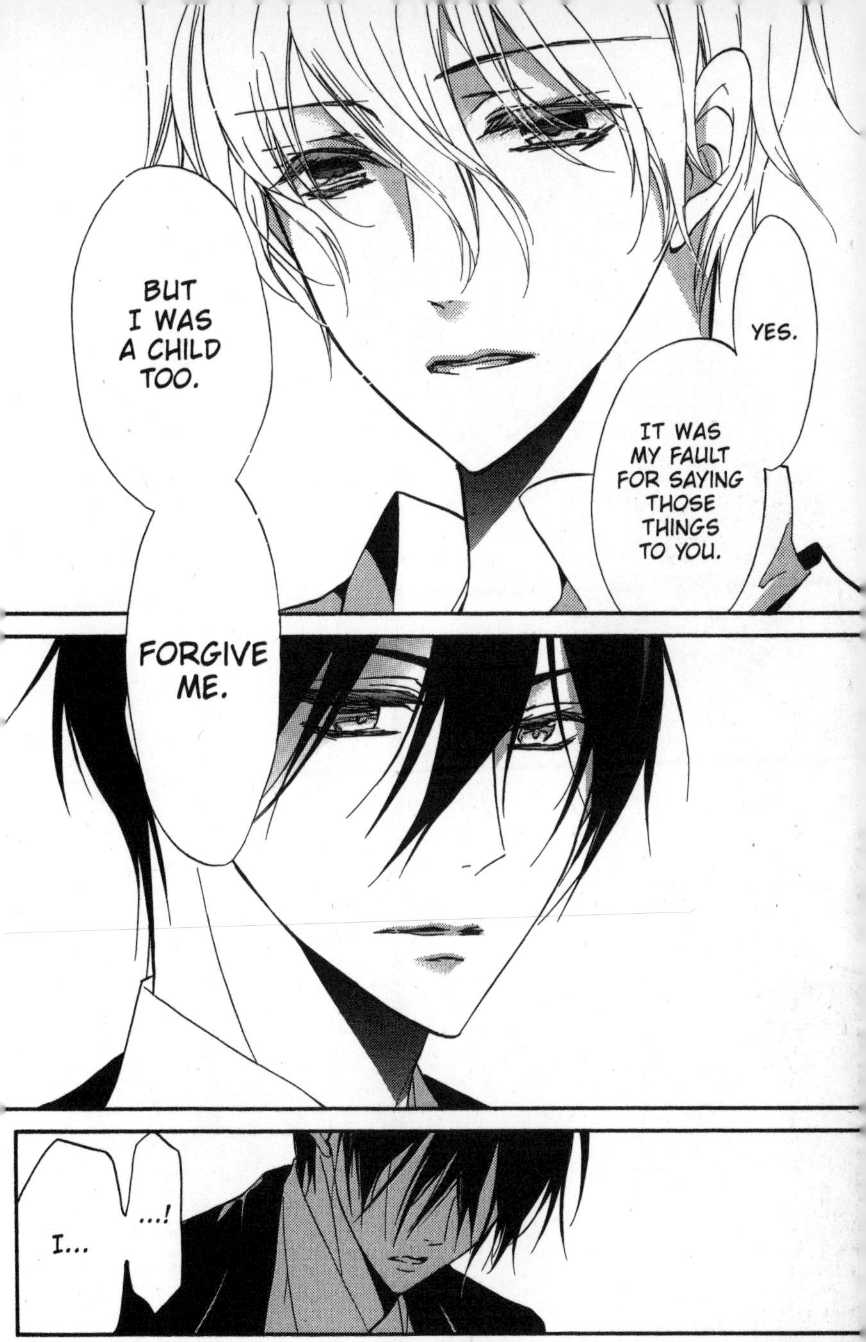
YES.
IT WAS MY FAULT FOR SAYING THOSE THINGS TO YOU.
BUT I WAS A CHILD TOO.
FORGIVE ME.
...!
I...

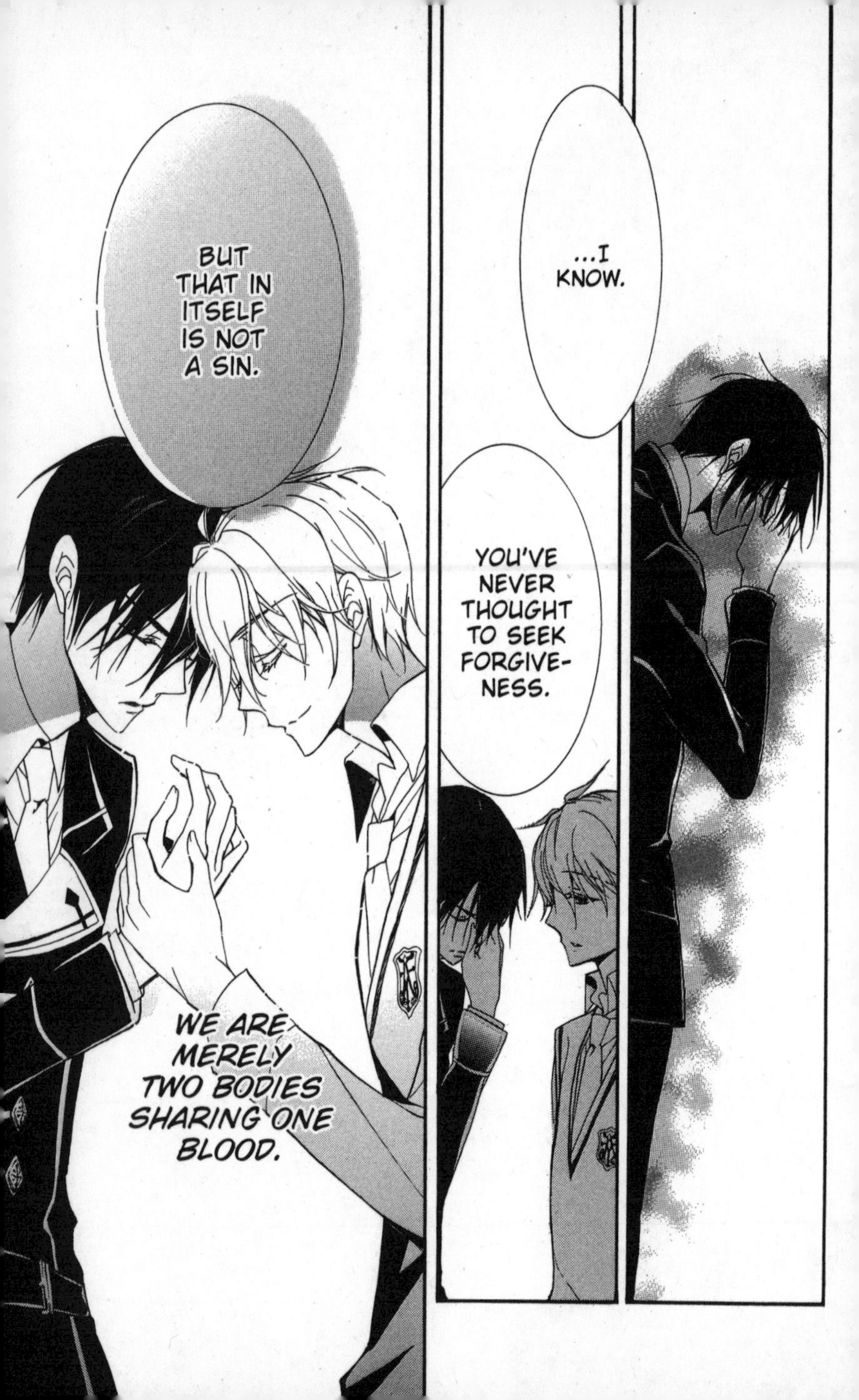
...I KNOW.
YOU'VE NEVER THOUGHT TO SEEK FORGIVE-NESS.
BUT THAT IN ITSELF IS NOT A SIN.
WE ARE MERELY TWO BODIES SHARING ONE BLOOD.

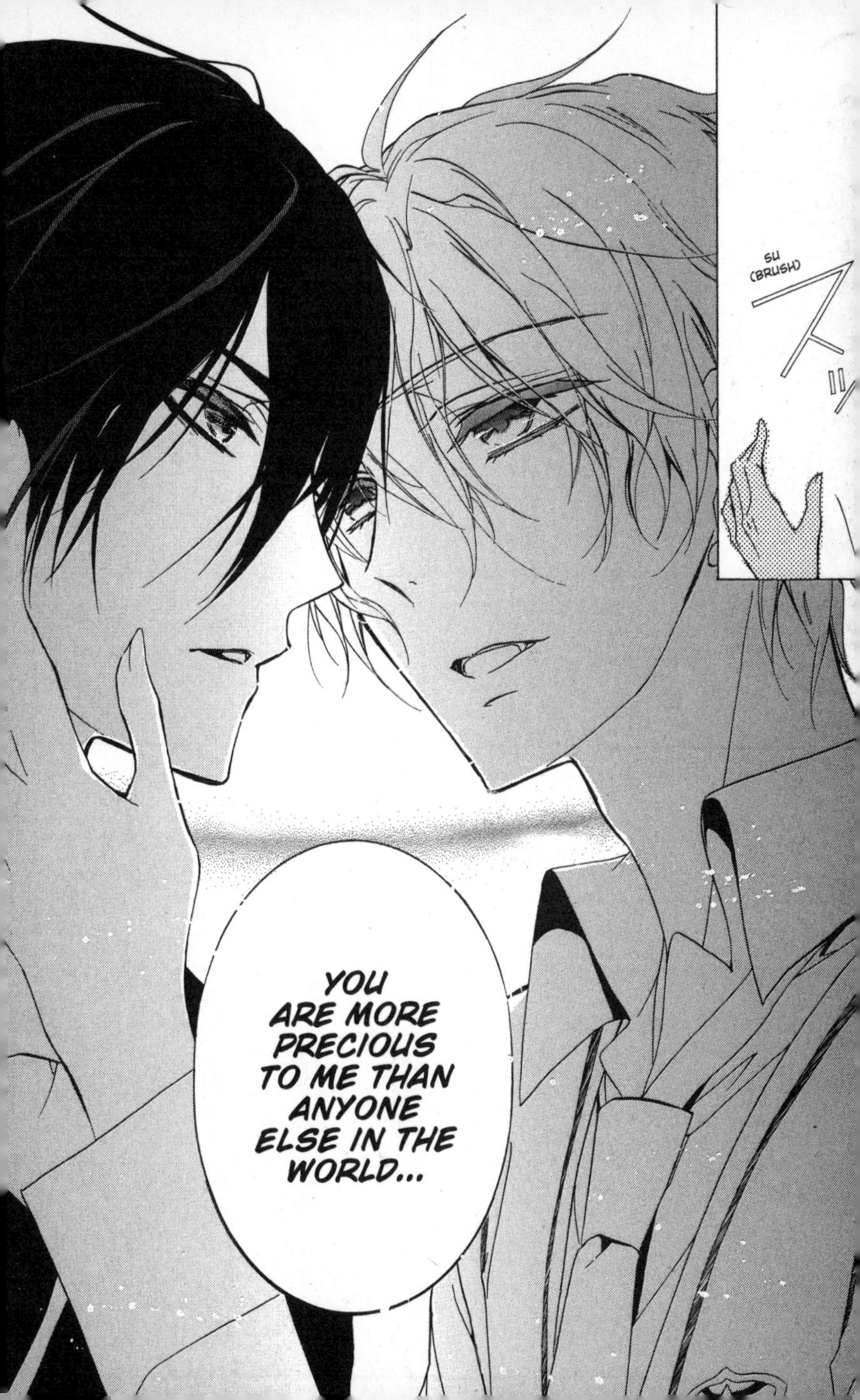
SU
(BRUSH)
YOU ARE MORE PRECIOUS TO ME THAN ANYONE ELSE IN THE WORLD...

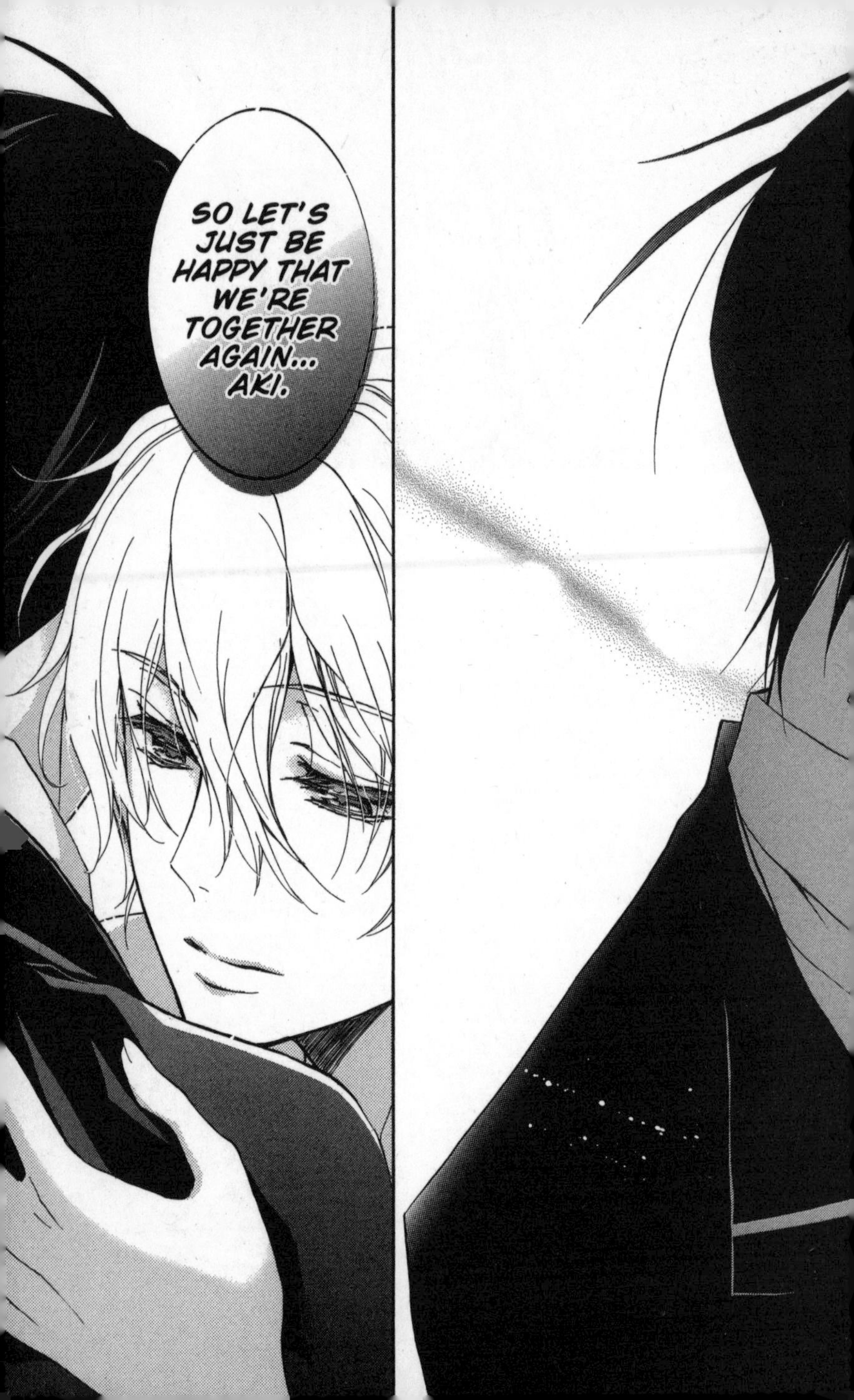
SO LET'S JUST BE HAPPY THAT WE'RE TOGETHER AGAIN... AKI.

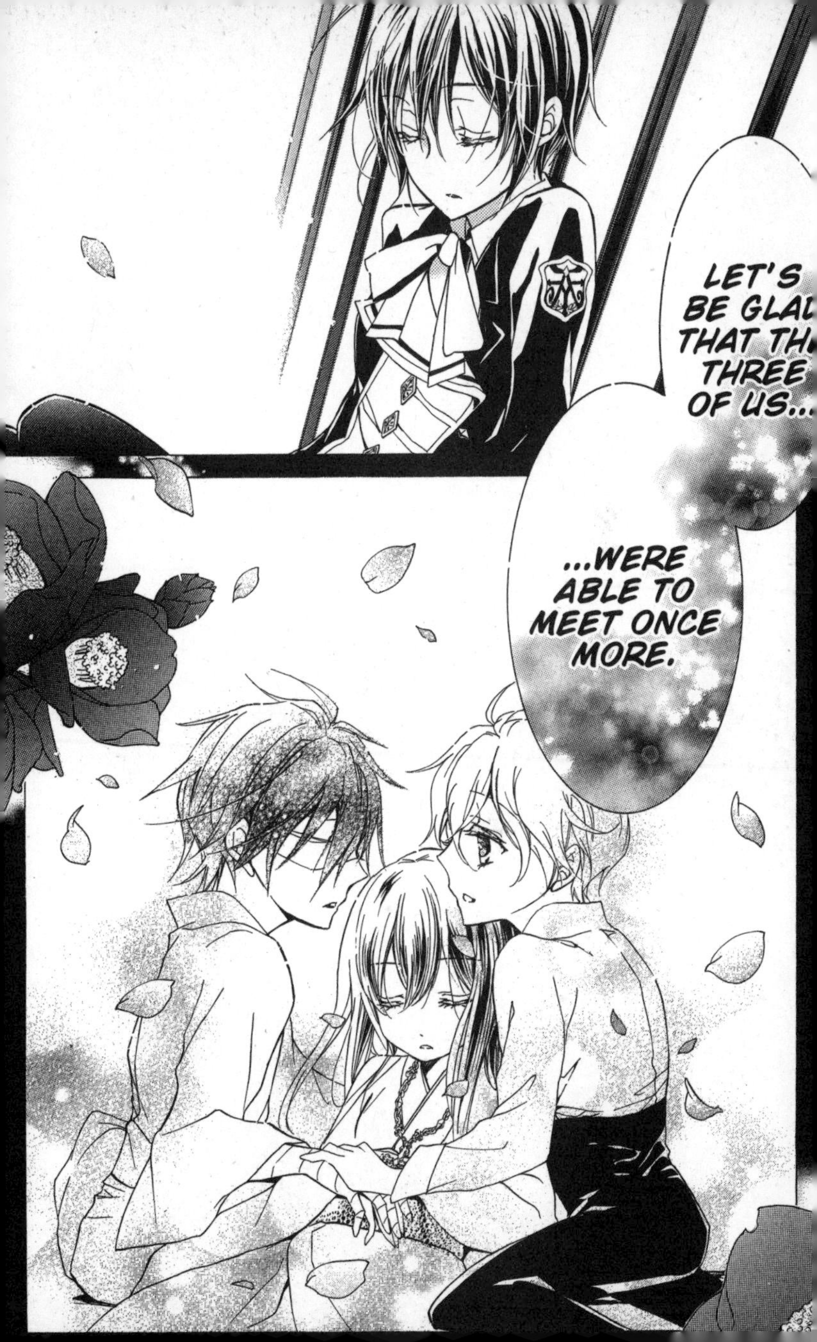
LET'S BE GLA THAT TH THREE OF US...
...WERE ABLE TO MEET ONCE MORE.

He's my only vampire

Aya Shouoto

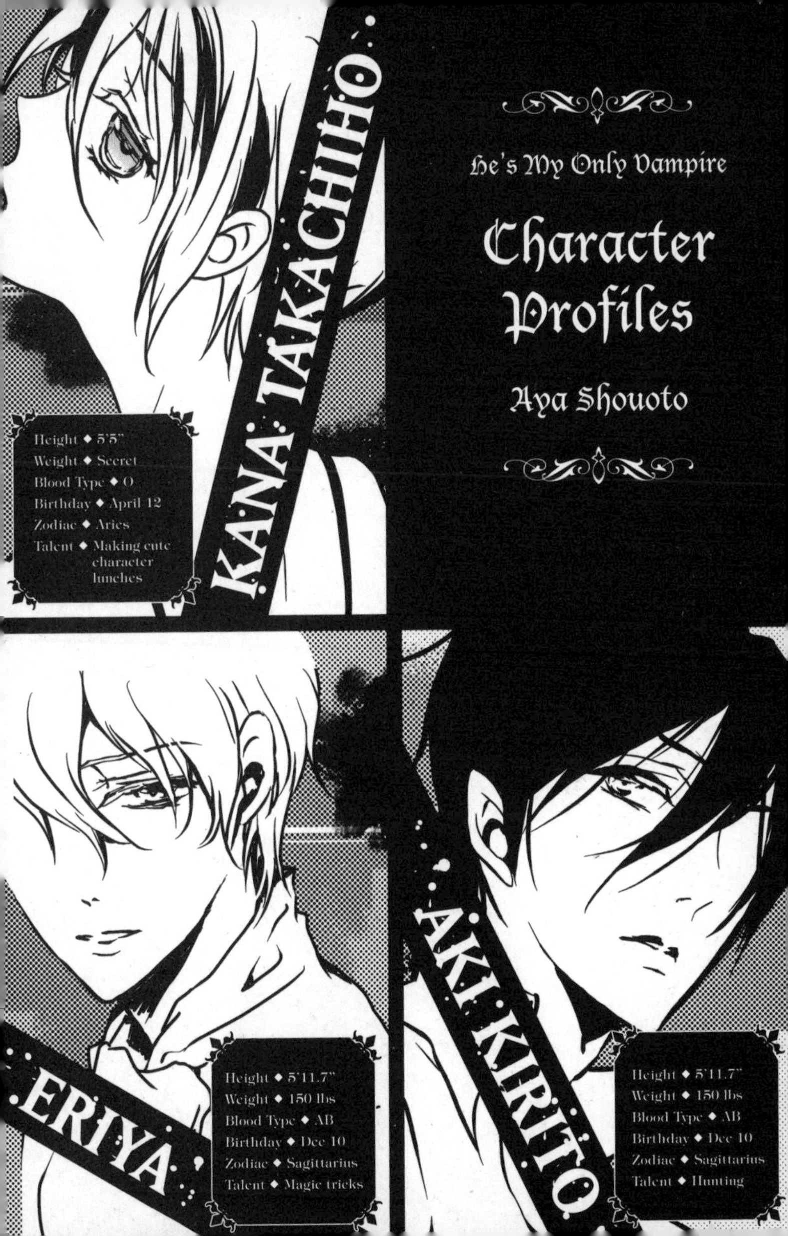
He's My Only Vampire
Character Profiles
Aya Shouoto
KANA TAKACHIHO
Height ◆ 5'5"
Weight ◆ Secret
Blood Type ◆ O
Birthday ◆ April 12
Zodiac ◆ Aries
Talent ◆ Making cute character lunches
AKI KIRITO
Height ◆ 5'11.7"
Weight ◆ 150 lbs
Blood Type ◆ AB
Birthday ◆ Dec 10
Zodiac ◆ Sagittarius
Talent ◆ Hunting
ERIYA
Height ◆ 5'11.7"
Weight ◆ 150 lbs
Blood Type ◆ AB
Birthday ◆ Dec 10
Zodiac ◆ Sagittarius
Talent ◆ Magic tricks

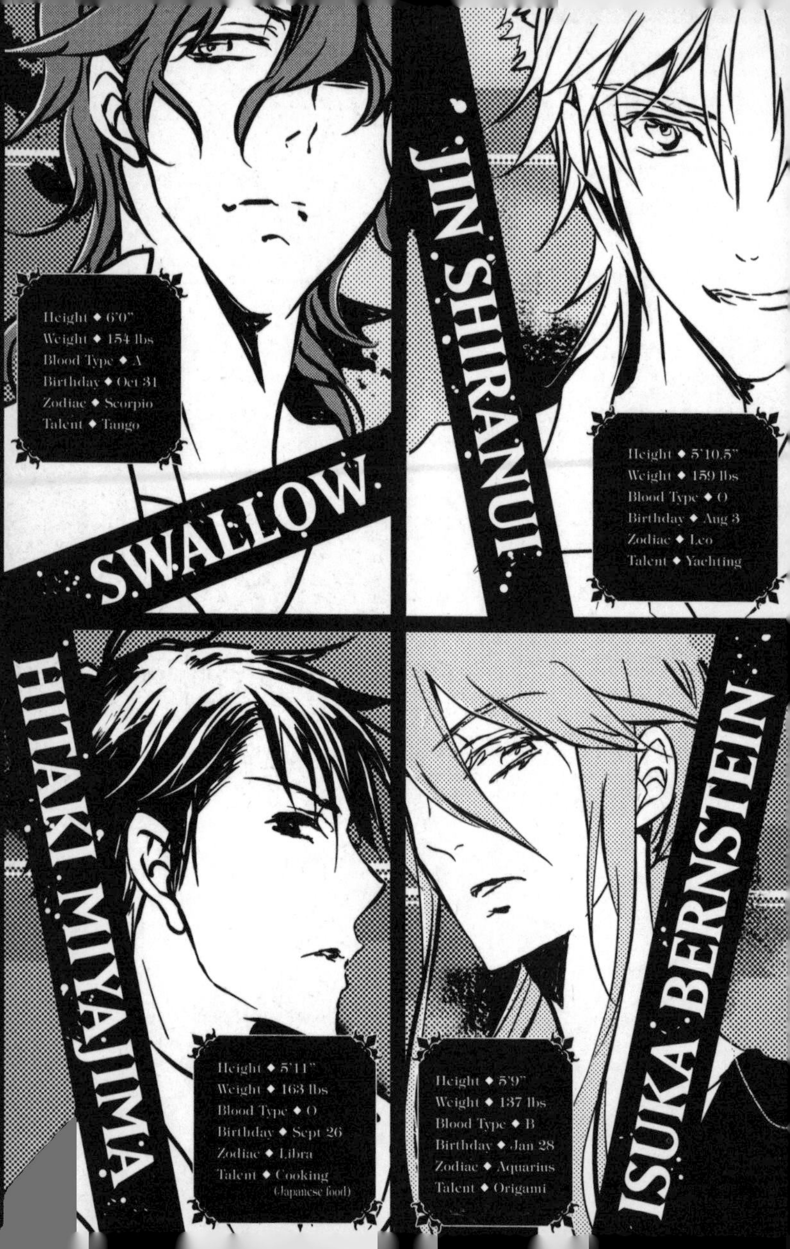
JIN SHIRANUI
Height ◆ 5'10.5"
Weight ◆ 159 lbs
Blood Type ◆ O
Birthday ◆ Aug 3
Zodiac ◆ Leo
Talent ◆ Yachting
SWALLOW
Height ◆ 6'0"
Weight ◆ 154 lbs
Blood Type ◆ A
Birthday ◆ Oct 31
Zodiac ◆ Scorpio
Talent ◆ Tango
ISUKA BERNSTEIN
Height ◆ 5'9"
Weight ◆ 137 lbs
Blood Type ◆ B
Birthday ◆ Jan 28
Zodiac ◆ Aquarius
Talent ◆ Origami
HITAKI MIYAJIMA
Height ◆ 5'11"
Weight ◆ 163 lbs
Blood Type ◆ O
Birthday ◆ Sept 26
Zodiac ◆ Libra
Talent ◆ Cooking
(Japanese food)

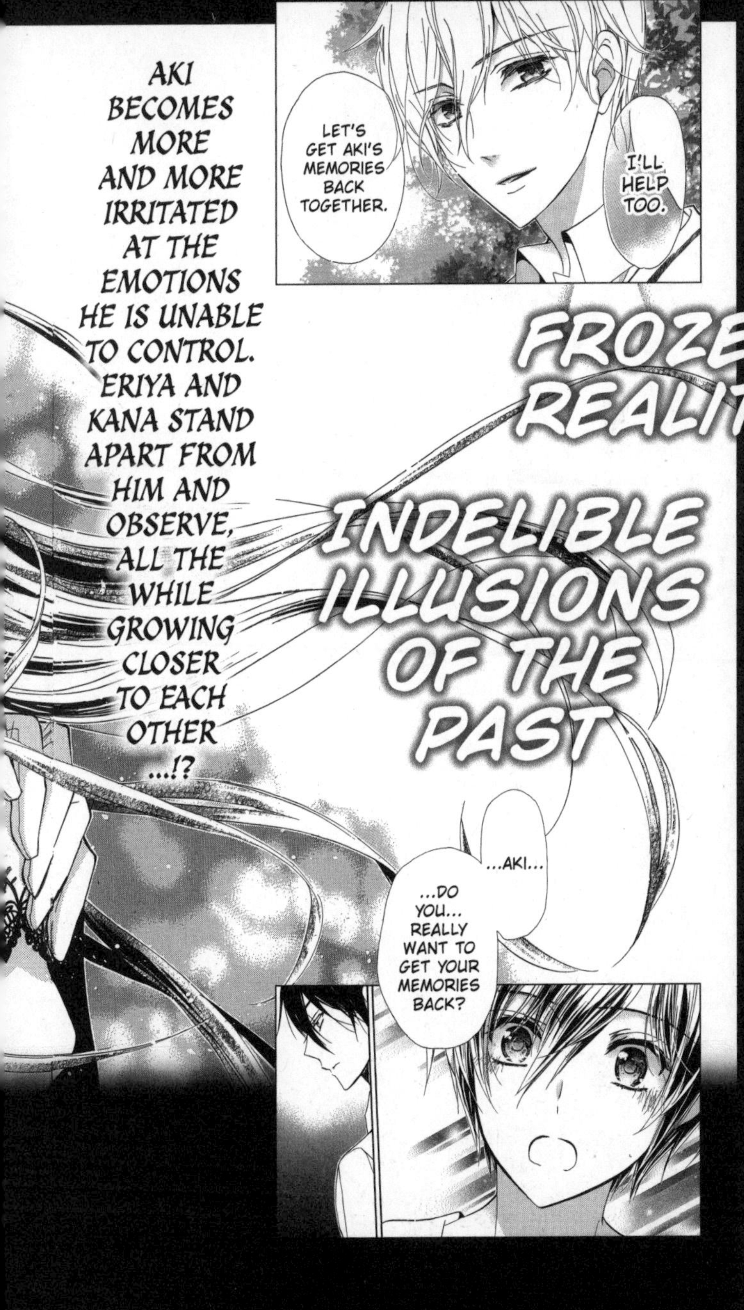
LET'S GET AKI'S MEMORIES BACK TOGETHER.
I'LL HELP TOO.
FROZEN REALITY
INDELIBLE ILLUSIONS OF THE PAST
AKI BECOMES MORE AND MORE IRRITATED AT THE EMOTIONS HE IS UNABLE TO CONTROL. ERIYA AND KANA STAND APART FROM HIM AND OBSERVE, ALL THE WHILE GROWING CLOSER TO EACH OTHER ...!?
...AKI...
...DO YOU... REALLY WANT TO GET YOUR MEMORIES BACK?

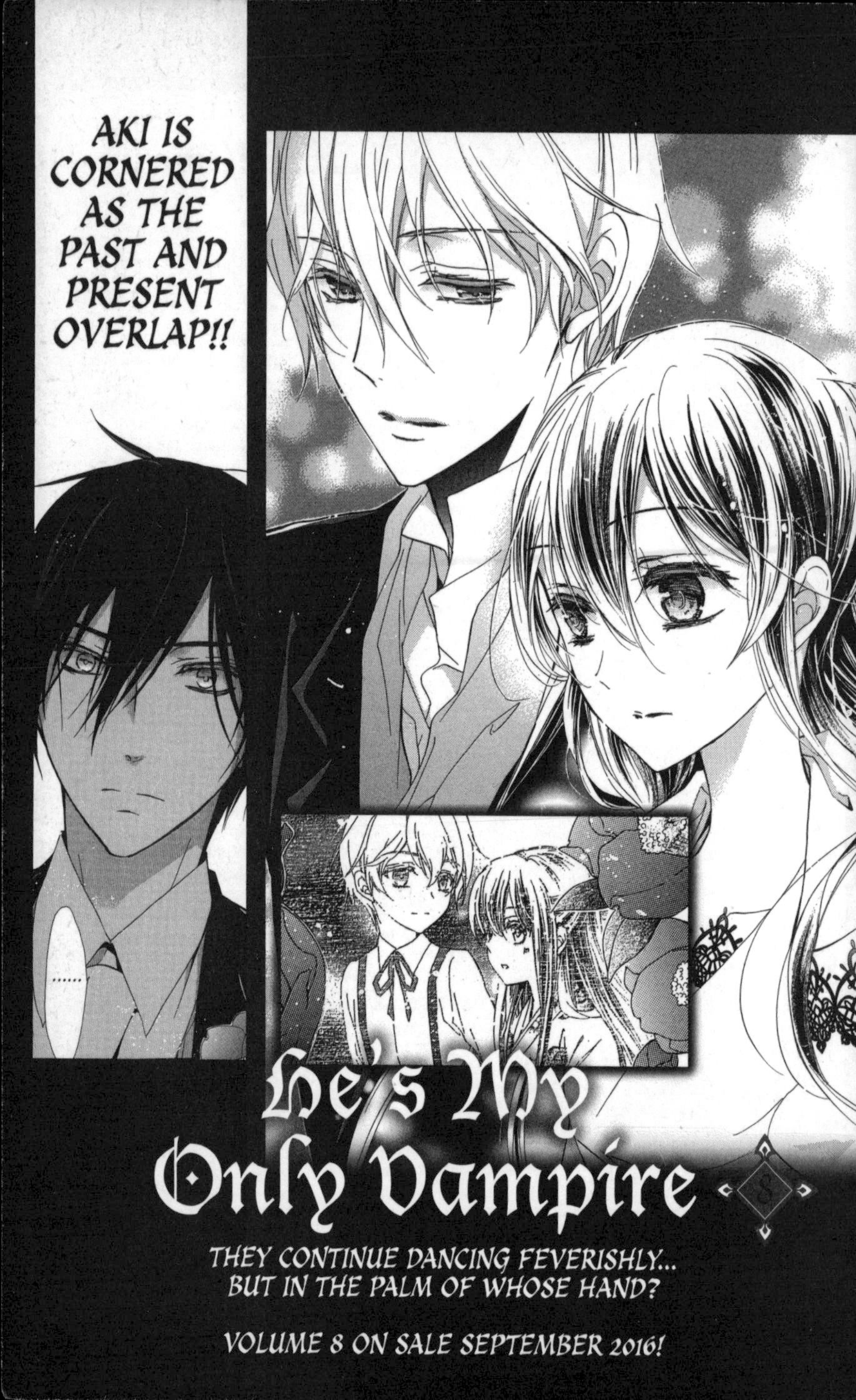
AKI IS CORNERED AS THE PAST AND PRESENT OVERLAP!!
......
He's My Only Vampire
8
THEY CONTINUE DANCING FEVERISHLY...
BUT IN THE PALM OF WHOSE HAND?
VOLUME 8 ON SALE SEPTEMBER 2016!

The Words of *He's My Only Vampire*

✝

Unlock the keywords of the dangerous yet beautiful world of *He's My Only Vampire*!

[Angel]
The true form of St. Agatha Academy's student council president, Isuka Bernstein, and vice president, Hitaki Miyajima, is that of angels. As beings aligned with the "Light," they are suspicious of Aki, who, as a being of Darkness, is their opposite.

[Curious Events Club]
A school club started by Kana in order to facilitate the gathering of information about STIGMAs. The CE Club will help resolve any type of trouble and is composed of Kana, Aki, and Jin.

[Dealer]
The title given to the judges of the Game. One is assigned to watch over every participant of the Game and has the power to punish any rule violations with an execution of the player. Aki's Dealer is Swallow.

[Electra]
A new drug that is spreading among the public. It is actually made from Aki's pure vampire blood and can turn humans into Lunatics.

[Emperor]
An elderly man with countless secrets, the Emperor is the absolute ruler of the Tsubakiins and the one who pulls all the strings from the shadows. He is referred to as the head of the Tsubakiins. It was he who educated the pureblood lord, Aki. He is also Eve's guardian. His true identity remains unknown and shrouded in mystery.

[Game]
The Game is a contest to gather the Seven STIGMAs and is centered around the city of Yagai, where Kana lives. The person who gathers all seven will be endowed with immense power and become the "Black Messiah." Aki is participating in this contest in order to gain the power to wake Eriya from his slumber.

[Lunatics]
When exposed to the scent of a pureblood vampire's blood, humans with darkness in their hearts transform into Lunatics under strong moonlight. Lunatics temporarily lose any sense of self and revert to beings of base instinct.

[Pureblood]
Purebloods have special powers even greater than that of a regular vampire. Their blood causes humans to go mad. They are beings both revered and feared. It is said that only a handful of them (including Aki) still exist.

[Soiree]
A private party the Tsubakiin clan hosts behind closed doors. It is ostensibly held to give leaders of certain industries a chance to mingle in an opulent setting, but in actuality, it is an opportunity for the Dark Nobility, who revere Aki's pure vampiric blood, to gather and worship during depraved "ceremonies."

[STIGMA]
STIGMAs are the embodiments of the Demonic Powers.

Anyone who can gather them all will gain enough power to rule the entire world should they choose. There are seven in total: Pride, Greed, Lust, Envy, Wrath, Gluttony, and Sloth.

[Thrall]
Thralls are special followers of pureblood vampires. Each pureblood may have only one thrall and cannot drink blood from any being but their own thrall. In short, a thrall is a pureblood's only possible prey. Thralls' bodies are almost invincible, though they may be injured by certain holy instruments. The relationship between a pureblood and thrall is so intimate that, if a thrall dies, its pureblood will die as well.

[Tsubakiin]
"Tsubakiin" is the name of the household that Aki and Eriya grew up in. It is a very old and respected name. The head of the Tsubakiins (who also controls many other great families in all but name) resides at Tsubakiin Manor, along with a large number of other members of the Tsubakiin clan, who possess a variety of special powers. The clan has long revered the pureblood vampire lord and reigns over the country's underworld.

[Woods]
The place Kana, Aki, and Eriya lived when they were children. The three were separated due to the great fire that occurred there seven years ago.

He's my only vampire
Aya Shouoto